Sisters in the Wilderness

Sisters in the Wilderness

The Lives of
Susanna Moodie
and
Catharine Parr Traill

Charlotte Gray

DUCKWORTH

First published in UK in 2001 by
Gerald Duckworth & Co. Ltd.
61 Frith Street
London
W1D 3JL
Tel: 020 7434 4242
Fax:020 7434 4420
Email: enquiries@duckworth-publishers.co.uk
www.ducknet.co.uk

First published in Canada in 1999 by the Penguin Group,
Penguin Books Canada Ltd, 10 Alcorn Avenue,
Toronto, Ontario, Canada M4V 3B2

Text design by Laura Brady

A CIP catalogue record for this book is available
from the British Library

ISBN 07156 3064 4

Printed in Great Britain by
Redwood Books Ltd, Trowbridge

This book is for my parents, Robert and Elizabeth Gray, with love.
It is also in affectionate memory of my father-in-law
Dr. Reginald Anderson (1910–1998).

Contents

Preface

A great river of emigrants flowed out of Britain in the nineteenth century. Between 1815 and 1889, over twelve million pioneers and convicts, slum kids and missionaries, governesses and soldiers, governors and judges boarded ship to go to the ends of the earth. Most of those who left the mother country were men, and by mid-century marriageable males were almost an endangered species at home. In January 1848, the *Plymouth Times* reported that there were "Forty single ladies for every single man in Weston-super-Mare."

Some of those who boarded the frigates and brigs, or in later years, the immeasurably faster steamers, assumed that they would return to the land of their birth once they had served British interests abroad. Many more, however, knew that they would never again see the families, communities and countryside they had left behind. For the rest of their lives they would be haunted by the sounds, sights and smells of their childhood—the chime of local church bells, the purple mist over Scottish moors, the acrid smoke from Guy Fawkes bonfires, the Norman cathedrals and the village pageants. In the backwoods of Canada, the hill towns of India, or on the sheep stations of Australia, an abrupt stab of nostalgia might at any moment pierce the heart of the man or woman who could never go home again. There is an ache of exile in every tale of emigration.

Nevertheless, passage abroad represented an escape for most of these British emigrants. There was so much to escape from. For those on the lowest rungs of the class system, emigration offered the promise of a new life in a new world. Each decade of the nineteenth century saw more upheavals for the labouring classes, as Britain lurched through the agricultural revolution, the economic slump after the Napoleonic Wars, and the industrial revolution. Forced off the land by the mechanisation of agriculture, the poor streamed into the new industrial cities. But conditions in the ironworks of Sheffield, the cotton factories of Manchester, the wool mills of Leeds or the engineering firms of Birmingham were appalling. Dirt, squalor, disease and hunger were endemic. Life for the urban poor was, in Charles Dickens's words, "one dem'd horrid grind".

Of all the British possessions overseas, the five principal North American colonies (Upper Canada, Lower Canada, Nova Scotia, New Brunswick, Prince Edward Island) held out the greatest promise. They were the closest and cheapest to get to, and land was affordable. Most of British North America was uncharted at the start of the century: vast areas were still unexplored when the Dominion of Canada was established in 1867. Moreover, the egalitarianism spawned in the American Revolution had travelled north. Canada was the land of opportunity, where no one had to doff his cap and every newcomer could reinvent him or herself if they so chose.

With good luck and hard work, a penniless Scots immigrant might establish a hardware store and watch his own sons expand the business into a mercantile empire that spanned the nation.

Susanna Moodie and Catharine Parr Traill crossed the Atlantic in

1832. The two Strickland sisters came from a far more comfortable background than the vast majority of those who packed up their possessions and headed off into the unknown. Susanna and Catharine had been raised in an Elizabethan manor house where they, their four sisters and two brothers benefited from an unusually good education from their parents. Their husbands, John Moodie and Thomas Traill, had signed up as officers in the Royal Scottish Fusiliers when they were still teenagers to fight in the Napoleonic Wars: after the 1815 Battle of Waterloo, each was discharged on half-pay. The Moodies and Traills travelled in relative ease as cabin passengers when they crossed the Atlantic, rather than in steerage where ragged children, screaming babies, sea-sick mothers and exhausted fathers were crammed like sardines.

Nevertheless, the same force that drove the steerage passengers away from their homeland also propelled the Strickland sisters. Emigration was an escape from poverty for these two women too—although in their case, it was the genteel poverty of the marginal middle-class rather than the grinding poverty of industrial slums and rural hardship. They left England because their means were too slender to support the standard of living to which they aspired. As Susanna wrote regretfully, "The half-pay of a subaltern officer, managed with the most rigid economy, is too small to supply the wants of a family, and if a man is of good family, not enough to maintain his original standing in society." As half-pay officers, John Moodie and Thomas Traill were eligible for land grants in Upper Canada, so the two couples set off to pioneer in the wilderness. They assumed that they would take their place amongst the landed gentry of the New World.

Unbelievable hardship awaited the genteel emigrants. There was no landed gentry in the New World. The two husbands had to hack down trees, clear bush, build homes and establish farms in the middle of an uncleared forest. The two wives lived in leaking log-houses with dirt floors, faced childbirth alone in the woods, and dealt with the threat of forest fires, wild animals, frostbite and starvation. The sisters they had left behind in England could not begin to imagine the exhausting and harrowing experiences experienced by pioneers in the Canadian bush.

John and Thomas lacked both the physical stamina and the skills for the tasks that faced them. Susanna and Catharine were tougher and more competent than their husbands: they rose to meet the challenges. But what sets them apart from nearly all the other women who left the British Isles was that they were, and remained, professional writers. By the time they arrived in Canada, both were accustomed to a disciplined routine of writing, and had an intellectual need to capture their experiences in the written word. Each managed to continue the career on which she had embarked during her younger days in England.

Back in England, the two sisters had published poetry, romantic fiction and children's stories that fit into the Regency tradition of women's writing. Most of it was insipid and conventional. Once in Canada, while they were evolving from ingenuous British emigrants to sturdy Canadian immigrants, they were also finding new voices. Despite the incredibly hard work of surviving and raising families in the backwoods, they carved out time each day to write themselves into visibility. After days spent cooking, baking, planting, harvesting, sewing, washing and bottling, each woman would light a home-made candle and sharpen a quill pen. In letters home and magazine articles, they would describe the pattern of their daily lives and their fellow pioneers. There was scarcely a publishing industry in Canada when the sisters arrived, and most of their neighbours were illiterate. Yet they persevered.

The Strickland sisters who remained in England helped to find publishers in London for the manuscripts that arrived by post from Canada. There was a sturdy British readership for tales of life in the colonies, but most contemporary accounts were by men like John Mitford Bowker, who arrived in South Africa in the late 1820s, or George Fletcher Moore, who settled in Australia in the 1830s. Female emigrants were more likely to record their experiences for their families back home in private letters—letters which, in many cases, were read, collected, and then forgotten in dusty attics, perhaps to be discovered years later and published. So the Strickland sisters' books had the appeal, during their own lifetime, of being both well-written and unusual in the insights they gave into colonial life. They sold well.

Shortly after I myself arrived in Canada from England in 1978, I came across *Roughing It in the Bush*, Susanna's best known book. Her reactions and observations resonated with me, despite the 150 years that had elapsed between our transatlantic crossings. Although I had come not to a raw young colony but to a wealthy settled country, I identified with her homesickness, and her inability to understand her Yankee neighbours. Like her, I found little charm in an Ontario landscape that was a bleak contrast to the gentle English countryside. Years later, I discovered Catharine Parr Traill's book *The Backwoods of Canada*, and was captivated by Catharine's sunny temperament. Her unpretentious pragmatism was a characteristic that, after years of friendships with Canadian women, I now see as a dominant Canadian trait.

The sisters' ability to speak to contemporary readers helps explain Catharine's and Susanna's powerful hold on the contemporary Canadian imagination. Their names and books have endured. This is partly because there are so few records of what life was like for British pioneers in the unexplored backwoods of Upper Canada. But it is primarily because the personality of each sister reverberates through her best books. Over the course of their long lives, the two sisters laid the foundations of a literary tradition that still endures in Canada: the pioneer woman who displays extraordinary courage, resourcefulness and humour, and who discovers her own strength as she overcomes adversity. Her sturdy figure has marched through the pages of some of the best-known Canadian writers of the last 100 years, from to Lucy Maud Montgomery (author of *Anne of Green Gables*) to Robertson Davies. The motto of this literary archetype comes directly from Catharine Parr Traill's *The Canadian Settler's Guide:* "In cases of emergency, it is folly to fold one's hands and sit down to bewail in abject terror. It is better to be up and doing."

But Susanna and Catharine didn't just develop one of the most striking archetypes in Canadian literature. They themselves appear in the fiction and non-fiction of contemporary Canadian writers.

Susanna Moodie is held in particular esteem by two of Canada's most eminent women writers: Carol Shields and Margaret Atwood. One of the earliest novels by Carol Shields features a writer who is completing a biography of Susanna Moodie, and is intrigued by the contradictions in Susanna's character. "Dare I suggest a hormone imbalance?" ponders the biographer, a sensible and witty woman. "Psychological scarring?... She was so shrewd about her fellow Canadians that she enraged them, but nevertheless seemed to have had little real understanding of herself."

Margaret Atwood is the Canadian writer who has done most to shape the popular perception of Susanna Moodie. Atwood's long and productive relationship with Susanna began when she found *Roughing It in the Bush* in her family bookcase. In 1970, she published *The Journals of Susanna Moodie*, a powerful cycle of poetry in which Atwood uses Susanna's experiences as the basis for meditations on pioneer life, human dislocation, and fear of the unknown.

After we had crossed the long illness
    that was the ocean, we sailed up-river...

We left behind one by one
the cities rotting with cholera,
one by one our civilized
distinctions

and entered a large darkness.

It was our own
ignorance we entered.
      — from "Further Arrivals."
      (© Margaret Atwood, *The Journals of Susanna Moodie*, 1970, used by permission of Oxford University Press)

Atwood returned to Susanna Moodie in her ninth novel, *Alias Grace* (1996), which was short-listed for the Booker Prize. The novel is based on a true story that Atwood first discovered in Susanna's book, *Life in the Clearings versus the Bush:* the story of Grace Marks, the "celebrated murderess". Susanna's account of Grace's crime was third-hand, taken largely from newspapers and much embellished with Susanna's taste for melodrama. "Mrs. Moodie is a literary lady," the disapproving Reverend Verringer pronounces in the novel, "and like all such, and indeed like the sex in general, she is inclined to [embroider.]"

Catharine Parr Traill appears, as a model of humanity and creativity, in *The Diviners*, by another well-known Canadian novelist, Margaret Laurence. "Saint Catharine! Where are you now that we need you!" cries out the heroine, Morag Gunn. Catharine's ability to rise above hardship, and make the best of every situation, is a comfort to Laurence's twentieth century heroine adrift in a hostile world. "Imagine naming flowers which have never been named before!" reflects Morag. "Like the Garden of Eden. Power! Ecstasy! I christen thee Butter-and-Eggs!"

However, in their own books and the books in which they have walk-on parts, Susanna and Catharine remain elusive. Writers in the twentieth century tried to deduce the personalities of the two women from their published works. I wondered, as any writer must, what were the women behind the authorial voices *really* like? When Susanna and Catharine were not carefully shaping their own images for their readers, how did they behave? What were their private thoughts and feelings? How much did the blood relationship between these two women mean to each of them? How did they relate to their husbands and children? And the sisters they had left behind in England?

I found the answers to these questions in three recently published volumes of their correspondence, and in their personal papers held in various archives (principally in the National Archives of Canada and the National Library of Canada). In the unvarnished prose of old journals and yellowing letters, a different picture of each sister emerges. I learnt of Susanna's quiet competence, even as she put on paper her sense of

XVI *Sisters in the Wilderness*

helplessness in the woods. I read about the disasters and family trials behind the brave face Catharine always wore. I realised how much the sisters relied on each other, as a link with the Old Country and as a source of support for each other's creative efforts. I understood the importance to both Catharine and Susanna of a third sister, the intimidating Agnes Strickland in England. One hundred years ago, Agnes Strickland was one of the best-known authors in Britain: her thirty-three biographies of queens and princesses were on the bookshelves of every well-stocked library. Today, she is almost forgotten, and the two Canadian sisters, whose lives horrified her, are celebrated in the land they eventually learnt to call "home".

The sisters came alive for me, as flesh-and-blood women at the centres of their families. There is much more to both of them than they ever allowed their own readers to know. Most of all, I began to understand the stamina, talent and determination that allowed two English ladies to overcome the hardships of pioneer life and lay the foundations of a literary tradition in the Great Dominion of the North. They never achieved their hopes of joining the Canadian land-owning gentry, but they did leave a powerful legacy in Canadian cultural life.

Sisters in the Wilderness

Prelude

February 1834

Tall, dense pine trees loomed over the Moodies, blocking any glimpse of the night sky, as they wearily clambered down from the heavy, horse-drawn sleigh. Susanna, John and their two little girls were exhausted, hungry and chilled to the bone. For eighteen hours they had lurched across packed snow and frozen swamp and through thick, silent forest. Now they had finally arrived at the home of Susanna's sister Catharine Parr Traill and her husband Thomas, just north of the little Upper Canadian town of Peterborough. Golden light flooded out of the log cabin's open door: Susanna stumbled towards its promise of warmth and shelter—and reunion with her beloved sister.

Was it really less than two years since the sisters had last seen each other? It felt like half a lifetime. Back then, the two young women had been rising stars in the lively literary world of Regency London. They had more than enough talent and education to become serious writers: only the straitened circumstances of their own family, and their husbands' poor prospects, had held them back. Persuaded by their husbands that they would have a better future in the colonies, they had said goodbye to each other on the pebble beach of Southwold, in Suffolk. Then each couple had made their own way across the Atlantic, towards Upper Canada, for a new life in a New World.

So far, however, the New World had proved more hostile than they had ever imagined. As Susanna huddled in the sleigh throughout that long February day, she wondered whether she would ever be able to carve a comfortable life out of this wilderness, let alone achieve the success as an author she had once dreamed of. "I gazed through tears upon the singularly savage scene around me," she wrote years later in her most famous book, *Roughing It in the Bush*, "and secretly marvelled, 'What brought me here?'" Catharine had found the landscape equally overpowering, admitting in her first Canadian book, *The Backwoods of Canada*, that "the long and unbroken line of woods . . . insensibly inspires a feeling of gloom almost touching on sadness."

Could these two women ever come to terms with Canada? In 1834, it seemed unlikely. During their first eighteen months in the colony, they had not even managed to see one another. Poor communications, primitive roads, family responsibilities and the relentless daily demands of pioneer farms had kept them apart, although only fifty miles separated them. But now, at least, they would have each other. Close allies since childhood, they would at last be able to share their fears and lift each other's morale.

When Susanna appeared in the doorway of her cabin, Catharine rushed to embrace her. Tears sprang to Susanna's eyes as she heard her sister's voice and felt Catharine's arms encircle her. The two young women clung to each other in an explosion of joy. Years later, Susanna wrote: "I never enjoyed more heartily a warm welcome after a long day of intense fatigue, than I did that night of my first sojourn in the backwoods."

Chapter 1

New Beginnings

The childhood of Catharine Parr Traill and Susanna Moodie in the early 1800s was very similar to that of Jane Austen, born a quarter of a century earlier. Like her, they grew up in rural England, with its settled rhythms and reassuring continuity. And like the Austen family in Hampshire, the Stricklands didn't quite fit into the society of prosperous landowners who were their neighbours in Suffolk. Thomas Strickland, father of Catharine and Susanna, had lifted his family out of the lower reaches of gentility, but failed to slot his children safely into the ranks of East Anglia's landed gentry. As a result, the Strickland girls, like Jane Austen and her sister Cassandra, felt themselves to be on the margins of county society and became acutely attuned to social nuance. The sense during their childhood of being outsiders affected each of them in different ways.

Neither Thomas nor his wife was native to Suffolk. Susanna's and

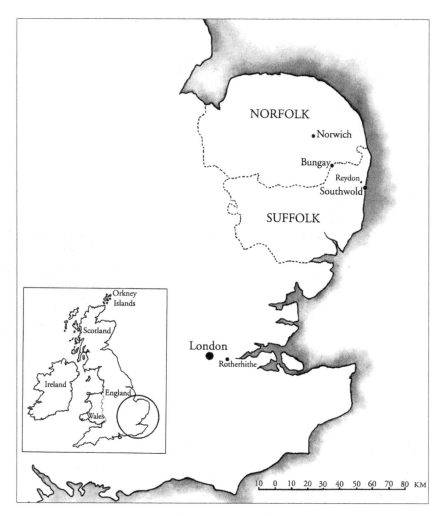

Suffolk, in the early nineteenth century, was a county of sleepy villages and medieval churches.

Catharine's father was born in 1758 in London, to a respectable but penniless family that had drifted south from Yorkshire. As a teenager, he joined a shipping company called Hallet and Wells, and he spent most of his early adult life in the east end of the smoky, noisy city. Thomas rose in the firm to become master and sole manager of the Greenland docks near Rotherhithe, and the owner of several properties in the east end of London.

Thomas Strickland was married in 1789 to Susanna Butt, a grand-niece of Sir Isaac Newton, the great English mathematician and astronomer. But the first Mrs. Strickland died in 1790, within a few months of their marriage. Three years later, when he was thirty-five, Thomas Strickland married again, this time to twenty-one-year-old Elizabeth Homer. It was a productive match. In the first ten years of marriage, Thomas and Elizabeth had six daughters: Elizabeth (known as Eliza) arrived in 1794, Agnes in 1796, Sarah (known as Thay) in 1798, Jane in 1800, Catharine Parr (named after Henry VIII's sixth wife, with whom there was a vague ancestral link) in 1802 and Susanna in 1803. Two sons subsequently took their places in the nursery—Samuel in 1805 and Thomas in 1807—but they were never players in their sisters' nursery games.

Thomas Strickland didn't really enjoy the bustle of Rotherhithe: his heart lay in his library, not his wharves. He took particular pride in the books and memorabilia once owned by Newton that his first wife had brought into his household. And he suffered from gout—an excruciatingly painful complaint. For health reasons, and with hopes of bettering his social position, Thomas decided in 1803 to leave the city and move to Suffolk.

Thomas Strickland's decision to move to a bucolic county north of London and reinvent himself as a country squire was typical of his age—although it probably didn't seem so to him. In 1803, the country was simmering uncomfortably under George III, the third inadequate Hanoverian monarch in a row. It was also fighting one of the greatest enemies it had ever faced: France's Napoleon Bonaparte, whose forces challenged the Duke of Wellington on land and Admiral Horatio Nelson at sea. But the preceding century had seen changes in Britain that had shaken the traditions of centuries. Brilliant prime ministers such as Robert Walpole and William Pitt had successfully transferred power from hereditary aristocrats to elected representatives; demand for an extension of the franchise beyond wealthy landowners was starting to build. Robert Clive's victories in India had established British rule there, and the American War of Independence had eliminated British control of thirteen colonies. There had been a rush of inventions, such as Richard Arkwright's water-powered spinning machine and James Watt's steam engine. In 1785 *The Times* was established; in 1802, the English physicist John Dalton introduced atomic theory into chemistry. As Britain embarked on the new century, it was alive with new thinking, new intellectual movements and a new sense of possibility. It was on the brink of the Industrial Revolution, which would make Britain the wealthiest nation in the world. The social strata were shifting, and there was new room for upward mobility.

In Suffolk, there was a surprising turnover of estates at the top of the social hierarchy as members of a new class—nouveaux riches—bought up old manor houses. The industrialist John Crowley, who owned England's largest ironworks, in County Durham, two hundred miles north of London, had set himself up in a mansion in the sleepy old Suffolk village of Barking. One of London's richest malt distillers, Samuel Kent, had settled into a stately hall on the River Lark at Fornham St. Genevieve. The district in which Thomas Strickland decided to set himself up was the Waveney Valley in eastern Suffolk. By late 1803, he was renting Stowe House, a Georgian manor on a hill over-looking the town of Bungay.

Suffolk was attractive to people like Thomas Strickland because the comfortably rounded bulge of land jutting into the North Sea has always been one of the most beautiful corners of England. Suffolk shares with Norfolk, its northern neighbour, vistas of flat fields, scattered villages and meandering streams. The gentle features and wide skies of Suffolk at the time of the Stricklands are best captured on the canvases of two of England's greatest landscape painters, John Constable and Thomas Gainsborough. Curlews endlessly wheel round in the sky; silvery light slants onto still water; yellow fields are spangled with the brilliant vermilion of poppies. In 1803, the county's most dramatic features were man-made and on a human scale. Inland, there were medieval flint-and-stone churches, and brick windmills with creaking sails. Along the coastline, there were lighthouses to warn North Sea fishing fleets and collier brigs of the shifting sandbanks on the East Anglian shore. Even today, little has changed—Suffolk prides itself on the way it ambles through history, at least a century behind the rest of England.

Five of the Strickland daughters were born by the time the family moved to Suffolk, and Susanna arrived within the first few months. In later years, Catharine was to recall Stowe House as "our Eden," and to compress memories of every season and childhood delight into her ecstatic descriptions of the house and grounds. "The banks of the stream were lined with sweet purple violets, primroses, and the little sun-bright celandine: from this slender streamlet we children drank the most delicious draughts from Nature's own chalice, the hollow of our hands, or sipped its pure waters, like the fairies we read of, from the acorn cups that strewed the grass. . . . Later on there was a good store of wild strawberries, which we gathered and strung upon a stalk of grass to carry home to our mother as a peace-offering for torn frocks and soiled pinafores."

During the years at Stowe House the children were happily enclosed in two overlapping but self-contained worlds—their own close-knit family, and the timeless routines of rural Suffolk. During the mornings, they congregated in the brick-paved parlour for lessons. The elder children acted out scenes from Shakespeare, or studied Greek and Latin under their father's supervision, while the younger children were taught to read by their mother. Elizabeth and Thomas were strict parents who insisted that their children's education be well grounded in history, geography, mathematics and the theology and morality of the Church of England. Disobedience was punished by solitary confinement, without dinner. Thomas wanted his daughters as well as his sons to be self-reliant. His fourth daughter, Jane, never forgot his lessons. "'Persevere and you must succeed,' was one of his maxims," she recalled years later. "'God helps those who help themselves.' When his right hand was disabled by gout, he used his left hand to write with—such was our father."

After their mornings in the schoolroom, the Stricklands spent the afternoons around the garden and farmland, or accompanied their parents on local errands. With their mother, they would visit Bungay, a market town with a romantic ruined castle on the hill above it. Every Thursday, there was a lively market in the cobbled square by the seventeenth-century Butter Cross, a local stone monument. The town had a full complement of artisans who kept the local economy going, and whose workshops were irresistible draws for curious children. Harness-makers, wheelwrights, brick-makers, potters, basket-weavers, coopers, blacksmiths and farriers—the young Stricklands could watch their carriage horses being shod, or their cooking pots repaired, by men who had learned their skills from their fathers. They could eavesdrop on the old men who gathered in the sunshine for a "mardle" (as a casual chat was known locally) or count the grain sacks being unloaded for grinding in one of the local windmills.

With their father and his manservant, Lockwood, the children might set off on fishing expeditions along the River Waveney. The Waveney, which loops lazily around the town of Bungay and is still the haunt of otters, snipe and duck, was a favourite destination two hundred years ago for local eel-fishers. Their method of catching their prey was called "eel-babbing" and was unique to this little pocket of England. Worms spiced with a tasty mixture of dung were threaded onto a special kind of wool. The wool line was then fixed to a rod and dropped in the Waveney's shallow waters, where an eel might snatch at the worm and get the wool caught in its teeth. Practised babbers swore by this technique, which saved them the slimy, frustrating job of removing a hook from the eel's mouth. Thomas Strickland and his children would walk down to the Waveney in the late evening to watch the babbers at work. But Thomas himself was a rod-and-fly gentleman, whose fishing bible was Isaac Walton's *The Compleat Angler*. He would read aloud passages to Catharine when he took her fishing, and his first-edition copy of Walton's classic would become one of her most treasured possessions.

Thomas was often incapacitated by gout, and his wife would be too busy nursing him to pursue her children's education. Then the girls had to amuse themselves. "In the long winter evenings we gathered around the fire and the elder ones would tell long stories bearing upon some point of history but embellished according to the invisible genius of their fertile minds," Catharine recalled years later. "These improvised histories were continued night after night. New characters introduced and new events. And often this amusement gave place to the reading aloud [of] Shakespeare's tragedies . . ." As the logs flamed in the stone fireplace and kept at bay the darkness beyond the hearth, Agnes Strickland—who, though the second eldest, was the dominant and by far the most theatrical of the brood—kept her five sisters enthralled as she recited from memory Hamlet's soliloquy, "To be or not to be," or John of Gaunt's stirring invocation from *Richard II*: "This royal throne of kings, this sceptered isle . . ." Or else she stage-managed a whole production, with herself—tall and deep-voiced—as male lead and Sarah, the prettiest of the sisters, as Ophelia, Juliet or Viola.

It was an extraordinarily intense family of literary youngsters: they spent far more time with each other than with any other children and had all read more by the age of ten than most girls of their era and class read in a lifetime. Of the six sisters, five would become published authors. In later years, Catharine found the comparison of the Stricklands with another literary sisterhood of the nineteenth century irresistible. "Began reading for the second time the life of Charlotte Bronte," she wrote in her journal when she was fifty-eight. "There is so much in this book that reminds me of our own early years—were I to write a history of the childhood of the Strickland family . . . how many things there would be that would remind the reader of the early days of the Brontes."

During these years, Thomas Strickland's investments continued to prosper. He still owned property in Rotherhithe which yielded some income, and he had also entered into a partnership with a coach-maker in Norwich, the chief city in Norfolk. He bought a townhouse within the city walls, on a cobbled street near the lovely medieval church of St. Giles. And in 1808 he purchased a gentleman's residence eighteen

Reydon Hall

The girls revelled in the well-stocked library and dusty attics of Reydon Hall, Suffolk.

miles southeast of Bungay, about a mile from the Suffolk coast. During a particularly cold spell in January, the Stricklands left Bungay and moved to Reydon Hall.

Reydon Hall is a solid brick manor still considered one of the most attractive houses in the county. Built in 1682, it has mullioned windows, fancy curved Dutch gables on its third floor and rambling grounds. At the front of the house during the Stricklands' ownership was a broad sweep of driveway hidden from the road by a thick stand of oak, chestnut and ash trees; to the rear, extensive lawns dotted with old sycamore trees gave way to the Reydon woods, owned by the Earl of Stradbroke. Inside the Hall there were three spacious reception rooms, several bedrooms, a stone-flagged kitchen and servants' quarters. The writing desk of General Wolfe, hero of the Plains of Abraham, took pride of place in the drawing room; how Thomas had acquired this treasure is uncertain. In the best tradition of noble mansions, the Hall even boasted a third-floor garret reputed to house a ghost called "Old Martin." The bedrooms were low-ceilinged and pokey, and there were constant problems with a leaky roof. Nonetheless, its old brick glowed with warmth, and even today, after countless additions and renovations, its beautiful scalloped gables and elaborate double chimneys lend Reydon Hall considerable grace. The house affirmed that Thomas Strickland had arrived in Suffolk society.

Thomas and Elizabeth now divided their time between Reydon Hall and Norwich, where their two sons went to the fee-paying Norwich Grammar School. They frequently took their two oldest girls with them, leaving the younger ones at home in the charge of the servants. "Reading was our chief resource," Catharine would recall in later years. "We ran-sacked the library for books, we dipped into old magazines of the last century. . . . We tried history, the drama, voyages and travels, of which latter there was a huge folio. We even tried 'Locke on the Human Unders-tanding.' We wanted to be very learned . . ." They combed through back numbers of the *Astrologer's Magazine* for tales of witchcraft and ghosts, which they then retold with great relish to the cook and housemaid until the latter were convinced they would meet Old Martin on the stairs. To relieve the boredom of dull, dark winter days, the two youngest girls decided to write a novel for children. Careless of old Martin's ghost, in the dusty attic they unearthed a supply of paper in a chest with massive brass hinges and locks—left behind, according to family legend, by a young Indian prince who had been sent to England as an ambassador to the Royal Court.

Susanna's interest in the novel flagged. But even as a youngster, Catharine was the kind of person who liked to finish anything she began. She plodded on with the story entitled "The Swiss Herd-boy and his Alpine Marmot," which enthralled Susanna and Sarah. However, Mrs. Strickland and Eliza—the bad-tempered eldest sister who always regarded herself as a third parent to the youngest children—discovered Catharine's manuscript one day when they had returned from Norwich. They were horrified that Catharine was "scribbling such trash" and confiscated it. Susanna, who was far too headstrong to accept rebuke meekly, was outraged. Catharine, a much more easygoing child, made less of a fuss—and was allowed to keep her manuscript when she promised to use it for curling papers.

A flat-bottomed wherry making its way down the winding River Waveney.

On fine days, the girls often left their books behind and walked between dense hawthorn hedgerows to Southwold, a mile from Reydon. In those days, Southwold was a busy fishing village with its own cod fleet and a reputation as a smuggler's haven. Great black-sailed wherries—slow, flat-bottomed boats that could navigate East Anglia's shallow, silty rivers—brought sackloads of corn and barley into the harbour, where they were transferred to London-bound brigs and schooners with heavy, seaworthy keels. Barrels of malt were unloaded onto the quay and trundled off to the local brewery, owned by the Adnam family. The Stricklands could watch all this maritime activity, visit the library and shops, or on summer evenings cheer their brother Sam's successes when he played cricket for the Southwold village team. They could brave the stiff sea breezes and, clutching their bonnets to their heads, climb up Gun Hill overlooking Sole Bay and inspect the ancient cannon there. Or they could walk along the miles of flat pebble beach. "We loved to watch the advance and recoil of the waves, the busy fishermen among the nets and boats, and the happy children on the sands," Catharine later recalled. "But there was a greater fascination still to us in the search for treasures left by the flood-tide or cast upon the shore by the ever restless waves." Shining pebbles, bits of jet or amber swept south from the Yorkshire coast, shells and fossils accumulated along the window ledges of the children's bedrooms.

Most of the information about the Stricklands' Suffolk childhood comes from Catharine herself, who at the end of her life wrote out her memories for her grandchildren. Her account reflects her own sunny view of life, and her preference for "bright glad thoughts" over dreary memories of reduced circumstances. Catharine had an enviable sense of her self and confidence in her place in the world. Throughout her life, she radiated grace, good cheer and affection for everyone around her. Her sister Sarah spoke of her as "the Katie . . . the pet of the household." Her blue eyes always sparkled with happiness and curiosity about the world. She had a warm smile and an air of stolid contentment, and even as a baby Catharine "never cried like other children—indeed we used to say that Katie never saw a sorrowful day—for if anything went wrong she just shut her eyes and the tears fell from under the long lashes and rolled down her cheeks like pearls into her lap. We all adored her."

The key to this sense of self-worth and extraordinary invulnerability must be the unusual relationship she had with her father. Catharine's sisters all acknowledged that she was her father's favourite child. No matter how irritable Thomas Strickland might be with the gout, or the noise and mess made by his large brood, he never snapped at Katie. She was such an easy companion: Katie listened attentively to others, and always fit in with other people's plans. As a result, her parents and siblings loved to be around her. "My father idolized her," Sarah told a great-niece decades later. Katie was his chosen companion for fishing trips and walks through the woods, during which he would impart his own serious interest in botany to his daughter by revealing the mysteries of plant and wildlife to her.

Thomas's affection gave his beloved Katie a psychological cushion against misfortune. It also nourished an interest in natural history that was at the same time an intellectual stimulus, a distraction from setbacks and a confirmation of her deep and simple Christian faith. "It is fortunate for me that my love of natural history enables me to draw amusement from objects that are deemed by many unworthy of attention," she wrote. "The simplest weed that grows in my path, or the fly that flutters about me, are subjects for reflection, admiration and delight." Catharine's love of natural history was an extension of her belief in a benevolent and omnipotent God. Her mind was steeped in religion in a way that is difficult to grasp today. Her religious beliefs were quintessentially early-nineteenth-century—romantic, rather sentimental and absolutely trusting. In future years, Catharine would rely on her love of nature, the beauties of which she saw as the expression of God's will, to carry her through one disaster after another. "Strength was always given to me when it was needed," she noted at the end of her life. "In great troubles and losses, God is very Good."

It must have been hard for Susanna to watch her father and sister disappear together. As the youngest daughter, she might have expected to occupy the niche of family favourite. Instead, she felt like the runt of the female litter, excluded from one of the most important relationships in her small world. She reacted to this exclusion with defiance rather than submission. While Catharine played with dolls and learned to identify birds and press flowers, Susanna collected frogs, toads and lizards. She spun impossible tales of seeing snakes and crocodiles in the Suffolk hedgerows, just to shock her father. Tired of being told, when she was naughty, that "Boney will come and catch you," Susanna declared that she was madly in love with Napoleon Bonaparte. Thomas Strickland was horrified that his youngest daughter should admire the Corsican monster who was Britain's mortal enemy. One night in 1815, when the Strickland family was sitting around the dining-room table, a neighbour ran in shouting, "Boney has escaped from Elba!" Susanna whooped for joy. Her enraged father immediately sent her to her bedroom.

A miniature of Susanna, painted by her cousin Thomas Cheesman when she was in her early twenties, reveals a young woman with a dimpled chin, wide grey eyes ablaze with spirit and an expression of nervous anticipation. Red-haired and short-tempered, she could be careless of others' feelings. Her elder sisters found her "a curly-headed emotional creature, rather Keatsian in appearance." Susanna admitted to a friend that she was "the creature of extremes, the child of impulse." She poured much of her uncertainty and sense of being unloved into childish poems—poems that, when she was in her fifties, she described as "the overflowing of a young warm heart, keenly alive to the beauties of creation."

All in all, the Strickland sisters enjoyed an idyllic childhood. But it came to a crashing halt in 1818. War with France had drawn to a triumphant close in 1815 with Britain's victory at Waterloo. But in the aftermath of the Napoleonic wars, England lurched into a severe depression. The economic downturn menaced the kind of mercantile enterprises in which Thomas Strickland had invested. Thomas had made the mistake of guaranteeing a loan to his Norwich partner to keep a business afloat in bad times. When the business collapsed, his capital was wiped out. The shock of near-bankruptcy triggered his death at the relatively young age of sixty.

Elizabeth Strickland, now forty-six, was left a widow, with a meagre income, six unmarried daughters (three still in their teens) and two sons, thirteen and eleven, still at an expensive grammar school.

Chapter 2

"The Scribbling Fever"

Elizabeth Strickland was determined not to let the family's social status slip after her husband's death in 1818. Until she herself died forty-six years later, at the robust age of ninety-two, she continued to live at Reydon Hall and cling to the position Thomas had established for them. In the early years of her widowhood, she even maintained the house in Norwich so the boys could carry on attending school there, and she sent her daughters Eliza, Agnes and Catharine to run that household. But with the loss of the family breadwinner, the Stricklands were plunged into a penny-pinching existence behind the brave front. Cooks, maids and gardeners all disappeared, and so did General Wolfe's desk and the elegant carriage. The family tended the vegetable garden, and went out less and less.

Keeping up appearances was a strain on Mrs. Strickland; her temperament soured and she took to her bed. Many of the rooms of Reydon

Hall were closed up, and one guest would remember that it smelled of "rats and dampness and mould." When the girls travelled anywhere, they either had to borrow a neighbour's donkey to pull their donkey cart or take the public coach. Invitations from neighbouring gentry dried up, since the Stricklands were unable to return the hospitality. Nor was there any hope of staying abreast of the rapidly changing fashions of the 1820s. This was an era when female clothing was increasingly influenced by Romantic attitudes. Puffy sleeves, tightly corseted waists and wide girlish skirts, in flower-bed colours of lilac and rose, transformed women into fragile Fragonard heroines, dependent on male protection. But Susanna and Catharine could barely afford to renew their wardrobes, let alone play out a fantasy that had little to do with the threadbare reality of their lives.

The lives of the Strickland sisters were now constricted by genteel poverty and rural isolation. They were excluded from the masculine world of army, navy, commerce or politics. Their brothers both embraced one of the few options open to gentlemen without means as soon as they were old enough to flee the stifling matriarchy of Reydon Hall. Both set off to settle in the colonies. Sam was barely twenty years old when, in 1825, a family friend encouraged him to cross the Atlantic and try his hand at farming in the colony of Upper Canada. Within a few months, young Thomas too was gone, on his way to India and a life in Britain's merchant fleet. After their brothers' departure, the Strickland girls had few opportunities to meet men of the standing required for marriage. Socially, they fell between two stools—they were not wealthy enough to claim membership in the

Catharine Parr Strickland, sweet-tempered and placid, was her father's favourite child.

landed gentry class, but their residence in the country meant they were excluded from the new urban merchant class.

Catharine and Susanna were sixteen and fifteen when their father died. In the crisis of quiet desperation that followed, they forged a close alliance, based on their position as the two youngest daughters and on their shared love of reading. Both clung to the catalogue of family maxims—a belief that the darkest hour comes before the dawn, and a certainty that God helps those who help themselves. The difference in their personalities reinforced their reliance on each other. Catharine wrote of herself, "I think that I have a happy faculty of forgetting past sorrows and only remembering the pleasures," and she often found herself reassuring her sensitive younger sister when Susanna plunged into the depths of despair. Only Catharine could cope with Susanna's emotional intensity. While Susanna resented Catharine's imperturbable patience, she also adored her. "I know I would rather give up the pen," Susanna wrote to a friend in 1829, "than lose the affection of my beloved sister Catharine, who is dearer to me than all the world—my monitress, my dear and faithful friend."

Susanna Strickland was impulsive and defiant, with a wicked sense of humour.

At the same time, Catharine enjoyed the fact that Susanna was, in her younger sister's own words, a "wild Suffolk girl so full of romance." Susanna could infuse placid Catharine with her own giddy *joie de vivre*. "Possibly it was the contrast between us that had the effect of binding us nearer to one another," Catharine mused later in life. The primal bonds between the two women—far stronger than either felt for their four sisters and two brothers—were deep-rooted and comforting to both.

In Norwich, Catharine was a frequent visitor at the city library, and she was soon venturing "once more to indulge the scribbling fever." At first, she didn't see her little stories as a way to make money. Nor did her sisters, although by now both Agnes and Eliza (her contempt for "trash" notwithstanding) were experimenting with poetry and simple literary sketches. Their mother, clinging to respectability, would have decreed that it was unthinkable for a gentlewoman to consider earning her living. This was, after all, the era in which Jane Austen, the parson's daughter from Hampshire, covered her notebooks with a piece of muslin when she heard somebody approach her room, and when the Norwich writer Harriet Martineau wrote her articles for a church magazine in her freezing bedroom between five and seven o'clock in the morning so her mother wouldn't discover what she was up to. It was dangerous for a woman even to suggest that she had a brain: the eighteenth-century writer Lady Mary Wortley Montagu had once advised her daughter to hide her intellect "with as much solicitude as she would hide crookedness or lameness."

Yet Catharine, Susanna and their sisters were aware of the intellectual ferment of the age in which they lived. Their father's own library, inherited from Sir Isaac Newton, was out-of-date by the time they were old enough to take down the leatherbound volumes. Nevertheless, it contained enough early examples of Enlightenment thinking—the works of John Locke, several accounts of exotic travel and Sir Isaac Newton's own scientific publications—to give them a sense of what was happening in the wider world. All the old institutions were under scrutiny—religion, monarchy, slavery and patriarchy. With their father's death and their plunge into genteel penury, the sisters had a particular interest in some of the new thinking about women's lives, such as Mary Wollstonecraft's *Vindication of the Rights of Women*, first published in 1792. Wollstonecraft (who died in childbirth in 1797, before Catharine and Susanna were born) passionately championed women's claim to equal treatment in the spheres of education, the professions, the law and politics.

The boldness of Wollstonecraft's thinking was anathema to estab-lishment figures such as Horace Walpole, who dismissed the author and her followers as "hyenas in petticoats." Nevertheless, Wollstonecraft's legacy directly touched the Strickland sisters' lives. The spread of liter-acy among women during the previous hundred years meant that Woll-stonecraft's manifesto was widely read. And, thanks in part to her success, publishers realized that there was a growing market for works by lady authors. The tradition of women writers in England began to gather momentum: gentlewomen were producing belles-lettres, travel memoirs and domestic tales. Fanny Burney had already published four successful novels, the best-known of which was *Camilla*, depicting the lives of virtuous but inexperienced girls entering society. By 1815 Jane Austen had two bestsellers to her name (*Sense and Sensibility* and *Pride and Prejudice*) and had been invited to dedicate her new novel, *Emma,* to the Prince Regent. Writing was beginning to be both respectable and lucra-tive for women.

England had not yet been engulfed in the claustrophobic glorification of the family, and the idea of woman as the "angel in the house," that would later characterize middle-class attitudes in Victorian Britain. Regency London was permeated with the elegance, extravagance and sartorial splendour that defined the age. It was a jolly, if exhausting, time to be alive, for both men and women. The preferred literary style was urbane and fastidious, and women excelled at it.

For the Stricklands, stuck in East Anglia, opportunities for women with literary ambitions still seemed hopelessly out of reach. But one day an old friend of Thomas Strickland's came to visit, and chanced upon a children's story about a highland piper that Catharine had written. When he left, he took it with him and showed it to a publisher in London. To Catharine's delight, the friend arrived a month later and pressed five golden guineas into her hands. The publisher wished to produce a little book under the title *The Blind Highland Piper and Other Tales*. Five guineas was a considerable sum in those days, enough to finance a trip to

Agnes, the brilliant and bossy elder sister, was the first of the Stricklands to see her work in print.

London. It was particularly exciting for a young woman who had no expectations of legacies or marriage settlements. Catharine's success encouraged the literary efforts of four of her sisters: Eliza, Agnes, Jane and Susanna. All five began to see that writing might offer an escape from their pinched circumstances, and an opportunity to shape better lives for themselves. Only pretty Sarah, known within the family as "the baker" because she made such delightfully light loaves, never showed any interest in publication.

By the early 1820s, the Strickland girls had secured a limited entrée into the kind of London literary circles where Mary Wollstonecraft's ideas were debated and Fanny Burney's latest novel discussed. Their second cousin, Rebecca Leverton, was a wealthy widow who held court in the elegant terraced house in Bedford Square bequeathed to her by her husband, Thomas Leverton, the square's architect. Bedford Square was one of the "best addresses" in the newly built district of Bloomsbury. Rebecca often invited her cousins to stay with her. She certainly appreciated their willingness to run errands and bring glasses of warm milk to her before she rose each morning, but she also tried to expand their horizons. Catharine particularly enjoyed the visits. "I am indeed very happy and enjoy the society of my London friends," she wrote to her friend James Bird, a well-known poet who ran a stationery shop in the Suffolk village of Yoxford, and his wife Emma. "Mrs. Leverton takes me abroad in the carriage everyday to shew me some building or public place of note. . . . I am so enchanted with [Westminster] Abbey that I could stand for hours looking on it."

A less grand, but more exciting, connection was the artist Thomas Cheesman. Cheesman, whom the girls referred to affectionately as "Coz," was a colourful character in a grubby artist's smock who moved in somewhat raffish circles. His house in Newman Street was cluttered with musical instruments, books and half-finished paintings. Cheesman was a man ahead of his time, who encouraged Agnes and Susanna (the two most determined writers) to press ahead with their literary ambitions.

Agnes, who had been twenty-two when her father died, moved to London in the early 1820s to capitalize on her literary connections and potential. She was the first Strickland in print: in 1817, the year before Catharine earned her first five guineas, Agnes had published a poem about Queen Charlotte's death in a Norfolk newspaper. The success of this florid eulogy to royalty catapulted Agnes into rather grand circles, and she never looked back. Soon she was mixing with minor aristocrats, dropping names and insisting that, in addition to the family connection with Catherine Parr, she had the Stuart blood of Scottish kings. With the sense of theatre acquired during their childhood dramatic evenings, and with an imperious toss of her well-dressed silky black hair, Agnes always enjoyed making an entrance at social events. She expended as much creative energy on her appearance as on her literary output. "Last week I was obliged to assist the mantua maker in making and altering my robes," she wrote to a Suffolk friend. "Fitting and refitting, frilling and grilling . . . chased from the secret chambers of my brain a multitude of excellent ideas which had I been at leisure to have instituted would have furnished employment for a month."

A third ally in the young women's pursuit of publication was an old friend of their father's, Thomas Harral, who had moved from Suffolk to London to edit a fashionable magazine entitled *La Belle Assemblée.* Harral's daughter, Anna Laura, was one of Susanna's best friends; his son Francis was Catharine's first serious beau. Harral introduced the Stricklands to various writers and poets in the capital, and he gave them advice on how to get published. Through Harral, Susanna met a man who quickly became a father figure. Thomas Pringle was a Scottish poet and outspoken leader of the Anti-Slavery League. He found the admiration of a clever, lively young woman immensely flattering, and he frequently invited her to stay with him and his family in their townhouse in the Finsbury district of London, or in their country home in Hampstead. Pringle indulged Susanna, praised her poems and encouraged her to question convention. In turn, Susanna adored him, and she wrote to him daily when they were apart. It was an intoxicating relationship: a mix of paternal and erotic affection. Susanna took to calling Pringle "Papa."

With the help of people like Harral and Pringle, the Stricklands were able to take full advantage of the latest literary fashion—literary "annuals." These lavishly bound, expensive anthologies offered short narratives of love and chivalry. Specially commissioned steel engravings depicted pensive maidens gazing at the heavens, or sitting in solitude by a roaring sea. To a modern reader, the annuals offer only sentimentality and bad writing; to the Stricklands, they offered liberation. They gave women the opportunity to support themselves. For example, Mary Shelley (Wollstonecraft's daughter, the author of *Frankenstein* and the wife of Percy Bysshe Shelley) earned enough money from the gushing romances she contributed to *The Keepsake*, edited by Lady Blessington, to keep her son in school at Harrow.

By 1829, five of the six Strickland sisters—Eliza, Agnes, Jane, Catharine and Susanna—had established toeholds in London's literary cliffs. Eliza, who always hated Reydon Hall, was living in a furnished room in London and editing *The Court Journal,* a jaunty and rather snobbish periodical stuffed with fashion tips, gossip about the royal court and theatre notices. Agnes was publishing rapture-filled epic poetry and being mentioned as a writer of considerable promise (although a waspish reviewer suggested that "'poems long and legendary' are above the calibre of your muse"). Catharine quietly and methodically published a children's book almost every year from 1825 onwards. Her income steadily rose, so that by 1830 she was being paid more than twelve pounds for *The Sketchbook of a Young Naturalist*. It is hard to estimate what this is worth in modern terms: the working rule for British historians is to multiply early-nineteenth-century values by fifty to render them in late-twentieth-century terms. Any equivalence is crude, since there were fluctuations within decades and the cost of services rose much more rapidly than the cost of manufactured goods. But Catharine was probably earning roughly six hundred pounds for each book in today's money. Her annual income of twelve pounds would have made a significant difference to life at Reydon Hall, but it would not have been enough to live on in an era when an English farm labourer earned about thirty pounds a year.

In addition, there was a Strickland assembly line for the production of poetry, reviews and stories which regularly appeared in several of the seventeen annuals being published. The sisters often co-wrote stories, and several times an editor would attribute a certain piece to the wrong sister. Payment was meagre for most of these pieces, and the letters that the women wrote to their editors suggest more craven gratitude than aggressive pursuit of a fair fee. But anything was better than nothing. "I should be enabled to leave a sum for home expenses in Mamma's hands," a hopeful Catharine wrote to Susanna, in one note about a few shillings that were due for a particular article.

The Stricklands' contributions to glossy anthologies were terribly conventional. Maidens swooned, lions roared, Byronic heroes martyred themselves. For Eliza, Catharine and Jane, this was enough. But Agnes and Susanna pushed at the limits of convention. Competition crackled between these two young women. Each recognized in the other a talent for expression that their sisters could never claim. All their lives, Susanna and Agnes envied each other's successes even as they exchanged congratulations on achievements. The edge of competition was blunted only by the difference in their writing styles. At this stage, Susanna was pouring more and more of her creative energy into verse. She was also using, in some of her stories for *La Belle Assemblée*, a first-person narrative voice, which allowed her to include her own wit, and interest in magic and spiritualism, in her sketches of Suffolk characters. Agnes was going in a different direction. Acknowledging that she couldn't make it as a poet, she had begun to interest herself in the past and to haunt the newly completed British Museum. Amongst its untidy piles of still-uncatalogued collections of state and private records, she took her first step towards her lifetime avocation: history.

As Susanna approached her late twenties, she became increasingly irritated by the dainty constraints of the glossy anthologies. At the same time, she was enmeshed in religious doubts. She was a young woman in search of herself, torn between her literary aspirations and a fierce religious faith. A close friend told Susanna that she sounded like "a mad woman and a fanatic" when she gave vent to the intensity of her emotions. Perhaps the young writer was simply disgusted by the vicar of Reydon's preference for "huntin' and fishin'" over giving sermons; perhaps she was swept away by the fervently anti-establishment views of her hero, Thomas Pringle, a Methodist. Pringle denounced Tory smugness with histrionic passion. For whatever reason, in 1830, Susanna turned her back on the pomp and rituals of the Church of England, whose comfortable pews were occupied each Sunday by the carriage set, and was admitted into a Nonconformist congregation in a village church three miles from Reydon. Most of her co-worshippers were farmers and their labourers, who arrived on foot or in creaking hay-wagons.

Mrs. Strickland and her three elder daughters, who were all busy clinging to the upper rungs of society, were horrified. This was a most unconventional step for a young woman of Susanna's breeding. They had already had to deal with the fact that the fourth Strickland sister, Sarah, had also become a Dissenter. But Sarah's conversion was less threatening than Susanna's, since it had remained a private matter. The family knew that Susanna, unlike demure Sarah, would immediately rush into print, to embarrass her relatives with fervent proclamations of her new allegiance and criticisms of the spiritually slack. Sure enough, Susanna soon published an ambitious and heartfelt poem entitled "Enthusiasm." She belittled "men of pleasure" in this epic work and glorified "the unlearned and those of low estate" who, with their simple faith, are the only Christians who will attain salvation. Agnes was mortified, wondering what her smart friends would think. It wasn't the last time that Susanna would embarrass her.

Susanna was not only taking an unconventional spiritual path, she was also being politicized. Thanks to Thomas Pringle, she was increasingly involved in the abolitionist movement—as radical a political movement in the early nineteenth century as feminism would be in the mid-twentieth century. Pringle invited Susanna to transcribe the stories of two former slaves from British colonies, a twenty-four-year-old man called Ashton Warner from St. Vincent, and a forty-year-old woman, Mary Prince, from Bermuda. Mary, now working in the Pringle household, dictated "a recital of revolting cruelty" to the impressionable young Susanna, who carefully wrote down and shaped the narrative of exploitation. Susanna downplayed the project's importance in a letter to a friend: "It is a pathetic little history and is now printing in the form of a pamphlet to be laid before the Houses of Parliament. Of course my name does not appear." But the impressionable twenty-seven-year-old was gripped by Mary's account of physical and sexual brutalities at the hands of her masters. She had seen with her own eyes the appalling criss-cross of scars, evidence of repeated lashings, on the older woman's back. Mary Prince was a tough, outspoken survivor, but her experiences as a malnourished, poor, powerless woman in a distant British colony fed Susanna's fascination with the darker side of human existence. When Susanna subsequently published Ashton Warner's story, she reproached her fellow countrymen with the "gross injustice and awful criminality of a free nation suffering such an abomination as negro slavery to exist in her dominions."

Susanna's letters reveal how much she enjoyed mingling with publishers, essayists and writers when they congregated in the Pringles' London drawing room. She was flattered when the intelligentsia made a fuss of her, assuring James Bird with blatantly false modesty, "I am almost sick of flattering encomiums on my genius. How these men in London do talk. I learn daily to laugh at their fine love speeches." She was eager for friendship with other "bluestockings," as women writers were often called. Most of all, the ambition to be a much-published, well-known author—a path on which her sister Agnes was already launched—began to burn in her with a frightening fierceness. Although the Strickland girls were raised to respect intellectual achievement, they were also brought up to be docile wives to whomever they might marry. Susanna was both intoxicated and embarrassed by her hunger for fame—a hunger, she worried, that was "not only a weak but a criminal passion." Her angst cannot have been helped by the fact that she was now over twenty-five and, like all her sisters, seemed fated for spinsterhood.

Rivalry between Agnes and Susanna continued to seethe as Susanna began to catch up with her sister's success. The two women managed a temporary truce in 1830 when they co-produced a small pamphlet entitled *Patriotic Songs*, including eight poems, four by each sister, that celebrated England and the monarchy. King William IV was so impressed that he called its authors "an ornament to our country." And Catharine was relieved to see Agnes and Susanna on better terms. "Could I tell you the joy that fills my heart at the reunion of two sisters, you would rejoice," wrote the family peacemaker to "kindest and most affectionate Susy." "May no worldly consideration, no prejudice, no contradiction of opinion on indifferent subjects ever disturb your love."

Then, in May 1830, Lieutenant John Dunbar Moodie, an exuberant and cheerful thirty-three-year-old Scot who had just returned from South Africa to look for a wife, turned up at the home of his old friend Thomas Pringle. Soon, he and Susanna were taking walks together on Hampstead Heath, sharing their love of music and reading aloud to each other. Within two months of John's arrival, Susanna's interest in theological debate had been overtaken by her enthusiasm for the dashing lieutenant. In the words of her sister Catharine, she had "become a convert to Lieutenant Dunbar Moodie." And John Moodie was petitioning Mrs. Thomas Strickland for her youngest daughter's hand in marriage.

Chapter 3

Sweet Dreams

ohn Dunbar Moodie marched into Susanna Strickland's life with the verve of a fife-and-drum band. He appeared to offer everything Susanna wanted in a lover. He could match her emotional intensity, and (like her sister Catharine) he could lift her spirits with his infectious optimism and zest for life. Short and stocky, with unruly dark hair, John was just too damn cheerful and healthy to fit the languid ideal of the era, but there was an attractive gallantry to him. He had a score of thrilling anecdotes about his military experiences in the Napoleonic wars and his adventures on the South African veldt, where he had settled after he left the army. As Susanna's mother noted approvingly, he was a "gentleman of family and high moral character." And the Scotsman, who was six years older than Susanna, played the flute, composed poetry and wrote the most beautiful love letters. "I feel we cannot live but in each other's arms," he told his "beloved Susie" within weeks of meeting her. "My whole soul is absorbed in one sweet dream of you—you must and shall be mine . . . I care for no luxuries, dearest, let me but press you to my heart and I will live upon those dear lips, and these worldly cares would be forgotten . . ."

His passion was enough to persuade Susanna, her mother and her older sisters to overlook what Mrs. Strickland politely referred to as an "income too confined to support a wife." The wolf was not far from the door for John Dunbar Moodie. He belonged to a class disastrously familiar to mothers of eligible daughters in early-nineteenth-century England: officers who had defended King and country during the Napoleonic wars and had now been pensioned off on half-pay; at any time, they could be recalled for active service. Britain's wars with France in the late-eighteenth and early-nineteenth centuries had been a boon for younger sons of impoverished gentry. Fighting "Boney" had given them an income and a way of life otherwise unavailable.

The youngest of five sons of an ancient but obscure Scottish family, John Moodie was born in 1797 on his family's estate on the bleak and craggy Isle of Hoy in the Orkneys. Melsetter, the family seat, was a large, ugly brick manor house, built about forty years earlier and already heavily mortgaged. John's eldest brother, Benjamin, sold it at the first opportunity. John joined the army as soon as he was old enough: at sixteen, he became a second-lieutenant in the 21st Royal (Northern) Fusiliers. But within two years he had been wounded in the left wrist during an engagement on Dutch soil and retired on half-pay, with few prospects and little education. His income would barely cover the needs of a bachelor of modest tastes—and though John wasn't extravagant, throughout his life he was immoderately generous to those he loved.

In 1817, John's brother Benjamin Moodie had emigrated to the Cape Colony, at the southern tip of Africa. The British government was offering free passage and a hundred acres of land to anyone who would settle the land and quell the Bantus, or "Kaffirs," as the settlers contemptuously called them (*kaffir* means "infidel" in Arabic). So in 1819 John decided to join Ben. The following year, a third brother, Donald, sailed off to the Cape as well. John Dunbar Moodie spent eleven years farming the red soil of southern Africa, and there were aspects of life in the colony that he loved. Rising at dawn and shouldering his rifle, he would ride out across the open grasslands to hunt elephants and "sea-cows," as the Boers called hippopotamus. But it was a miserable and lonely existence for a sociable man in his twenties: speaking broken Dutch to his Boer neighbours in the Groote Valley, scratching a subsistence living from the dry and stony terrain and repelling Bantu raids on his livestock. "I lived for years without companionship, for my nearest English neighbour was twenty-five miles off. . . . My very ideas became confused and limited, for want of intellectual companions to strike out new lights." John dreaded the idea that he might turn into another crusty, sunburnt old misanthrope, grumbling to newcomers about the way that Westminster ignored South Africa's potential. So in 1830, he returned to England, "with the resolution of placing my domestic matters on a more comfortable footing."

Within weeks of his return, John Moodie had secured Susanna's heart. Within months, he had her mother's permission to marry his beloved. But he faced a monumental challenge: how could he afford a wife? There were so few avenues open to a young man who was neither rich nor landed, and who had neither the skill nor the inclination to set himself up as a merchant of some sort. John resorted to a tactic popular amongst penniless young men of his day, as well as several heroes of novels by Jane Austen, William Thackeray and Anthony Trollope. He turned to his rich relatives, in hopes of a settlement or promise of future legacy. He rushed up to Scotland to visit a smattering of elderly and, he hoped, benevolent uncles, but kept in touch with his beloved Susie in daily letters.

The ardour in those letters burns as brightly today as it did when he sharpened his goose quill and dipped it into the ink: "Believe me you are indeed with me when I lie down and when I rise my thoughts are still with you—you still are present in my dreams with your smiles and the looks you wore when first I loved you." In page after page, John described to his fiancée the tortuous process of chasing family money from elderly relatives. They all seemed to be ensnared by debts, complicated entails on their properties and lawsuits. But John was never one to let setbacks lower his spirits; he quickly moved on to exuberant, thigh-slapping descriptions of various adventures. "My old craze for boat sailing seized me one day," began a five-page account of a terrifying sail, in which John was nearly shipwrecked in the Pentland Firth. Despite a savage storm, and the inexperience of his young companion, John managed to haul his dinghy off the rocks. He then took refuge in the harbour at Hoy, his birthplace. The locals greeted him rapturously, to his delight. "A poor old woman near a hundred years of age, who had been a servant of my grandfather's, sent her grand-daughter to me with a pair of worsted stockings. . . . Ah! my Susie had you been with me this would indeed have been one of the happiest moments of my life."

John's inclination to revel in danger and regale listeners with his adventures was a mixed blessing. His intention had been to sweep his bride off her feet. He wanted to take her back to his property in South Africa immediately after they were married and he had wangled some capital out of his family. At first, Susanna fell in with these plans and worked harder than ever to churn out stories for the annuals. "I must depend on my wits to buy my wedding clothes," she explained to friends. But although John's braggadocio about shooting elephants and leopards at the Cape, not to mention his spine-tingling descriptions of snakes, amused the habitués of London drawing rooms, they started to unnerve Susanna. While John was scouring Scotland for rich relatives, she got cold feet. She began to wonder whether the literary lions of London weren't more her style than the tawny-maned lions of South Africa. She asked herself why she would move to a colony in which slavery was still permitted, when the Mary Prince story had made her a fervent abolitionist. In January 1831, while John was still in Scotland, she abruptly broke off the engagement: "I have changed my mind. You may call me a jilt or a flirt or what you please. . . . I will neither marry a soldier nor leave my country for ever . . ."

What happened to the great love affair? Susanna, it seems, had found herself in a very modern dilemma. She had recognized that if she followed her heart, she would probably be abandoning her ambitions. "[I] feel happy that I am once more my own mistress," she admitted to a confidant. Her writing career had taken off: that year she had managed to place stories in several publications, including Harral's monthly, *La Belle Assemblée*, the weekly *Athenaeum* and the annuals *The Amulet, Friendship's Offering* and *Juvenile Forget-Me-Not*. She was meeting or corresponding with kindred spirits such as Mary Russell Mitford, a single woman sixteen years her senior who was supporting herself as a professional writer. And the more Susanna heard about the empty, arid grasslands of the Cape, the less attractive they sounded—especially when she compared them to the streets of London.

It is not difficult to imagine the appeal to Susanna Strickland of the London of the early nineteenth century. In the second half of the eighteenth century, the capital had been transformed from a conglomeration of villages, such as Westminster and Chelsea, linked by muddy lanes and narrow streets, into a magnificent city traversed by paved roads. Six new bridges across the Thames River, built between 1750 and 1827, had supplemented London Bridge, and by unclogging the city's arteries had enormously increased commerce. The population had doubled in the previous fifty years: with two million citizens, it was now not only the largest city in the world but also its principal financial exchange, the "Rialto of the age" in James Morris's phrase. Private developers had built grandiose terraces of large houses, like the Nash Terraces on the south side of Regent's Park, and elegant rows of shops along Oxford Street and Bond Street. Men of business and letters congregated in the coffee houses, book shops and clubs of Piccadilly. Susanna could wander down busy thoroughfares, listening to the noisy cries of vendors selling lavender, cherries, hot loaves or gingerbread, as she admired shop windows full of the latest furniture designs or Paris fashions.

Moreover, the world was opening up for talented young women like the Strickland sisters. The capital was exploding with the kind of cultural activities in which, following the example set by Mary Wollstonecraft, Fanny Burney, Jane Austen, Maria Edgeworth and Mary Russell Mitford, Susanna could envisage a future. Elizabeth was already editing her periodical; Agnes was frequently mentioned as a "poetess" in society columns; Catharine was a popular writer of children's books. The booksellers, engravers and publishers who had offices in St. Paul's Churchyard, Paternoster Row, Ludgate Hill and Fleet Street were eager for material. The introduction of steam printing after 1814 had lowered costs and multiplied the number of copies of a publication that could be printed in a short time. There were close to three hundred newspapers circulating through the United Kingdom. Did Susanna really want to exchange this buzz of literary activity for the isolation of a South African farm, surrounded by hostile "Kaffirs" and truculent Boers? Did she really want to leave a city in which women were playing an increasingly important public role to live in a country that still endorsed the inhumane practices that Mary Prince had described?

It is clear that "Papa" Pringle influenced Susanna's decision to forsake romance and devote herself to the literary life. Thomas and Margaret Pringle had lived in South Africa for seven years; that's where they had met John Dunbar Moodie. But they had returned to England in 1826, sickened by the way the British government condoned slavery in the colony and exasperated by the way it blew hot and cold in its policies towards the Boer majority. Thomas attached more importance to his hopes for Susanna than to his friendship with Moodie. He painted a dispiriting picture of colonial life to his young protegée and encouraged her to reconsider her engagement. A young woman of her talent, he argued, would thrive in the publishing world—especially with himself as her mentor. "By the strong recommendation of my friends," Susanna reported home, "I have been induced to board with a family for the next three months and to try my fortune in the world of letters. . . . I hope to get on and prosper." Her new London lodgings were in Middleton Square, in the district of Finsbury—a respectable but unassuming address. Like Islington to its north, and Bloomsbury to its west,

Finsbury was a pleasant neighbourhood of spacious Georgian squares, filled with flower-beds, trees and lawns and surrounded by beautifully proportioned terraces of four- or five-storeyed houses. Susanna's rooms overlooked the newly consecrated St. Mark's, a fine stone church with a splendid tower. And she was just around the corner from "Papa" Pringle, in Claremont Square.

At first, Susanna found her independence stimulating. "All my friends promise to call upon me in my new home!" She reeled off to her Suffolk friends James and Emma Bird a catalogue of the distinguished writers she had met, and the invitations to "grand converzationes" she had received. She watched a ragtag political demonstration in the streets of Islington, which she told James Bird would have made him laugh himself "into pleurisy." Finsbury was a neighbourhood peopled with literary and artistic types, such as the cartoonist William Cruikshank. "We often met and had a chat about things," she would recall in later years. "He was a wonderful man in his way." One of her neighbours was Edward Irving, a prominent preacher

Middleton Square

For three exhilarating months in 1832, Susanna lived
the life of a bluestocking in Middleton Square, London.

who ranted from the pulpit in a strong Scottish accent about the need for more ritual in church services. Susanna fought through his crowds of admirers to hear him perform. "It was worth enduring a state of suffocation to see and hear him. . . . I never took my eyes from off this strange apparition. . . . Imagine a tall man with high aquiline features and a complexion darkly brilliant with long raven love locks hanging down to his waist, his sleeves so short as to show part of his naked arms and his person arrayed in the costume of old reformers." In addition to lively letters to friends, she turned out an amazing volume of work—book reviews, stories, songs, poems. Her self-doubt, and her ambivalence about success vanished. At the Pringles' weekly receptions, Susanna glowed as distinguished editors pointed her out to each other as one of the brightest among the new women writers.

Susanna was particularly entertained by the egos and behaviour of those—like Irving, Pringle and the editors of the various annuals—who made their living by their wits. She observed the affectations of the young member of Parliament Edward Lytton, her exact contemporary but already an established dandy and the successful author (under his pen name Bulwer-Lytton) of two successful novels. She never forgot her first glimpse of the historian Thomas Carlyle, "but he was such a crabbed looking man that I did not care to make his acquaintance," she told an interviewer years later. She had felt on the margins of family life as a child, while sweet-tempered Catharine got all the attention. Now, as a woman, and as someone uncertain about her own social status, she once again felt like an outsider in London's *beau monde*. Nobody observes her fellow human beings with a more acid clarity than someone who feels she doesn't really belong in the magic circle, and Susanna's whole life had prepared her for this role. In letters she polished a style of cool amusement that echoes Jane Austen's delicious sense of irony. "There is to me a charm in literary society which none other can give," Susanna wrote to a friend, "were it only for the sake of studying more closely the imperfections of temper and the curious manner in which vanity displays itself in persons of superior mind and intellect."

After a few weeks of trying to support herself, however, the pressure to produce and the battles to secure adequate payment began to erode Susanna's confidence. "A single woman of good fortune is always respectable, and may be as sensible and pleasant as anybody else," Jane Austen had written in *Emma*, a few years earlier. "But a single woman with a very narrow income must be a ridiculous disagreeable old maid! the proper sport of boys and girls!" When Susanna was in a good mood, she believed she could conquer the world. But when her spirits sank, nightmares of penury, spinsterhood and emotional starvation shrank her horizons. She had only to look at her three eldest sisters for a vision of a bluestocking future. Elizabeth lived a cramped existence, between her furnished London room and the crowded editorial offices of *The Court Journal.* Agnes was constantly worrying about how to afford the finery she needed for her smart parties. And Jane remained cooped up at Reydon Hall, keeping house on a pittance, scrambling for fees from annuals and caring for their increasingly crabby mother.

When Susanna's letter breaking off their engagement finally reached John in Scotland, he was shattered by her abrupt rejection. He rushed south to win her back. Assuring her that he loved her far too much to lose her, he declared that if the wildlife of South Africa struck such terror in her, he would abandon all plans to return there. He must have arrived soon after Susanna's resolve to be her own mistress had started to flag and his passionate wooing soon bore fruit. Susanna recognized that, as Mrs. John Dunbar Moodie, she would at least escape the old maid stigma, if not poverty. She was reminded that she and John thought alike in many ways: both were vehemently opposed to slavery, expected deference from their social inferiors, but felt that manners were at least as important as money. And the physical presence of her suitor rekindled the ardour that had flamed so brightly the previous summer. His humour and cheerful energy provided a reassuring contrast to her self-doubt and pessimism. John made her laugh at her own uncertainties. Susanna's determination to be independent wilted in the heat of his desire, and she agreed that they should get married as soon as possible.

In the early nineteenth century, weddings were usually modest affairs. Perhaps that is why only Catharine, of all Susanna's sisters, arrived to celebrate this occasion. In the absence of Susanna's family, the Pringles showed their support for their young friend. Mrs. Pringle helped Susanna assemble an outfit for the wedding and entertained the little party to breakfast before the ceremony on April 4, 1831. The gathering at their Finsbury house was a modest but joyful affair—probably without liquor, given Mr. Pringle's low church leanings, but with no shortage of elegant speeches and good wishes. Then Thomas Pringle helped the bride into his carriage and drove with her to the splendid Greek revival parish church of St. Pancras, Woburn Place. Sitting next to the coachman was feisty Mary Prince, the former slave who had dictated her story to Susanna. "Black Mary," Susanna remembered, "had treated herself with a complete new suit . . . to see her dear Missie and Biographer wed." Catharine Strickland acted as bridesmaid. At the altar stood Moodie, nervous until the very last moment that Susanna might get cold feet again. Thomas Pringle had evidently overcome his disappointment at Susanna's decision, and he led her up the aisle, between the Ionian columns, to the awaiting bridegroom.

Catharine, who had watched her sister vacillate between her writing ambitions and her love for John Moodie, knew that Susanna was still uncertain about marriage. "The dear girl kept up her spirits pretty well though at times a shade of care came over her brow but she rallied as much as possible," she told the Birds a couple of days later. "What do you now think of the vagaries of woman-kind?"

Three days later, Susanna wrote to the same friends a letter in which she protested far too vehemently that she had no lingering doubts. "I assure you that, instead of feeling the least regret at the step I was taking, if a tear trembled in my eye, it was one of joy and I pronounced the fatal obey with the firm determination to keep it." But she acknowledged that "the fatal obey" had already cramped her ambitions. "My blue stockings, since I became a wife, have turned so pale that I think they will soon be quite white, or at least only tinged with a hue of London smoke."

After their wedding, the Moodies spent a few weeks in Finsbury. Susanna continued to mingle with her literary friends and write for the annuals. John had just published an account of his adventures as a youthful soldier (*A Narrative of the Campaign of 1814*) and was now negotiating with the publisher Richard Bentley about a book on his experiences in South Africa. It would finally appear in 1835, under the title *Ten Years in South Africa, Including a Particular Description of the Wild Sports,* and consisted of enthusiastic descriptions of shootin' with the boys, interspersed with a few brief throat-clearing passages about farming methods. John and Susanna were already finding it hard to make ends meet, and the question of how to support themselves became more acute in early summer when Susanna realized that she was pregnant. They decided to reduce their costs by leaving London and renting a cottage in Southwold so that Susanna could be near her mother, sisters and friends.

Susanna never enjoyed her pregnancies; she was afflicted with nausea and a general lassitude. Nevertheless, she and John enjoyed receiving her sisters and the local "Grandees," as Susanna termed Suffolk's gentry. "Even Mamma forgets her resolution of never leaving home and honors our little mansion with her presence," she noted. Neither John nor Susanna dared look much beyond the birth of their baby. They had no money and no prospects, and there were few opportunities in England for a man of John's skills. But then a surprise visitor turned up on their doorstep. It was Robert Reid, a successful settler in Upper Canada whose daughter was the wife of Susanna's brother Samuel. Sam had flourished in Canada as an employee of the Canada Company, a London-based organization that had bought up vast tracts of Crown land in Upper Canada to sell to incoming settlers. Sam had been a superintendent of Canada Company projects around Guelph, in the triangle of Upper Canada that jutted down towards Lake Erie, before moving east to the newly settled town of Peterborough, north of Rice Lake, of which the Reid family had been founders. Reid was gung-ho on the advantages of emigration. He boasted to the young couple about his own history—how, after a struggle of twelve years, he had the satisfaction of a family of ten children all now in a position to become wealthy landowners. Reid promised the young couple "independence and comfort on the other side of the water, and even wealth after a few years' toil."

Reid's rosy picture of prospects in Upper Canada was only one element in the flood of propaganda about emigration then circulating around Britain. England was now in a crippling agricultural depression. The prices of wheat and barley had fallen by more than half between 1812 and 1830. At least one in ten of the British people was a pauper, for whom emigration offered the *only* escape from poverty. All around Southwold, tenant farmers were defaulting on their rents, and agricultural labourers were being thrown out of their cottages and into parish poorhouses. In the coal mines of the Midlands, naked women pulled wagons through the shafts to earn a few pennies. In the factories of the north, children of eight or nine were working twelve-hour days. Of course, the Moodies were in a different class from these casualties of the faltering economy—but they too were its victims.

The Moodies began to consider crossing the Atlantic as a way to maintain their social position despite their cramped income. By now they had realized that, even outside London, to live in the style to which an English gentleman aspired they needed at least one thousand pounds a year. John's military pension of a hundred pounds a year, and their combined but unpredictable earnings as writers, would never amount to that sum. So when a public meeting about the advantages of emigration to Canada was advertised, John was amongst those who flocked to Norwich to hear it. He was accompanied by his friend and Southwold neighbour Thomas Wales.

The lecture was given by one of the chief Canada-boosters, William Cattermole from nearby Bungay. Cattermole had a financial interest in extolling all the golden opportunities in the New World: he was an agent of the same Canada Company that Sam had worked for, and he received a bonus for every emigrant he recruited. Cattermole rhapsodized about the cheapness and fertility of the land available to those who braved the high seas. He spoke of Canada's salubrious climate, its fertile soil, commercial advantages, great water access, its proximity to the mother country and its exemption from taxation. He told of land yielding forty bushels to the acre and log houses raised in a single day with the help of friends and neighbours. He insisted that society in York (which eventually became Toronto, but was then a muddy, ramshackle settlement) was "equal to any provincial town in Britain." His lectures and pamphlets made Upper Canada sound like Virginia—a warm, welcoming landscape with civilized people tending fruit trees and arranging flowers.

Cattermole was not the only huckster selling rainbows. A volume entitled *The Emigrant's Guide to Upper Canada* by a Captain Charles Stuart should have been renamed *The Pilgrim's Guide to the Celestial Regions,* according to another settler, E.A.Talbot. Salesmen like Cattermole and Stuart presented the gloomy acres that were available in the most attractive language, and soon John was musing about the possibility of an "estate" in the New World, as if he were talking about a grouse moor in Scotland. Neither Cattermole nor Stuart mentioned the monumentally hard work required to clear the land of dense forest growth, the total absence of everything most English people considered essential to their comfort, or the loneliness and poverty that settlers faced in the early years.

The combination of Reid's anecdotes and Cattermole's gush, plus the cheerful letters that arrived at Reydon Hall from Sam Strickland, captivated John Moodie. He decided that, if he couldn't return to South Africa, Canada was an acceptable alternative. Retired and half-pay officers were eligible for free grants of several hundred acres of land there, in the hopes that, in the event of invasion from the south, they would form the core of an instant defence force. It was only twenty years since the Americans had mounted an invasion of Upper Canada, and relations between the United States and Britain remained uneasy. John, being the type who was convinced he could make a go of any adventure, began to muse on the excitements of life as a landowner in Upper Canada. He grumbled about their cramped life in Southwold and complained to his sister-in-law Agnes that he was "Suffolkating." Agnes

THE EMIGRANTS WELCOME TO CANADA.

London cartoonists warned gullible emigrants that the promises of bucksters like William Cattermole were worthless.

BIRDER'S® WORLD MAGAZINE

DD3

KALMBACH PUBLISHING CO.

21027 Crossroads Circle, P.O. Box 1612, Waukesha, WI 53187-1612

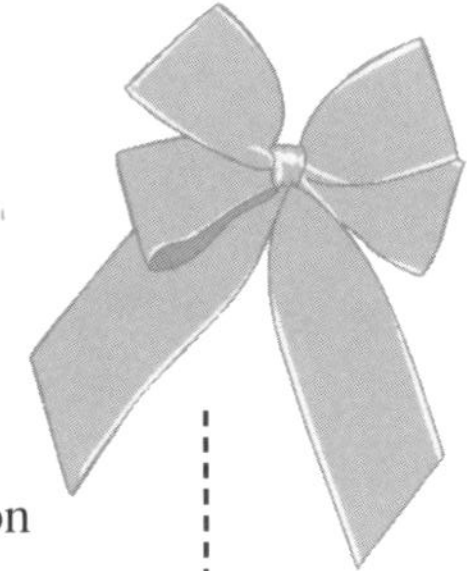

A special magazine gift subscription

has been ordered for you by

Mom and "Marni" Mom"

Enjoy many hours of

pleasurable and informative reading!

For

Nancy and Dan.

GC2003DR

couldn't imagine why anybody would want to live in a colony where there were no theatres, libraries or stately homes. But she always had a soft spot for "brother Moodie," so she didn't try to discourage him.

The prospect of emigration appalled Susanna. She did not want to leave England. She shared many of Agnes's reservations about a land with no history, no literature and no cultural life. But she had to admit that she and John were going nowhere in England, and there would be little they could promise their children for the future. And she knew that she would meet her brother in Canada, instead of South Africa's lions, elephants and snakes. "You must not be surprised at our flight in the spring," she confided to her friends the Birds. John set about getting letters of recommendations to various Upper Canadian nabobs in order to smooth his path through the colony. Letters of introduction, establishing the holder's social standing, were crucial door-openers for gentlemen emigrants to a society where jobs were allocated by patronage. With a letter from the right patron, a half-pay officer could get his name on the list of candidates for such desirable appointments as customs officer, postmaster or sheriff. John started to play the patronage game even before he crossed the Atlantic.

News that the Moodies were planning to emigrate shook Susanna's sister Catharine to the core. Throughout the stormy progress of the Moodie romance, Catharine had been quietly nursing a broken heart. For more than a year, she had been in love with Francis Harral, son of the editor of *La Belle Assemblée.* When the romance went off the rails, Catharine sank into a depression and was barely able to write. At the Moodies' wedding, Susanna noticed that "my dear Katy [looked] but so so."

Realizing that Catharine was in a bad way, the Stricklands' widowed cousin, Rebecca Leverton, swept her off first to Bath, then to Oxford and finally to her country house in Herefordshire. Throughout the fall of 1831, Catharine obediently and passively trailed after her relative through fashionable drawing rooms. "Mrs. Leverton is very kind to me and treats me with the greatest confidence as a friend and a child at the same time," she reported. But when she heard about the Moodies' intentions, Catharine snapped into action. She made plans to return to Suffolk to see Susanna, "as I could not endure the thought of parting from her at a distance and possibly for years, perhaps for life."

Catharine returned to Reydon Hall, and every afternoon, often with Jane or Agnes, strolled along to Southwold where the Moodies were installed in a cottage overlooking the grey North Sea. The newlyweds were the perfect advertisement for marriage: John played his flute and made his sisters-in-law laugh, while Susanna beamed with unaccustomed happiness. And Catharine was not the only visitor to the clifftop cottage: soon after the Moodies moved to Southwold, Thomas Traill, an old friend of John's, came to stay with them. Like John, Thomas was a Presbyterian Scot and a half-pay officer who came from the impoverished Orkney gentry. Both had served in the Royal (Northern) Fusiliers during the final years of the Napoleonic wars. The Traill family estate, Westove, near the little town of Kirkwall, was as run-down and mortgaged as the Moodie estate had

Thomas Traill had served in the Napoleonic wars with John Moodie: in 1832, he was a balding widower of uncertain means.

been. Westove had once been a seat of considerable wealth, yielding an annual income of 18,000 to 30,000 pounds (equivalent to at least a million pounds today) from its harvest of sea-kelp, which was used in the manufacture of glass. But when straw, a far cheaper alternative, was discovered to be equally effective as a chemical reagent and source of potash, Traill fortunes plummeted. Unfortunately, the Traills went on living like lords for some years, saddling the estate with a pile of hopeless debts. Now Thomas could expect no dividends from Westove's farms or its sea-kelp harvest.

John and Thomas were complete opposites in looks and personality. Where John Moodie was short, bearded and plump, Thomas Traill was tall, thin, balding and clean-shaven. While John was jovial and energetic, Thomas was reserved and sedentary. John enjoyed a convivial pipe of tobacco surrounded by friends; Thomas silently took snuff. John always had a smile on his face; a gloomy expression characterized Thomas. While John Moodie liked to see himself as a man of action, Thomas Traill saw himself as a scholar—he had attended Wadham College, Oxford, spoke several languages and adored highbrow chat with fellow intellectuals. One of his closest friends was John Lockhart, son-in-law and biographer of Britain's hugely successful novelist Sir Walter Scott. And while John Moodie had presented himself to Susanna free of family responsibilities, Thomas Traill arrived on the scene in 1831 as a thirty-eight-year-old newly widowed father of two teenage boys. He had left his sons, Walter and John, with a relative in Scotland and moved to London, like his fellow officer John Dunbar Moodie, to find some congenial company and, perhaps, a wife.

As the winter winds whistled across Southwold beach, and Susanna Moodie awaited the arrival of her baby, it didn't take long for Thomas and Catharine to become close. Both were lonely and recovering from the abrupt end of cherished relationships. Both were great readers. Catharine's serenity and optimism were irresistible to Thomas, who himself admitted of his own temperament, "I am not disposed to be sanguine about anything." He recognized that her kindness and unshakable faith offered him a sense of security that he had never been able to achieve for himself. And Catharine found in Thomas what she had feared she would lose in Susanna's departure—a close friend who offered companionship, and who needed her.

The atmosphere in the Moodies' cottage was charged with the sexual chemistry between Susanna and John. John had already learned to tiptoe around Susanna's moodiness while overwhelming her with lusty affection. "Ah, he is so kind, so good, so indulgent to all my wayward fits," Susanna wrote of her husband soon after their wedding, "that I look up to him as to my guardian Angel. I seem to lose my own identity in him, and become indifferent to every thing else in the world . . . my heart will never grow old or cold to him." What could be a better advertisement for marriage than the picture of John and Susanna so passionately in love, and so excited about the impending arrival of their first child? Their parlour was a hothouse for the budding romance between Catharine and Thomas, neither of whom could spontaneously generate the erotic intensity that characterized the Moodies.

The Moodies were overjoyed to see Catharine blossom in the glow of Thomas's love. But Catharine's mother and sister Agnes disapproved strongly of her suitor. Now that their mother rarely ventured beyond the kitchen gardens of Reydon Hall, the Strickland sisters all turned to Agnes for approval. Agnes, a take-charge kind of person, did not think much of Thomas. He was nine years older than Catharine, and had none of John Moodie's *joie de vivre* to offset his shortcomings. He lacked the manly virtues of energy, courage and decisiveness that Catharine's father, Thomas Strickland, had embodied. Furthermore, he was encumbered with debts, teenage children and a morose temperament.

Catharine's docile temper aside, she had a will powerful enough to make up for her fiancé's reticence. She was determined not to let her bossy older sister or anybody else sabotage this relationship. And besides, both Catharine and Thomas were infected by the Canada-mania that had captured the Moodies. Susanna and Catharine began to discuss the notion of leaving England *together*—waving goodbye to their own pinched circumstances and their husbands' failing Scottish fortunes and venturing overseas to meet again with their brother Samuel. They helped each other collect the clothes they would need for a voyage across the ocean and a new life in the New World: flannel petticoats, sturdy boots, knitted stockings, warm cloaks.

Events moved quickly through 1832. In late February, after a long and painful labour, Susanna and John's first baby was born. John doted on his "dab-chick," as he called his daughter. She was christened Catherine Mary Josephine at St. Edmund's Church, Southwold. A couple of months later, on May 13, Thomas and Catharine were married in Reydon's squat little parish church, St. Margaret's. Agnes and Jane Strickland acted as bridesmaids as Catharine floated up the aisle on John Moodie's arm. Mrs. Strickland sat in the front pew, her teeth gritted with disapproval. At the altar rail, Thomas slipped onto Catharine's finger the thin gold band that in the years ahead she would never remove even for a moment—neither when she was elbow-deep in laundry suds, nor when her hands were knotted and swollen with arthritis. In later years, Agnes recalled the Traills' marriage as a most upsetting affair, from which her mother never really recovered. But Catharine insisted in a letter to James Bird that, "My dear husband is . . . all that a faithful heart can desire in a partner for life."

By the end of the month, both the Traills and the Moodies had said their goodbyes at Reydon Hall. The Traills left first. On a long, curving Suffolk beach, Catharine and Susanna clung to each other, both wondering whether they would survive to meet again on another continent. Thomas finally persuaded his wife to join him in the rowboat, and they were carried out to *The City of London*, the little steamer that paddled up the east coast of England and southern Scotland each week, calling in at all the seaside towns between London and Leith, the little port close to Edinburgh. Out at sea, Catharine stood at the rail of the steamer. She slipped her hand into her husband's, but she never took her eyes off the figure on the beach.

From Leith, the Traills travelled on to Thomas's birthplace in the Orkneys, so that Thomas could introduce his new wife to his family and at the same time inform them of his plans to emigrate. One of his cousins told Thomas that Catharine was "a lovely, bright, sunny thing to take out to the untracked wilds of a new country." But the hard-headed islanders knew that the Thomas Traills had little alternative. Within a few weeks, Thomas and Catharine were in the port of Greenock, outside Glasgow on Scotland's west coast, looking for a ship to take them across the Atlantic.

Days after the Traills left, it was the Moodies' turn. Susanna stood on the coastal steamer's deck and listened for the last time to the bells of St. Edmund's, summoning parishioners in the little village of Southwold to morning service. Slipping out of sight were the windmills and church towers of her childhood, and the bright green fields filled with spring wheat. "To leave England at all was dreadful," she would write later. "To leave her at such a season was doubly so." The Moodies, with their ten-week-old baby, intended to sail directly to North America.

Both couples were bound for the mouth of the St. Lawrence River—that vast waterway described by every travel writer of the time as "mightier than an ocean." The lands and towns ahead of them were little more than a catalogue of unfamiliar names: Newfoundland, Grosse Ile, Quebec, Montreal, Cobourg, York. Neither Susanna Moodie nor Catharine Parr Traill would ever again see her homeland, or her mother and sisters. Left to herself, Susanna would have regarded emigration as a one-way trip over the edge of the world. But Catharine had none of Susanna's dread of the unknown: she rather liked the idea of starting out afresh. In 1826, she had even published a little children's adventure story, entitled "The Young Emigrants," based upon letters from some family friends who had settled in Upper Canada. Catharine's enthusiasm diluted Susanna's fears. The prospect of emigration was not nearly so intimidating if it was a family affair. Susanna and Catharine could dream of taking their places within the landed gentry of Upper Canada, where their own children would be assured of a future.

Chapter 4

Flapping Sails

For most of the thousands of people who left the British Isles during the early nineteenth century, emigration meant the chance of a new and better life. They were escaping grinding hardship in their native land; they were fleeing the disease, starvation and hopelessness that engulfed Britain's labouring classes at the end of the Napoleonic wars. *Anything* was better than what they were leaving behind, and William Cattermole's descriptions of the New World made emigration even more attractive.

But in any century, even the most optimistic emigrant is also entering exile—from her history, her roots, her place within her community. And the two young Strickland women were not fleeing starvation; they were both leaving comfortable, if threadbare, lives and promising literary careers. They were emigrating to better their families' prospects, but plenty of young ladies like themselves remained in England, scraping by on slender means.

Catharine, and to a lesser extent Susanna, convinced herself that emigration was the start of an adventure. In fact, what choice did either have, when their husbands insisted that emigration was the only option? In departing England, though, both women lost their social and psychological moorings and were cast adrift. Both continued to call England "home" in the years to come, and they yearned for the country from which genteel poverty had exiled them. "Home! the word had ceased to belong to my *present*—it was doomed to live for ever in the *past*," Susanna wrote. "For what emigrant ever regarded the country of his exile as his home? The heart acknowledges no other home than the land of its birth." Powerful waves of nostalgia for a vanished world would regularly overwhelm them. Reydon Hall—its kitchen, library, lawns, sycamore tree; the surrounding fields and the pale Suffolk sky—remained locked in their memories, preserved for ever in the amber of loss. Half a century later, they would still catch glimpses of childhood bedrooms in their dreams, or vividly recall autumn bonfires in the kitchen garden if they smelled wood smoke. Being wrenched from one's homeland leaves deep scars in the psyche of every emigrant in any era: Susanna and Catharine bore these scars for the rest of their long lives.

The Moodies were the first to leave Britain. The coastal steamer from London deposited them at Leith, the little harbour close to Edinburgh, and John conceived the bright idea of starting their transatlantic voyage from there. Though Glasgow was the usual departure point for North America, if they sailed out of Leith instead, they could simply pay a porter to carry all their worldly goods from the steamship's hold to that of a sailing ship on a neighbouring wharf, rather than packing everything onto a public coach to then bump and rattle over forty miles of dusty, potholed highway to Glasgow. The departure from Leith might even allow John, as they rounded Duncansby Head in the far north, a last glimpse of the Old Man of Hoy—the unclimbable red sandstone mountain, encircled by screeching seabirds, that had dominated his boyhood in the Orkneys. And so their minds were made up.

John was never a man to weigh his options wisely, and this decision was not a wise one. It meant that the Moodies would have to sail round the northern tip of Scotland, guaranteeing them a slower, stormier passage. It also meant that they didn't have many vessels to choose from.

John Moodie marched up and down the harbour, chatting to any nautical types who were hanging around the wharves or drinking in the quayside taverns below Leith's Martello tower. Leith was both a flourishing fishing port and a centre of trade with other seafaring European nations, including the Scandinavian countries, Russia, Holland, France, Spain and Portugal. The names of its crooked, cobbled streets—Elbe, Baltic, Cadiz and Madeira—reflected its cosmopolitan links. Its tall stone warehouses bulged with Danish barley, Norwegian timber, Russian tallow and flax, Dutch clocks, European wines and North American rice, rum and animal pelts.

Several dozen smacks, brigs and schooners were tied up at the stone quays. John soon discovered the handful of wooden sailing ships bound for Quebec City. He talked to their captains, all of whom were hungry for genteel passengers who would pay full rates to fill cabins. At Susanna's urging, he booked his small family onto a ninety-two-ton, one-masted brig, the *Anne*, which had a monosyllabic and dour Scottish captain called Rodgers and a crew of seven. Seventy-two passengers were contracted to travel in steerage. The Moodie party consisted of Susanna, John, three-month-old Katie and Hannah, a nursemaid Mrs. Strickland insisted they take with them, as well as James Bird, the eleven-year-old son of their Suffolk friends, who was being sent to acquire pioneer skills in the New World. They were the only cabin passengers.

Susanna was assailed by misgivings as she surveyed those who would be travelling below decks. There were so many people in steerage, and they were so poor. She, her sister and their husbands were crossing the Atlantic in a year when the flood tide of emigrants to Canada was at its peak. Some 52,000 would be landed in Quebec City in 1832, during a shipping season that lasted only two months. In addition to choosing the worst route, the Moodies had also chosen the worst year to travel.

Altogether, 655,747 people sailed away from British shores between 1831 and 1841, nearly three times as many as had emigrated during the previous ten years. Creaking timbers, captains bellowing orders, waves slapping against hulls, the whip of rigging in the wind—the docks at Southampton, Woolwich, Liverpool and Glasgow vibrated with the hullabaloo of transporting the huge outflow of people. Steerage passengers outnumbered cabin passengers (usually referred to as "colonists," to underline the class difference) by about fifty to one. The five colonies in British North America (Upper Canada, Lower Canada, Nova Scotia, New Brunswick and Prince Edward Island), particularly Upper Canada in this period, were the most popular destinations for both rich and poor. Canada-bound emigrants didn't have to face the dreadful prospect of convict neighbours in Australia, of loneliness in the Cape Colony, of tropical diseases in the Indian subcontinent or the cruel practices of slavery (by now considered utterly unchristian, but not abolished until 1834) in the West Indies. And the voyage to Canada was shorter than the alternatives. In the 1830s, vessels were expected to take an average of six to seven weeks to reach Quebec City from Britain's west coast ports, compared to twelve to fifteen weeks to reach Australia, and five to six months to reach India. All these sailing times were approximate and varied according the wind and weather.

If Susanna winced at the number of emigrants on her ship, she was even more appalled at the conditions in which they were obliged to travel. Steerage-class passengers had a miserable time. The *Anne* was a relatively small boat, and its seventy-two cheap-fare passengers were crammed into a space only sixty feet long by ten feet wide and five and a half feet high. On the eastward passage across the Atlantic, timber plugged this space; now, on the westward voyage, it was filled with double rows of berths made of rough planks hastily nailed together. Baggage, utensils and food supplies jammed the aisle, and there was little ventilation. Children played in the fetid darkness; dirty bilge water slopped across the floor; rats swarmed up from the hold. On long, storm-plagued voyages, the smell of unwashed bodies, rotting food and vomit was suffocating. Emigrant ships were supposed to feed all their passengers, but few captains bothered to load sufficient supplies of biscuit, flour, salt pork and fresh water to last the whole voyage. When the daily provisions were distributed, they were almost always too meagre and often spoiled.

The worst of the emigrant ships came from Ireland's twenty-one ports, carrying the wretched cargo of refugees from famine, fever and the regular failures of the potato crop. By the mid-nineteenth century, the boats had earned the nickname "coffin ships." But the brigs, brigantines and schooners leaving Scotland's eighteen ports or England's thirty-six carried their own burdens of misery. And in the event of a shipwreck, steerage-class passengers usually drowned; lifeboats were provided for cabin-class passengers only. Life in steerage was awful. "Sir, a ship is worse than a jail," wrote that cynical realist Dr. Samuel Johnson. "There is, in jail, better air, better company, better conveniency of every kind: and a ship has the additional disadvantage of being in danger."

The *Anne's* sails were hoist on July 1. A week later she had weathered the storms off Scotland's eastern coast and was into the Atlantic Ocean. During the first days at sea, Susanna revelled in the lack of demands on her. Within the past four months, she had faced a bewildering series of changes: the birth of her first child, preparing everything she might need for a future in an unknown land, saying farewell to her mother and sisters whom she might never see ever again. Now she could catch her breath. She could finally give little Katie all her attention. She could nurse her in the privacy of the cabin with no interruptions. When the weather was good, she might sit out on the deck and watch the waves. She played with Captain Rodgers's Scottish terrier, Oscar, who had made eleven transatlantic voyages and whose mate had a litter of three puppies during the voyage: "When my arms were tired with nursing, I had only to lay my baby on my cloak on deck, and tell Oscar to watch her, and the good dog would lie down by her and suffer her to tangle his long curls in her little hands in the most approved baby fashion, without offering the least opposition."

The Moodies' maidservant took care of all the laundry, which was done in an iron tub on deck once a week. And cabin passengers ate with the captain, so Susanna didn't have to conserve or prepare food. Instead, she tucked into meals of hard biscuit, ham, corned beef, fresh eggs, fowl, cabbage and potatoes. Cabin passengers drank ale or porter, rather than the increasingly rank "fresh" water or the stewed black tea that was served to the sailors. Most vessels carried a few hens, kept penned up in the longboat, to provide fresh eggs in the early weeks and fresh chicken as the voyage drew to an end. Some ships even boasted a cow on deck, to provide fresh milk—although the *Anne* was too small for such a luxury.

It didn't take long, however, for John Dunbar Moodie to get bored. He was always trying to find something to occupy himself with. Sometimes he trailed a fishing line behind the vessel, hoping to hook a silvery bonito, which might be hauled up onto the deck and eagerly eaten at dinner. Sometimes he amused himself by training his rifle on sea birds that hovered over the ship. He talked to some steerage passengers, swapping war stories with an old Scotch dragoon called Mackenzie. He marvelled at the way the sailors shinnied up and down the rigging. He borrowed the captain's telescope and spent hours gazing at the horizon, hoping to see land, another vessel, a whale, shark, porpoise or flying fish—*anything* to break the monotony. On a couple of clear nights, he made Susanna stir from her berth and come and view the brilliant light show in the sky—the Northern Lights, which he hadn't seen since he'd lived in the Orkneys.

Susanna was amused by her husband's eager impatience for action, but she secretly rejoiced that there were no other cabin passengers to join John on wild exploits. On the waterfront in Leith, they had heard tales of gentlemen who would take off a in rowboat from the ship in which they were crossing the Atlantic to fish, and were abandoned when the ship's sails finally caught a wind. Another transatlantic traveller, John Howard, recorded in his diary in 1832 that, when he and some other passengers en route to Quebec on the *Emperor Alexander* took a little excursion from their vessel in a dinghy, they were "so intent on our sport that we did not observe that a breeze had sprung up." Howard described how, "looking around for our ship, we found that she had sailed at least five miles from us. . . . We therefore threw off our coats and [started to row] but all to no purpose as the ship began to disappear from our view." After the desperate party had nearly given up hope of rescue, and as the rays of the setting sun illuminated the *Emperor Alexander's* sails on the distant horizon, the ship finally changed direction and returned to collect them. "The captain was standing on the poop. I took my gun and had a great mind to shoot at him, but at that moment we observed our wives imploring him to take us on board." If John Dunbar Moodie been a fellow passenger of Howard's, he would certainly have been amongst those who were nearly lost because they had rowed off to shoot at puffins and other "curious web-footed birds."

The voyage of the *Anne* dragged on. The sun rose and set, rose and set, over the empty Atlantic, and progress was agonizingly slow in the baffling winds. After only three weeks, fresh water was rationed. Soon Susanna herself could barely conceal her impatience. She tried to write a story about a woman who emigrated from England to Canada but was unable to finish it. She buried herself in Voltaire's *History of Charles XII*. She was forced to wean Katie because of "a severe indisposition," probably seasickness. The Moodies did not suffer the disasters many transatlantic travellers faced in this period: the *Anne* did not catch fire, nor was it shipwrecked or driven off course by a raging storm. Susanna did not record any fearful epidemics of measles, typhoid, cholera or fever below decks that might have put little Katie in danger. But she could hardly bear the boredom.

Five weeks into the voyage, the *Anne* was becalmed on the Grand Banks, off Newfoundland. There she sat, sails flapping empty, for three long weeks. By now, Susanna was almost screaming with ennui. The Grand Banks fogs were notorious. Another emigrant stuck in a similar fog

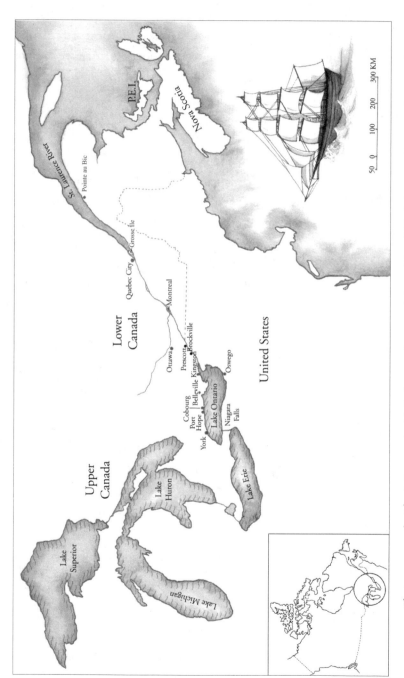

The journey across the Atlantic Ocean, and up the St. Lawrence River into the heart of British North America, took two months.

described how his boat got so lost that he and some crew members jumped into a dinghy to take depth soundings: "During our absence kettles, bells and bugles were kept sounding terrifically on board the good ship, or we should never have found it again, for at twenty yards' distance we lost sight of her. I shall never forget the vast magnifying effect of the mist on the ship, her spread sails, shrouds and cordage. She loomed into sight an immense white mass, filling half the heavens."

Supplies were dwindling on the *Anne*, but the dense fog meant that passengers and crew could not see any of the Newfoundland fishing boats strung along the Banks. Other transatlantic vessels managed to augment their rations with fish, either caught by their own crew or purchased from fishermen. "Our fishing goes on with great success," a colonist who also crossed in 1832 noted in her diary. "The Captain has just succeeded in catching an immense cod-fish [weighing] 40 lbs. Amongst the captures of this day is a Hollybut, 70 lbs weight; we are to have it for dinner." But there were no monster cod or halibut on the *Anne*, and after close to two months at sea, the steerage passengers were starving and the cabin passengers were down to hard biscuit. Not that Susanna cared; she was wretchedly seasick in the sullen swell. As she clung to the deck rail and stared out into the gloom, she was in limbo, adrift between two worlds, two lives. If only the pebble beaches and crumbling cliffs of the Suffolk seashore would loom out through the fog, rather than icebergs—stark, ghostly and entirely unfamiliar.

In the last week of August, the *Anne* sailed into the Gulf of St. Lawrence. As the sun climbed in the sky and the morning mist cleared to reveal Lower Canada's wild, rocky shores, the Moodies' spirits lifted. Susanna and John stood hand-in-hand at the rail. Susanna was almost overcome by the splendour of the mountains on the north shore—"they loomed out like mighty giants—Titans of the earth, in all their rugged and awful beauty." She looked up and down the huge waterway: "never had I beheld so many striking objects blended into one mighty whole! Nature had lavished all her noblest features in producing that enchanting scene." She liked the look of the small whitewashed houses on the shores close to Quebec City, and the neat churches with their silver tin roofs and slender spires against the backcloth of "dense, interminable forest." Her excitement blossomed on August 30, when the captain finally dropped anchor off Grosse Ile, the quarantine station thirty-three miles below Quebec City. From the deck of the *Anne*, Susanna watched the bustle of people and boats on the island, heard the sounds of laughter and shouting from the shore and watched the blue smoke from dozens of little cooking fires spiral into the clear sky. After nine weeks of being confined to a ship scarcely more than a hundred feet long, it looked like a "perfect paradise" to her. Visions of fresh bread and butter danced in her head.

This was the first year of operation for the Grosse Ile quarantine station. Before 1832, ships had sailed directly to Quebec City's docks. A surgeon would then come on board for a cursory check for fever among the passengers that might infect the city's residents. But by the late 1820s, the Quebec City authorities were exasperated by the incoming tide of destitute paupers who spread epidemics of typhoid, measles or cholera as soon as they stepped ashore. A few months before the Moodies' arrival, the health authorities of Lower Canada had hastily tacked together some wooden sheds on Grosse Ile and decreed that all vessels must stop there. All steerage passengers were obliged to disembark, to be inspected for disease. Every piece of sheet or blanket that had been used during the crossing had to be taken ashore to be washed; straw bedding was thrown overboard. The sick were herded into the sheds, which looked like animal pens, and held there until they either died or recovered. Within days of its opening, Grosse Ile was known as "the Isle of Death." Its busiest residents were the coffin-makers.

Susanna Moodie knew nothing of the island's fearsome reputation as she watched the steerage passengers climb into boats to be rowed over to dry land. The Moodie party did not have to go ashore because, as cabin passengers, they were not considered health risks. Only their bedding had to be sent to Grosse Ile, to be washed by their maidservant. Susanna resented being told to stay on the *Anne*, particularly when John gleefully joined the disembarkation. She was even more chagrined when the captain and her husband returned and told her that they had been unable to replenish their stores, or buy Susanna the loaf of fresh bread they had promised her, because the provision ship from Quebec City had not yet arrived.

Eventually Susanna did go ashore. And she discovered that the perfect paradise was actually a "revolting scene"—a seething mass of shrieking, dirty, half-naked people. Thousands of emigrants jostled each other at river's edge as they tried to wash all their bedding and clothes. Women trampled ragged blankets in the dirty water while yelling at their kids. "I shrank, with feelings almost akin to fear, from the hard-featured, sun-burnt harpies, as they elbowed rudely past me." Even the Scottish labourers who had travelled steerage on the *Anne,* and been perfectly respectful during the voyage, were "infected with the same spirit of unsubordination and misrule, and were just as insolent and noisy as the rest." It was a rude shock. Her dismay was intensified as she watched a huge, wild-eyed Irishman, flourishing a shillelagh and wearing only a tat-tered greatcoat, leap over the rocks shouting, "Whurrah! my boys! Shure we'll all be jontlemen!"

Relief had surged through the steerage passengers as they stepped on dry land. They were finally released from the noisy, smelly, dirty claus-trophobia of the ship's hold. But Susanna was incapable of empathizing with them. From birth, she had lived in a world of neatly segmented social hierarchies, in which everyone knew the social class they belonged to and regarded other classes almost as separate species. Now, for the first time in her life, there was no invisible membrane between the cabin-passenger gentry and the lower orders. She was looking at a fragmented world of uncertainty. As Susanna struggled to get her bearings in this vision of purgatory, she had her first taste of emigration as exile—exile from the society in which, even though she often felt marginal, she had always known where she belonged. When she tried to express her horror, she sounded impossibly hoity-toity. But it was much more complicated than that: Susanna was trying to protect herself from chaos.

Even in London, Susanna had rarely strayed into the slums of the city's east end or south bank. She had seen poverty, but the closest she had come to scenes of raw humanity, fighting for survival, was in Mary Prince's story, or in Hogarth's series *Gin Lane*, the richly detailed engravings of mass depravity and mayhem that were exhibited in the windows of London's print shops. And so, as she looked around her at Grosse Ile, Susanna's shock was mixed with horrified interest. How could she not recall the description of an uncivilized world she had read in the leather-bound copy of Hobbes's *Leviathan* in her father's library? "No arts; no letters; no society; and which is worst of all, continual fear and danger of violent death; and the life of man, solitary, poor, nasty, brutish and short." The sight of Hobbes's words made flesh fascinated Susanna the voyeur. The dark underbelly of the human condition—murder, madness, rage, despair—stimulated her imagination, as it would on many occasions in the future. She left Grosse Ile to return to the *Anne* only when she heard that there would be a decent meal of bread, butter, beef, onions and potatoes on board.

Two days later, the *Anne* left the quarantine station behind and sailed towards Quebec City. Safely back on deck, and at a remove from sun-drenched harpies and wild Irishmen, Susanna regained her equilibrium. She relaxed in the sunshine, contemplating spectacular scenery instead of the human terrors of the New World. Only a few months earlier she had gushed for London annuals over imaginary landscapes. Now, stunned by her first sight of the Montmorency Falls and Quebec City perched high on the rocky cliffs, she resorted to the lush vocabulary of Wordsworth and the Romantic poets for the reality: "Nature has lavished all her grandest elements to form this astonishing panorama. There frowns the cloud-capped mountain, and below, the cataract foams and thunders; wood, and rock, and river combine to lend their aid in making the picture perfect, and worthy of its Divine Originator." She continued to keep reality at arm's length when the *Anne* dropped anchor below the Citadel: she would not step ashore. Ostensibly, this was because cholera raged in the city—although this didn't prevent John Dunbar Moodie, accompanied by young James Bird, from jumping into a rowboat and disappearing to explore Quebec's winding streets.

The harbour below Quebec City was jammed with ships, and in the middle of the night, disaster struck. A large three-masted vessel, the *Horsley Hill*, with three hundred Irish immigrants aboard, collided with the *Anne* in the dark. There was an ear-splitting crash as the larger vessel's bowsprit came thundering down on the *Anne*, threatening to swamp her. Passengers on the threatened ship swarmed onto the deck, screaming with fear, and Captain Rodgers was immediately surrounded by several frantic women clinging to his knees.

Susanna was lying in her cabin when the pandemonium erupted. Grabbing her baby, she hurried out onto the deck to see what had happened and quickly took in the scene: the towering bulk of the *Horsley Hill*, looming out of the darkness over the *Anne;* the hysterical women immobilizing the captain. She heard the cracks of splitting timbers, the splash of waves, the confused shouting of sailors. Immediately, she rose to the occasion and ordered the women to follow her below deck. Ignoring the foul smell of unwashed bodies and vomit, she made them sit still and pray quietly. By sheer force of personality, and despite her own alarm, she remained cool and in command. "British sailors never leave women to perish," she told her companions, with apparently unshakable assurance. Until close to dawn, her authority held. The incident must have reassured Susanna that, even in the New World's melting pot of peoples, the natural authority of the educated classes held sway and she could make herself heard.

Although the Traills began their Atlantic crossing a week after the Moodies, they made far better time. After leaving Thomas's relatives in the Orkneys, they went directly to the port of Greenock, outside Glasgow. There Thomas paid fifteen pounds each for his and Catharine's cabin passage to Montreal in a fast-sailing brig, the *Rowley*. The *Rowley* was not a regular passenger ship: its hold was filled with a cargo of rum, brandy and sugar. The Traills' only companions were two young men and the captain's goldfinch.

Catharine had fallen very sick just before embarkation and was unwell for much of the voyage. At one point both the captain and the steward feared that she would die before landfall. But she gradually recovered, and in letters home describing the crossing, her chief complaint about the voyage was boredom. "I can only compare the monotony of it to being weather-bound in some country inn," she wrote to her mother. She didn't even have Voltaire to fall back on, as Susanna had, let alone a new-born baby. "I have already made myself acquainted with all the books worth reading in the ship's library: unfortunately, it is chiefly made up with old novels and musty romances."

The most unnerving fact for Catharine was the way Thomas sank into gloom. Thomas was singularly ill-equipped to deal with the voyage. Despite his bookish interests, he had not furnished himself with a library to last six weeks. He had none of John Moodie's interest in catching fish, shooting birds or chatting up the crew and passengers. Instead, he moped. Catharine tried to convince herself that Thomas's low spirits were a typically male response to cramped quarters: "Where a man is confined to a small space, such as the deck and the cabin of a trading vessel, with nothing to see, nothing to hear, nothing to do, and nothing to read, he is really a very pitiable creature." She resorted to playing the role she had so often played within the Strickland family: the resilient optimist, who raised everybody's spirits. When a long-faced Thomas started pacing the deck, she rose from the bench where she was sitting and sewing and walked alongside him, her arm linked through his. She enthused about all their plans for the future and the excitements that awaited them in Upper Canada. But there was a hard-headed realist underneath the Pollyanna cheerfulness. She realized that this was an inauspicious start to their marriage and emigration. She confided to her mother that the plans she had described with such gusto "in all probability will never be realised."

Catharine's first introduction to the New World was far more pleasant than her sister's. While the *Rowley* was anchored close to the south shore of the St. Lawrence about two hundred miles from Quebec City, awaiting a pilot, Thomas rowed ashore with the captain onto a little promontory called Pointe au Bic. He returned with an armful of flowers. After five weeks at sea, without a glimpse of anything green and growing, Catharine the amateur botanist was overjoyed. Her eyes filled with tears as she took the bouquet from Thomas and buried her face in it. She identified some of the blossoms, such as the sweet peas and wild roses, but realized with excitement that others were entirely unfamiliar. What was the name of this white orchid? Or these small yellow-and-white flowers? Were they unique to the New World, and how would she ever be able to learn their names? She carefully carried them off to the cabin and flattened them out between the pages of her Bible to preserve them. To a student of nature, the prospect of finding and identifying new species was thrilling.

When the *Rowley* arrived at Grosse Ile, its passengers were all forbidden to step ashore since none had travelled steerage. Catharine was not plunged into the dirty, hungry, shrieking crowd of new emigrants, as her sister Susanna had been; she did not see them cavorting around on the rocks or doing their stinking wash at the water's edge. Susanna's "perfect paradise" was all Catharine saw—a happy, colourful scene in the distance that reminded her of a fairground, with clothes waving in the wind, women basking in the sunshine and children chasing each other through the water. She didn't believe the customs officer who told her that what she was looking at was really "every variety of disease, vice, poverty, filth and famine." Similarly, she never went ashore at Quebec City, because of the cholera there. All she could do was marvel at the scenery. With only European experience to go by, she happily assumed that the stands of old trees on the sparsely populated south shore hid "pretty villas and houses." At the end of the day, the sound of church bells rang across the water through the warm summer air, summoning citizens to evening prayer. As she sat on board the *Rowley,* Catharine could still imagine that Canada was a land of milk and honey—particularly when the captain reappeared from the customs inspection with a basket of ripe apples for her, plus fresh meat, vegetables, bread, butter and milk.

In late August 1832, Thomas and Catharine finally stepped off the *Rowley* and onto Canadian soil in Montreal, then the largest city in British North America. Situated where the Ottawa River flowed into the mighty St. Lawrence, it had been the centre of the fur trade for over a century. It could not compare with the cities that Catharine knew best, London or even Norwich, with their ancient churches and palaces. It didn't have properly paved streets or decent drains, and there were uneasy relations between the English-speakers and French-speakers who made up, in about equal numbers, its population of thirty thousand. However, it could already boast a handsome Catholic cathedral, plus several massive stone colleges, nunneries, barracks and bank buildings. And the Scots merchants who ran all the shipping and trading companies housed themselves in mansions quite grand enough to compete with the merchants of the Old World.

None of this wealth was apparent, though, when the Traills arrived, and the newcomers were not impressed by the city. They found themselves enveloped in the foul smell of open sewers as they walked through narrow, garbage-strewn streets to the Hotel Nelson, on Place Jacques Cartier. The 1832 cholera epidemic had swept through Montreal, wiping out whole families and orphaning infants. Catharine was horrified by the mean houses, the ragged street urchins, the drunken emigrants lurching through the town, the overcrowded boarding houses. She urged Thomas to clear their luggage through customs as quickly as possible, so they could travel on to Upper Canada.

Perhaps the customs officials were too overworked. Perhaps Thomas let himself be elbowed aside by other, pushier colonists. Either way, the Traills' bags were stuck in the customs warehouse. In the sultry heat of late August, Catharine did not have enough energy for sightseeing. She was still not completely recovered from the sickness she had contracted while in Scotland and was apprehensive of further infection. So she remained at the hotel while they waited, and got to know her fellow guests and the hotel staff.

Finally, after two long days, the Traills' bags were released from customs. But by then, Catharine's fears had been realized: she was fever-ish, sweating, writhing with stomach cramps and throwing up repeatedly. Cholera had struck.

Thomas had no idea what to do. But Catharine's sweet nature had captivated the hotel staff, who found her a refreshing contrast to the imperious or condescending English women they usually had to serve. The housekeeper and maids appreciated her gentle manners and genuine interest in their families, their backgrounds, and their views on life in Montreal. The landlady's sister, Jane Taylor, came to Catharine's rescue. She despatched Thomas to find a physician and, oblivious to the risks of contagion, settled down to nurse Catharine through the crisis. When the doctor arrived, he quickly applied the finest remedies known to the nine-teenth century—bleeding, an emetic and some opium to dull the pain, none of which had any impact on the infection. It was Jane Taylor's round-the-clock nursing and concern that Catharine should never become dehydrated (coupled with Catharine's strong constitution) that probably saved her life. At the same time, Jane soothed Thomas, who was frantic with worry. Almost miraculously, Catharine did begin to recover. Within a week, although she was still frail, she was pronounced well enough to travel on to Upper Canada.

The cholera episode—Catharine's first experience of her new fellow countrymen—confirmed her faith in the essential humanity of all the different people she met. Her sister Susanna felt lost in a country with no established order. Susanna's first impression of Canada was of a frightening chaos, peopled by rude illiterates, amongst whom her exquis-ite sense of social nuance was useless. Catharine's first impression could not have been more different. She had enjoyed kindness from strangers, and she had survived the cholera because people she barely knew had taken it upon themselves to nurse her. Emigration gave Catharine new friends, new plants and the excitement of a new life.

Chapter 5

Land of Stumps

What did it remind them of? What was it *like?* It is hard to imagine the feelings of these two women in their first few weeks in North America. They could as well have landed on a new planet as a new continent. They lived in an era of hearsay; they'd had no photographs or travel documentaries to help them visualize the colonies. Their mental images of British North America had been shaped by the huckster promises of William Cattermole and a few romanticized engravings of Quebec City, Niagara Falls and similar sights, which made Canada look like a depopulated Switzerland. Neither woman had any experience of travel; all they knew were the picturesque villages and softly rolling countryside of the south of England. Now, as each couple travelled separately up the St. Lawrence River towards Upper Canada, Susanna and Catharine groped for familiar landmarks or reference points. Was it like Hampshire? Or Kent?

Their husbands were a little more worldly: as Orkneymen, they were blasé about raging waves, bare peaks and dense forest. Thomas Traill had travelled extensively in Europe with his first wife, and John Moodie had spent a decade in South Africa. But even they were unprepared for the scale of Canada—distances so great they took days to cover, rivers as wide as the English Channel, lakes as vast as oceans.

The culture shock was slow to hit them. Montreal and Quebec—the first two cities they had glimpsed—were as crowded, clamorous and cosmopolitan as Leith and Greenock. They had thrived since the early eighteenth century on the fur trade and, more recently, the lumber business. Soldiers, sailors, merchants, money-lenders, colonial officials and domestic servants milled around their cobbled squares. Their wharves were piled high with masts, spars, planks, boards, shingles, clapboards, laths, barrel staves and squared timbers, bound for markets as distant as Britain and the West Indies. For Susanna and Catharine, the only difference between Montreal's docks and their father's old stamping ground at London's Greenland docks was that most of Montreal's dock workers spoke French.

But the newcomers left the prosperous, well-populated cities of Lower Canada behind them as fast as possible. They were bound for Upper Canada, where former officers in the British army, like Thomas Traill and John Moodie, were eligible for free land. They were anxious to reach their destination quickly in order to take up their land grants and get a roof over their heads in the few weeks before the Upper Canadian winter closed in. So from Montreal, each couple spent three days hopscotching between steamboats and stagecoaches, according to the navigability of the St. Lawrence. First they clambered onto a stagecoach to Lachine, to avoid the turbulent water just above Montreal. After a few hours' bumping over rutted roads, they climbed out of the coach and boarded a steamer. They paddled up the river as far as Cornwall, where they disembarked to stay the night. The following morning they got back into a stagecoach and took the road alongside the Long Sault rapids. Once at Prescott, well above the foaming water, they embarked on another steamer, which toot-tooted its way past Brockville, through the Thousand Islands and (while the passengers slept) into Lake Ontario.

The sisters' rosy expectations of Upper Canadian society were not based exclusively on William Cattermole's promises. They knew that the colony rested firmly on British laws and traditions. British currency circulated through the colony (alongside, for the sake of convenience, American dollars); the lieutenant-governor, who ran the colony, was appointed by the British crown; lawyers trained at British universities ran its legal system; the Anglican Church, usually represented by the forbidding, lace-cuffed figure of Bishop John Strachan, owned vast swaths of land and was enormously important in the colony's affairs. All major decisions were made by the British government in Westminster. By the time the sisters arrived in 1832, the Legislative Assembly was already an arena for fierce debate between the "Family Compact," a small group of wealthy families who clustered around the King's representatives, and the Reformers, who demanded a larger role for elected representatives in the colony's government. William Lyon Mackenzie, an outspoken member of the Reformers, had made his newspaper, *The Colonial Advocate*, a leading voice of the Reform movement. Nevertheless, in the taverns along the St. Lawrence the sisters saw men raising their tankards to King William IV, and on board the lake steamer, they were comforted by the familiar accents of the Old Country.

For all its British laws and traditions, however, Upper Canada still consisted of fewer than a quarter of a million immigrants spread over a vast territory that only its native people really understood. Its immense emptiness was scarcely scratched by the influx of Loyalists and British immigrants. As Susanna and Catharine travelled west from Montreal, they had seen what settlers called "the Front": the busy little towns that clung to the north shore of the St. Lawrence and consisted, for the most part, of a grist mill, a sawmill, a church, one or two stores and an inn. Only a handful, such as Brockville and Kingston, also boasted a smithy, a newspaper and a couple of lawyers. York, the administrative centre of

Upper Canada that would be renamed Toronto, was still a squalid water-front settlement of fewer than nine thousand residents—tiny compared to Quebec City and Montreal. To the north of the Front lay the "Back Townships," the surveyed tracts of impenetrable swamps and forests of pine, oak and maple. Scattered through the thousands of acres of silent forest were bush farms consisting of log huts, barns, laboriously ploughed fields, newly planted orchards and stumps—endless acres of stumps. Once a settler had chopped down the trees on the land he had acquired, he had to wait at least seven years before the huge, ugly stumps were sufficiently rotten to pull out of the earth. Roads connecting these bush farms were either virtually impassable or nonexistent. Even those who acquired their land free had to use their own capital to buy the implements they needed to clear it, and ploughs and hoes were costly. Because labour was in short supply in the under-populated colony, if a gentleman immigrant chose to employ others to prepare his land and plant his crops, he could expect to pay at least twice the wage he would have paid in Britain. Luxury goods were unattainable; only flour, whisky and salt pork were cheap and available. Survival was a back-breaking, soul-destroying struggle.

Before Catharine had even left Montreal, a disappointed settler, on his way back to England, had warned her that most of Mr. Cattermole's promises of an easy life for settlers were utter make-believe. "I found I had been vilely deceived," the angry Englishman moaned. "Such land, such a country—I would not live in it for all I could see!" It took new-comers, he insisted, at least five years of back-breaking toil to clear their land and build a decent home before they could begin to think of plant-ing flower gardens. But Catharine decided that the young man simply hadn't tried hard enough, and she paid no attention. The next day, as she jolted her way westward in the stagecoach, she was reassured by what she saw. Land along the Front had been farmed for several years, so that attractive white frame houses had replaced log cabins, and well-established orchards were heavy with apples, plums and crab apples. "I am delighted with the neatness, cleanliness and comfort of the cottages and farms," she bubbled. She noted with pleasure familiar flowers—goldenrod, and purple-spiked valerian "as plentiful as the bugloss is in our light sandy fields in England." She talked to the landlady at a tavern about the hanks of home-dyed wool that hung on fences to dry, and the clay ovens that stood close to many dwellings: "At first I could not make out what these funny little round buildings, perched upon four posts, could be; and I took them for bee-hives till I spied a good woman drawing some nice hot loaves out of one."

But even sunny-tempered Catharine could not ignore the rough-and-ready manners of some of her new acquaintances. After a lifetime of hat-doffing deference from social inferiors in Britain, she was shocked by the attitude of the Loyalist innkeeper in Cornwall: "Our host seemed perfectly indifferent as to the comfort of his guests, leaving them to wait on themselves or go without what they wanted." She admitted that she had been warned about the "odious manner ascribed, though doubtless too generally, to the American." She was equally upset when a large, rude man jammed himself into the stagecoach on the Cornwall to Prescott leg of the journey, squashing up the other nine passengers so uncomfortably that she herself was "literally bruised black and blue." The Loyalists, who made up the majority of residents of the Front in the early 1830s, were full-fledged North Americans: they had been on the continent for several generations, members of a society that valued achievement over education or wealth. They had no time for genteel immigrants who assumed that a British colony would respect the British class system. Their pioneer individualism jarred on class-conscious English nerves. But Catharine made the best of these circumstances, and praised the tavern-keepers at the Prescott inn to the skies: "the female servants were all English, and seemed to vie with each other in attention to us."

Susanna didn't have Catharine's ability to overlook the disturbing evidence that Upper Canada was not a northern Eden. Although never as sensitive to landscape as her sister, she shared Catharine's pleasure in the scenery on the journey west (*anything* was better than the "watery waste" of the long sea voyage she had endured). But Susanna's primary focus was always people, and she was appalled by many of her fellow passengers on the steamer, especially the Irish drunk who lay outside the ladies' cabin all night, singing and ranting about "the political state of the Emerald Isle." She was unnerved by the way that servants sat at table with their employers, and common labourers took pleasure in lippy talk with the gentry to whom, in England, they would have tugged their forelocks. And she was horrified when she and John met Tom Wales, the Suffolk friend with whom John had gone to hear Cattermole's lectures, who had arrived in the colony two months earlier. Like many of the new European arrivals, Wales was shivering with "the ague"—a malarial fever spread by mosquitoes which left its victims feverish and weak. Like the disappointed Englishman whom Catharine had met in Montreal, Tom Wales was hellbent on getting back to England as fast as he could. He gave Susanna an earful about the bush—hideous roads, swarms of

Cobourg in 1838: this sketch, completed by the artist William Bartlett six years after the sisters passed through the little town, includes the newly-opened Victoria College (centre).

black-flies, swamp fever, thieving land agents and a disgusting diet of potatoes and pork fat.

As the Traills had arrived in Lower Canada two weeks before the Moodies, the two families travelled separately up the St. Lawrence River. Thomas and Catharine arrived in Cobourg—their jumping-off point for the backwoods—a week before John and Susanna.

The couples had agreed that they would eventually rendezvous at Sam Strickland's home in the township of Douro, two days' journey north of Cobourg. Communications were so bad in the colony that not only was there no way that each couple could track the other's moves, but Sam Strickland didn't even know his two sisters were about to arrive on his doorstep.

Cobourg gave Catharine and Susanna their first real taste of Upper Canada. During his East Anglian lecture tour, Cattermole had described the town as a "handsome and thriving place [with] stores in abundance . . . hatters, shoemakers, and every other convenience which a wealthy, grain-purchasing, money-making generation could desire." And it certainly had pretensions. It had shrugged off its early nickname, "Hardscrabble," and with flag-waving pride renamed itself Cobourg, in a misspelled tribute to Prince Leopold of Saxe-Coburg-Saalfeld, who had married Princess Charlotte, only child of the future King George IV, in 1816. Princess Charlotte was heir to the British throne; had she not died a year after her marriage, Upper Canada's Cobourg might have revelled in royal patronage. Unfortunately, when another German prince entered the British royal family, he paid no attention to the little colonial namesake. Prince Albert of Saxe-Coburg-Gotha, husband of Queen Victoria, had little interest in Britain's overseas possessions.

Most of the original population of Cobourg was composed of Loyalists, who had lived in North America for several generations but had fled north during the 1790s after the American War of Independence. Next to arrive, during the 1820s, was a wave of half-pay British officers interested in free land and a new start. By 1832, Cobourg had a population of around one thousand and aspirations to a cultural life. There was a printing office and a book society. James McCarroll, a talented Irishman who had recently immigrated with his father, had just opened a music school promising "the sublime studies of such spirits as Carolin, Weber, Mozart, Haydn, Handel, &c." There were regular tea parties for which the wives of Cobourg's leading citizens dressed up in their best flounces and furs to discuss the same topics that would have galvanized similar gatherings in England—new brides, new babies and the servant problem. There was a Methodist Academy. A sandy beach gently curved around the bay, cradling the high-masted lake schooners as they bobbed about on the water. Cobourg's weekly newspaper, the *Cobourg Star* ("a friend and welcome guest at every fireside"), was edited by R.D. Chatterton, an English journalist familiar with both Susanna's poetry and the London literati that Susanna and Catharine had left behind. The Reverend Mr. McAulay gave his sermons in St. Peter's Anglican Church in such a fruity English accent that he might have been standing in the pulpit of the church in Reydon. Catharine insisted that Cobourg lived up to expectations. She wrote home happily about its "very pretty church and select society," and commented that "many families of respectability [had] fixed their residences in or near the town."

This was raw Upper Canada, however, not pastoral England. Beyond the cleared fields surrounding the little lakeshore town was the gloomy, impenetrable bush. Black bears often strolled through backyards. No newcomer could ignore the town's gimcrack appearance: most of its one hundred and fifty houses were little more than wooden shanties. And to anyone familiar with Suffolk's ecclesiastical gems, St. Peter's looked more like a cowshed than an Anglican church. The only two buildings of any substance were the new stone courthouse on the town's outskirts and a splendid brick mansion recently erected by the lawyer George Boulton. There was such a shortage of coins in the colony that half the money in circulation in the Cobourg stores consisted of brass buttons torn off discarded uniforms. And there always seemed to be at least one dishevelled pioneer making an exhibition of himself in the middle of town, half-sozzled at eleven o'clock in the morning. Cobourg boasted three taverns and several distilleries, but only two churches.

Susanna was far less generous—and more incisive—than her sister in her assessment of Cobourg. It didn't take her long to realize that Cobourg's culture was skin-deep. Her heart sank as she heard how the book society read Walter Scott's novels or Lord Byron's poetry over and over again, because it took at least two years for the latest London best-seller to arrive. Her nose crinkled as she took in the shabby state, including perspiration stains, of many of the ladies' gowns. Her eyes widened as she glanced through the pages of the *Cobourg Star*. She was horrified by "the freedom of the press [which is] enjoyed to an extent in this province unknown in more civilized communities." Upper Canadian periodicals were notorious for the abuse and invective they heaped upon their targets. "It is the commonest thing in the world," Susanna noted with alarm, "to hear one editor abusing, like a pickpocket, an opposition brother; calling him a reptile, a crawling thing, a calumniator, a hired vendor of lies, and his paper a smut-machine." Even William Lyon Mackenzie, in *The Colonial Advocate*, deplored the fact that the hundreds of newspapers circulating in Upper Canada had become the "dernier resort of the venal, the profligate and the unprincipled in society." For Susanna, this kind of invective was a far cry from *La Belle Assemblée* and *The Court Journal*.

The Traills spent only the night of August 31, 1832, in Cobourg. An autumnal chill had crept into the evening air, and the pressure to keep moving was strong. More urgently, Catharine had realized that Thomas was not an ideal pioneer. Thomas was a sweet, gentle man, but easily defeated by circumstance. All his erudition was useless in a crisis, as her cholera episode in Montreal had demonstrated. He was hopelessly impractical: if he tried to nail a trunk closed, he always hit his finger with the hammer. On the journey up the St. Lawrence, Thomas had sunk into an increasingly gloomy silence as his wife enthused about the scenery. Catharine began to understand that the success and happiness of her marriage would depend on her own initiative and energy. She knew

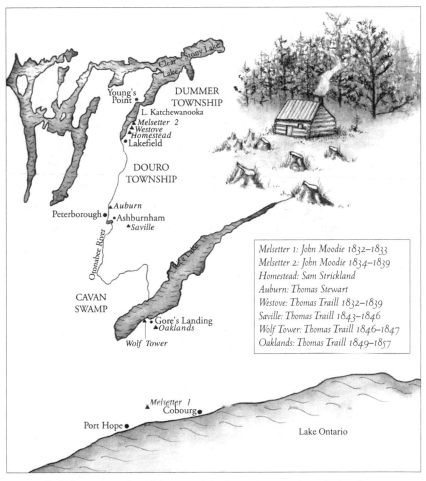

Melsetter 1: John Moodie 1832–1833
Melsetter 2: John Moodie 1834–1839
Homestead: Sam Strickland
Auburn: Thomas Stewart
Westove: Thomas Traill 1832–1839
Saville: Thomas Traill 1843–1846
Wolf Tower: Thomas Traill 1846–1847
Oaklands: Thomas Traill 1849–1857

The back country north of Cobourg was a landscape of swamps, forests, bush and rivers.

that she could not manage alone. So she insisted that she and Thomas should embark on the last leg of their journey—the thirty-eight miles north to Peterborough—as soon as possible. From Peterborough, they would get in touch with Samuel, who was living eleven miles further north, on the Otonobee River.

Sam, his wife Mary and their two small children had settled north of Peterborough only a year earlier, some months after Sam had terminated his employment with the Canada Company. Samuel Strickland was just the kind of person that any new immigrant, with no experience of the colony, would value as a close neighbour. Within months of acquiring land, Sam had cleared twenty-five acres and built a decent house. He had huge advantages over either of his brothers-in-law. Several years younger than both Thomas and John, he was a strong, resourceful man who had now lived in Upper Canada for seven years and had acquired all the necessary practical skills. He could use and care for oxen, make ox-yokes and axe handles, cut and stack hay, build zigzag fences and split logs. Like his sister Agnes in England, he was a take-charge kind of person. His forte was organizing "bees"—the community working sessions at which neighbours would pool their labour for the benefit of one of their members. What's more, Sam revelled in the pioneer life. A barrel of a man, he loved hunting and practical jokes. (He once buried a porcupine in a barrel of nails, then invited anybody who came along to take a free handful.) Catharine hoped that capable Sam might teach scholarly Tom how to work with his hands.

Douro Township had a further attraction for the Traills: it had a reputation as a little island of gentility amidst the uncouth stumps. The name itself caused a flutter in the breast of every British military man: Douro was named after the Battle of the Douro River in the Peninsular War. The township, which covered about fifty square miles, stretched from the banks of the Otonobee River in the west to the edge of Dummer Township in the east. It had good water communications, thanks to the river, and in its southwestern corner there was the rapidly growing settlement of Peterborough, with a population of over seven hundred people. Two Anglo-Irish gentlemen—Sam's father-in-law, Robert Reid, and Reid's brother-in-law, Thomas Alexander Stewart—were amongst the founders of Peterborough and lived with their large families on its northern edge. Sam Strickland had bought land close to the Reids immediately after he left the Canada Company. He had then sold that land and, with the proceeds, bought more uncleared acres farther north, where the Otonabee River widened out and became a long skinny lake called Lake Katchawanooka, or "Lake of the Waterfalls." (The lake was also referred to as "Katchewanook" and "Katchiwano" in this period, before its name was regularized on provincial maps.) The Strickland farm on Lake Katchewanooka was the first dwelling in the community originally known as North Douro, and eventually renamed Lakefield.

Thirty-five miles to the north, on Sturgeon Lake, there was a second covey of gentlefolk. Of the six settlers there, four were university-educated, one had attended an English military college and the last had "half a dozen silver spoons and a wife who plays the guitar," according to one of the group, John Langton from Lancashire. Patrick Shirreff, a Scottish farmer who travelled throughout North America in the early 1830s, recorded that the society of the Peterborough region was reputed to be "the most polished and aristocratic in Canada." What Shirreff implied was that there were far fewer loudmouthed Loyalists here than on the Front. The British class system had been partly transplanted to the Peterborough region—which meant that Catharine and Thomas would feel comfortably at home in its upper ranks. Thomas might find a kindred spirit amongst the bookish Sturgeon Lake crowd.

Catharine's creeping anxiety about what lay ahead was evident in her account of the journey from the Front into the back country that she sent home to her mother. Girlish enthusiasm faded from her descriptions of a countryside that looked increasingly foreign. Although the gentle hills north of Cobourg reminded her of Gloucestershire, she deplored the "zigzag fences of split timber [which were] very offensive to my eye. I look in vain for the rich hedgerows of my native country." As the afternoon wore on, and the woods each side of the road thickened, she began to wonder how any settler could clear the ground and build a log house within a single day, as Mr. Cattermole had airily promised.

Today, we can barely conceive how barbaric Catharine must have found the British North American frontier of 170 years ago. There are no sepia photographs to kindle our imaginations; only a few amateurish sketches capture the immensity of the wilderness. Ancient stands of white pine, many over one hundred feet tall and with trunks five or six feet across, dwarfed the puny efforts of early settlers to tame the dense undergrowth of cedar and birch. Soon these giants would be felled by greedy lumber crews, eager to feed the appetite of Britain's Royal Navy for squared timbers and masts. But in 1832, the mighty trees towered like malevolent sentinels over a landscape broken up only by swamps, rivers, rocky outcrops, lakes and clearings created by forest fires. Often the only sound in the dead of a bitter winter night was the howling of wolves; often the nearest habitation was several miles away, through almost impenetrable bush.

Catharine huddled closer to Thomas as the horse-drawn wagon rumbled on. When they arrived at Rice Lake, her curiosity was whetted by the sight of an Indian village inhabited by Chippewa people (known today as Ojibwe, or in their own language, Anishanabeg). But her appetite for tourism was quenched when she got thoroughly chilled by driving rain as they crossed the lake on a grubby little steamer. Then the steamer, which continued up the Otonabee River, ran aground four miles below Peterborough. The men on the rowboat that eventually arrived to rescue them had consumed a whole keg of whisky and were "sullen and gloomy." After an ugly row with the passengers, the men took off into the night, leaving Catharine and Thomas stranded in the woods. "We were nearly three miles below Peterborough, and how I was to walk this distance, weakened as I was by recent illness and fatigue of our long travelling, I knew not."

Luckily, one of their fellow passengers knew where he was going. In response to Catharine's entreaties, he guided them through the dense forest to safety. It was an ordeal. At one point, Catharine lost her footing in the dark as she crossed a stream and fell into knee-deep water. And when they finally reached Peterborough, they found the principal inn there completely full. Thomas stood helplessly by as his shivering, wretched wife tearfully explained their predicament to the landlady. Catharine's gentle nature (plus the promise of a handsome reward from the Traills' savings) made instant friends: "we received every kindness and attention that we required from mine host and hostess," she reported in her weekly letter back to Reydon Hall. The innkeeper and

Travel in the New World was a rude shock for English gentry. Henry James Warre (1819–1898) contrasted his elegant Montreal sleigh (bottom sketch) with the bone-shaking experience of winter travel on country roads.

his wife "relinquished their own bed for our accommodation, contenting themselves with a shakedown before the kitchen fire."

The following morning, a message was sent to Sam Strickland that his sister had arrived in Peterborough with her new husband. It took the boy who delivered the message all day to make his laborious way through the forests, along the roughly marked eleven-mile trail. Two days after Catharine and Thomas had reached Peterborough, a breathless and excited Sam arrived by canoe from his farm, after shooting the rapids of the Otonabee River, for a noisy reunion at the inn. He soon got Thomas organized. Thanks to Sam, Thomas had already secured a land grant of some waterfront acres on Lake Katchewanooka. Now his brother-in-law persuaded Thomas to spend some of his meagre capital on more acres that adjoined Sam's land, so their two farms would be contiguous.

Within three months of leaving the British Isles, the Traills had begun backwoods life with a wonderful advantage: they didn't have to start from scratch. They had a neighbour who knew what he was doing, and who could lend them the agricultural implements (axes, ploughs, scythes) with which they were completely unfamiliar. Moreover, unlike most early settlers, they were able to spend their first year in the bush not in a leaky, cramped shanty but first as guests of various friends in Peterborough, and then in a sturdy log cabin near the Stricklands that had been abandoned by another family.

The Stricklands' hospitality sweetened the Traills' first taste of pioneer life. The Reids and Stewarts formed a little clique into which Catharine—generous, kind and always willing to lend a hand with jam-making and bread-baking—was soon absorbed. During the early weeks in Peterborough, Catharine quickly became close friends with Dublin-born Frances Stewart, who was eight years older than she was and already the mother of eight children (she would have eleven children altogether, all of whom would survive childhood). Frances shared all Catharine's religious, literary and botanical interests. A relative by marriage of the novelist Maria Edgeworth, Frances and her husband Thomas had moved to the unbroken bush of Douro Township ten years earlier, when Peterborough scarcely

Irish-born Frances Stewart became a close friend to Catharine as soon as the Traills arrived in Douro Township.

existed. Frances knew all too well how wretched a woman like Catharine would feel as she faced the rigours of life in the backwoods. In 1823, Frances herself had written home: "This place is so lonely that in spite of all my efforts to keep them off, clouds of dismal thoughts fly and lower over me. I have not seen a woman except those in our party for over five months, and only three times anyone in the shape of a companion."

Frances, a spry little woman with a ready smile, quickly became Catharine's confidante, ready to comfort her when she unburdened herself about her homesickness for East Anglia, her impatience that letters from home took more than two months to reach her, her unhappiness that there was no church at which she could attend services. However bad Catharine found the bush, she had to acknowledge that her new friend had found Upper Canada in a far more raw state. Frances had drawn on her deep faith in a protective God to sustain her, and on her extensive knowledge of natural science (she had studied chemistry, botany and geology as a child) to catalogue the plants around her.

During the 1820s, the Stewarts had watched the local population swell and had built themselves a comfortable log house on the Otonabee River, a home they named Auburn. By the time the Traills arrived in Peterborough, Auburn's every shelf and wall was lined with collections of dried flowers and grasses, Indian bows and arrows, dried skins of small furry animals, bear claws, eagle wings, antlers, fossils, rock and crystal specimens and Indian pottery. All winter a huge fire blazed in the hearth, while children played on the floor and an infant slept in an Indian cradle.

Frances provided Catharine with the support Thomas could never offer and Catharine knew she could never ask of him. Auburn became Catharine's haven, and an example of what she wanted to create in the backwoods. At Auburn, she could play Frances's piano (the only one for miles around) and compare specimens of flora and fauna with her friend. Soon it became a game for the Stewart children to present her with bits of moss, curious leaves or petrified shells. "Ooh, Mrs. Traill," they would say, mimicking her enthusiasm, "Here's a wee mite." Catharine learned from Frances "how much could be done by practical usefulness to make a home in the lonely woods the abode of peace and comfort even by delicately-nurtured women, and energetic, refined and educated men."

After the Traills moved the eleven miles north, to Lake Katche-wanooka, Catharine saw much less of Frances. The long walk along a roughly blazed trail was not an inviting prospect, particularly in the short winter days. It was too easy to get lost. Catharine was soon absorbed into another circle of pioneers: the Stricklands, Shairpes and Caddys, who were hacking a living out of the untamed bush. The presence of another woman was a huge boost to the women in this pioneer settlement, all of whom were locked in an exhausting and endlessly fertile cycle of annual childbirth. Catharine's sister-in-law Mary Reid Strickland already had three children and was pregnant with her fourth (eventually she would have fourteen babies, three of whom would die as infants). And in June 1833, Catharine's own first baby was born. Newborn James was "the joy of my heart and the delight of my eyes," as Catharine described him to the Birds, in Suffolk.

By the time the new cabin on the Traills' own property was finally ready for occupancy in December 1833, Catharine had recovered her optimistic belief that she and Thomas could conquer the wilderness. Scarcely a day went by without her sitting down to write lengthy descriptions of life in Upper Canada to her mother and sisters in England. The letters brim over with the same cheerful enthusiasm that, by now, Catharine had decided it was her marital duty to provide for her husband.

Chapter 6

"Yankee Savages"

The mere thought of the wilderness appalled Susanna. The Moodies arrived at Cobourg on September 9, a week after the Traills had left. During her first few days there, she was so depressed by gruesome tales of the back country from Tom Wales and others that she decided even the skin-deep "civilization" of a small town was preferable to the bush. After all, unlike Catharine, she already had a small baby to care for. And Cobourg, with its newspaper and library, offered more hope of a literary career than some backwoods settlement could ever promise.

It didn't take long to persuade John that they should stay put for a while. Her husband was easily convinced that he would do better to try land speculation rather than backwoods farming. Gregarious and chatty, he felt he had more hope of succeeding as an enthusiastic salesman than as an ignorant farmer. So he shelved his original intention of immediately applying for the free land to which he was entitled, especially since all the available plots close to the Front had been taken up years earlier. Instead of following the Traills into the back country, the Moodies looked around for a property they could afford where the land had already been cleared and buildings erected.

John and Susanna settled into Cobourg's Steamboat Hotel. The talk in the saloon was all of lots and concessions, acreage and mortgages. John was soon in the thick of it, buying drinks for all the promoters who hung around the smoky parlour, convinced he was going to get a good deal. By the end of September, the Moodies had plunged into the set-tlers' life: John paid three hundred pounds to a land-dealer for a cleared two-hundred-acre farm on the edge of Hamilton Township, eight miles west of Cobourg and four miles east of the smaller waterside settlement of Port Hope. (At this stage, when both dollars and pounds were cir-culating, the exchange rate was roughly five dollars to the pound. As a general rule, early eighteenth-century amounts in Upper Canada should be multiplied by one hundred to determine their contemporary equiva-lent—although, like the British rule, this is a rough-and-ready approxi-mation. Three hundred pounds in 1832 would therefore be worth about $150,000 today.) With his usual blithe optimism, he named his Canadian "estate" Melsetter, after the Orkney home in which he was raised.

Hamilton Township remains today, 170 years later, an inviting land-scape of rich pastures, gentle hills and bubbling streams, with a view of the distant lake from the high points. The land John had acquired was cleared, not just of bush, but even of stumps. Its two log houses and frame barn were already built. Although the purchase of Melsetter took a big bite out of his limited capital, in theory John Moodie had made a sound investment. In practice, however, the deal was a disastrous, because John hadn't known enough to ensure that he had both immediate occu-pancy and title to the farm. He quickly discovered that the log house was still occupied by the previous owner, Joseph Harris, who had gone bank-rupt but refused to move himself, his wife and eight children out. John agreed to rent, sight-unseen, another, smaller dwelling on the property.

Susanna, her baby and Hannah the maidservant cheerfully waved goodbye to the Steamboat Hotel and set off in a covered carriage to take possession of their new home. But her spirits sank as the carriage bounced along the uneven road, a steady rain began to fall and Hannah launched into a non-stop grumble about the dark woods that menaced them on all sides. Finally the carriage rocked to a halt as they crested a steep hill, and the driver pointed out a miserable hut below them. Susanna gazed at the tumbledown shanty with horror and insisted that it couldn't be their future home—it was no better than a pigsty. "You were raised in the old country, I guess," the driver sneered at her. "You have much to learn, and more, perhaps, than you'll like to know, before the winter is over."

When John Moodie arrived a few minutes later, with their luggage in two wagons, Susanna was perched on the edge of an abandoned trough, ashen with horror. But with John's encouragement, she pulled herself together. She was soon helping sort out their home, while the rain beat down on the roof and blew through the open doorway. She found the door buried under some debris at the back of the house, and John got it back on its hinges. Hannah swept out a year's worth of animal droppings and old straw. James, their manservant, and Tom Wales, who had accompanied them, unloaded the wagon, stored their trunks in the loft and lit a fire in the fireplace. All the while, little Katie lay in the feeding trough, yelling her lungs out. For all the bustle and progress, it was a grim beginning to life in Upper Canada.

The Moodies were still sorting out their new home when their first visitor arrived. The door was flung open, and there appeared a young woman with "sharp, knowing-looking features, a forward, impudent carriage, and a pert, flippant voice," according to Susanna. "The creature was dressed in a ragged, dirty purple stuff gown, cut very low in the neck, with an old red cotton handkerchief tied over her head: her uncombed, tangled locks falling over her thin inquisitive face, in a state of perfect nature." The visitor was Emily Seaton, daughter of Roswell Seaton (or "Old Satan," as Susanna called him), a local reprobate who had nothing but contempt for inexperienced British settlers. Susanna quickly discovered that the "Yankee damsel" had come to "borrow" a decanter of whisky. In the next few weeks, the visitor returned to "borrow" tea, sugar, candles, starch, blueing, irons, pots, the new plough, a spade and trowel—on the false assumption that, as the young woman pointed out, "You old country folks . . . have *stacks* of money." The items were either never repaid or returned in such poor condition that they were useless. Susanna had no idea how to deter the "Yankee savages" from purloining her supplies and implements. Her neighbours' borrowing habits reduced her to tears of frustration.

The Moodies' maidservant, Hannah, did not stay long, nor did any of her successors. It was a hard life, and there were plenty of homes crying out for servants that could offer a more comfortable situation. Susanna's insistence that she was not going to compromise her standards, and that master and servant must eat separately even though they now lived in a one-room cabin rather than Reydon Hall, didn't help. Without a servant, Susanna was regularly faced with menial tasks that she had never performed at home and now had to master. On her first attempt at laundry, she scrubbed the skin off her wrists without getting the clothes clean. On her first attempt at baking bread, she produced a leaden, burnt lump. "Oh Mrs. Moodie," Tom Wales snickered. "I hope you make better books than bread." The days seemed endless as she sat by a crackling fire and tried to ignore the snow falling steadily. Tom Wales left, desperate to return to England even though his pockets were empty and his health broken. Homesickness triggered uncontrollable bouts of tears in the early weeks. On one occasion, when John was away in Cobourg or Peterborough, Susanna faced the terror of being left overnight, alone but for her baby, while wolves howled and her last candle spluttered into darkness: "Cold, heart-weary and faint, I sat and cried."

After a wretched winter, first in the hut and then in another small cabin nearby, the Moodies finally took possession of their farmhouse the following June. They found it overrun by mice (they trapped fourteen the first night), fleas and large black ants. "Old Joe," as the Moodies called Joseph Harris, and his brood had left a dead skunk in a cupboard as a farewell gift. But no sooner had the Moodies cleaned up the mess than gullible John made another miscalculation.

Acknowledging his own ignorance of farming methods, John adopted a well-known pioneer strategy and agreed to "share" the farm with another couple. The Moodies would provide the land, implements, live-stock and seed, while the other couple would do all the manual work and share the produce. But the couple cheated the Moodies ruthlessly, steal-ing their potatoes, apples, seed corn and even their rooster and ruining their implements. "All the money we expended on the farm was entirely for these people's benefit, for by the joint contrivances very little of the crops fell to our share; and when any division was made, it was always when Moodie was absent from home and there was no person present to see fair play," Susanna wrote. Even more upsetting for Susanna was the wife's wagging tongue. "We no longer had any privacy," Susanna com-plained. "Our servants were cross-questioned, and our family affairs can-vassed by these gossiping people, who spread about a thousand falsehoods regarding us. I was so much disgusted with this shareship, that I would gladly have given them all the proceeds of the farm to get rid of them."

Throughout these trials, Susanna began to get a sense of herself as a woman of fortitude. In England, after their father's death, the Strickland sisters had realized that they would have to live by their wits. They couldn't afford to comport themselves in the manner of the helpless creatures they wrote about for the London annuals. And yet each had tried to radiate the delicate femininity common to fashionable ladies. To abandon the appearance of sweet vulnerability would have been to risk social censure. In Canada, however, delicate femininity was worse than useless when a wolf threatened the chicken coop, or when a cow's udder was swollen with milk. When Susanna finally overcame her own fear and milked the Moodies' red heifer, she was overwhelmed with a sense of achievement. She insisted that she was "prouder of that milk than many an author of the best thing he ever wrote, whether in verse or prose." It was, she acknowledged, "a useful lesson of independence."

*In letters filled with closely-woven handwriting, Susanna
recorded her first impressions of British North America.*

In her day-to-day existence, Susanna had little time to miss the pleasures of literary London. She was even busier after June 1833, when her
second daughter, Agnes, was born. Susanna was far too gritty a woman
to let adversity overcome her. Although she downplayed her achievements in the self-deprecating manner of middle-class Englishwomen,
Susanna was young and strong and capable. Day to day, she organized
her little household, sewed clothes for her family, made sure there was
food on the table and took an interest in even those neighbours she came
to dislike intensely: "I tried to conceal my blue stockings beneath the
long conventional robes of the tamest commonplace."

Yet all this time, Susanna never stopped thinking of herself as a
writer, first and foremost. With baby Aggie in her arms and little Katie
crawling around her feet, she would sharpen her goose-quill pen and
write long letters to her family in England, just as Catharine was doing

thirty-two miles away. Postage, which was paid by the recipient not the sender, was charged by the number of sheets used, so when Susanna had covered one side of the paper, like most correspondents of the time, she would turn it and write across her own writing. Occasionally, she would even turn it to write diagonally across the two layers she had already composed. In some letters, she described their circumstances with grim realism. In response to one outpouring of misery, her sister Agnes replied, "I grieve that you should be the tenants of a comfortless hut and exposed to so many hardships and privations." At other times, Susanna adopted a more jaunty tone: "We were quite charmed [with] your pretty letter," Agnes wrote approvingly.

Susanna's chief preoccupation was to transform her life into literature. On scraps of paper she jotted down sketches of her neighbours and poems that expressed her emotions. Her creativity was fuelled by rage and impatience. Into the edgy, amusing tales of the uncouth settlers amongst whom she found herself she poured her contempt for the illiterate. On other occasions, she would try to capture in verse her impressions and experiences of her new life:

Oh! land of waters, how my spirit tires,
In the dark prison of thy boundless woods . . .
Though vast the features that compose thy frame,
Turn where we will, the landscape's still the same.

Susanna was too much of a professional to lock her outpourings away—she wanted to be published. As soon as she arrived in Cobourg, she wrote to editors in York, Montreal and New York, with examples of her verse. Introducing herself as Susanna Strickland to the editor of the *Albion*, published in New York, she offered two of the poems she had written since she'd arrived in Canada. One described the sound of sleigh bells in winter; the second, more doleful, dealt with an emigrant's nostalgia for "the music of our native shore." Susanna made it clear to the editor that, in her opinion, Canada was a living death for writers.

There was, as yet, no Canadian literature, and there were precious few publishers in Upper Canada. Everybody was far too busy struggling to feed their families and cheating their neighbours "to pay much attention to the cultivation of literature." But she insisted that the demands of family life in a log cabin had not dampened her own poetic inspirations, "which in my own beautiful and beloved land were a never failing source of amusement and delight."

The *Albion*'s editor published several poems. Susanna's morale soared to see her name in print again (although she was never paid). Publication in a New York paper, then as now, meant that Canadians noticed the talent in their own backyard. R.D. Chatterton, editor of the Cobourg *Star*, suddenly decided that he wanted to reprint her poems. Alongside the "chaste and beautiful Songs," Chatterton extolled the "racy, and pure English style of the fair authoress." But he bristled at Susanna's disparaging comments about Canadians and complaints that her muse had received "little respect . . . in the wilds of Canada." The editor of Cobourg's main newspaper was not prepared to admit that his town lacked class. "This apathy must arise from other causes than those she somewhat captiously alludes to, for our experience has convinced us that a want of taste can by no means be imputed to the inhabitants of this province." There was, however, a grim truth in Susanna's complaint. She had found no soul-mates amongst the vulgar "Yankees" or monosyllabic hunters of Hamilton Township. She hungered for the kind of female companionship that she had enjoyed with her own sisters, particularly Catharine. She was suffering an emigrant's most bitter complaint: the only kind of readers with whom she felt in tune were in the land she had left behind.

It was her sister Agnes who, with her usual bluntness, brought Susanna's predicament home to her. Early in the summer of 1833 a long letter arrived from London, in Agnes's sloping, rapid scrawl, which began: "You would like to hear my literary news, you say." Agnes then proceeded to reel off various triumphs. "I had a poem in the *Souvenirs*: 'Uncle Gregory's Will' and the 'Insect Travellers' were in the *Offering*,

and I had a religious poem in the [journal of the] Missionary Council."
Agnes's cheerful bragging reminded Susanna of everything she had once
enjoyed, now so far away—new books, intellectual gossip, the company
of fellow writers. The titles of all those annuals, eagerly publishing
Agnes's stories, made Susanna's practical achievements in the bush look
like hard slog for little reward. Susanna knew that Agnes would dismiss
all her newfound pioneer skills as "servants' work." Agnes was obviously well on her way to high eminence in the literary world, while
Susanna had spun into oblivion. Agnes was winning their sisterly competition for recognition.

Agnes had some inkling of Susanna's misery at finding herself in "a
land of strangers," so, with the bossy benevolence Susanna remembered
so well, she went on to offer some unasked-for advice on how her emigrant sisters could occupy their "free time." "Penny magazines are all
the rage. They are very nice publications made up of selections of a
useful nature from various authors on subjects of history, natural history, letters or novels, and I think you or Kate might edit a Canadian
penny magazine on the same plan and make a good income if you could
enter into an agreement with an honest bookseller. The *Penny Magazine*
which started this time twelvemonth [ago] now pays the enormous
income of 200,000 pounds, but if you could make but five pounds a
week it would be worthwhile trying and you could put in poetry from
your books and mine."

As Susanna sat in her chilly wooden cabin, far from anything her
English sisters would consider "civilization," she didn't know whether to
laugh or cry. Agnes obviously had no idea of her sisters' circumstances.
As if Susanna and Katie, living two days' journey from each other, could
find enough material "of a useful nature" for a magazine, or even a single
honest bookseller who could help them! Susanna couldn't even imagine
which of her fellow Upper Canadians would buy it. Moreover, Susanna
had no interest in producing a how-to book for settlers. She wanted to
write the kinds of religious poems and romantic stories that Agnes was
so successfully getting into print. Susanna would much rather be writing

about "a noble deer" pursued by a pack of wolves "like so many black devils" than transcribe the recipe for venison pie.

As the Moodies' second year in the colony began, their prospects grew bleaker. Susanna had found some outlets for her creativity but hadn't secured any income. And, despite her temporary triumphs, she was still subject to intense bouts of homesickness. She felt trapped by her babies and her circumstances, unable even to visit her sister near Peterborough because travelling was so difficult for most of the year. On the occasions when Agnes's letters arrived, her tears would flow for hours. Thanks to John's mismanagement, they were running out of money, and the farm was nowhere near providing them with a livelihood. John was digging himself deeper and

A drawing of a goldfinch and thistle by Susanna. Although she didn't share her sister's interest in natural history, flower painting was a relief from the hard work of pioneering.

deeper into debt with the Cobourg moneylenders in order to buy equipment and hire men. He worried constantly that soon they would be unable to afford to feed themselves. And he felt helpless as Susanna raged that her feelings for Canada were the same as those "the condemned criminal entertains for his cell—his only hope of escape being through the portals of the grave."

Desperate to make Susanna happy, and convinced that they needed a new start, John made a snap decision. They must move. Had he spent the next few years getting the Hamilton farm working well, his investment would have paid off handsomely. Despite the short-term problems, the farm was a prosperous one in a desirable location. John could have participated in the growing export of wheat to England, and he would have watched land values climb. But John didn't give it a chance. Once he had decided something wasn't working, he was always impatient to move on. After barely a year in Hamilton Township, he elected to sell the property.

Leaving Susanna and the two little girls at Melsetter, John made the difficult journey to visit Sam and Catharine and their families on Lake Katchewanooka. He still had not taken advantage of his right to a free land grant, so now, impetuous as ever, he got his brother-in-law Sam Strickland to secure sixty-six uncleared acres on the banks of the lake, close to the Traills. On his return, he set about to convince Susanna that they should uproot themselves from Hamilton Township. Title to military land grants, he argued persuasively, expired unless the land was settled within two years of purchase. They had better get moving. Besides, if they left the Front, they could say goodbye to their unpleasant American neighbours who had jeered at their manners. Around Peterborough, Moodie insisted, the state of society was "more congenial to our European tastes and habits."

In an unexpected *volte-face*, Susanna suddenly had second thoughts about packing up all their possessions. By now she had "nested" at Melsetter: "It was a beautiful, picturesque spot and . . . I had learned to love it; it was much against my wish that it was sold." Unlike her husband, she probably had a better business sense for Melsetter's potential. But she was never able to resist her husband's enthusiasms. "To the Woods! To the Woods!" sang out John, seizing Susanna in his arms and waltzing her round the kitchen. In late 1833, each of the six Strickland sisters had received a much-anticipated seven-hundred-pound legacy from an uncle in England. This was a fortune for Susanna and Catharine in Upper Canada, where labourers earned sixty pounds a year and two hundred pounds was considered a comfortable annual income. It allowed John to pay off most of his debts to Yankees, grasping land speculators and unforgiving merchants in Cobourg, and begin to daydream about his new "estate" amongst the gentry of Douro Township.

In the early weeks of 1834, John and Susanna waited impatiently for the snow on the road north to be packed sufficiently hard for them to travel. John booked the local carrier to transport them in two wagons, mounted on runners. One morning, in the chilly pre-dawn darkness of early February, John, Susanna, the carrier and his son loaded the two little girls, the maidservant, kitchen table and chairs, farming implements, chickens, clothes, the big iron bake kettle, pots and pans—and Susanna's precious Coalport tea service—into the two wagons and headed north. A long, cold day of being jostled and thrown about, as the wagons rolled across the frozen ruts, stretched ahead of the Moodies.

The journey was a nightmare. The Moodies travelled nearly fifty miles that day, from Cobourg on Lake Ontario, via Port Hope, over the marshy, thickly wooded area then known as the Cavan swamp. They had hoped to stop for the night on the far side of the swamp, in Peterborough, then a sprawl of wooden houses and a few stone buildings including an inn. But the two brothers hired to drive them were eager to keep going and accomplish the whole distance within a day. So from Peterborough, as a blood-red sun dropped below the white horizon, they followed the roaring, surging Otonabee River eleven miles north towards the new settlement on the banks of Lake Katchewanooka.

On and on the sleighs rattled and bumped, over the frozen ridges of the icy track, between high snowbanks. Sometimes the two sleighs slid smoothly over the ground; other times, the Moodies were thrown violently forward as the sleigh runners hit a rock or tree stump protruding through the packed snow. The full moon, which had allowed Susanna to see the road ahead, clouded over. The cold grew more intense. The wind rose.

As the night wore on, Susanna gripped the side of the sleigh and concentrated with grim determination on a single point in the future: their arrival at Lake Katchewanooka. The Moodies were expecting to stay there with Sam. Susanna could remember her brother only as an ebullient, curly-haired teenager, who had left England to make his fortune in the New World in 1826, though she knew from her husband John's visits to Sam the previous fall that he was now married and comfortably settled. All she could think about was the first sight of his cheerful face, and the moment when she would step out of the cumbersome, hateful sleigh and be embraced by her own flesh and blood. She knew her beloved sister Catharine was in the same area, but she wasn't sure when she would see her. She was too cold and exhausted by travel to think of anything beyond the prospect of Sam's hearth. When the sleigh finally drew up outside a solid log house, with lighted windows, she could barely wait to uncurl her cramped, stiff body.

Before she had time to clamber down from the sleigh, however, Sam emerged from his log house. He yelled a hearty greeting but immediately told the driver they were not stopping yet. Blithely oblivious to his sister's exhaustion, and careless of the misery in her face, he told her that she was expected at her sister's, a further ten minutes down the road. All Susanna heard was that the journey was not yet over. She buried her face in the fur of her dog and wept.

A further upset lay ahead. When the first heavily laden sleigh was in sight of their destination, the driver pulled the horses up to a slithery, unexpected stop. The road ahead was completely blocked by the massive trunk of a fallen pine tree. The second sleigh nearly cannoned into the back of the first. The first driver urged his horses to jump the obstruction: the sleigh with its human cargo teetered for a minute on the top of the trunk, then slid safely across. When the second sleigh reached the top of the log, however, it hung poised there for a second and then, in ghastly slow motion, tipped gradually onto its side and finally fell to the ground with a dreadful crash. The sleigh landed heavily on the wooden crates it had carried. The frozen darkness was filled with the sounds of wood splitting, glass breaking and china smashing. Iron cooking pots that had been tied to the top of the pile of crates rolled across the road. Fragments of wood, pottery and bone china spilled out into the snow. Not one piece of the precious Coalport tea service survived the calamity.

Susanna Moodie had loved her elegant teapot, with its pattern of gold leaves and blue ribbons and flowers. During the first months in their Hamilton Township cabin, when her spirits were low, she would take this symbol of gentility down from a high shelf and cradle it in her arms. She would remember the way that her mother, back home at Reydon Hall, took tea at four o'clock every afternoon. Mrs. Strickland herself had given the Moodies the Coalport tea service as a wedding present. Susanna had carefully transported the teapot, plus the matching milk jug, slop bowl, sugar bowl with its own dainty lid, and six cups and deep saucers, across the ocean and over hundred of miles of mud roads and forest tracks. And now one of the few remaining links with her vanished way of life—the life of an English gentlewoman, who held translucent china cups in smooth white hands—was smashed beyond repair. There was no hope of replacing it in the wilderness.

Chapter 7

"Halcyon Days in the Bush"

The sisters' reunion was intensely emotional. Susanna's arrival after such a long cold journey was like a dream: Catharine's familiar, loving voice; the smoky warmth of the Traills' log house; the wonderful sense of being amongst family again. After the hugs and tears, there was a chance to admire each other's offspring. It was February 1834, and Catharine had not seen Susanna's daughter Katie, now two, since they'd parted in Suffolk, and she was eager to fuss over eight-month-old Agnes, while Susanna immediately took to little James Traill, a plump nine-month-old who watched the new arrivals with silent curiosity.

Best of all was the joy of being with a kindred spirit—someone who shared the same values, memories, sense of humour and history. Their reunion promised a return to the companionship of their childhood. Isolated from each other, the two sisters had coped with a society foreign to everything they had known. Catharine had forged ahead, buoyed up by her motto: "Hope! Resolution! and Perseverance!"—a slogan given added force, as her husband pointed out, "because you not only recommend the maxim but practise it also." But Susanna, who lacked her sister's flexibility, still struggled to adapt to the manners and customs of the New World.

Now, however, each sister had a sympathetic audience. Safe in their family solidarity, and their shared assumption of a social hierarchy, they could hardly wait to compare notes on all their new experiences. They didn't have to *explain* things to each other—why they found Yankees cold or Irish immigrants feckless. Peals of laughter rang out as the sisters tried to top each other's catalogue of disasters.

Catharine giggled at the way that the Americans she had met talked: their "nasal twang," and their habit of using the word "fix" not in the precise English sense of "mend" but as a catch-all term for doing any kind of work. Susanna regaled Catharine with tales of her neighbours and servants in Hamilton Township. Susanna was a much better raconteur than her sister; her stories always had a rhythm and a punchline. "I wish nature had not given me such a quick perception of the ridiculous," she once admitted, "such a perverse inclination to laugh in the wrong place." Her ear for regional and class accents made her a brilliant mimic. She replayed an argument between Bell, a Scottish maidservant who used to work for the Moodies, and John Monaghan, an Irish lad who had arrived on their doorstep. First she imitated the indignant Bell, insisting in an exaggerated Scottish accent, "I winna be fashed aboot him," because she regarded the boy as a Papist robber. Next, Susanna switched into an Irish lilt as she imitated the pathetic John, claiming he was beaten by his former master: "Shure the marks are on my showlthers yet."

Catharine's gentle anecdotes reflected her inability to "read" the people in Upper Canada, as anyone in England could unconsciously "read" their fellow countrymen by their body-language, accents and attitudes. Catharine always saw the best in people and was rarely censorious. She had been warned about the "odious manners" of native-born

Americans, but once she had got to know a few Yankees, she was agreeably surprised to find them "for the most part, polite, well-behaved people." Susanna, in contrast, was unsettled both by her failure to understand the strangers she met and by her inability to position them in relation to herself. So her vivid descriptions of dishonest land-dealers, thieving neighbours and disappearing servants were designed to shore up her flagging sense of superiority to all these uncouth strangers, as well as to entertain her audience. She called Uncle Joe, the bankrupt farmer from whom John had bought the Hamilton Township property, a "weasel-faced Yankee." She described the neighbour whose family constantly borrowed articles from the Moodies and never returned them as a "bony, red-headed ruffianly American squatter."

Susanna was impressed with the Traills' newly completed log house, which they had named Westove, after the Traill family property in the Orkneys. In a humid summer it benefitted from the breeze off the lake because it was set on a little peninsula, referred to by Catharine as "the Point." On the ground floor there was a kitchen, a large parlour with a bedroom off it, a pantry and a storage closet. Thomas had hung maps and prints on the parlour walls; Catharine sewed curtains of green cambric and white muslin for the windows. An open staircase led to an upper floor that would later be divided into three bedrooms. Below the kitchen was a cellar in which potatoes, turnips, carrots and onions could be stored through the winter. The rooms were dark; windows were small, to ensure a warm interior during Canadian winters. But through a small pane of glass in the parlour door there was a view of Lake Katchawanooka.

Susanna was less delighted, however, with her first sight of the real "bush," as opposed to the cleared land close to the Front. The clearing around the Traills' house "was very small," she noted, "and only just reclaimed from the wilderness, and the greater part of it was covered with piles of brushwood to be burnt the first dry days of spring. The charred and blackened stumps on the few acres that had been cleared during the preceding year were everything but picturesque; and

*A bush farm in the 1830s: the sight of corduroy roads and acres of stumps discouraged many settlers. (*Bush Farms near Chatham*: watercolour by Philip J. Bainbrigge.)*

I concluded, as I turned away, disgusted, from the prospect before me, that there was very little beauty to be found in the backwoods."

The two sisters spent the first weeks of 1834 sitting together in front of the Traills' Franklin stove, nursing their babies and reestablishing their old intimacy. The snow melted slowly that spring in the Peterborough district. John Dunbar Moodie supervised work on his own cedar log cabin, about one mile north along the shoreline from the Traills' residence. Then he turned to the question of how to clear his land. He had extended his sixty-six-acre holding on Lake Katchewanooka by spending more of Susanna's legacy on a further three hundred acres (paying, he admitted to Tom and Sam, an outrageous price for some of this uncleared land). He spent yet more of the legacy on the tools and labourers to help clear the property. Each labourer was paid on a piecework basis: eleven to twelve dollars for chopping, logging and fencing an acre of hardwood land, and fourteen dollars if pine, spruce and hemlock predominated. His spending didn't concern his wife; Susanna trusted his judgment. Besides, it was easy for her to shrug off any worries in Catharine's company. Catharine enthused about how beautiful the summers were and laughingly dismissed Susanna's fears of wild beasts bounding out of the woods.

Soon the two women were strolling down the newly trodden path through the forest to inspect progress on the Moodie log house. It was larger than the Traills', and the ground floor was already partitioned into a parlour, kitchen and two small bedrooms. A fire was lit in the stove, and there was a plume of smoke from the chimney. Despite its dirt floors and the chinks in its walls, it was "a palace when compared to the miserable hut we had wintered in during the severe winter of 1833," observed Susanna. "I regarded it with complacency as my future home."

As the days lengthened, and the ice on Lake Katchewanooka turned grey and rotten, Catharine wrote home to tell their mother that, "My dear sister and her husband are comfortably settled in their new abode . . . we often see them." The two women spent a lot of time reminiscing about Suffolk. They liked to chat about "sweet, never-to-be-forgotten home, and cheat ourselves into the fond belief that, at no very distant time we may again retrace its fertile fields and flowery dales."

By the first week in May, the maples, oaks and birches around the Moodies' and Traills' cabins were in leaf. Soon there was a carpet of trilliums and lady's-slippers on the forest floor. At the lake's edge, the pale spikes of wild rice waved gently in the breeze. John Moodie bought a canoe, to which (ever the Orkney lad) he attached a keel and sail. Whenever possible, he and Susanna would skim across the lake's surface. Susanna's letters home were now almost as chirpy as Catharine's, as she began to see the landscape through her sister's eyes. There was no more talk of "gloomy woods." Susanna rhapsodized about "the august grandeur of the vast forest" which cast "a magic spell upon our spirits." Her poetry reflected her happiness:

Come, launch the light canoe;
The breeze is fresh and strong;

The summer skies are blue,
And 'tis joy to float along."

One of the most memorable expeditions the Moodies ever made was up Lake Katchewanooka into Clear Lake and from there to Stony Lake (or Stoney Lake, as it is still sometimes spelled). John, Susanna and their two little girls set off at dawn and arrived after a couple of hours at Young's Point Falls, where the jovial Irish miller, Mr. Young, invited them to dine with his family. To Susanna's amazement, his two daughters produced a lavish feast of "bush dainties," including "an indescribable variety of roast and boiled, of fish, flesh and fowl," plus "pumpkin, raspberry, cherry and currant pies, with fresh butter and green cheese (as the new cream-cheese is called), molasses, preserves and pickled cucumber." The Moodies left their daughters with the Young family and paddled on through Clear Lake, an "unrivalled brightness of water [which] spread out its azure mirror before us." At length, the Moodies reached Stony Lake—a dramatic piece of water lodged in a geological fold, where the stark granite of the Canadian Shield meets the soft sandstone of the St. Lawrence Valley. "Oh, what a magnificent scene of wild and lonely grandeur burst upon us as we swept round the little peninsula, and the whole majesty of Stony Lake broke upon us at once," Susanna wrote later in *Roughing It in the Bush*. "Imagine a large sheet of water some fifteen miles in breadth and twenty-five in length, taken up by islands of every size and shape, from the lofty naked rock of red granite to the rounded hill, covered with oak-trees to its summit: while others were level with the waters, and of a rich emerald green, only fringed with a growth of aquatic shrubs and flowers. Never did my eyes rest on a more lovely or beautiful scene. Not a vestige of man, or of his works, was there."

Susanna was right: Stony Lake was almost pristine wilderness. Its shores were still untouched by loggers, and only a handful of settlers had ever paddled across its surface, threading their way through its picturesque isles. The local Chippewa treasured the lake as a source of birchbark, wampum grass, wild onions and game. They venerated its tranquillity and tried to keep Europeans away by telling them stories about rattlesnakes and wild beasts. Now Susanna stared around her at the landscape, "savage and grand in its primeval beauty." She admitted to herself that, "filled with the love of Nature, my heart forgot for the time the love of home."

Susanna was already expecting her third child when she arrived at Lake Katchewanooka. Encouraged by the good reports of immigrant life that reached England from both of her sisters, Agnes Strickland composed some cheerful verses in doggerel for her brother-in-law, John:

It affords me much pleasure,
To hear how your treasure,
Increases in land and in money.
And I give you great joy
On your hopes of a boy
To feed on your butter and honey.
And in the meanwhile,
Baby Aggie's sweet smile,
And Katie's gay prattle must be
A fund of sweet mirth
As you sit by your hearth,
With Susie at breakfast or tea.

John's hopes for a boy were answered: in August 1834, John Alexander Dunbar (always known as Dunbar) was born.

Both Susanna and Catharine had come to childbearing relatively late, but now they too were caught up in the exhausting cycle of frequent pregnancies and births. Susanna would have seven babies within eleven years, her first when she was twenty-nine and her last when she was forty. Most of her pregnancies were difficult and her labours were long; she often thought she was going to die. Catharine spaced out her nine pregnancies a little more: she was thirty-one when James was born and forty-six when the last of her children arrived, in 1848. No letters survive describing the backwoods births, when doctors were always miles away and women had to rely on friends like Frances Stewart (and later Catharine herself) to be midwives. Neither woman would have written such letters: in the nineteenth century, the messy business of childbirth was *never* mentioned in polite society or literature. In Britain during this period, an allusion to a woman being "with child" or "lying in" was considered the height of indelicacy. (During the early 1830s came the first whimsical mentions of babies being found under gooseberry bushes.) The modern imagination recoils from the idea of giving birth in a log house, with the wind howling outside, flickering candles providing the only light and raw whisky the sole source of pain relief. The bush abounded with stories of women who died either during childbirth, or because puerperal fever set in afterwards, or because the strain of too many pregnancies caused heart disease.

Motherhood came as naturally to Catharine as breathing. It was the most meaningful activity in her life. She was always prepared to give more love than she took, and she saw no conflict between her family and her impulse to write. Since her first child didn't arrive until after she had reached Peterborough, and while she was staying with friends, she had been able to enjoy her first few weeks with him. She always hugged and kissed all her babies and treated her offspring as children long after they had grown up. Thomas was a distant parent, but Catharine made up for him. She taught her toddlers little prayers, and she read to them as they got older. She made her daughters rag dolls out of scraps of fabric. She led her brood on long, exciting walks through the forest, showing them where the deer gathered at the water's edge and how to collect frog spawn. Soon the window sills and shelves were as loaded with treasures as the window ledge of Catharine's Reydon Hall bedroom had been. The Traill children responded to their mother with deep affection, mixed (as they got older) with exasperation provoked by her suffocating love. The Traill cabin exuded warmth, with its constant smell of baking, its patchwork quilts (Catharine was an expert quilter, who loved quilting bees) and a fire that blazed brightly in its hearth.

Catharine's homemaking gifts even succeeded in cheering up Thomas, for whom life in the backwoods was proving a ghastly disappointment.

The dynamics in the Moodie cabin, a mile down the lakeshore, were quite different. John was an indulgent, loving father who could always be persuaded to play a tune on his flute or get down on hands and knees and pretend to be a bear. But Susanna was never entirely at ease as a mother. Tense and emotionally needy, she could never embrace her maternal role whole-heartedly. The writing impulse gnawed at her; she did not put her children's needs first in the same unthinking way that Catharine did. She was not a natural hugger like Catharine, and although she loved her babies, she resented their demands. It had been hard enough to make the journey from Reydon Hall to Cobourg with a baby in her arms—now she had to organize her new log house with two little girls underfoot, plus a newborn infant. She taught her family to read, but she didn't have Catharine's patience with their temper tantrums or squabbles. Dolls irritated her: as a child she had preferred frogs, and she thought rag dolls were a silly waste of time. She and her daughter Agnes often clashed, since little Aggie was just as willful as her mother. It didn't take Aggie long to discover that Aunt Traill's cabin was more convivial, and that Aunt Traill always seemed to have more time for her than her own mother did. The Moodie children scampered along the forest path to the Traill cabin whenever the opportunity arose.

There was plenty of love in the Moodie household, but most of it was the passion that still flamed between John and Susanna. As John kept reminding her, they had come to the colony for the sake of their children—to give them a future they could not afford in England. Susanna had been much too wrapped up in her love for John to question his decision to emigrate. Instead, consciously or unconsciously, all her life she resented her children for her exile—and even as small children, they knew it.

During the first few years in the backwoods, the Traill and Moodie households usually had a hired man and a maidservant apiece to help with the domestic and yard work. Nevertheless, both women had to do far more than their mother ever did at Reydon Hall. In the mornings there were stoves to stoke, chickens to feed, eggs to collect, babies to feed and dress, porridge to make (John Moodie always relished his "pouritch," particularly if there was a little cream to pour on it). Then there was all the baking to be done—the bread, pies and cakes required to feed not just growing families but also the hired help in the fields. Kitchen gardens—with carefully tended rows of potatoes, peas, carrots, squash and onions—needed weeding and watering from late April onwards. Once a week, each woman heated iron cauldrons of water in which to do laundry; in summer, it could be rinsed in the lake. Once all the sheets and garments were washed, with caustic lye soap that took the skin off hands, they had to be hung to dry. The weather had to be very bad indeed before a pioneer wife decided to keep the wet laundry inside and drape it over cabin partitions, fogging the place with clammy humidity. Far better to hang it outside where it froze as it dried, then bring in the shirts, aprons, gowns, sheets and underwear (all stiff as boards) and fold them on the kitchen table.

Afternoons were the times to socialize. Susanna's prickly distrust of strangers had subsided now that she was securely entrenched amongst like-minded British gentlefolk. There were two other families besides the Stricklands, Traills and Moodies who lived close to Lake Katchewanooka: Lieutenant Alexander Shairp and his wife Emilia, and Lieutenant-Colonel John Caddy and his wife Hannah. The women often gathered for tea in the afternoon. Their heads were always bent over their needlework, as they had to clothe their whole families. Boys and men wore grey flannel shirts and homespun trousers; girls and women wore long, full-skirted dresses (wool in winter, calico in summer), covered with gaily patterned cotton aprons. Since there were no paper patterns, the women would unstitch an old garment and cut the new cloth according to these pieces. As they sewed and mended, they compared notes on how to make butter and cheese from the scrawny cows most families kept, how to make candles from mutton fat, which berries made the best jam or how to bake good bread with gritty flour. They kept each other informed about who was travelling to Peterborough or across Rice Lake to Cobourg or Port Hope and might pick up supplies of tea, rice or dried fruit. They eagerly peppered visitors and newcomers with questions. Was the colonial government going to improve the roads? Had cholera struck again in Lower Canada? Were conditions in the Old Country just as bad as when they left? Was King William IV still alive?

On other days, Susanna and Catharine would take their children on expeditions to collect flowers and catch butterflies. Frances Stewart had lent Catharine two guides with which to educate herself about North American plants. One, published in London in 1814, was a scientific tome entitled *Flora Americae Septentrionalis (North American Flora)* by Frederick Pursh; the other was an *Essay on Comparative Agriculture; or A Brief Examination into the State of Agriculture As It Now Exists in Great Britain and Canada*, by J.E. Burton, published in Montreal in 1828. Both books fell far short of Catharine's needs as she struggled to identify new species of plants. Like Frances Stewart, she started to keep careful notes concerning her specimens and observations. When each family got back to their cabins, the women would lay out their finds. Catharine would carefully pack up the moths and insects she had caught, or plant seeds she had dried, to send to sisters Jane and Sarah in England. She deeply regretted that she had not paid more attention to her elder sister Elizabeth's instruction in painting before she left home. Now she enviously watched Susanna as her youngest sister got out her pens and paints to execute exquisitely precise sketches of flowers she had collected or birds she had seen.

Pioneer families ate early, so it was soon time to pack up such erudite pursuits and prepare dinner. The basic diet in winter was monotonous: pea soup and pork, potatoes and bread, and perhaps some preserved fruit while supplies lasted through the long winter. Anything that had to be purchased in Peterborough was an expensive luxury. The trick to survival, physical and financial, was to be self-sufficient. In summer the children were sent off to pick wild strawberries, blackberries, gooseberries, red and black currants, huckleberries, grapes and blueberries, which their mothers would then stew. ("A dish of raspberries and milk, with sugar, or a pie, gives many an emigrant family a supper," Catharine suggested.) And there were often special delicacies. During a pause in farm routines, the men might take time to shoot deer or game birds, or catch fish in the lake. If an Indian woman arrived at the door, there was also the possibility of duck or venison.

Members of the local Indian band started calling on the settlers within a few days of each woman's arrival north of Peterborough. Frances Stewart had told Catharine that when the first Europeans settled in the area, they regarded the Indians as "strange, wild, foreign savages . . . rolled in blankets, red leggings and mocassins covering their feet and legs; long black hair hanging loose and matted over their faces and shoulders, restless black eyes peering everywhere." The "Chippewa Indians," as the sisters called them, had been established in the area for nearly 150 years. They supported themselves by trapping, hunting, fishing and gathering edible plants. Once the settlers began to clear the land, the Indians were happy to start trading goods with them. In exchange for baskets, mats, ducks or venison, they took such European treats as pork, flour, potatoes or clothing. Susanna's quilted petticoat was particularly coveted by her visitors. Sometimes they asked to borrow household items. "Once a squaw came to borrow a washing-tub, but not understanding her language, I could not for some time discover the object of her solicitude," Catharine wrote home. "At last she took up a corner of her blanket, and pointing to some soap, began rubbing it between her two hands, initiated the action of washing, then laughed, and pointed to the tub; she then held up two fingers, to intimate it was for two days she needed the loan." The tub was returned punctually.

The Strickland sisters had arrived in Upper Canada with a romanticized image of the colony's native people. The eighteenth-century travel literature in their father's library at Reydon Hall was liberally sprinkled with references to "the Noble Savage": travellers wrote about native peoples in North America in the same tone as they used for ruins in Europe, as though they were charming and exotic remnants of a disappearing culture. Philosophers and poets, from Rousseau to Wordsworth, had extolled native people's freedom and self-reliance as a dignified alternative to the grasping cruelty of "civilization." Many of the authors had never actually met a native, but they imparted to emigrants like the Stricklands a fuzzy belief in their innate goodness. So Susanna and Catharine approached their Chippewa neighbours with rosy expectations, and they weren't disappointed. They made regular calls on the band's camp along the lakeshore. They enjoyed hearing their new friends singing hymns on Sundays (the band had been converted to Christianity by a Methodist missionary a few years earlier). They got to know several members of the band quite well: Peter, the chief, his wife, Mrs. Peter, and various hunters, young men and children. Both sisters conversed easily with the women in the camp who, like themselves, were pregnant, nursing babies and teaching older children how to behave. These shared female experiences forged a bond between English and Indian women much stronger than any rapport established between an Indian hunter and a newly arrived Englishman.

Each sister was intrigued by different aspects of the native way of life. Catharine was fascinated by the Chippewa habit of carrying children in specially woven baskets fastened to their mothers' shoulders with deerskin straps, and infants in flat cradles strapped to their backs. "I have seen the picture of the Virgin and Child in some of the old illuminated missals," remarked Catharine, "not unlike the figure of a papouse in its swaddling-clothes." Catharine embraced these neighbours with unqualified friendship and adopted many of their customs: she wore deerskin moccasins in the snow, and she dosed her children with *arum alropurpureum* when they had diarrhea. She was also impressed with the exquisite native craftsmanship. It wasn't long before letter cases and flower stands decorated with quillwork, and knife trays and work baskets made of birchbark, were scattered all over her parlour, and a miniature birchbark canoe was soon on its way to Sarah Strickland, in England.

Susanna found her Chippewa neighbours honest and grateful for any kindness shown to them. She deplored the way that most white settlers treated the natives. Indians met with more approval than Susanna accorded many settlers. She allowed any Indian visitor to sit at the table with her, although she still wouldn't permit her Irish servants the same privilege. "An Indian is Nature's gentleman—never familiar, coarse or vulgar," proclaimed "Moodie's squaw," as the Indians called her. She delighted in the nicknames in their own language that the Indians had given some settlers: *muckakee*, meaning bullfrog, for an odious braggart, and *segoskee*, or rising sun, for a young man with a red face.

But Susanna was incapable of the simple warmth that her sister found so easy and the lack of prejudice that real friendship with these "dark strangers" would require. European to her marrow, Susanna found the Chippewa men ugly: "with very coarse and repulsive features. The fore-head is low and retreating, the observing faculties large, the intellectual ones scarcely developed; the ears large, and standing off from the face, the eyes looking towards the temples, keen, snake-like, and far apart . . . the jaw-bone projecting, massy and brutal." She decided that their tents were dirty and that the native women who slept with white men were immoral. And close encounters with the Chippewa convinced her that the talents and good qualities of Indians "have been somewhat overrated, and invested with a poetical interest which they scarcely deserve," by many of their armchair admirers in the Old Country.

On Catharine's receipt of the legacy from the sisters' English uncle, Thomas Traill, like John Moodie, had immediately embarked on ambitious plans. An energetic settler working by himself could clear only four acres a year, so Thomas hired men to clear the bush on his acreage, despite the high cost of labour. He contracted additional men to build a granary, stable, dairy, chicken house and a verandah in front of his house, to improve the interior and to prepare beds for flowers and vegetables. Throughout the mid-1830s, Thomas Traill and John Moodie continued to chop, fell and clear the trees from their acres. Then they prepared the ground for crops by dragging a heavy iron plough over the rocky ground (carefully avoiding any boulders or stumps that would break its teeth). If they planted the seed too early, it might get caught in the late frost. If they left it too late, the growing season might be too short and the crop destroyed by rain. The only crops that proved reliable were the root vegetables, particularly potatoes, that every settler's wife planted close to her cabin.

Both John and Thomas were grimly aware that wrenching a desirable "estate" from the dense backwoods was a monumental task. Thomas's spirits sagged as he stared out at his rotting stumps and realized how quickly his capital was disappearing. But he tried not to worry Catharine, who wrote home, "My husband is become more reconciled to the country, and I daily feel my attachment to it strengthening." John was too much of an optimist to be anything other than sanguine about the future, and Susanna described this period as "the halcyon days of the bush."

The demands on both men and women in the bush were endless: there were always crops to harvest, maple sap to boil for syrup and sugar, apples to dry, fruit to bottle, fences to build or mend, potatoes to plant, candles to make. But even in the busiest season, Catharine found time to pull a crudely made wooden chair up to the scrubbed pine kitchen table and write in her journal or begin a letter home. Her account of their "Robinson Crusoe sort of life" filled pages and pages of precious vellum paper with her neat, sloping script. She was a compulsive scribbler who wrote the way she talked—in a warm, happy gush. Nothing deterred her from her prolixity. "Brevity in epistolary correspondence is not one of my excellences," she sheepishly admitted.

She wrote about the shortage of basic supplies such as tea and milk, and the dire state of the roads. She described how her clothes crackled with static electricity during a January cold snap, and how she had developed a taste for maple sugar in her tea. She enthused about Sam's skill at spearing fish in the lake, and the elegance of Indian quillwork. In her eyes, snow always twinkled like diamonds; a flock of snow buntings sparkled like "stars of silver," even the bonfires of brushwood were "a magnificent sight." She wrote about "bright sunbeams and blue cloudless sky"; pretty ducks "skimming along the . . . pine-fringed shores";

honeysuckle, St.-John's-wort and the magnificent water-lily, which "in all its virgin beauty expands its snowy bosom to the sun and genial air." She asked her family to send her some seeds from the primroses and violets that grew around Reydon Hall, so that she might introduce them into the backwoods.

Catharine could make the best of anything. Even the ugly, immovable stumps, which marched over the Traills' newly cleared property like an army of angry dwarves, acquired their own flattering metaphor. In her letter to England, Catharine described how in winter each stump sported its "turban of snow."

At one level, Catharine's enthusiasm was genuine. She had never been as fond of metropolitan life as her sisters Eliza, Agnes and Susanna and had always preferred to watch the seasons gently blend into each other in Suffolk. In Upper Canada, she now had the far more dramatic cycle of seasons, and a vast new array of plants, to record.

Similarly, she "never was a votary at the shrine of luxury or fashion," unlike Agnes and Susanna. She had hated the necessity, when visiting London, of getting dressed up in a full chemise, linen drawers, petticoat-bodice, whalebone corset and six or seven petticoats under a wide-skirted gown. The whole outfit (including bonnet, laced boots, heavy wool shawl and gloves) would have weighed close to twenty pounds, and it made every outing an exhausting challenge. In the backwoods, Catharine simply pulled on enough garments for warmth and respectability before venturing outside. "We do what we like; we dress as we find most suitable and most convenient; we are totally without the fear of any Mr. or Mrs. Grundy; and having shaken off the trammels of Grundyism, we laugh at the absurdity of those who voluntarily forge afresh and hug their chains."

But there was a bleak self-justification underlying Catharine's upbeat tone. Catharine knew that her mother and elder sisters would find Upper Canada appallingly primitive, and that they would be disgusted at the lack of regard for social status. She acknowledged that it was "a hard country for the poor gentleman, whose habits have rendered him unfit for manual labour." She admitted to her mother how women of any class who had left England for Canada were "discontented and unhappy. They miss the little domestic comforts they had been used to enjoy; they regret the friends and relations they left in the old country; and they cannot endure the loneliness of the backwoods." When her mother implied by return of post that she shared Catharine's regret at her "exile," Catharine shot back: "Let the assurance that I am not less happy than when I left my native land console you for my absence."

There was an additional reason for Catharine's relentless good cheer. She knew that if she allowed herself to linger on the discomforts of their new life, she would be falling in with Thomas's pessimism. Catharine was deluding herself when she wrote that her husband was reconciling himself to the new country after the arrival of her legacy. Her husband didn't have anything like his wife's get-up-and-go. Thomas's physical and psychological health were both crumbling. After a couple of years in the colony, his back was bent and his sparse hair iron grey. Wherever he looked, all he could see were more trees to be cut down, more bush to be cleared. He longed to go home. If he had to stay in Upper Canada, he would have preferred to cultivate an orchard and rear sheep. But it would be years before his land was ready for anything less demanding than potatoes, wheat and pigs. He was in his early forties, and feeling his age—but he had nobody with whom to share the work-load. So he started to borrow money, digging himself into debt, in order to hire Irish labourers to help clear his land. He worked alongside the men, chopping, clearing the underbrush, making brush heaps, logging, burning the fallow ground, sowing and harrowing his first crop.

Thomas had few psychological resources to protect him from the leaden depressions into which he sank with increasing regularity. He never learned to enjoy the Canadian landscape that his wife had grown so fond of. The quiet pleasures of canoeing, fishing or contemplation of a brilliant sunset had no appeal for him. There was no time for the only pursuit he really enjoyed: reading. Daylight had gone before he dragged himself back to the log house for his dinner each evening. He was far too weary to try reading by the light of a candle or whale oil lamp. Occasionally he managed to set pen to paper and write to the two sons he had left behind in the Orkneys, with his first wife's father. He suggested, with customary diffidence, that they might join him in Upper Canada. In 1833, Walter Traill was eighteen and John was fourteen— young lads who could have taken much of the labour from his shoulders. But neither boy was in the least interested in becoming an unpaid labourer for his father. Walter had already decided to study medicine, and didn't even bother to reply to his father's letters.

A hundred and fifty years ago, nobody understood the bleak reality of chronic depression. Catharine was too compassionate a woman to fix to her husband's condition one of the derogatory diagnoses of the day—moral frailty, unmanly weakness. But she recognized that if she herself admitted feelings of defeat or failure, Thomas's spirits would utterly collapse. And she knew that Agnes, in England, would be unable to restrain herself from telling Catharine that she had only herself to blame, for rushing into a precipitate marriage with an impractical, middle-aged widower. So Catharine insisted to her family that she was going to be "cheerful and contented for the sake of my beloved partner." She was not going to "sadden him by useless regrets." Her lush descriptions of Upper Canada's matchless scenery, flora and fauna allowed her to turn a blind eye to everything that was going wrong. She immersed herself in her love of nature, as she had learned to do at her father's side when Thomas Strickland had walked his little daughter along the Suffolk paths.

Few of Catharine's original letters home from this period have survived. But most of her observations were published in her own lifetime, thanks to her sister Agnes. Catharine had seen her elder sister's letter to Susanna suggesting that the two Canadian sisters might collaborate on a magazine containing information "of a useful nature." Either she or Agnes must have realized that Catharine's letters home would make an attractive publication. Agnes certainly liked the idea, and she and her sister Jane edited

Catharine's correspondence into a publishable manuscript. This was no mean task at a time when manuscripts were carefully copied out in long-hand, especially as Catharine's handwriting was not always easy to follow. Jane complained to Catharine about a later manuscript that "though the work is a very interesting one you had left it imperfect in construction and there was an immensity to do—Agnes who looked over it sometimes was as puzzled as myself." The cleaned-up draft was then sent to Charles Knight, a London publisher. Knight agreed to bring the manuscript out in January 1836 as part of his "Library of Entertaining Knowledge." It appeared under the title *The Backwoods of Canada: Being Letters from the Wife of an Emigrant Officer, Illustrative of the Domestic Economy of British America.*

The book was pitched to the "wives and daughters of emigrants of the higher class" who would become the "pioneers of civilization in the wilderness." *The Backwoods of Canada* painted a light-hearted picture of an active, satisfying life for women who were prepared to discard anything "pertaining to the artificial refinement of fashionable life in England" and concentrate on domestic duties and botany. It reads well today, because it is as informative, lively and cheerful as its author must have been. Her sunny personality almost leaps off every page: she devoted only two paragraphs to her attack of cholera, but required forty pages of text to describe the fauna and flora she discovered during her first few months in the bush. Catharine altered several of the details of her emigration (the name of the boat on which the Traills crossed the Atlantic was changed from the *Rowley* to the *Laurel*) and made the best of all the worst moments, such as the grim journey from Rice Lake to Peterborough. There are only fleeting references to her husband: his name is never mentioned.

All Catharine's upbeat pretense, for Reydon consumption, about her less-than-perfect marriage and precipitate decision to emigrate now became the gloss over the hardships of pioneer life. When *The Backwoods of Canada* was first published in England, it sold so well that Catharine was asked to add some extra information for later editions. (She supplied a how-to chapter on pickling vegetables and making maple sugar, soap and candles, plus some statistics on immigration.)

For all their difficulties, in their first four years in Canada, the Moodies and Traills had scarcely tasted the real hardships of pioneer life. They still had a little capital to draw on, and they could still dream that they were gracefully helping to establish a New World squirearchy.

Chapter 8

"A little red-haired baboon"

"Canada is the land of hope," Catharine assured her family back home, after she had been in the colony for three years. "Everything is going forward; it is scarcely possible for arts, sciences, agriculture, manufactures, to retrogade; they must keep advancing."

There were reasons other than Catharine's incurable optimism for this happy prognosis. The Canada-mania in the British Isles during the early 1830s had meant a rush of people across the Atlantic. With all these new settlers taming the bush, establishing communities, bringing crops to market and buying supplies for their farms, how could the colony's economy not grow and thrive? As the frontier was rapidly pushed west, how could colonial governors and their masters in London not invest further in Canadian roads and canals? Any fool, argued the colonists, could see that this was the way to fortify British North America against its rapacious neighbour to the south.

British canal-building was one of the wonders of the early-nineteenth-century world. A spider's web of beautifully maintained waterways already covered the map of England. By the time the Moodies and the Traills crossed the Atlantic, the British were busy exporting their canal know-how to Canada to strengthen their territorial possessions there. In 1825, the first vessel passed through the Lachine Canal, avoiding the rapids south of the island of Montreal. Four years later, the new 27-mile Welland Canal allowed ships loaded with lumber and grain to bypass the Niagara Falls and the turbulent Gorge and enter Lake Ontario from Lake Erie. But the most impressive feat of canal engineering was opened in 1832. At enormous cost in both lives and money, the 125-mile Rideau Canal system, with forty-seven locks, was hacked out of granite to link Kingston (British military headquarters in North America) to the Ottawa River. The first two canals improved commerce within the northern half of the continent; the third strengthened Canada's defences against the United States.

These successes sparked a rash of proposals for similar colony-building projects. Douro Township was a district ripe for rapid settlement and growth, and well situated for the development of a waterway. There was already talk in Toronto (formerly York), the seat of government for Upper Canada, of a canal system to link Lake Huron to Lake Ontario and the St. Lawrence River. Lake Katchewanooka, on which the Traill and Moodie properties perched, would be part of the route. Such a waterway would allow vessels from Lake Huron to make their way into Lake Simcoe, across the present-day Kawartha Lakes, down the Otonabee River, across Rice Lake, and from there down the Trent River to the Bay of Quinte, close to Belleville. The proposed canal system would give settlers easy access to supplies for their settlements and markets for their products. It would open up a vast area of back country for development and at the same time boost existing settlements on its banks. Various eager investors were already building mills, taverns and solid stone houses in Peterborough, in anticipation of a bonanza. The township had even agreed to plug the worst potholes in the corduroy roads (made with logs laid crosswise to the traffic) that linked the scattered settlements. "Sooner or later there is little doubt but that it will be carried into effect," Catharine Parr Trail boasted.

Unfortunately, there was a great deal of doubt. For all its promise, the economy of Upper Canada remained primitive, weak and entirely dependent on logging and agriculture. Nothing could happen without the hard labour of new immigrants. As John Moodie noted in a long article he wrote for an English newspaper in 1836, Canada's *"present* prosperity and progress in improvement must depend *chiefly* upon emigration and the expenditure of imported capital." But the supply of willing labourers began to drop off in the mid-1830s. Cholera was devastating the populations of the Old World. Immigrant ships continued to unload human cargo at Grosse Ile, but immigrants eager to tame the bush did not materialize in the numbers expected. Far more of the newcomers, particularly those from the middle or upper classes, gravitated to established communities like Toronto, Kingston, London and Belleville.

Beneath the ebb and flow of immigration, however, was another, more corrosive cause for Canada's slow rate of growth. The British government was losing interest in its colony. England was no longer the depressed country that the sisters had left behind; Britain was finally emerging from its post-Napoleonic doldrums. The puffing, clanking, booming age of the railways had begun, and the mother country was being transformed into the wealthiest nation on earth. Far-sighted capitalists preferred to invest in British coal mines, railways and factories instead of distant and doubtful engineering projects.

A new class had stepped onto the British stage: the industrialists, whose entrepreneurial skills and muscular ambitions made the cities of the Midlands and the north—cities like Sheffield, Leeds, Birmingham and Manchester—hum. These "masters of the new manufacturing machine," in historian Donald Creighton's phrase, were men who "sought world markets and the traffic of the Seven Seas." They were free-traders, with all the contempt for victims of such policies that free traders always display. They had no time for underpopulated colonies—like Upper

Canada, the Cape Colony or Australia—that needed British subsidies for defence or administration. They were impatient with Canadian colonists who wouldn't cut the umbilical cord with the mother country, and who relied on shipping monopolies and tariff preferences to protect their transatlantic trade. These ambitious manufacturers were more interested in the giant market in the United States than in sparsely populated British North America.

At the same time that Britain was turning its back on its North American possessions, tensions were emerging within the colony itself. The interests of the governed were visibly diverging from those of the governors.

The titular ruler of Upper Canada was the lieutenant-governor, a well-born Englishman (usually the possessor of a title, several military honours or at the very least a coat of arms for his carriage) sent by Westminister to Toronto to run the colony's affairs. The actual governors were his local advisers—the clergymen, officers, officials and landowners of the Family Compact whose idea of government was entirely feudal. Members of this local oligarchy were linked by blood, marriage or at least allegiance to the Church of England. Comfortably ensconced in their impressive stone mansions in Toronto, members of the Family Compact dominated the judiciary, the Executive Council and the Legislative Council (neither of which was elected) and much of the House of Assembly (the elected lower house, which was virtually powerless). They dispensed favours to their friends and directed British policy to their own advantage.

The Traills and the Moodies would have loved to belong to this exclusive élite of families like the Boultons, Jarvises and Powells. They felt connected to them by virtue of their education and background, and they yearned to be recipients of their patronage. Either Thomas Traill or John Dunbar Moodie would have been ecstatic to get his hands on a government job like local land registrar, which gave its holder an income. Thomas Traill was overjoyed when he was appointed a justice of the peace. Even though remuneration was derisory—a small proportion of the fees charged for performing marriages or the fines levied for minor crimes—the office bestowed on its holder a dab of prestige.

However, neither the Moodies nor the Traills had the wherewithal to join the exalted ranks of bigwigs in the colonial capital. Both couples were stuck in the backwoods because that was where they could get free land. Like everybody else who was roughing it in the bush—from rude Yankees to Anglo-Irish gentlefolk, from Irish paupers to Scottish labourers—they were the governed. And like the rest of the backwoods settlers in the late 1830s, the sisters and their husbands faced mounting problems: crop failures, a shortage of money, a slow-down in immigration, struggles with inadequate transportation facilities.

By now, the diminutive and hot-tempered Scottish-born journalist William Lyon Mackenzie had emerged as the backwoodsman's champion. Part hustler, part prophet, "Little Mac" had been galvanizing opposition to the Family Compact since the early 1820s, first as the outspoken editor of *The Colonial Advocate* and then as an elected member of

A brilliant demagogue, William Lyon Mackenzie (1795–1861) was a hero in the backwoods, but a thorn in the flesh of Toronto's Family Compact.

the legislature of Upper Canada. In more recent Canadian history, only Newfoundland's Joey Smallwood can match Mackenzie for populist wizardry—demonic fluency, fierce energy, fearlessness against the odds and an ability to fill the air with honey and gall. By the time the Traills and Moodies were settled in Douro Township, Mackenzie was busy inflaming the ragged (and often illiterate) backwoodsmen with his passionate Tory-bashing and his stinging criticism of the Toronto nabobs. Speaking from schoolhouse steps or the back of farm carts, he ranted about dishonest officials, corrupt clergy and lace-cuffed place-seekers. He pointed out that Upper Canada was a stagnant backwater compared to the United States, where newcomers had a say in their country's future and easy access to land. On the main streets of every small town in Toronto's hinterland, he accused the Family Compact of ruling Upper Canada "according to its own pleasure" and committing "acts of tyranny and oppression." His voice shrill with indignation, and his red wig repeatedly sliding off his bald head, he made personal attacks on his political enemies. He insisted that people like Henry Boulton, the Attorney-General of Upper Canada, and John Beverley Robinson, Chief Justice, "surround the Lieutenant-Governor, and mould him like wax to their will."

The Traills and Moodies had plenty of reasons to agree with the substance of Little Mac's tirades. They had firsthand experience of the sluggish development of the backwoods. But they were so blinded by their social prejudices and eagerness to cling to "establishment" values that they failed to see that Little Mac was talking about their own plight. They couldn't see that the colonial administration was impervious to problems faced by families like theirs. They didn't understand that their own community would never thrive, or their own land rise in value, unless the colonial government stepped in to encourage settlement and invest in better transportation systems—measures the Family Compact had no desire to initiate.

To people like Traill and Moodie, William Lyon Mackenzie was a dangerous radical and a troublemaker who challenged all their most dearly held principles of social order. Another gentleman farmer in the Peterborough region, John Langton, spoke for his ilk when he dismissed Mackenzie as a "little factious wretch. . . . He is a little red-haired man about five foot nothing, and extremely like a baboon." Mackenzie's followers, in the considered opinion of John Moodie, were "under the influence of the most odious selfishness." Moodie was too busy detecting a strain of republicanism in the Radicals' demand for representative government to appreciate Mackenzie's diagnosis of the colony's problems. Little Mac's followers were, in Susanna's words, "a set of monsters," traitors to the British flag and "enemies of my beloved country." And the agitation of the Radicals meant a further drop in immigration to Upper Canada from the mid-1830s, with jarring consequences for life around Peterborough.

The legacies to Susanna and Catharine had been substantial, yet the money ran like sand through the fingers of John Moodie and Thomas Traill. The tranquillity of the "halcyon days of the bush," as Susanna had described her first months on Lake Katchewanooka, began to evaporate as the two men exhausted their capital and ran out of cash. Part of the problem was that neither the Moodie nor the Traill property yielded enough wheat or lumber to sell at market. Their crops were so scanty that there was barely enough wheat to last them until Christmas, let alone to leave a bag of flour with the miller in payment for his services. But even better harvests would not have saved the families from the consequences of a major depression throughout North America in the mid-1830s, which brought economic stagnation to the backwoods. By the fall of 1835, Susanna had sold most of her own clothes (with the exception of her wedding dress and the handmade baby clothes Mrs. Strickland had sent from England) so that she could pay her servants. Soon the only servants who remained were ones who had nowhere else to go and stayed on without wages. The hired men disappeared; the ambitious plans for outbuildings were shelved; each family began to retrench.

Hunger and want hovered like harpies over the little cabins in the woods. And all four adults—Thomas and Catharine, John and Susanna—began to look around for other ways to make money. At first it was a quiet search. It rapidly became desperate.

Susanna had continued to write poetry and sketches. She sent them off to two New York–based publications, the *Albion* and the *North American Magazine,* and several Toronto–based periodicals, including the *Canadian Magazine* and the *Canadian Literary Magazine*. They were well received by editors who appreciated the "former Susanna Strickland." The American poet Sumner Lincoln Fairfield, editor of the *North American Magazine,* described Susanna as having "genius as lofty as her heart is pure." Susanna's relief at this recognition was almost craven. She replied to Fairfield in January 1835: "Though residing in a small log hut, in the backwoods of Upper Canada, and constantly engaged in the everyday cares of domestic life, I am not so wholly indifferent to praise, as not to feel highly gratified when the spontaneous outpourings of a mind, vividly alive to the beauties of Nature, meets with the approbation of men, of superior worth and genius." But poetry did not put bread on the Moodie table. Fairfield's payments did not even cover the cost of Susanna's paper and pens.

Catharine was also finding that writing did not pay. *The Backwoods of Canada* was enthusiastically reviewed when it appeared in London early in 1836. The London *Spectator* praised the author's elegance of mind, modesty and "sound practical views," and declared that "it would be difficult to decide whether [the book] was more entertaining or useful." The London *Athenaeum* was enchanted by the author, who "is obviously endowed with life's best blessings—an observant eye, joined to a cheerful and thankful heart." It recommended the book "for its spirit and truth." The book was excerpted in several magazines and journals, and noted in *Tait's Edinburgh Magazine* as "written by a lady, who has set a stout heart to a steep hill, . . . and who by spirit, activity, and good humour, has surmounted her difficulties, or converted them into pleasantries." It had immediately become required reading for any English gentlewoman considering emigration to British North America, and its sales helped to keep Mr. Charles Knight's shaky publishing house afloat.

Yet the author received only 110 pounds for the copyright to the book, and no royalties on sales. Stuck in the remote depths of a colony, Catharine had little leverage on Charles Knight. The ingenuous optimism that saturates *The Backwoods of Canada* drained away, as the author realized that her bestseller was not going to rescue her from the woods.

By now, the sisters' husbands were dismally discouraged. Both families were afflicted with malaria, which was rampant on the frontier, where settlers were struggling to drain mosquito-infested swamps. After a few days of sweating and shivers, most of the family members recovered fully. But the disease "threw a gloom" on Thomas's spirits, according to Catharine, which he lacked the stamina to shake off. Both men had additional family responsibilities. The Moodies now had four children: Katie, Aggie, Dunbar, and Donald, who was born in May 1836. By 1837, Catharine was the mother of James, four; Katharine Agnes Strickland (Kate), one; and newborn Thomas Henry Strickland (Harry). There were a lot of mouths to feed on a few acres of wheat and potatoes.

Thomas Traill would willingly have sold his farm to the first bidder. Unfortunately, there were no takers. Thomas informed relatives in the Orkneys, in 1836, that "land has been nearly unsaleable for the last two years." He described his predicament in ghastly detail, adding mournfully that he wished they had emigrated to the West Indies instead of Canada. Then he threw out a pathetic appeal for "anything like a Consulship at some small Foreign Port [where I might live] a life more suitable to my tastes and habits." The last sentence of his letter is suffused with despair: "But I must live and die, far from many of those that I love most dearly."

John Dunbar Moodie was in an even worse predicament than his brother-in-law. He had fewer cleared acres and more debts. In yet another of his impetuous business decisions, he had sold his military commission back to his regiment (which would quickly sell it to another bidder), which meant that he no longer had his military half-pay, one hundred pounds a year, to help him scrape by. With the lump sum he had received in return, he'd bought stock in a Cobourg steamboat company. It was soon obvious that the steamboat stock was worthless, but by then John had used it as surety for various loans. John rarely revealed his anxieties; he knew that this would shake Susanna, who depended on his emotional stability. But he too began to explore other options for their future. First, he tried to interest publishers in the idea of a book about emigration to Upper Canada, similar to his recently published *Ten Years in South Africa*. Next, after seeing an advertisement from the Texas Land Company in the *Albion*, he considered abandoning Upper Canada and moving to Texas. A few months later, he tried a different tack. He wrote to Sir Francis Bond Head, the newly appointed Lieutenant-Governor of Upper Canada, describing his struggles with "embarrassments and difficulties of no ordinary description" and appealing to him for a government appointment that might shield his family from "distress or ruin." But nothing came of any of these efforts.

Every few weeks, a letter would arrive for Susanna from Agnes Strickland, in England. Although she often enclosed some entirely inappropriate gift, such as silk stockings ("only worn once at court"), Agnes was acutely aware of her sisters' deteriorating fortunes and dwindling hopes. She always tried to send her letters with someone travelling to the colony, since the Moodies' could barely afford to pay for the letters she sent them through the mail. Carefully wrapped in the folded paper (envelopes were still not in use) were two or three silver coins for the children. John and Susanna were too close to starvation to do anything other than spend the precious coins on desperately needed essentials.

Susanna, like Catharine, was a resourceful, practical woman. She was a better cook than her sister, and just as accomplished at preserving cabbage, pickling cucumbers, smoking bacon and plucking wildfowl. When presented with dead squirrels, she could transform them into pies, stews or roasts without a twitch of distaste. When they could no longer afford tea or coffee, she recalled a recipe for dandelion-root coffee in the

Albion and promptly went out to dig up some roots. "The coffee proved excellent"; a supply was sent over to the Traills. But things went from bad to worse, and during the bitterly severe winter of 1836, Susanna's children were weak with hunger. Overcoming her kneejerk English sentimentality about pet animals, Susanna slaughtered her daughter Katie's pet pig, Spot. She noted with remorse, however, that while her family fell on the pork, their dog Hector, who had been Spot's boon companion, could not bring himself even to gnaw on one of Spot's bones.

Susanna and Catharine clung to each other in hardship. When the Traills were afflicted with "the ague," as settlers always called malaria, Catharine noted that, "but for the prompt assistance of . . . Susanna, I know not what would have become of us in our sore trouble." In return, Catharine sent over bread and maple cakes for the Moodie family. Kitchen utensils and farming implements were shuttled between the two log houses.

Relations between the two brothers-in-law were less amicable. They were such different characters that, when things were going badly, it was almost inevitable that Thomas's lugubrious pessimism would irritate easygoing John, while John's consistently bad judgment about business matters would exasperate Thomas. Thomas was annoyed when the Moodies borrowed, and broke, the Traills' sugar kettle (although they had it mended for him). For some time, there was a distinct chill between the two men. This pained their wives, who knew their kinship was too valuable to disrupt with petty squabbles. Eventually, Thomas apologized to his brother-in-law: "I again express my sincere and bitter regret at ever having given you any uneasiness, the more particularly at a time when you had more than enough to annoy you otherwise. I hope we shall hence forward live as friends and brothers."

As the decade drew on and harvests failed, in damp little log cabins scattered through the bush, settlers were starving. Those from genteel backgrounds, like the Moodies and Traills, were the most vulnerable: unlike working-class immigrants, they didn't have the manual skills to farm for themselves, and they no longer had any money to pay others to work in the fields. Despair drove many to drink. News of the most hopeless cases travelled quickly from settlement to settlement.

Susanna heard about one half-pay officer in nearby Dummer Township, an epauletted and decorated veteran of military service in India, who was so depressed by the dreary cycle of isolation, poverty and crop failures that "the fatal whiskey-bottle became his refuge from gloomy thoughts." Captain Frederick Lloyd finally deserted his wife Ella altogether and headed south. Susanna organized an expedition to take bread, gingerbread, sugar, tea and home-cured ham to the abandoned wife and her seven children. Since John was away, she asked Thomas, her brother-in-law, to accompany them. Thomas, Susanna and her friend Emilia Shairp, whose cabin was close to the Moodies', walked for miles in the bitter January cold through the "tangled maze of closely-interwoven cedars, fallen trees and loose-scattered masses of rock." When they finally arrived at their destination, Susanna saw a picture of utter desolation—a woman struggling to maintain her dignity while watching her children shiver and weep with hunger. They had exhausted their supply of potatoes, which was all they had eaten for weeks. Susanna stared at the wan, emaciated figure in a thin muslin gown ("the most inappropriate garment for the rigours of the season, but . . . the only decent one that she retained"). She looked at two little boys cowering under the coverings of a crudely made bed in the corner "to conceal their wants from the eyes of the stranger." She stuttered out a formal greeting: "I hoped that, as I was the wife of an officer, and, like her, a resident in the bush, and well-acquainted with its trials and privations, she would look upon me as a friend." The little family fell on the sackload of supplies with gratitude. As Susanna watched, she must have wondered whether this was what the future held for her.

Chapter 9

A Call to Arms

In early December 1837, Sam Strickland was too intent on keeping the heavy iron plough steady to notice the young lad racing over the hill towards him, waving a piece of paper. As dusk settled on the grey landscape, snowflakes began to swirl around the horns of the lumbering oxen. Sam urged Buck and Bright forward. He was late planting, and he knew that once he had finished his own field, he would have to help at his sister Susanna's farm. John Moodie had broken his foot while sowing his winter wheat and was limping around on homemade crutches.

The excited cries of James Caddy, his neighbour's son, finally caught Sam's attention, and he grabbed the paper from the panting youth. It was a proclamation dated December 5, two days earlier, from the Lieutenant-Governor of the province, Sir Francis Bond Head. Rebellion had broken out in the colony. The Lieutenant-Governor called upon the loyal militia of Upper Canada to assist in putting down an armed uprising. Toronto was under siege, James blurted out between gasps for air. William Lyon Mackenzie was at the head of a ragtag army of rebels. Shod in clogs and armed with rifles, pikes and pitchforks, they were marching down Yonge Street. Little Mac was challenging the rule of law, the authority of the British crown and the power of the Westminster-appointed governor. There was even talk, young Caddy breathlessly added, that Toronto had already been burned to the ground, Bond Head killed and war declared between Upper Canadians and the Yankees.

This was shocking news. Douro Township's gentlemen immigrants were too distant from Toronto to know that Bond Head was an arrogant fool who had misjudged the strength of popular feeling and had helped provoke the uprising by treating Mackenzie as nothing more than a raving madman. At the various harvest festivals and Strickland family celebrations along Lake Katchewanooka that fall, Little Mac had been regarded as a bit of a joke. "Mackenzie's treason," in Catharine's words, "had been like the annoying buzz of a mosquito ever in the public ears."

Now Mackenzie had co-ordinated his offensive with an uprising of the Patriotes in Lower Canada, led by Louis-Joseph Papineau, who were also demanding more control over the colonial government. Taking advantage of Bond Head's ill-advised decision to send his troops to Montreal, to quell the Patriotes there, Little Mac had launched an attack on a defenceless Toronto.

Within hours, eager to support the Crown, Sam Strickland had said goodbye to his family and set off through the December night to Peterborough, to join the Peterborough Volunteers. By the following morning, Thomas Traill was marching alongside Sam down the rutted cart-track towards Port Hope. A day later, John Moodie had shouldered his knapsack and limped on his crutches the eleven miles to Peterborough, where he borrowed a horse and rode on to Port Hope at the head of two hundred more loyal volunteers. For Thomas and John, the call to arms was thrilling. Soldiering was their business. Soldiering meant the jangle of harness, the bark of orders, the acknowledgment of their officer status—as well as regular meals and jovial male companionship.

It meant an escape, albeit temporary, from the backwoods and suffocating poverty. Both men dearly loved their wives, but the opportunity to defend the interests of the motherland was irresistible. It had an extra piquancy in 1837, because Britain had a new monarch, Victoria. For the first time in their lives, the rallying cry for these soldiers was "God save the Queen!"

For Catharine Parr Traill and Susanna Moodie, however, the news was appalling. Dutiful feelings of loyalty to British interests were swept aside by dismay at the prospect of their husbands' prolonged absence. They had infants to nurse and children to feed, and now they would also have to do the men's work in the dead of winter—keeping fires lit, woodpiles filled, animals fed and paths cleared. The snowstorm had continued all night; weeks of freezing temperatures and snowdrifts lay ahead. "God preserve us from the fearful consequences of a civil warfare," Catharine confided to her journal. "O, my God, the Father of all mercies, grant that he may return in safety to those dear babes and their anxious mother." The backwoods reverberated with rumours: Toronto was beseiged by sixty thousand men; four hundred Indians had attacked the city and slaughtered all the inhabitants; American soldiers were crossing the border in support of Mackenzie. The two women were terrified that armed rebels might burst out of the forest at any moment, intent on rape, pillage and murder. "Became so restless and impatient I felt in a perfect fever," Catharine wrote in her journal. Susanna and her children moved into the Traills' cabin.

In fact, the rebellion fizzled out almost before it began. There were scarcely any casualties, and William Lyon Mackenzie was forced to flee across the border. Bond Head offered a reward of one thousand pounds for his capture. When news reached the little settlement north of Peterborough that the men would soon be home, Catharine escorted Susanna home in the horse-drawn sleigh. With the children swathed in buffalo rugs, the two women wrapped themselves up in a blanket together and started laughing hysterically in the cold night air. Suffused with relief that their husbands were safe, they were overcome with the

PROCLAMATION.

BY His Excellency SIR FRANCIS BOND HEAD, Baronet, Lieutenant Governor of Upper Canada, &c. &c.

To the Queen's Faithful Subjects in Upper Canada.

In a time of profound peace, while every one was quietly following his occupations, feeling secure under the protection of our Laws, a band of Rebels, instigated by a few malignant and disloyal men, has had the wickedness and audacity to assemble with Arms, and to attack and Murder the Queen's Subjects on the Highway—to Burn and Destroy their Property—to Rob the Public Mails—and to threaten to Plunder the Banks—and to Fire the City of Toronto.

Brave and Loyal People of Upper Canada, we have been long suffering from the acts and endeavours of concealed Traitors, but this is the first time that Rebellion has dared to show itself openly in the land, in the absence of invasion by any Foreign Enemy.

Let every man do his duty now, and it will be the last time that we or our children shall see our lives or properties endangered, or the Authority of our Gracious Queen insulted by such treacherous and ungrateful men. MILITIA-MEN OF UPPER CANADA, no Country has ever shewn a finer example of Loyalty and Spirit than YOU have given upon this sudden call of Duty. Young and old of all ranks, are flocking to the Standard of their Country. What has taken place will enable our Queen to know Her Friends from Her Enemies—a public enemy is never so dangerous as a concealed Traitor—and now my friends let us complete well what is begun—let us not return to our rest till Treason and Traitors are revealed to the light of day, and rendered harmless throughout the land.

Be vigilant, patient and active—leave punishment to the Laws—our first object is, to arrest and secure all those who have been guilty of Rebellion, Murder and Robbery.—And to aid us in this, a Reward is hereby offered of

One Thousand Pounds,

to any one who will apprehend, and deliver up to Justice, WILLIAM LYON MACKENZIE ; and FIVE HUNDRED POUNDS to any one who will apprehend, and deliver up to Justice, DAVID GIBSON—or SAMUEL LOUNT—or JESSE LLOYD—or SILAS FLETCHER—and the same reward and a free pardon will be given to any of their accomplices who will render this public service, except he or they shall have committed, in his own person, the crime of Murder or Arson.

And all, but the Leaders above-named, who have been seduced to join in this unnatural Rebellion, are hereby called to return to their duty to their Sovereign—to obey the Laws—and to live henceforward as good and faithful Subjects—and they will find the Government of their Queen as indulgent as it is just.

GOD SAVE THE QUEEN.

Thursday, 3 o'clock, P. M.
7th Dec.

☞ The Party of Rebels, under their Chief Leaders, is wholly dispersed, and flying before the Loyal Militia. The only thing that remains to be done, is to find them, and arrest them.

R. STANTON, Printer to the QUEEN'S Most Excellent Majesty.

humour, as Catharine noted in her journal, of finding themselves "not a whit less happy than if we had been rolling along in a carriage with a splendid pair of bays instead of slowly creeping along at a funereal pace in the rudest of all vehicles with the most ungraceful and uncouth of all steeds." Thomas and John were back on their farms only days after they had left.

Despite its comic-opera aspect, the rebellion had stirred everybody up. Susanna wrote an anthem calling on the "Freemen of Canada" to fight the "base insurgents." Fifty years before Rudyard Kipling, she tapped into the British appetite for triumphant patriotism. It was soon on the lips of every soldier in Bond Head's ragged defence force. The second of its five verses made it plain that the loyalty of true Canadians, wherever they were born, must lie with the motherland:

What though your bones may never lie
Beneath dear Albion's hallow'd sod,
Spurn the base wretch who dare defy,
In arms, his country and his God!
Whose callous bosom cannot feel
That he who acts a traitor's part,
Remorselessly uplifts the steel
To plunge it in a parent's heart.

The rousing words were accompanied by banging pot lids and waving fists as Susanna's children marched around the kitchen reciting the anthem, while their father accompanied them on his flute.

The triumphant suppression of the '37 Uprising infused the Christmas celebrations two weeks later with additional jubilation. Catharine decorated her cabin with even more ingenuity than usual, threading dried cranberries onto pine boughs to simulate the red holly berries she had gathered as a girl in Suffolk. Her daughter Katie made a hemlock wreath and twisted her precious coral beads (which her mother had refused to sell) around the boughs. Catharine scrounged supplies from her brother

Sam to ensure a feast, and by the time the Moodie family arrived in their sleigh, the Traills' table was laden with the weight of roast duck, potatoes, vegetables carefully preserved four months earlier, pies, preserves and breads. While Thomas and John toasted the new Queen in treacle beer (made from treacle, hops, bran and water), Catharine distributed maple sugar sweets to the children.

After dinner, the two families went outside to play in the newly fallen snow. Both men were now limping, since awkward Thomas had fallen off his mount and sprained his ankle at a meeting of the militia in Peterborough a few days earlier. Though the men were unable to pull the children on their homemade sleds along the snowy paths through the woods, the two Strickland sisters, as usual, compensated for their husbands' handicaps.

It was only when night fell, and the women sat beside the Franklin stove nursing their infants and reminiscing about Reydon Christmases, that a sadder note crept in. They recalled jubilant wassailing parties while their father was still alive, when the Hall was thronged with merrymaking neighbours and attentive servants. They thought of their four older sisters in England. They remembered how, after their father's death, Agnes always took charge of celebrations, while gentle Sarah quietly produced a delicious dinner despite their straitened circumstances. "Our Christmas meetings at best are but a melancholy imitation of those social hours," sighed Catharine. "Their chief charm arises here from the retrospect of the past and from the long train of affectionate remembrances that crowd thick and fast upon each other."

The taste of military life had given new energy to both John and Thomas. Both hated farming and knew they were failures as frontier pioneers. Now they had tasted again a life based on professional, rather than manual, skills. Their brother-in-law Sam Strickland, who had never served in the regular army, was happy to return to pioneering, but neither John nor Thomas could bear the thought of slogging through another miserable year in the bush. John Moodie was forty-one, and Thomas Traill forty-five: too old for heavy labour. The short-lived uprising of 1837 had opened a new chapter for both the Moodies and the Traills.

John Moodie was the first to find an escape route. He was under pressure from creditors in both Peterborough and Cobourg; if he could acquire a salary, he could finally pay off some debts. So when the government in Toronto announced the creation of several new regiments to defend the colony, Moodie immediately volunteered. His energetic cheeriness charmed the military authorities and wangled him a captain's commission in the Queen's Own Regiment. By late January 1838, he was back in Toronto, three days' journey from Peterborough, sitting in the New British Coffee House on York Street, or strolling along King Street admiring the Georgian terraces and brick market buildings that had sprung up in the previous decade. It was a welcome change of circumstances, especially since, according to the Sturgeon Lake settler John Langton, military officers were "as thick as blackberries" on the streets of Toronto. A mood of carnival buoyancy prevailed; there was no end to the old friends to be discovered and toasts to be drunk.

A month later, Moodie was posted to the Niagara Region, even farther from his family. His regiment was positioned to repel incursions from rebels now based across the border. Mackenzie had assembled a small army in Buffalo of American sympathizers anxious to join Mac's crusade to "free" Canada. The border raids of these wild-eyed Yankees were costing far more in casualties and damage than the original uprising had done.

With at least one hundred miles between them, John and Susanna had to rely on the mail service to maintain their intimacy, as they had in the months before their marriage. In the densely written lines of their letters, we can glimpse the strength of their love for each other, and their mutual dependence. "I have been so bothered and hurried about with parades, drills, and other duties," John wrote to his "dearest Susie" from Toronto, "that I have not till this moment been able to settle myself sufficiently to write to you and our sweet babes. God bless you all. How I long to clasp you to my heart, my own good old wife, and to kiss my dear honest hearted Katie my light hearted Aggy, and sly Dunnie and my gentle generous Donald." As the weeks of separation dragged on, even the delights of a regular income palled: "Do write me soon, my dearest Susie and tell me all about my dear children. I could not live long without seeing you all . . . I am tolerably sick of *Militia Soldiering* and shall be right glad to get back to my old woman and our dear brats again." In every letter, John sent his wife as much money as he could afford. "Now my dear Susie do not stint yourself of comforts for I cannot bear to be pampered up while you are suffering any privation."

Susanna was equally lonely: "I have shed more tears since you have been away than during the whole period of our marriage," she wrote to her "dearest Moodie." "I wish you were here." A few months later, she confessed to John, "I long to be with you—to see, to speak to you, to hold you to my heart once more. . . . There are times when I almost wish I could love you less. This weary longing after you makes my life pass away like a dream." She missed both John's physical presence and his ability to lighten her mood: "I dreamt you returned last night and I was so glad, but you pushed me away, and said you had taken a vow of celibacy and meant to live alone, and I burst into such fits of laughing that I awoke."

The passion of their marriage was undimmed, despite the hardships of the past seven years and the arrival of four children. John was still, as Susanna wrote years later in *Roughing It in the Bush,* "my light of life." Their letters pulsate with buoyancy and desire, but unslaked libido is only half the story. John and Susanna were more than man and wife. They were united in a friendship that was unusual by nineteenth-century standards, and is refreshing to a twentieth-century reader. They took each other seriously as writers: whenever possible, Susanna showed John her work before she sent it to the publishers. John was terribly proud of his clever wife and always encouraged her literary ambitions. While he was in Toronto, he managed to sell several of Susanna's patriotic ballads, as well as some of his own poems, to *The Palladium,* a Toronto newspaper published by a Rice Lake acquaintance of the Moodies, Charles Fothergill.

Soon after John disappeared to Toronto, Susanna realized she was expecting a fifth child. A woman of Susanna's age and class in England during this period would have been treated as an invalid; her "delicate state" would have required her to avoid exercise or excitement. But by 1838, Susanna had left such feeble behaviour far behind. She and her youngsters were alone in the bush with only Jenny, an illiterate Irish servant, to help her. This pregnancy appears to have given her a rush of energy. As soon as the sap started flowing, she organized Jenny to make maple sugar. Once the snow had melted, Susanna sowed the spring crops and planted her garden with a wide assortment of vegetables, including melon and cucumber. Thomas Traill could only envy his neighbour's achievements. "She is farther advanced than her brother or me, or indeed any of the neighbours," he wrote to John Moodie. "I am happy to say that all your children look fat, fair and flourishing as do mine, and you will find on your return which I hope will be soon that everything has been managed admirably in your absence and every difficulty met with energy, constancy and courage. I am proud to do justice to the worth and value of your most excellent wife. She is indeed a treasure of which you may be proud." Thomas found himself asking if he could borrow Jenny to help him plant potatoes.

Thanks to John's military pay, the Moodies were nibbling away at their debts to Peterborough merchants and to various labourers. But Susanna worried constantly about the hundreds of dollars they still owed. Even after a hard day of field work, she busied herself at night with anything that might bring in some cash. She painted birds and butterflies onto the hard bracket fungus fans that grew on trees, then gave the finished works to her brother Sam to sell to his Peterborough cronies. Invited to contribute to a new Montreal publication, the *Literary Garland*, she wrote late into the night, by the uncertain light of old rags dipped in pork lard and stuffed into the mouth of a bottle. The *Literary Garland*, published by John Lovell, was the first successful literary magazine in British North America, and it was also the first to pay its contributors. Susanna shed tears of pride and relief when her first payment arrived, in the form of a crumpled twenty-dollar bill. And she took her courage in her hands and composed a letter to the new Lieutenant-Governor of Upper Canada, Sir George Arthur, in which she described her family's circumstances and requested that John should be allowed to continue in the regiment, "which, by enabling him to pay our debts, would rescue us from our present misery."

In August, John Moodie's regiment was disbanded and John returned from the front. Soon after the Moodies' joyful reunion, a third son, John Strickland, was born safely. Susanna's hard work resulted in the most abundant crops the Moodies had ever reaped. "The harvest was the happiest we ever spent in the bush. We had enough of the common necessaries of life," Susanna noted. In the evenings, she and John resumed their old habit of taking gentle sails across the lake. But John was now out of a job, and the dark cloud of debt hovered over the family. Susanna didn't tell her husband about the petition on his behalf that she had sent to Sir George Arthur. Although the Moodie marriage was much more intimate than that of the Traills, Susanna, like Catharine, recognized the frailty of the male ego. She shrank from any suggestion that she might appear the more decisive or resilient partner. "Proud and sensitive as he was," she wrote affectionately of her husband, "and averse to asking the least favour of the great, I was dreadfully afraid that the act I had just done would be displeasing to him."

The Lieutenant-Governor never directly acknowledged Susanna's letter. As the days shortened and the temperature dropped, Susanna's spirits fell. But in late October, good news arrived: John Moodie received a letter from Toronto appointing him temporary paymaster to the militia regiments stationed along Lake Ontario and in the Bay of Quinte. The salary of 325 pounds a year was more than Susanna had dared hope for. By December, John was living in Belleville, a well-established lakefront community between Kingston and Cobourg, a journey of ninety-five miles from his family. Susanna was facing her second winter alone in the bush.

Susanna did not relish another separation from John, but they had agreed that she should stay in the backwoods because it was uncertain how long the paymaster job would last. Both assumed Susanna would manage fine: the children were healthy, the Traills were nearby, and Susanna had proved the previous winter that she could handle the farm by herself. Susanna and her children spent Christmas with the Traills, and Catharine produced a delicious roast goose, fattened on wild rice, and plum pudding. The children spent the afternoon sliding down a snowbank. "It was a Christmas treat to watch those joyous faces, buoyant with mirth, and brightened by the keen air, through the frosty panes," Catharine would recall sixteen years later. As they had done the previous Christmas, the two sisters indulged in a few tears as they recalled memories of "home, country and friends from whom we were for ever parted," but Catharine reassured Susanna that their sisters in England would be thinking of them and "some kind voice would murmur, 'Ah would they were here.'" At the end of the celebration, Catharine helped Susanna pile her five youngsters into the horsedrawn sleigh for the journey home; the children immediately fell asleep "and we were left in silence to enjoy the peculiar beauties of that snow clad scene by the dreamy light that stole down upon our narrow road through the snow laden branches above our heads."

Susanna was still nursing little Johnnie. Her left breast had begun to ache on Christmas Day: within forty-eight hours it was inflamed and throbbing. "I was in great agony, and did little else but cry and groan until the following Sunday," Susanna later wrote to John. "Kind Traill went himself after dark and brought up the Dr. at three o'clock in the bitter cold morning. He put the lancet immediately into my breast, and I was able to turn and move my left arm for the first time for ten days, for I lay like a crushed snake on my back unable to move or even to be raised forward without the most piteous cries. You may imagine what I suffered when I tell you that more than half a pint of matter must have followed the cut of the lancet, and the wound has continued to discharge ever since. I was often quite out of my senses, and only recovered to weep over the probability that I might never see my beloved husband again."

Dr. Hutchison, a gruff Scottish practitioner from Peterborough, was shocked to see a wellborn Englishwoman sick and alone except for her small children and an illiterate Irish servant. He looked round the forlorn, cold, dirty room, feebly lighted by the wretched lamp, and said to Susanna: "In the name of God! Mrs. Moodie get out of this."

As Dr. Hutchison had pointed out, the log cabin that Susanna had once regarded as "a palace" was showing its age. Wood smoke had blackened the interior and left a sooty residue on every surface. The log walls had shrunk and shifted as they'd dried and aged, leaving big chinks to be plugged with rags and old paper. The stovepipes were so brittle that Susanna never dared light a blazing fire. The cups were chipped; the blankets on the bed were worn; mice had nibbled away the covers of the small library of books; there was scarcely any firewood left, and the supply of candles was almost exhausted. It was all Susanna could do to survive from day to day, as winter gales roared around her clearing in the woods. She had barely recovered from her grotesquely infected breast abscess when two-year-old Donald fell onto the corner of the iron stove and gashed his head open. "Jenny called out that he was killed, and for a moment when I saw his ghastly face, the blood pouring in a torrent from the frightful wound, I thought so too. . . . After some time I succeeded in staunching the blood with very warm water, and then I examined his head and I felt convinced his skull was not fractured though I saw the bone plainly."

Donald's head had not yet had time to heal properly when a third disaster struck the Moodie household: scarlet fever. First Donald was taken with "sudden inflammation on the lungs, attended with violent fever and every symptom of croup." Within twenty-four hours, the baby was similarly afflicted. Johnnie "was to all appearance dead," Susanna later wrote to her husband. "All sense appeared to have fled. His jaws were relaxed, the foam was running from his mouth and my lovely dear's beautiful limbs fell over my arms a dead weight. I burst into an agony of tears." Dr. Hutchison refused to come this time: the roads were almost impassable, and besides, there was little he could do—the fever was killing children throughout the district. Helped by Jenny, Susanna nursed her two children with warm baths, castor oil and hot mustard poultices on their chests. Then, as soon as she was sure they were out of danger, she collapsed with influenza herself.

During all these troubles, Susanna learned a powerful lesson. Although she was not nearly as popular in the settlement as her sister, her neighbours rushed to help her. A wealthy and childless young Scots woman, Mary Hague, realized that five-year-old Agnes was getting on Susanna's nerves with her constant singing and screaming, so she swept her off to her own house in Peterborough and kept her for the rest of that year. Aggie was soon skipping around in new shoes and a pretty dress, showing off newly acquired reading skills and visiting her mother only reluctantly. Susanna admitted to John, "My heart yearns for my poor noisy little pet," but she was relieved to have her off her hands. Another neighbour, Hannah Caddy (mother of James, who had given Bond Head's proclamation to Sam), took four-year-old Dunbar for a few weeks. Susanna's friend Emilia Shairp, with whom she had walked to Dummer, moved into the Moodie cottage to help Susanna through her own sicknesses. And often, when the Moodie pantry was bare, a silent Indian would slip out of the woods and leave a brace of duck, or a haunch of venison, on the doorstep. "They [were] true friends to us in our dire necessity," Susanna would recall in later years.

Common humanity, Susanna realized, was a far more attractive and useful quality than the class consciousness she had brought with her from England. "You must become poor yourself before you can fully appreciate the good qualities of the poor—before you can sympathise with them, and fully recognise them as your brethren in the flesh," she wrote in *Roughing It in the Bush*, primly adding, "Their benevolence to each other, exercised amidst want and privation, as far surpasses the munificence of the rich towards them, as the exalted philanthropy of Christ and His disciples does the Christianity of the present day." Never again would she bad-mouth Hannah Caddy, she promised John, for being a common old fusspot: "She is really a most generous affectionate woman, and I begin to be very sorry that I ever suffered my prejudices to overlook her real merit." In Belleville, John worried incessantly about his little family and fretted about how he could ever repay so much kindness. "My Dear you quite distress me with the accounts of the kindness of my neighbours. . . . These things are enough to make me *bankrupt* in gratitude."

The Traills did as much as they could for Susanna during these difficult months. But they had their own problems. Catharine had just had her fourth child, a second daughter she named Annie, who was a sickly baby. Thomas was nearly at the end of his tether, because he had been unable to follow John Moodie's lead and secure a an officer's commision in the Peterborough regiment. His creditors were pressing him for payment, and he was desperate to sell his farm. But land values had collapsed after the Rebellion. Susanna told John that she thought poor Thomas had "been treated very ill. I hope poor things they will get something soon." The previous December, trying to help her brother-in-law in the same way that, she presumed, she had helped her own husband, she had written to Sir George Arthur, explaining that her sister's circumstances "so nearly resemble my own that we may truly be called sisters in misfortune." She reminded the Lieutenant-Governor that Catharine had done the colony a great service by encouraging immigrants with her "cheerful volume," *The Backwoods of Canada.* "The work, which has brought great emolument to the publishers, has done little towards administering to the wants of the poor Author, who is struggling in the Backwoods with four infant children and contending with difficulties which would scarcely be credited by Your Excellency." But still no appointments or commissions came Thomas's way.

Perhaps Thomas Traill wasn't offered a job because the threat of war had passed. Perhaps his age and his reputation as a thinker, rather than a doer, worked against him. Perhaps knowledge of his incapacitating depressions was now widespread. Susanna reported to John that her brother-in-law was "in wretched spirits." As Catharine, almost single-handedly, kept the household going, she looked around desperately for a way out. She knew her husband could not take another year in the backwoods: they must move into a town, where he could mix with other educated gentlemen and perhaps secure a government job. When a newly arrived Anglican priest, the Reverend Henry Hulbert Wolseley, put in an offer of four hundred pounds for the Traill property, she urged Thomas to accept, it although it was small return for all the money they had invested. In March 1839, Thomas accepted the offer and finally escaped from the bush, and the family moved into Ashburnham, a village across the Otonabee River from Peterborough. But they still had no source of income other than Thomas's military pension of about one hundred pounds a year, and Thomas's petitions for an administrative appointment in the district also fell on deaf ears. Only the intercession of George Boulton, the wealthy Cobourg lawyer, prevented the bank from foreclosing on Thomas's debts, which the four hundred pounds from the farm sale had scarcely dented.

The Traills' move was a major wrench for both Susanna and Catharine. After five years, the mile-long path that linked their two homes in the forest had become so well-trodden that the roots of the pine trees along its margins stuck out of the ground, tripping up unwary travellers. Living as neighbours, each sister took for granted the availability of the other for casual chats and visits. "The insects were very troublesome coming through the wood from my sister Moodie's," noted Catharine in her journal in July 1836. A few days later she wrote, "Went up to my sister's in the canoe. My sister gave me a nice [cranberry] pie." Their children ran in and out of each other's homes, and knew their cousins as well as they knew their own siblings. Whenever a letter arrived from Reydon Hall, telling of Agnes's publications, their mother's health or events in Southwold, the sisters would read it together over a cup of tea.

Eleven miles now separated the sisters. Weeks or often months would stretch between encounters. Indeed, for the rest of their lives they would live in different towns. On visits to each other, they could revive their old companionship. In letters, they could exchange news of their children, books and English sisters. But they never again had the day-to-day comfort of each other's support.

In Peterborough, Catharine found someone to help fill the gap that Susanna had left in her life. She was able to resume her close friendship with Frances Stewart, the resourceful Anglo-Irish settler whom she'd met when she'd first arrived in Peterborough, and with whom she had kept up a lively correspondence about books and botany. But Catharine didn't like to reveal to outsiders the truth of her husband's lengthy depressions, which Susanna had seen first-hand. Catharine still loved Thomas for the gentle, graceful man he was in good times, but she yearned to have a family member close by to whom she might unburden her soul. "I seem to need some one to speak to and interchange friendly thoughts with from time to time," she acknowledged.

The parting was much worse for Susanna, who would have to watch a stranger move into the log cabin where she had so often gone for comfort. After the Traills had piled all their possessions onto a hired sled, she wrote a poignant note to John: "The dear Traills are gone—I am doubly lonely now. Many tears have I shed for their removal, we have been on such happy terms all winter." She had always enjoyed talking about books with Thomas, and had come to rely on his chivalry; he had been much more solicitous in hard times than Sam, her brusque brother. Whenever he'd been going into Peterborough, Thomas had checked whether Susanna needed anything. When he left Lake Katchewanooka, he brought her the stove out of the Traills' cabin. The family "have been so kind to me, especially poor Traill. One knows not the value of a friend till one is left alone in this weary world. The poor children quite fret after their good Aunt." But it was Susanna who longed most intensely for Catharine's presence. Without her sister, Susanna "felt more solitary than ever" in "the green prison of the woods."

Each month seemed to bring a new crisis. In March, the sheriff's officer turned up to seize the Moodies' cattle, in payment of a debt that John had contracted years earlier in Cobourg. Susanna was both flustered and outraged. She first tried to dismiss the officer with all the hauteur she could muster by insisting (truthfully) that the debt had been paid. When he wouldn't budge from her doorstep, she flung a thick shawl round herself, picked up her baby and imperiously ordered the officer to accompany her to the house of her brother. Sam Strickland was a leading citizen in the area whose credit was a great deal better than his brother-in-law's, and the officer didn't want to offend him. So when Susanna, her spine stiff and her face flushed with rage, strode off through the woods, the officer meekly followed her across the Traill property to the Strickland farmhouse, two miles away. Luckily, Sam was home, and he agreed to guarantee the debt if the sheriff would back off for two weeks while payment was confirmed. "I hope you will lose no time in setting the affair to rights and write me as soon as possible to alleviate my anxiety," Susanna wrote John. She was constantly being dunned by creditors. "Oh heaven keep me from being left in these miserable circumstances another year. Such another winter as the last will pile the turf over my head."

In Belleville, John was wracked with guilt over the miseries of "my poor old widow in the bush." He wrote: "I am grieved My Dearest to hear of your sufferings, and God knows how anxious I am that it might be in my power to relieve you from your comfortless situation." In painstaking detail, he described his efforts to do a bang-up job on the regimental accounts, in the hopes of getting a permanent position. He continued to hope that the steamboat stock might finally increase in value, so he could get some cash for his shares. And he tried to cheer Susanna with optimistic schemes for their future. He was already planning to buy a two-hundred-acre farm on the Bay of Quinte, writing with his usual confidence, "This is the most desirable situation in Upper Canada in my opinion in every respect excepting the population which is very much disaffected." He wrote to the Lieutenant-Governor, asking to be considered as a candidate for the newly established position of sheriff for the District of Hastings, based in Belleville. His hopes were raised when his letter was acknowledged with a promise that Sir George Arthur would consider him, "not only on your own account, but from the esteem and respect he entertains for Mrs. Moodie." Ever the romantic, John also made the kind of gestures that always appealed to a woman who, despite her circumstances, loved pretty things. He bought her a soft woollen shawl (it cost six dollars they could ill afford). And he sent a parcel of new shoes, and bolts of fabric, so she could make their children some desperately needed clothes.

Susanna soldiered grimly on through the trials. She knew John was doing his best to get them out of the bush, so she rarely allowed the physical and emotional ordeals to trigger any reproaches to her absent husband. When the parcel of shoes and fabric arrived, she quickly acknowledged it: "You guessed the length of my foot *exactly*. No wonder—you know it so well, for surely if any man ever knew how to please a poor silly woman 'tis yourself." She began to fantasize about co-editing, with John, a newspaper in a larger town: "I could take all the light reading Tales, poetry &tc. and you the political and statistical details." Once again, her physical need for her husband ripples through the letter. "A state of widowhood does not suit my ardent affections . . . Oh do come soon—my heart aches to see you once again my own beloved one."

With Catharine gone, Susanna had no one to talk to, no one to tell about how drained she felt at the end of the day. She was not the kind of woman who shared her problems with casual acquaintances. She was, however, a writer. The previous winter she had discovered that composing articles for the *Literary Garland* was "a great refreshment to me, instead of an additional fatigue. I forgot the hardships and privations of my lot whilst rousing into action, after long disuse, the powers and energies of my mind." Now, during the harshest winter she would ever know, she burned to articulate her experience on paper, and explore her grief and fears within the discipline of the written word. She had to get her emotions *out*. So when loneliness overwhelmed her, and she felt her heart would burst with the need to tell John how she felt, she would get out of bed, light a candle and write a lengthy *cri de coeur*. By the time she had finished, the page would be crisscrossed with her outpourings and damp with tears. She would stare, mesmerized, at the pattern that her pen had made on the spongy homemade paper. After a deep, slow sigh, she would pick up her despondent litany and hold it over the guttering flame of the candle. The paper would blacken and flame up; then the sooty ashes would float down onto the table. With dry eyes, Susanna would return to her bed.

Only when there was a gap of more than a couple of weeks between her husband's letters did her morale falter. She reread old letters, in which John described convivial evenings with his commanding officer, Baron de Rottenburg, at which everyone got drunk and "sundry missiles such as decanters, candlesticks, glasses &tc, were discharged." Then her self-control broke, and the bitter reproaches erupted in letters that were sent. In July she wrote, "Surely dearest, we cannot have become indifferent to you that you should leave us in this dreadful state of uncertainty as to your plans and present situation. . . . Night comes, and no word from you, and I take poor little Johnnie into my arms and . . . bathe his innocent face with tears. Cruel Moodie, one short sentence which would tell me you are well [and] would remove this miserable state of anxiety. . . . While I had you to comfort and support me all trials seemed light, but left to myself, in this solitude, with only old Jenny to speak to and hearing so seldom of you makes a life a burden to me."

John still had not secured a permanent position in Belleville, and by July, the separation had become too much for both of them. John returned home for a brief reunion, and to help his overworked wife with the harvest. But he was back in Belleville by September, desperately lobbying Baron de Rottenburg for a new position. Susanna knew that if she had to spend a third winter alone in the woods, she would go mad: "Another long separation from you would almost break my heart." She clung to her belief that "God would provide for us, as He had hitherto done," if she demonstrated enough faith.

Perhaps it was her faith that did the trick; perhaps it was John's persistence. In October 1839, John wrote a euphoric letter home to tell her he had been appointed sheriff of Victoria District. "Come down as soon as I let you know that I have a house for you," he wrote to Susanna. "I really long to kiss you all again."

Conflicting emotions swept over Susanna as she held John's letter in her hand. Her prayers had been answered, but she was not overjoyed. She always hated change: she had wept as she left Southwold, and she was miserable when they had left their first Canadian home, in Hamilton Township. John was always confident that every move would improve their situation, and this time, he assured her that she would thrive in the society of Belleville. But would she? She looked down at her shabby skirts and passed a chapped hand over her untidy, greying hair. During her years in the bush, she had rarely looked in a mirror. The backwoods had transformed her from a vivacious young lady into a capable, but haggard, matron. She had railed against her isolation in the bush, but now she told herself that she preferred solitude: "I did not like to be dragged from it to mingle in gay scenes, in a busy town, and with gaily-dressed people. I was no longer fit for the world." John knew his Susie well enough to realize that she was anxious that she and her family would be regarded as ignorant yokels by the sophisticates of Belleville. He quickly sent her another parcel of fabric, so she could sew new clothes for herself and her children.

Susanna swallowed her doubts and began to organize the move. There was a lot to do, but as usual she systematically and efficiently accomplished the task. She sold their stock, implements and household furniture, disposed of the livestock and made the necessary arrangements to lease the farm and leave the backwoods. Then she and the children sat back and waited for the onset of winter. There had to be a good base of packed snow on the corduroy roads before the two sleighs that John had hired in Belleville could make their way north to collect her. They waited and waited, and no flakes fell. On Christmas Day, her eldest son Dunbar looked out the window at the bright sunshine glittering on the ice of Lake Katchawanooka and groaned, "Winter never means to come this year! It will never snow again."

It was six more days before a savage winter gale swept across the landscape. The following morning, Dunbar looked out at trees, lake and distant woods covered in a thick white mantle. The same afternoon, the

Belleville sleighs arrived (the storm had hit the lakefront a few days earlier). Blowing on their frozen hands, Susanna and Jenny quickly loaded their belongings. In the midst of all the confusion, Sam Strickland arrived and announced that he would transport his sister and her children to Belleville in his well-sprung lumber sleigh, which meant they would have a much more comfortable journey. Susanna always relaxed around her large, noisy, capable brother. Soon they were both laughing as they watched Katie try to squeeze the old cat Peppermint into a basket. Sister and brother were convulsed when Jenny appeared, balancing on her head no fewer than four hats—a drawn silk bonnet, a calico cap, a beribboned straw sunhat and a grey beaver-fur hat. "For God's sake take all that tomfoolery from your head," Sam instructed her between guffaws. "We shall be the laughing stock of every village we pass through." Faithful Jenny had stuck with the Moodies through all their tribulations, but as Susanna prepared to reenter "civilization," the social gulf suddenly yawned between mistress and servant. Susanna sent Jenny ahead on the uncomfortable hired sleigh.

A last wave of nostalgia washed over Susanna as she took a final look back. She saw the log cabin in which she had given birth to her three sons; she gazed at the snake fence she had constructed with her own hands around her garden, and at the lonely lake beyond. She realized that her Chippewa friends had silently materialized in the clearing: with tears running down her cheeks, she kissed the women and their babies in an affectionate farewell. Daylight was nearly gone, and Sam had no time for his sister's sentimentality. He hurried her onto the seat next to him, shot a quick glance backwards to make sure children, baskets and bags were safely stowed and gave a loud "Giddyup" to the horses.

Susanna was mute as the sleigh slid through the incredible pall of the winter landscape. Tears ran silently down her face as she listened to the jangle of the horses' bridles, the rhythmic *chunk-chunk-chunk* of their hooves, the slither of runners on hard-packed snow, the rustle of dried leaves still clinging to the trees. Cold air entered the travellers' nostrils like knives; the horses' heads were soon white with frost. The party spent that night in Peterborough, where Susanna was able to arrange for the return of little Aggie to her own family after close to a year with Mary Hague.

In town, Susanna had a jarring insight into her children's ignorance of any life beyond their hardscrabble solitude in a backwoods cabin. As the loaded wagon entered the main street, five-year-old Dunbar stared in amazement at buildings that nestled up against each other. "Are the houses come to see one another?" he asked. "How did they all meet here?"

Chapter 10

Belligerent Belleville

By the admittedly modest standards of Upper Canada in 1840, Belleville was close to the acme of sophistication, with far more class and culture than Cobourg or Peterborough. It was large (the most important settlement between Kingston and Toronto) and well established (its Loyalist founders could trace their history in Upper Canada back three generations). It had been named after Lady Bella Gore, the beautiful young wife of Governor Francis Gore, in 1816, and its ladies prided themselves that their fashionable attire was less than a year behind London's.

Belleville's economy was thriving, thanks to two flour mills, two carding mills, four sawmills, three breweries, seven blacksmiths' shops and two tanneries. At its wharves, sailboats bringing goods from northern New York State via the Bay of Quinte jostled with fishing boats and steamers carrying passengers along the lakefront. Its twenty-six shops

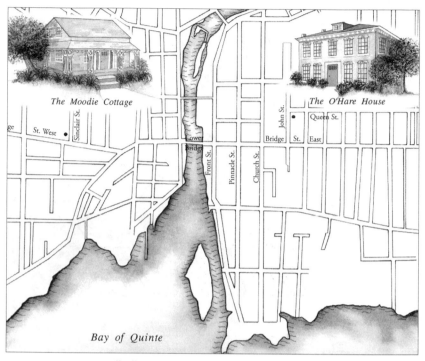

The Moodie Cottage

The O'Hare House

Bay of Quinte

*In 1840, Belleville was one of the most important towns in Upper Canada,
with a good harbour and a growing population.*

and twelve grocery stores carried imported goods from the United
States, the West Indies and Europe, as well as locally grown produce.
The town had at least one bookstore and a circulating library, and on
Sundays, its 1,700 citizens had four churches to choose from: Presbyterian, Methodist, Roman Catholic and Anglican. While Belleville's
finest families lived in solid limestone houses with large sash windows,
the town still had no sidewalks, and pigs roamed freely along the muddy
streets, gobbling up the garbage. But residents of Belleville were confident that they were in the vanguard of colonial progress: every seventh
house had a streetlight in front of it, which was lit on moonless nights so
that pedestrians could avoid the puddles and pigshit.

Underneath this urbane surface, however, seethed all the most vicious
emotions of the raw young colony. Every kind of prejudice flourished in
the town: Tories versus Reformers, Methodists versus Anglicans, Irish

versus Scots, Protestants versus Catholics. Belleville's numerous Irish Protestants had established one of the most active Orange Lodges in the province, and they commemorated the defeat of the Catholics in the 1690 Battle of the Boyne with bloodthirsty glee. All over Upper Canada, Orange Lodges were well on their way to becoming the most important club in every small town—boisterous, populist and passionately pro-British. But the Belleville Orange Lodge was particularly forceful.

By the time John Dunbar Moodie had secured a permanent job in Belleville, he was well aware that the town pulsed with bad blood. As he strode down Front Street in his military uniform, he endured the catcalls of those who had supported the rebels in '37. In Mrs. Margaret Simpson's smoky tavern on the waterfront, he heard the Scots immigrants sneer at the "Paddies" and watched the Irish immigrants come to blows with the "damn Yankees." He was at the opening of Belleville's most imposing new building—the county jail—which immediately filled up with drunks, debtors, cheats, violent criminals and thieves. The level of partisan sniping and name-calling was enough to discourage even an

Mrs. Margaret Simpson's tavern, where the Montreal–Toronto coaches
changed horses, buzzed with partisan gossip

optimist like John. "I sometimes wish I could clear out from this un-happy distracted country where I see nothing but ultra selfish Toryism or Revolutionary Radicalism," he wrote in 1839. "The people in this part of the country are split into some three or four factions—The Catholics harbouring dark designs under an hypocritical profession of loyalty and Orangemen goading them on to rebellion by claiming all the loyalty in the country to themselves—while the native Canadians [second- and third-generation immigrant families] are hugging the loaves and fishes as their own peculiar perquisite, agreeing with the others on hardly any one point but in hatred of the Scotch and their Church."

In the early days of 1840, however, John was too eager to see Susanna and their five children to dwell on Belleville's shortcomings. He had a new job and a new house, and he was going to make a new start in the new decade! He strutted past the unpainted frame houses that sprawled untidily along Bridge Street and Front Street, the two main streets that intersected on the banks of the Moira River, carefully avoiding the pot-holes and happily greeting passers-by. He was good at remembering names, and he delighted in offering cheery hellos to every lawyer, mer-chant, housewife and child he bumped into. Short and plump, his vest straining across his belly and his ready smile almost obscured by his mutton-chop whiskers, he radiated geniality. At last, after two years of almost constant separation, he could dream about cosy evenings with his family grouped around the fireside in the pretty, neat little cottage he had rented and furnished. He could imagine Susanna's relief that she no longer had to struggle out in the chill of a January morning to milk the cows; instead, she could purchase staples at a store. He could almost hear little Agnes and Katie singing nursery rhymes as he accompanied them on his flute. He smiled as he imagined his three sons chasing chickens in their yard. Most of all, John longed to show Susanna the china tea ser-vice he had recently purchased. There could be no more satisfactory symbol of Susanna's release from the backwoods, he fervently believed, than the chance to return to the old Reydon Hall custom of taking tea at four o'clock each afternoon in bone china cups.

On the third day of January, Susanna, Jenny and the children arrived in Belleville after a long and freezing journey from Peterborough through Cobourg. Thin-lipped with cold, Susanna was tearful and nauseated, and in no mood to be cheered up by bone china. Her first bit of news for John, as she pressed little Johnnie, now fifteen months, into her husband's arms, was that she was once again expecting a baby. John had made a brief visit home the previous November—just long enough to conceive their sixth child.

Although Susanna didn't welcome another pregnancy, both she and John were proud of their rapidly expanding family. Had she wanted to, Susanna could undoubtedly have learned about natural abortificeants (her Indian friends might have told her about the effectiveness of oil of cedar, hellebore or ergot of rye). But birth control and terminations were rarely considered by Canadians of this period. A brood of eight or ten children provided a ready supply of much-needed cheap labour for the farm, even if it did put a huge strain on the mother's health. Even in larger towns like Belleville, the birth rate remained high until the late nineteenth century, because children were still regarded as insurance for the future. One of the ditties popular in the colony suggested that:

> Of all the crops a man can raise
> Or stock that he employs,
> None yields such profit and such praise
> As a crop of Girls and Boys.

The following day, Susanna set off to explore Belleville. She was deeply disappointed, and irritated by what she perceived as its pretensions. She had hoped for a thriving market town like Bungay or Southwold, with cobbled streets and charming stone cottages. Instead she found "an insignificant, dirty-looking place" in which the frame houses were "put up in the most unartistic and irregular fashion." Large sections of Front Street remained unpaved, and the slabs of limestone on the paved sections were laid so carelessly that pedestrians

Susanna considered St. Thomas's Anglican Church "an eye-sore."

were constantly tripping and falling. Susanna harrumphed that the "paving committee had been composed of shoe-makers," because so many shoes got destroyed in falls or stuck in the deep, mud-filled pot-holes. Her relief at the prospect of regular Sunday worship was diluted by her disgust at the brick-and-frame "eyesore" that was St. Thomas's Anglican Church. St. Andrew's Presbyterian Church, on the same block, was an even shabbier wooden building. John's assurance that at least five households boasted pianos did not raise her spirits. Only the cedar-fringed banks and "rapid, sparkling" water of the Moira River, which thousands of logs floated down each spring, brought a smile to her face. The river reminded her of the Otonabee. Faced with the gossipy little community of Belleville, Susanna grew quite nostalgic for the privacy of her cabin on Lake Katchewanooka.

As sheriff of Victoria County, John was in a sensitive position. His job was to keep the peace among the various factions. This meant, in his view, staying aloof from the ethnic, sectarian and political schisms within the populace. He might have managed to stay away from ethnic and sectarian squabbles, but there was no hope of avoiding the political quarrels. A chasm separated the Tories, who swore undying loyalty to the British crown, and the Reformers, who felt that the colony should be given a greater degree of control over its own affairs. John tried to stay on the fence, by attending both the Anglican and the Presbyterian churches, and by appointing as his deputy sheriffs one Tory and one Reformer. But "however moderate your views might be," Susanna discovered, "to belong to the one was to incur the dislike and ill-will of the other."

While John had to deal with Belleville's frock-coated lawyers and merchants, who pursued their public vendettas through elections, legal cases and business practices, Susanna had to deal with their wives. Many were the kind of educated women for whose company she had hungered in the wilderness. But now she discovered that Belleville wives "entered deeply into this party hostility; and those who . . . might have become friends and agreeable companions, kept aloof, rarely taking notice of each other when accidentally thrown together." Her hands still roughened by field work, she also found them snobbish and superficial: she deplored their love of finery and their sneering disregard for farmers and "mechanics." In fact, she found herself in the unfamiliar position of scorning their hoity-toity pretensions, which were remarkably similar to those with which she had arrived in Canada.

A chilly social reception was only the start of the Moodies' problems. The knives were out for the new sheriff before he'd even set foot in the courthouse. There were a lot of civic offices attached to the new Victoria District, but the permanent, full-time office of sheriff was the plum. Although the sheriff's job had no salary attached, its holder could expect an income of at least $200 a year from fees received for serving writs and subpoenas. This was a very modest income for a professional man: John had earned 325 pounds a year as paymaster to the militia, and a successful lawyer in Upper Canada might bring in $1,000 a year. However, the real money for John came from the sheriff's right to keep any proceeds from the sale of impounded property and any court-imposed fines he collected. Income from these sources could amount to five or six times the total of fees received. The prospect of an annual income of more than $1000 meant that various Belleville worthies had been competing for the office long before the district was formally established. The strongest candidate was Thomas Parker, a Tory bully who was the former deputy sheriff of the Midland District (which then included what would later become the Victoria District) and the Belleville agent of the Commercial Bank in Toronto.

Parker was desperate to be sheriff because he was close to bankruptcy. He thought he had the job in the bag. When he heard that some *arriviste* half-pay Scot, who knew little about Belleville and nothing about municipal politics, had upstaged him, he was mad as hell. And so were all his friends. Anglican Tories to a man, they decided that the newcomer must be a Reformer and a Presbyterian, and that it was their civic duty to prove he was an incompetent sheriff. Knowing that the Moodies were chronically hard up, Parker played a vicious cat-and-mouse game with John. He and his Tory pals delayed payments to the sheriff on trumped-up grounds and brought nuisance lawsuits against him, which never came to anything but cost John money. John was soon begging the Toronto authorities for an additional appointment: "At present I am hardly able to support my family with the most rigid economy."

On top of all this unpleasantness, John had a messy start to the new job. Because he would be handling public funds, he had to produce two letters from people who would act as guarantors for him. But they had to be men known to the Toronto authorities—which was a challenge for John, who had rarely met any of the colony's prominent lawyers, merchants and landowners while he was stuck in the backwoods. He first nominated his two brothers-in-law, Thomas Traill and Sam Strickland, but after several weeks he heard that they didn't meet the exacting standards of the Toronto bureaucrats. As time ticked on, he grew anxious that his appointment wouldn't be confirmed before the first Quarter Sessions were due to be held in Belleville's new courthouse. He produced a second pair of guarantors, and then a third. The second pair of guarantors was finally accepted, and, at the last moment, John was sworn in and documented as sheriff. But his cheery self-confidence was punctured. He was sure that Thomas Parker was already denigrating him to the government. In a letter to Sir George Arthur in February 1840, ostensibly thanking the Governor for the job, John rushed to defend himself from any base accusations that might have reached Toronto ears. The Governor assured him that "Mr. Parker has not made any communication of the kind, directly or indirectly."

Initially, Susanna kept her distance from the tiresome infighting of Belleville citizens and concentrated on her children and her writing. Now that she was out of the woods, she wanted to reestablish herself as a professional writer so that she could supplement the family income. She had more time: she no longer had to care for livestock (though, like most town-dwellers, she still kept chickens and had a vegetable garden), and much of the arduous work of childcare, cleaning, laundry, cooking and baking had been delegated to the series of young Irish maids who had taken Jenny's place. And Susanna finally had in the New World an editor who valued her work—John Lovell, the most famous printer-publisher in nineteenth-century Canada, who had first approached her two years earlier to contribute to his *Literary Garland*.

Lovell's support was just the encouragement she needed. He paid according to the quantity of pages (five pounds per sheet) rather than offering a set fee for each contribution, and he printed anything she sent him. The poems, serialized novels and short stories that Susanna produced were written for an English (or at least a British-educated) audience. She assumed that her readers—for the most part, the merchant élites of Montreal and Toronto—would prefer European settings and fastidious heroes. She also sent works that she had written twenty years earlier, in Suffolk. And she began to play with the idea of shaping some of her experiences of the past eight years—her first impressions of Canada, the early months in Hamilton Township, the ups and downs of life in Douro—into sketches for publication.

Alongside her literary compositions, Susanna wrote personal letters to Lovell with all her family news ("I have been busy preparing my boys' winter clothing"). Once or twice she and John even managed a trip to Montreal to see her editor and visit with his wife, Sara, and their family in their elegant townhouse on St. Catharine Street. "She was a pleasant companion," Sara would recall. She admired Susanna's skill with water colours, and was amazed to hear that this English lady often had little Johnnie on her knee as she composed articles. Nostalgia for London tugged at Susanna as she glimpsed the cultured life of Montreal in the 1840s, with its concerts, theatres and soirées.

Susanna entrusted Lovell with the realization of one of her greatest dreams—the purchase of an inexpensive piano. In the backwoods, a piano had become the symbol of the lost state of gentility. Nothing had underlined their cultural and spiritual poverty so much as her inability to accompany herself on the piano when she taught her children the nursery rhymes and hymns of her youth. When Lovell secured one in Montreal and had it crated and shipped up the St. Lawrence to Belleville, Susanna was overjoyed. It almost made up for the ostentatious disregard that her Belleville neighbours continued to show for her literary achievements. At one point, one of her sons arrived home from school looking downcast; he said that another boy had jeered at him that "Mrs. Moodie invents lies, and gets paid for them."

In spite of their fresh start, sadness and misfortune continued to dog the Moodies. In July 1840, Susanna gave birth to a sickly little boy. Christened George Arthur, after their benefactor the Governor, he clung to life for only three weeks. It was an ill omen. Next, in December, the Moodies' rented cottage caught fire, and they lost their furniture, clothing and winter stores. They almost lost two-year-old Johnnie, too: he had hidden in the kitchen of the burning building and was rescued only seconds before the roof collapsed. The fire traumatized Susanna, who had suffered one house fire already in the Moodies' backwoods log cabin, and who was still mourning the death of her infant four months earlier: "The agony I endured for about half an hour [before Johnnie was found] I shall never forget." Had the calamity occurred in Douro Township, she would have rushed to her sister Catharine for solace.

Instead, she poured out her terrors in a letter to her mother and sisters in England. Astringent Agnes replied, "We were all much grieved to hear of your sad loss by fire and the distress it must have been to you and your lovely little flock, but if it had occurred before Moodie got the appointment it would have been of far more serious consequence."

By 1842, the Moodies had settled into a pleasant house on the corner of Bridge and Sinclair streets, on the western edge of Belleville. Built seven years earlier of local limestone, with a verandah across the front and a spacious and separate kitchen wing to the rear, it boasted the kind of features that have come to be known as "wilderness Georgian"—a graceful staircase curling upwards with a narrow banister, and a front door with sidelights and a deep cornice supported by four gently tapered pilasters. It was light-years away from the squalid log cabin in the backwoods, and it brought back happy memories to Susanna of the little clifftop Regency cottage in Southwold that she and John had lived in during their first year of marriage. It was the wrong side of town—the *haute bourgeoisie* of Belleville lived on the east side of the Moira, preferably on Church Street or John Street, at the top of the hill. But Susanna didn't care too much for gradations of status among small-town merchants She still regarded her refined English origins as all the rank she needed.

In later years, Susanna would look back on these years as being the most prosperous she and John ever enjoyed. They had (as she wrote to a friend in England) "many of the luxuries of life or such as are considered so in the Provinces," and the house was "a grand and comfortable home." She had at least two servants—a maid and a handyman—which allowed her to establish a household routine that included as much reading and writing as possible. She rose at six o'clock, hurriedly read some prayers with her children, organized breakfast, made whatever bread and pies were required for the day, then sat down to write. She wrote steadily until dinnertime, turning a deaf ear to interruptions from the maid or children. After an early evening meal, she took a walk, then made or mended clothes until the light was too dim for her to sew any longer.

Once the lamps were lit, she returned to whatever manuscript she was working on.

The worst tragedy of her life struck the family a couple of years after they had moved into the Bridge Street house. One night in June 1844, Susanna awoke to find her pillow drenched in tears. In her dream she had taken Johnnie, then five, to England, to visit her mother at Reydon Hall. Her older sister Jane had appeared and told Susanna that their mother had died years earlier, but that Susanna had never been told because her English relatives felt she already had so many sorrows of her own. Susanna was badly shaken by the dream and spent the following day wracked with homesickness and a strange sorrow.

She was so preoccupied that she scarcely noticed that little Johnnie, who had been watching his two elder brothers fishing in the Moira, was late home. Suddenly an older child rushed into the kitchen, shouting that Johnnie was missing. John Moodie rushed along Bridge Street to the river and pounded up and down the bank, calling his son's name into the deepening twilight. The child had been washing all the brook trout that

A memorial tablet for Susanna's two lost sons: "hope has faded from my heart."

his brothers had caught and had lost his balance as he leaned over the wooden wharf. Dunbar and Donald had been busy rewinding their lines and hadn't seen him leave them. Nobody had heard Johnnie's cries above the roar of the river. His father finally found the limp little body caught in the wooden supports of the wharf.

Susanna was devastated. The loss of her "lovely, laughing, rosy, dimpled child" was the "saddest and darkest [hour] in my sad eventful life." Johnnie's death plunged her into a despair deeper than she had ever known; she never entirely recovered her mirth and spontaneity. She brooded inconsolably for months and wrote heartfelt poetry about her loss.

But hope has faded from my heart—and joy
Lies buried in thy grave, my darling boy!

The tragedy had a profound impact on Susanna. It rooted her more firmly in her adopted land than any other experience. Johnnie was buried next to his infant brother George. Their mother visited their graves regularly. She grieved that these two sons would never see their mother's homeland. Her love for her lost little boys made Susanna begin to think of herself as the mother of Canadian children rather than the daughter of English gentry.

Against this backdrop of family misfortune, John had to contend with unending political sabotage. But Belleville's political battles brought an unexpected dividend when the Moodies met a politician for whom they would develop a lifelong admiration. This was Robert Baldwin, the Toronto lawyer who led the Reform Party.

In his time, Robert Baldwin was recognized as a giant amongst the young colony's statesmen. Today, his name is invariably invoked as "the father of Responsible Government," because he helped establish real democracy in Canada. (He is also remembered for a connection that would have surprised him: he was the grandfather of Robbie Ross, Oscar Wilde's first male lover.) Born in Toronto in 1804, Baldwin inherited

Robert Baldwin (1804–1858) was the father of Responsible Government and a close friend of the Moodies.

from his father, the Irish-born and immensely debonair Dr. William Baldwin, a large fortune, the extensive Spadina estate in the middle of Toronto and a sturdy belief that the government in Canada should be answerable to Canadian voters as well as to the government in London. In the aftermath of the 1837 Rebellion, the two Baldwins had made a forceful case for responsible government in the colony to Lord Durham, the Whig grandee sent out by the British government to investigate the troubled state of British North America. In the report that Lord Durham presented in 1839, the Baldwins were delighted to see that, alongside its recommendation for the union of Upper and Lower Canada (roughly, present-day Ontario and Quebec) into the United Provinces of Canada, it also proposed that the executive wing of government should be accountable to the elected legislature.

At first, Westminster refused this move to strengthen the colonial government, arguing that such a step would compromise British sovereignty. So Robert Baldwin spent the next twenty years championing responsible government in his native land. He also dedicated himself to implementing the kind of progressive policies that were only just beginning to be understood within the scattered settlements of the colony: linguistic and religious freedoms; a strong and non-denominational education system; and a firm partnership between English-speaking and

French-speaking citizens of the United Provinces. Much of today's Canadian political culture has its origins in the measured tolerance and broad-minded idealism of Robert Baldwin. He practised what he preached: he sent his four children to be educated in francophone schools in Lower Canada, and he forged a durable political partnership with Louis-Hippolyte Lafontaine, leader of the moderate reformers in Montreal. The two men served as joint premiers of the United Provinces between 1842 and 1843, and again between 1848 and 1851.

Yet Robert Baldwin was a reluctant politician who cut a poor figure on the hustings. A stilted orator, he was heavy and stooping, and he always had an unhealthy pallor. His opponents mocked (as historian Donald Creighton put it) his "solemn, slightly Pecksniffian air of conscious rectitude." Lord Sydenham, appointed Governor-General of British North America in 1839, described Baldwin as "such an ass!" Nevertheless, the public Baldwin personified the gentlemanly virtues to which John Moodie aspired—devotion to honour, duty and principle, and a fierce integrity in public office.

There was, however, another side to Robert Baldwin that appealed particularly to Susanna's fascination with darker, more complicated human emotions. The private Baldwin was intensely sensitive and had already suffered a painful epiphany by the time he met the Moodies. In 1836, his beloved wife Eliza, mother of his four children, had died after only nine years of marriage. Baldwin's grief was Gothic in its fervor, putting him in the galaxy of Canadian politicians whose private lives are as bizarre as their professional lives are bland. Robert Baldwin's determination to be reunited with his dead wife and share her pain was quite as weird as, a century later, Mackenzie King's determination to contact the spirit of his dead mother.

After Eliza Baldwin's death, her husband was subject to crippling bouts of depression that paralyzed him for weeks, even while he was co-premier of the United Provinces. He insisted that, at his death, his coffin should be chained to Eliza's. Most important, he asked that his body be operated on: "Let an incision be made into the cavity of the abdomen extending through the two upper thirds of the linea alba." It was a simulation of the primitive Caesarean section that Eliza had undergone for the birth of her fourth child, which had ultimately led to her death. When Robert Baldwin finally passed away, his daughter Maria ignored this gruesome instruction, but a month after the funeral (the largest ever seen in the colony), his son discovered the instruction in a pocket of one of his father's old jackets. In morbid obedience, he insisted that the corpse be exhumed so the ghastly procedure could be performed.

The Moodies first met Robert Baldwin when he was thirty-six, soon after their arrival in Belleville. Baldwin had come to Belleville because he wanted to represent Victoria District (renamed Hastings County in 1843) in the new United Provinces assembly. The Moodies were instantly drawn to someone who, like themselves, was furious to find himself squeezed between those who had taken up arms against legitimate authority and the blinkered upholders of British tradition and privilege. They were entirely in accord with a man who symbolized the landholding class, yet advocated gradual change. The Moodies' views were shifting. The tremendous adjustments they had made to survive in the backwoods and their newfound ability to hold their own in the New World had made them question the wisdom of decisions about the colony being made five thousand miles away in London, by strangers for whom Canada was just another British possession, along with India, Bermuda and New Zealand.

Along with Baldwin, the Moodies began to think that British North America would only flourish if its elected representatives, who knew the rural areas as well as the cities, had some say in how the colony should develop. But such cautious thoughts as these branded the Moodies as "traitors and rebels" within Belleville's professional circles, and no better than the malcontents who had marched down Yonge Street in 1837. Belleville's Loyalists, such as the Bensons and Dougalls, "arrogated the whole loyalty of the colony to themselves," noted a disgusted Susanna.

Baldwin often dropped by the Moodies' cottage during his campaigns. "If you have any regard for me, Mrs. Moodie," he said to Susanna one evening, "pray don't ask me to eat. I am sick of the sight of food." The custom throughout rural Canada was to ply any visitors with huge meals, and to take offence if they didn't stuff themselves. In the run-up to an election, Baldwin had daily been invited to dinners that featured ham, roast and boiled meat and fowl, puddings, custards and cakes, cheese and apple pie. Susanna thought it was hilarious that Baldwin's principal political supporters "literally almost killed him with kindness," and she was flattered that he treated her as someone who knew that such excess was unnecessary. At the Moodies' home, the distinguished Toronto lawyer preferred to bounce their children on his knee and talk earnestly about his vision of Canada as a bicultural nation. John valued Baldwin's "calm and forbearing spirit," and Susanna could never resist a clever, sentimental man who wrote poetry, repeatedly told her how much he admired her work and read her children's stories aloud to his own children. Baldwin made Susanna and John feel they had soul-mates beyond Belleville: enlightened and educated people who weren't mired in petty parochial disputes, and who believed Canada would one day be a major nation. Although John continued to insist that, as sheriff, he was above politics, in practice both he and Susanna were drawn into the Reformers' fold. Baldwin convinced them that responsible government was not synonymous with such nineteenth-century Canadian nightmares as mob rule or Washington-style republicanism.

John Moodie had a direct role to play in the elections in which Robert Baldwin was running because he was the returning officer, responsible for ensuring that voting was free and fair. This was a tough job in the early 1840s. Intimidation and bribery were rife. Each candidate had his own ballot box, and a voter would cast his ballot in full public view. Everyone could see who voted for whom. Rival candidates marched their supporters to the hustings "like the men-at-arms of two medieval private armies," in the words of Donald Creighton. John had to oversee two elections within his first two years in Belleville: one in March and April, 1841, and the next in October 1842. In both, Baldwin ran against Edmund Murney, a local lawyer. Anyone who ran into Murney on the street would have thought he was a pleasant and civilized fellow, but on a soapbox he was a fiend. He ranted against responsible government as a revolutionary plot, and he accused mild-mannered Robert Baldwin of being a Papist and a rebel.

Murney had the serried ranks of Tory Belleville behind him, including Thomas Parker, all the members of Belleville's Orange Lodge and George Benjamin, outspoken editor of the local newspaper, the *Intelligencer.* Both elections verged on riots. Baldwin was accused by his enemies of hiring a "large body of armed shanty-men, bullies and ruffians, armed with bludgeons, clubs and sticks" who prevented Murney supporters from reaching the hustings by their "threatening language and gestures." It is not clear whose supporters screamed the loudest and rudest insults, but there is no doubt that many voters on both sides were too scared to cast their votes at all. Baldwin was acknowledged to be the victor in 1841, and Murney in 1842. But the person most damaged by the turmoil and tension each time was Sheriff Moodie, who had failed to keep the peace. He was also accused by the Murney gang of showing bias towards Baldwin. George Benjamin charged him with "intimidation, perjury and partiality." He was summarily removed from the position of returning officer.

John and Susanna churned with outrage at the way they were being treated. John's letters to Robert Baldwin are littered with indignant references to the "low cunning and artful misrepresentations" of local enemies. He fulminated against Edmund Murney in 1842, and commented that, "Anything like fairness or straight forwardness with him is out of the question." But John and Susanna saved their most savage remarks for "the little Jew," as John referred to George Benjamin. Benjamin was probably no more hostile to Sheriff Moodie than most of Belleville's Tory establishment, but his criticisms had greater impact because he promoted them in the *Intelligencer.* There, according to John, he regularly "opined a lot in fine style" against the sheriff. Every Saturday, John's heart was in his mouth as he picked up the paper, wondering what slanders against him were contained in the weekly "smut machine" (as it was characterized by its rival, Kingston's *British Whig*). The editor of the *British Whig* had already noted that Benjamin did not tolerate any dissenting views on Belleville politics in his newspaper or his community "as he regards that field as entirely his own."

George Benjamin was one of the more intriguing characters in nineteenth-century Canada. He was born in Brighton, England, where his father, Emanuel Cohen, was the leading member of the town's Jewish community. The Cohens had twelve children: George's eldest brother, Levy, was founder and editor of the Brighton *Guardian*; two brothers emigrated to Australia; and one brother went to New York and became a physician. It is not clear why Moses Cohen, the second son, changed his first name to George and adopted his mother's maiden name as his surname, but it is clear that he was an ambitious lad, with a taste for adventure. He worked for a time on his brother's newspaper, but he quickly moved to Liverpool to engage in "commercial pursuits." By the time he stepped off a lake steamer onto the Toronto wharf in April 1834, the thirty-four-year-old Benjamin was widely travelled, spoke half a dozen languages and was accompanied by a pregnant fourteen-year-old girl whom he had married in New Orleans. Benjamin never advertised his Jewish background—he even managed to get himself elected grand

George Benjamin (1799–1864), Canada's first Jewish Member of Parliament, was cruelly caricatured in Susanna's writing

master of the Orange Order of British North America in 1846—but there was a Hebrew prayer book in the little leather satchel he carried.

Why did George Benjamin come to Canada? It was a surprising choice, given that Jewish immigrants were few and far between, and a British colony dominated by the Anglican Church tolerated less religious diversity than the United States. Yet the stocky and determined Benjamin must have heard about the colony's potential for a man with newspaper experience. Within five months of his arrival in Upper Canada, he and his wife Isabella were living in Belleville and Benjamin was about to open a new business. In September he published a prospectus announcing that he had "taken possession of the Press at Belleville" and was to be the editor and publisher of a newspaper under the name of the *Belleville Intelligencer and Hastings General Advertiser.* Some of Belleville's residents were aware that the paper's editor was Jewish, and Benjamin became the target of anti-Semitism in his own community. One sunny Friday in April 1836, he arrived at his office to discover that he had been hung in effigy in front of his own front door. The following week, Kingston's *British Whig* carried a poem that began:

Oh ladies all and gentlemen,
While I've nothing else to do,
I'll just sit down and sing a song,
About the Belleville Jew.

Both Benjamin and his newspaper were well established by the time the Moodies moved to town. In 1842, John could only wince at Benjamin's relentless attacks on him in the *Intelligencer.* But Susanna, far too spirited to turn the other cheek, decided to reply in kind. By now, Lovell's *Literary Garland* was selling well throughout the province, and Mrs. Moodie was one of its most prolific and popular contributors. She had an outlet for her anger. In 1843, she set to work on a manuscript that was to be her own sweet revenge on George Benjamin.

The manuscript in question was a four-part story entitled "Richard

Redpath. A Tale" for publication in 1843. The story began innocently enough, with the shipwreck of two English gentlemen, Richard and Robert Redpath, off Jamaica. Most of the tale then centres on the Jamaican slave trade, for information about which Susanna drew on the two booklets she had written about slaves while living with the Pringles in 1831. But in the third episode, the pace of the story picks up as Robert encounters the "Jew editor" of the Jamaica *Observer*, Benjamin Levi. Into the portrait of Levi, Susanna poured her detestation of George Benjamin's politics and her fury at the slanders spread about her husband by the *Intelligencer*. This was much harsher than the amusing malice that often tinged Susanna's character sketches. Despite Susanna's open-minded approach to both blacks, like Mary Prince, and native people, like the Chippewas near Peterborough, she smouldered with racism when she spoke of George Benjamin. The portrait of Levi resonated with the kind of anti-Semitism that characterized English society in the nineteenth century, and which kept Jews out of the Westminster Parliament until 1858. Benjamin Disraeli, the future British prime minister, was allowed to take his seat in 1837 only because, as a baptized Christian, he was prepared to swear the Christian oath of office.

Any Belleville citizen who picked up a copy of the *Literary Garland* in November 1843 would have instantly recognized George Benjamin in the description of Benjamin Levi. Like Benjamin, Levi was "a short, fat man, with broad shoulders, a head and neck like a bull" and an unusually large head covered in "a quantity of coarse, curling black hair." All Benjamin's defining features were given the most negative spin possible. The easy-going smile that Benjamin habitually wore was, in Levi, a "perpetual grin, which though meant for a smile, was but an acquired contortion to hide the evil workings of the spirit within." Benjamin's teeth, which he displayed every time he laughed, became "a malicious looking set of strong white teeth, which seemed as if they were formed to bite and worry his species." Benjamin's firm mouth was transmuted into a "hardened and audacious expression" that made Levi "an object of disgust and aversion." Moodie's local readers, instantly linking the fictitious Levi with the real Benjamin, would have learned that their newspaper editor was "a living, laughing, impersonation of gratuitous mischief" and a "sort of moral hyena."

Benjamin cannot have enjoyed the ridicule, particularly after it received even wider circulation when "Richard Redpath. A Story" was reprinted in the Toronto *Star*. Ten years later, it was reprinted yet again as part of a collection of Susanna's work entitled *Matrimonial Speculations*. There is no record of how much Susanna's attack wounded him; few issues of the 1840s *Intelligencer* have survived. The rule of thumb amongst Upper Canadian editors of the time was that, if you dished it out, you had to be prepared to take it, too. Benjamin had shrugged off other insults, such as the *British Whig's* description of him as "the slandering Belleville Jew." He had also taken steps to shield his family from overt prejudice by having most of his fourteen children baptized at St. Thomas's Anglican Church. (There would not be a synagogue in Belleville for another hundred years, but Benjamin carefully noted the births of his first eight children in the back of his Hebrew prayer book). He himself would be baptized a few months before his own death in 1864, and he was buried in St. Thomas's graveyard.

There was an obvious logic to the Moodies' decision to make a friend of Baldwin and an enemy of Benjamin, but their behaviour showed their hopeless lack of political smarts. As the 1840s drew to a close, it began to dawn on Susanna and John that Robert Baldwin's friendship was not going to assist John. Baldwin had no local roots in Belleville, and he had far too much on his mind to worry about the town's ineffective sheriff. After his defeat in Hastings in 1842, Baldwin changed constituencies and ran elsewhere for the rest of his career. With dogged loyalty, John Moodie continued to regard him as his patron. He wrote to him regularly, offering him advice on land and judicial reform. "My family— none of my children have forgotten you—still speak of you with great affection," he assured Baldwin in 1845. "Friends are scarce in these times, and we cannot afford to lose any." When Susanna gave birth to a fifth son in 1843, he was named Robert Baldwin Moodie. However, Baldwin did nothing to secure a new job for John where he might escape his persecutors. John yearned to be registrar of the Niagara region, but Baldwin was unwilling or unable to satisfy Moodie's petitions for help.

In contrast, George Benjamin, now a key player in Belleville, nursed his grudge against the Moodies. By now, Mrs. Moodie was a writer to be reckoned with: she was the most important and prolific contributor to the *Literary Garland,* her battle songs from the 1837 Uprising were still whistled on the streets of Upper Canada, and her sharp tongue was legendary within Belleville. Buoyed up by success, Susanna blithely assumed that her literary contretemps with Benjamin was par for the course in a life of letters. She even took a mischievous delight in her character Levi's wickedness. "I don't know what we should do without Benjamin Levi," remarks a character in the story. "He keeps us all alive." She was too taken with her creation to reconsider either the substance or the tone of her depiction. In 1854, she boasted to her London publisher that, "The Jew Editor is a true picture drawn from life which so closely resembles the original that it will be recognized by all who ever knew him, or fell under his lash, a man detested in his day and generation."

To George Benjamin, however, Susanna's story was not just an amusing little joke. He was not universally detested: he was a vigorous and imaginative politician who worked hard for his Belleville voters. In 1847 he was elected as the senior official in the area, responsible for all roads, schools and public works. And in 1856 he was elected as a Member of the Parliament of the United Provinces—the first Jew to sit in Parliament anywhere in the British Empire. John A. Macdonald, the Tory leader, told him that, "You may be a *leetle* wanting in *Suaviter.* However, your ability is well known to us all." As Benjamin's career went from strength to strength, and his influence grew, he waited for an opportunity to settle his scores with a sheriff he had always opposed and the writer who had penned such a venomous caricature.

Chapter 11

Barefoot Crusoes

While the Moodies were settling in Belleville, and making important friends and enemies, Catharine and Thomas Traill were living a hand-to-mouth existence. After leaving the bush in 1839, they had rented a little frame house in Ashburnham, the village on the opposite bank of the Otonabee River from Peterborough. The house had a reliable well and an orchard that Thomas looked after. Catharine spent hours in her garden, cultivating the potatoes, carrots, turnips, currants and melons that would see them through the winter. Even in the hardest times, she could never resist planting flowers, too—marigolds, sweet peas, poppies and pinks—to brighten the view from her kitchen window. She had her good friend, Frances Stewart, close by, and Frances's daughter Ellen Dunlop, to whom she also grew attached. She somehow found the few dollars required to hire a servant to help her with her four children and household chores. Her daughter Annie recalled of these years, "On the whole we were very comfortable."

But the family's only income was Thomas's annual military pension, as he was unable to secure a government job in neighbouring Peterborough. Susanna Moodie wrote of her brother-in-law: "He has had the mortification of seeing all the places filled up—some by men half his age—and himself passed up." Catharine scrambled for ways to supplement the family income. She started a small school, and she also began to act as the local nurse and midwife, relying heavily on the herbal remedies on which she was already an expert. Every week her daughter Katie took a basket of eggs, from the flock of about thirty chickens the Traills always kept in their backyard, to market, where they fetched about tenpence a dozen. Catharine also acquired a couple of geese, which she plucked regularly so she could sell the down ("the quills are not touched, so that the animal suffers but little from the operation"). But all this hard work yielded only pennies. Ever since the Traills and Moodies had arrived in Canada, the parcels that came regularly from Reydon Hall had been an important source of clothes and housekeeping items for each family. These days, Catharine was so dependent on her sisters' handouts that she wept with relief when their letters and gifts turned up at the Peterborough post office.

Agnes's letters to Catharine, and her activities in England, provide an interesting counterpoint to the lives of her sisters in Canada. Despite the Stricklands' lack of means and paucity of aristocratic connections, Agnes was enjoying extraordinary success. Her career as a biographer, which started only after her sisters had arrived in Canada, must have surprised them. In the Regency London that Susanna and Catharine had left behind, the British monarchy had been deeply unpopular. They could recall the intelligentsia sneering at George IV as a lazy drunk and William IV as "Silly Billy." But everything changed when the petite and prim figure of Victoria, eighteen years old, ascended the British throne in 1837. The young Queen was a magnet for public attention. Victoria's subjects wanted to know about their monarch's dresses, jewels and tastes; they adored her youth and aura of vulnerability, and the glamour of her wedding to Prince Albert of Saxe-Coburg-Gotha in 1840. Agnes, who had an acute eye for commercial opportunity, promptly produced a two-volume biography entitled *Victoria from Her Birth to Her Bridal.* The Queen herself was outraged by the book's numerous inaccuracies (she scribbled "Not true" in the margins of nearly every page of the copy presented to her, and deleted whole paragraphs). But Agnes had hit a public nerve, and from then on she was unstoppable.

Interest in the young Queen blossomed into a more general interest in female royalty, and Agnes Strickland was there to feed the appetite. Over the next three decades, she and her sister Elizabeth produced biographies of thirty-three queens (including both consorts and female monarchs, and covering England, Scotland and France). The two women worked hard and companionably on both the writing and the extensive research for each volume. They trod new ground in historical writing. (Agnes suppressed the error-ridden biography of Victoria, and none of her subsequent books contained careless mistakes). Eliza and Agnes never relied on secondary sources. They unearthed papers that had lain mouldering in private collections, and in this way they shone a public spotlight on women whom contemporary male historians had ignored. They wrote about the past from the point of view of its spouses and victims, as well as its heroes. Thomas Babington Macaulay, a politician and author of the monumental five-volume *History of England from the Accession of James II,* "detested their methods," according to Agnes's biographer, Una Pope-Hennessy: "The emphasis was distressingly different from what he was accustomed to, for with the entry into the closet and the bedchamber, history was no longer a pompous march of massy events engineered by massive men, but a succession of intimate and homely details from which generalisations were gradually built up."

The biographies made the Strickland name famous. However, only Agnes Strickland's name appeared as the author of each book. Eliza, who actually wrote more than half the individual biographies, regarded popular acclaim as vulgar and was happy to let Agnes take all the credit. She had no interest in swanning through literary salons. The two women spent their mornings together, burrowing away in the British Museum Library or royal archives. In the afternoons, Eliza avoided all unnecessary calls and refused all invitations: instead, in her rented room in Bayswater, she read, wrote or visited with old acquaintances. Agnes, in contrast, revelled in her newfound status and acclaim. When in London, she always managed to secure an invitation to stay with smart friends in Regent's Park or the West End. "The great gain [from the newly published third volume of the twelve-volume set *The Queens of England*] is that it has given me a grand place in society as well as literature," she wrote to her Canadian sisters in 1841. "Since I last wrote I have been down to Windsor and had a long morning in the Royal Library. . . . Yesterday I drank tea with Lady Bedingfield." Agnes was the premier royal biographer of her age.

From now on, Agnes's letters read like chapters from Thackeray's *Vanity Fair*. They were speckled with the names of minor aristocrats, junior politicians and the more literate members of the landed gentry. Agnes's tall, mannish figure and deep voice were soon well known within the *beau monde* of Britain. One evening she sat next to the Duke of Wellington: "My early enthusiasm in favour of the hero of a hundred fights has not abated one chit. He was not near as deaf as I had heard." She spent the summers writing at Reydon Hall, or as a guest in country houses. In 1846, a portrait of Agnes in the purple velvet dress she wore at court was hung in the Royal Academy. The artist, John Hayes, managed to soften the sitter's imperious expression into something closer to a fashionably feminine simper. Further honours glimmered in the ether. "Our little queen," as Agnes referred to Victoria with proprietorial pride, was even said to have murmured something about a royal pension. Apparently, biographical inaccuracies had been forgiven in the light of Agnes's deluge of deference.

Given that both Susanna and Catharine were as talented as their elder sister, and Susanna was just as ambitious as Agnes, both women must have asked themselves, as they read Agnes's accounts of literary accomplishments, "What if . . . ?" Had they remained in England, might they too have established themselves as successful authors? Was Agnes's success largely because she had remained "in real and single blessedness," as she smugly put it, so could devote her time to her books, rather than to husband and children? Agnes had found her metier in the field of royal biography. Might her younger sisters have equalled her triumphs in their own (very different) genres, or might they, at the very least, have ridden her coattails to prosperity?

Catharine did not envy her elder sister. Unlike Susanna, she had never nursed a personal rivalry with Agnes. She had no interest in hobnobbing with the likes of Lady Bedingfield; she lacked the vanity to desire a portrait by a Royal Academician. However, Catharine was finding it just as hard to make ends meet in Ashburnham as she had in the bush. Her little school had failed, and Thomas was again sinking into despair. She had already tried to get a further payment for *The Backwoods of Canada* with a heartfelt appeal to the publisher: "While her little volume is read with pleasure by the talented and wealthy, the writer and her infant family is struggling with poverty and oppressed by many cares." But this had only yielded a further fifteen pounds, bringing Catharine's total income from *Backwoods*—one of the most widely circulated and best-known books about Canada—to 125 pounds. As Catharine sat in her parlour in Ashburnham and read Agnes's letters, she began to hope that Agnes might help her again. It was Agnes who had found a publisher for *Backwoods* in 1836. Now that Agnes was such a celebrity, surely she could find a publisher for more sketches of life in Upper Canada by Catharine?

Agnes tried. There was every reason to anticipate a warm reception for a manuscript by Mrs. Traill. *The Backwoods of Canada* had been well reviewed, and its first printing of eleven thousand copies had sold quickly. It had been reprinted in 1838, 1839 and 1840, and translated into German in 1838 and French in 1843. Moreover, there was now a vogue for improving and educational material. In 1823, Dr. George Birkbeck had founded the first "Mechanics' Institute" in London—an early form of public library—to feed what he called "the universal appetite for instruction," and soon after, every city boasted a similar institute. As literacy spread in the new industrial towns of Victorian England, so did demand for the printed word. The wives of the newly wealthy manufacturing class were not only unprepared to run large family houses, with servants lurking behind green baize doors, they were also ignorant of the manners required in the polite society to which they had been elevated. Even a book with the unappetizing title *What to do with Cold Mutton* went into a second printing. There was an epidemic of encyclopedias for the common man, and of series with titles like Valpy's Family Classical Library, the Edinburgh Cabinet Library and The Library of Entertaining Knowledge, the series in which *Backwoods* had been published. Memoirs and travel books often commanded advances as high as 250 pounds and could make their publishers profits running into four figures.

If anyone could have helped Catharine, it would have been Agnes. Agnes knew the importance of personal contacts and self-promotion. She was an indefatigable hustler and a canny businesswoman: she harangued publishers to issue and distribute her books and secure good reviews for them. As her reputation grew, she negotiated a share of sales revenue in addition to a flat fee for every book she produced. But Agnes had no luck with her sister's manuscript. Her own success reflected the popular demand for history, but the new industrial class didn't want to read about remote forests and North American flora. Catharine was out of touch with English tastes and English publishers. She lived beyond the edge of the known universe for London literary types. Agnes confided to Susanna, "I have failed to obtain anything for [Catharine's] mss. as yet," and she decided that Catharine must dismember the manuscript and peddle the sketches piecemeal to various periodicals in Britain and Canada. Agnes did manage to place several of the sketches, including two to *Chambers's Edinburgh Journal*. But Catharine waited for months for payment, and there is no evidence that *Chambers* ever sent a fee to their Canadian contributor.

Traill fortunes spiralled downwards with each passing year. In 1840, a fifth baby was born, but Catharine's joy was short-lived: Mary Ellen Bridges Traill died before her first birthday. Catharine had another baby in 1841, a fourth daughter, named Mary Elizabeth Jane, who survived. But within months, Catharine was pregnant again, and her fifth daughter died as an infant in 1843. All her children were constantly sick with earaches, boils, coughs, burns, infected cuts—hardly surprising, since they were starved of protein and fresh fruit and vegetables for most of the year. "Anxious nightwatchings over the cradle of suffering infants have brought down my strength and health," wrote Catharine. No woman in this period took the survival of a child for granted. Both Catharine and Susanna drew heavily on the Christian certainty that their infants' short lives were not without purpose, and that their babies would live again in heaven. "They are . . . like sparks struck from the iron to sparkle fly upwards, gladden the eye by their brightness for an instant and be lost in space," Catharine believed. "Who can say how often the loss of the young child has been the light sent by God to guide the sorrowing parent to the mercy seat of Christ."

Although Catharine never forgot her dead babies, she had to suppress her own grief for her husband's sake. With each setback, despair weighed more heavily on Thomas. A crescendo of demands from creditors in England, Peterborough and Cobourg forced the Traills into financial crisis. Reluctantly, they left Ashburnham and moved into a run-down farmhouse three miles out of town. Catharine hoped they could achieve self-sufficiency on this modest acreage. Thomas put a down payment on the house and spent his scanty remaining funds on seed and livestock. Catharine insisted everything would be fine, planted yet another garden of marigolds and mallow, and named the house Saville—the name of one of the Traill properties in the Orkneys. Stuck in the bush once again, she drew heavily on her faith that the Lord would provide. She never revealed her loneliness to her husband, who had again withdrawn into the dark recesses of chronic depression. Instead, she fell back on her faith. As she dug and weeded in the kitchen garden, or lifted heavy cast-iron pans of porridge from the stove, she would pause briefly, straighten her aching back, close her eyes and utter silent prayers. She confided to Ellen Dunlop, "There is no privation I feel more than not having the means of going to church."

Susanna knew from Catharine's letters that the Traills were in a bad way. Catharine poured out her worries to Susanna: "I feel . . . like a vessel without a pilot drifting before an overwhelming storm on every side rocks and shoals and no friendly port in sight. . . . The game of life seems to me a difficult one to play . . ." Through mutual friends, Susanna heard how Catharine's six children (an eighth baby, William Edward, was born in 1844) were rarely able to leave the house because their clothes were in rags. James, thirteen, and nine-year-old Harry had only one pair of broken and patched boots between them, so they took it in turns to go out into the snowdrifts and bitter winds to find firewood or draw water from the well. The older girls, Kate (now ten) and Annie (eight) could not attend school because they had no shoes, and because Catharine, crippled with rheumatism, relied on them to do the work of the servants that she could no longer afford. Poor little Mary, her youngest daughter, suffered constantly from infected eyes and ears, and cried so much that she wore her mother's patience "to rags." The little girls helped wash and patch their worn garments, feed the baby, preserve fruits and vegetables and prepare the boiled potatoes, gruel and porridge that was their diet. The Traills were so poor that they could not even afford tallow for candles; at night, Catharine burned pine knots, rich in resin, to provide light.

Susanna could not leave her young family in Belleville to help Catharine, who was two days' journey away. But as often as possible, the Moodies sent the Traills packages of castoff clothes and supplies of tea and sugar. Susanna urged her sister to submit a steady flow of material to Lovell's *Literary Garland*. Grinding poverty was hardly the environment in which the composition of light-hearted articles and stories flourished, but with dogged professionalism, Catharine struggled on, acknowledging that the five-pounds-per sheet fee helped pay off "small annoying debts that we cannot leave unsettled."

When news of the Traills' move back to the bush reached Eliza, Agnes, Jane and Sarah Strickland, the English sisters were all anxious about Catharine. Unlike Susanna, however, they had no understanding of the brutal hardships she faced. Poverty for the childless Stricklands in Suffolk and London meant frayed cuffs and cheap cuts of meat. They couldn't even imagine the icy horror of barefoot children in a Canadian winter, the sad whimper of a hungry infant or the struggle of a mal-nourished ten-year-old boy to drag home firewood.

Agnes had never forgiven Catharine for marrying Thomas. She was convinced that all the Traills' troubles were his fault. "Ah, why did she involve her bright days in such a sea of trouble," Agnes wrote to Susanna in 1841, about Catharine. "There was neither hope nor reason in marry-ing such a man as our poor brother Traill notwithstanding his many amiable qualities . . . my heart bleeds at the sacrifice she has made." But a couple of years later, Agnes was jolted out of her complacency. A rumour reached England that the Traills were "in the last state of desti-tution and misery." Agnes was horrified, both by the heart-wrenching details of her sister's poverty and by the idea that her family was the sub-ject of gossip on her own side of the Atlantic. She quickly sent off sev-eral parcels of fabric and second-hand clothes. Agnes knew that her parcels were also precious to the Moodies in Belleville, but she explained to her youngest sister that, "The dire straits which poor Kate's circum-stances appear to have reached makes it imperatively necessary for me to make a personal sacrifice in order to send her some money, little enough but more than I can spare. Consequently, I have nothing to send for you except a little French cambric . . ."

Agnes resurrected all her old prejudices as she considered Catharine's problems. "Of course I must give to her who wants the means of existence as I knew she would with that disastrous and ill-judged marriage. . . . I wish I had not been so true a prophetess. It is heartbreaking to think of our poor Kate, who was so kind and deserv-ing of a better fate, becoming the victim of such a marriage. My only wonder is that she has kept the wolf from the door for so long. . . .

I think Mr. Traill's own kindred ought to try and help him." But Mr. Traill's own kindred in the Orkneys were already shouldering the responsibility of raising the two sons of his first marriage. They assumed that the grand and well-connected Agnes Strickland would subsidize the Traill ménage in Canada.

Sometimes Thomas must have felt singled out by misfortune. Fired up with fellow feeling for another Scottish immigrant, he had backed a loan for the young Scot to build a mill on the Otonabee River. The young man was drowned, and Thomas found himself obliged to pay his friend's debts. Even run-down, shabby Saville was now beyond his means. Catharine had to pack up her meagre possessions and move out before Thomas had a chance to harvest the crops he had planted. By now, the threat of bankruptcy had rendered him catatonic. "The harrassing state of uncertainty in which we are kept about our future plans is preying dreadfully on Traill's mind," Catharine wrote to Susanna in 1846, "nor can I rouse him from it."

Perhaps a benevolent deity did hover over the Traills, as Catharine believed, shielding her family from complete disaster. It must have seemed that way when the Reverend George Wilson Bridges, an eccentric English cleric, stepped into their lives to rescue them from homelessness. Somehow a copy of *The Backwoods of Canada* had found its way to Jamaica several years earlier, where it had fallen into the hands of Bridges, then rector of the Parish of St. Anne's. Bridges had just suffered a series of bizarre and devastating family tragedies. After nineteen years of what he had thought was a happy marriage, his wife had abruptly deserted him, his own family had turned against him, and his four daughters were drowned in a freak sailing accident. Bridges was left in Jamaica with a three-year-old son. Shattered by loss, Bridges read *The Backwoods of Canada* and decided to abandon the tropical climate and comforts of Jamaica for the chilly and tangled backwoods of Canada. Perhaps he was persuaded by the cheerful warmth of Catharine's observations, written long before hardship had ground her down. Perhaps a revulsion for the languid, self-indulgent white élite of Jamaican society propelled Bridges to seek a more bracing, self-sufficient life. Whatever the reason, he decided to make Mrs. Traill his model and follow her to Upper Canada. He wrote in a memoir that if he had not "gone wild he would doubtless have gone mad." In 1837, he arrived in the newly settled community of Gore's Landing, on the south shore of Rice Lake, twenty-two miles by road and steamer from Catharine.

George Bridges must have cut an extraordinary figure in the wilds of pre-Confederation Canada. A tall, bony man who swept about in brocaded robes and smoking jackets, he was completely out of place among its shabby-coated farmers and merchants. Bridges's idea of luxury was well-aged port; his neighbours' idea of luxury was enough chairs in their own homes for every family member to have a seat. Bridges's neighbours in Gore's Landing thought the newcomer was indeed mad when he started building a house on the lakeshore. Recklessly oblivious to the extremes of Canada's climate, Bridges hired local carpenters to erect a six-floored octagonal structure with barred windows and an underground entrance. Then he himself put together tables, chairs and shelves out of red cedar, so the whole house smelled like a Finnish sauna. When the peculiar residence was finished he invited his heroine to visit. In wine made by Bridges from local grapes, he and Catharine toasted his new home and she named it Wolf Tower.

Given Bridges's history (and his rumoured propensity for opium), it is not surprising that he didn't last long in the backwoods. His house was a stifling conservatory in the summer months, as the sun beat down on its glass windows, and a lethal icehouse in the winter, when freezing drafts whistled up its six levels and round its open floors. After four years, Bridges had had enough and once again walked away from his life, heading this time to England. But he stayed in touch with Catharine. When he heard how tough things had become for the Traills by April 1846, he offered them Wolf Tower as a rent-free residence.

The offer of free lodgings came in the nick of time for Catharine. She immediately wrote to Susanna, describing just how grim their circumstances had been before Bridges had stepped in: "My dear husband was fretting himself to death and me too, for both my health and spirits were sinking under the load of mental anxiety more on his account than the circumstances, and want of strengthening diet." She had run out of wood for the stove, flour to make bread, and meat or fish other than the perch that her sons caught in the Otonabee. But now Thomas had set off for Wolf Tower "in high spirits *for Traill*," with their nine-year-old Harry, to plant some spring wheat. A few days later, Catharine and the other five children, plus their furniture, two cows and two sheep, boarded a noisy steam-driven paddle-wheeler, the *Forester*, which took them from Peterborough down the Otonabee River and across Rice Lake to Gore's Landing.

"When I came to reside at Wolf Tower," Catharine would recall in later years, "I came in weak health having scarcely recovered from a long and terrible fit of illness, but so renovating did I find the free, healthy air of the beautiful hills that in a very short time I was quite strong and able to ramble about with my children among the picturesque glens and wild ravines of this romantic spot, revelling in this rich and rare flower garden of nature's own planting. The children were never weary of climbing the lofty sides of the hills that surrounded the ravine, forming the bed of one of those hill torrents to which they have given the name of 'The Valley of the Big Stone' from a huge boulder of grey granite that occupies the centre of it."

The romance of Wolf Tower lifted Catharine's spirits. In her mid-forties, Catharine was overweight and unhealthy, and on damp days she complained of aching joints. A network of broken spider veins covered her round cheeks, her blond hair was thinning and stringy, and her eyes were ringed with dark shadows. But now her gurgling laugh echoed up Wolf Tower's spiralling staircases, and she recovered the sparkle in her bright-blue eyes. During the warm summer months, she enjoyed teaching her children their letters in the fifth-floor conservatory, with its panoramic views of green hills and blue water. She persuaded the newly appointed Anglican minister of St. George's Church, Gore's Landing, to conduct open-air church services at the big grey lump of granite her children had named "the Big Stone." Catharine's eyes filled with happy tears as she looked around her and thought of the words of her favourite psalm: "The pastures of the wilderness drip; and the little hills rejoice on every side. The pastures are clothed with flocks: the valleys also stand so thick with grain that they laugh and sing." Perhaps the flocks were missing, and the grain was sparse, but as she always liked to insist, "The sight of green things is life to me."

As an adult, Annie Traill would recall that she and her siblings were "happy as larks" during these years: "We children used to scramble over the hills and ravines, delighting over the beautiful flowers and shrubs which grew so luxuriantly everywhere, and my dear mother, when able, used to accompany us." Agnes continued to send generous parcels, despite her exasperation with her brother-in-law. One year the parcel contained table cloths, children's books, German silver spoons, a metal teapot, two coats for the boys, needles, thread, a pair of cutting shears, towelling, a Scottish plaid gown for which Agnes had no more use, six pairs of white stockings, some boots for Catharine and lengths of calico, muslin, blue-check shirting and flannel. "Very acceptable the things will be," Catharine told Susanna, "for I was beginning to think with wonder how I would find clothing for these poor children, now reduced to worse than bareness." Agnes had also sent along the latest volume of her *Queens of England* series, and a copy of the *Juvenile Scrapbook: A Gage d'Amour for the Young*, an anthology edited by Jane Strickland which contained several pieces by Agnes.

In retrospect, Annie would realize how difficult her mother's life was during these years. She and her sister Kate did much of the baby care and domestic work, but "the burden fell on [mother] and she was not strong." James and Harry Traill, in their early teens, worked almost full-time in the fields, because Thomas was a wreck of his former self. Looking at the emaciated and melancholic figure who barely spoke above a clipped whisper, it was hard to believe he had once been a cosmopolitan, well-groomed gentleman. His teeth were stained and his hair matted; he looked haunted by anxieties. A Scottish visitor described Thomas as wearing "a shawl around his neck that one would not have picked out of the gutter and that had not been washed for a month—a nose very much smeared with snuff, hands and face evidently in want of soap and water yet with all this unprepossessing exterior evidently a kind hearted and well informed man." But Catharine, recalled Annie, was "ever cheerful and ready to tell stories or sing to our dear father in the evening."

With the onset of winter, it became evident that Wolf Tower was a hopelessly impractical residence to keep warm, and the Traills soon moved on. But they liked the area so much that they didn't move far. For the next couple of years, they rented another house, which they called Mount Ararat, near the Rice Lake Plains, as the lake's rolling south shore was known. Catharine's stamina, not to mention her good humour, was extraordinary: her ninth and last baby was born in 1848, when she was forty-five. (He was named Walter in memory of Thomas's oldest son, who had died at age thirty, three years earlier.) She was constantly bothered by excruciating attacks of rheumatism. "I cannot now lift my hand to my head without great pain," she wrote to Susanna in 1849, "nor can I put it back without being forced to scream out with the agonising pain I endure in moving it. . . . I suffer at times great pain in my right knee . . ." Yet her children could always bring a smile to her face. One day, her daughter Annie would later recall, her mother discovered that a set of silver teaspoons, each bearing the Traill family crest, had disappeared. The set was one of the few possessions from home that Thomas and Catharine still possessed. When Catharine questioned her children, each in turn denied that he or she had touched the precious spoons, until the inquisiton reached five-year-old William. The little boy confessed that he had planted the spoons in the garden, to make them grow. His father and elder brothers rushed outside to dig them up, but the child could not recall where he had buried them. They never turned up, but Catharine loved to tell the tale for the rest of her life.

In 1849, Catharine saw a wooden house just east of Gore's Landing that she decided they must buy. Oaklands was a large log cabin, which meant it had pokey windows and was dark inside, but it had a substantial stone chimney. It was also cheap, because it stood on the top of a windy hill and was miles from the woodlot. Raising the down payment was a problem for the penniless Traills, but Catharine found a way. For years, Thomas had clung to his officer's commission as the qualification that would secure for him the elusive government job. Now his wife persuaded him that, at fifty-two, he would do better to cash the commission in and use the proceeds to buy the house. Thomas raised some additional funds by borrowing from his brother-in-law Sam Strickland and from John Moodie. After ten wretched years of rented, borrowed or mortgaged houses, in 1849 the Traills once again had their own home. It was not ideal: bitterly cold north winds swept across the hills, reminding Catharine of the east winds that swept along the Norfolk coast in January, and Oaklands was a difficult house to heat. Catharine wrote to a friend one January, "We sit in the small parlour and keep but two fires, consequently the bedrooms are cold." But the Traills finally felt settled.

The move did little for Thomas, however, who remained in a permanent and paralyzing state of depression. "I cannot endure to see my poor husband so utterly cast down," Catharine wrote to Susanna in Belleville. "I wish that he could look beyond the present and remember that the brightest of earthly prospects endure but for a season—and it is the same with the trials and sorrows of life—they too come to an end."

From time to time in her own correspondence, Catharine reluctantly confided her own bouts of despair. "There is a cloud gathering over us that I see no means of averting," she told Frances Stewart in 1851. The following year, she wrote to Susanna of how she longed to visit her, and enjoy "the great comfort to me of seeing you and talking over many matters that I cannot write." But she was a resilient woman who had learned to escape gnawing anxieties by taking refuge in nature: the huge maple trees, the scampering chipmunks, the delicate saxifrage and white violets that she carefully pressed between layers of cotton in one of Thomas's books. She also knew what was expected of an English lady: she had seen how her own mother had coped with the loss of her husband when she was forty-six, how she had managed to put a brave face on adversity. Catherine rarely indulged in grumbles. Instead she forced herself to look on the bright side, reminding herself often that God's grace would protect her. In her daily entries in her journal, Catharine often sounds like the wife of a prosperous gentleman-farmer in Surrey. Gazing out at the distant lake, and watching a cloud of passenger pigeons career across the mother-of-pearl sky, she noted: "I know of no place more suitable for the residence of an English gentleman's family. There is hardly a lot of land that might not be converted into a park."

Catharine's determination to keep writing was unquenched, despite Agnes's failure to market her sequel to *The Backwoods of Canada*. She still wanted to publish a book in England, for the audience with whom she had been most popular when she lived there: children who shared her love of nature's bounty. She had been mulling over a particular idea for a young people's novel for nearly ten years. In 1837, she had copied into her journal an advertisement from the Cobourg *Star* that had sparked the idea. "50 pound REWARD," read the headline, and in smaller print below: "Lost on Saturday last the 29th of July on the road leading from Bowskill's mills to Foe's tavern, near the Rice Lake Plains a child about six years old the daughter of Mr. Thos. Eyre of Hamilton near Cobourg. She wore a blue plaid cotton frock and was without her bonnet. Whoever will return the child to her parents or give such information as may lead to her discovery shall receive the above reward. Thomas Eyre."

The spectre of children lost in the forest was common among Canada's early settlers. It was a real threat, when paths were few, forests dense, and children as young as five were sent off to find lost cattle or take a lunch-pail to men working in the bush. Contemporary newspapers were filled with such heartbreaking tales. The story in the Cobourg *Star* had a happy ending. Mr. Eyre's daughter (improbably called Jane) was found four days later, after a search involving nearly a thousand people. But there were plenty of other youngsters who were never seen again. Both Catharine and her sister Susanna collected anecdotes of such ghastly occurrences. The nightmare of missing youngsters struck to the core of their maternal beings. Such a prospect, in Susanna's view, was "more melancholy than the certainty of [the child's] death." It also symbolized the deeper anguish of leaving behind familiar scenes and losing oneself in new and unknown territory.

The details of Jane Eyre's disappearance haunted Catharine's imagination. She brooded over what it would be like to be the little girl who had wandered away from a picnic and suddenly realized that the sun was sinking and she could no longer hear human voices. She put herself in the place of the mother, screaming her child's name into the black wall of silent trees and beating her chest with anguish and self-reproach for having allowed the child out of her sight. By the time she arrived at Rice Lake, Catharine had sold two different versions of the story to *Chambers's Edinburgh Journal* and a third to the London annual *Home Circle*. (Like any professional writer, she had no scruples about recycling her material). By the time the third version appeared in 1849, Catharine was well launched on a full-length novel about children lost on the plains on the south shore of Rice Lake.

Catharine first developed the narrative of what was to be *Canadian Crusoes, A Tale of the Rice Lake Plains* as a story for her own children. During picnics at the Big Stone, or at bedtime in Wolf Tower, her brood would sit wide-eyed as their mother spun a tale about the world they lived in. The landscape she described was the landscape the Traill children knew—the Big Stone, the wild rice beds of Rice Lake, the local hills and ravines. In the evenings, Catharine would sit at her writing desk and put the story on paper. Writing was both therapy and catharsis for her, as it was for Susanna: an escape from day-to-day anxieties. In March 1850, Catharine reported to Ellen Dunlop, Frances Stewart's daughter, that "I have been writing a little now every night at my Canadian Crusoes, and hope if I keep tolerably well to have the volume ready by the middle of May. . . . I am in good hope of winning fifty pounds when it is ready and that cheers me up to persevere in my work." By September she was able to write to Ellen, "I have yesterday finished my arduous and fatigueing task of copying the MS of the Canadian Crusoes—354 pages besides some notes." Two weeks later, Catharine sent off her manuscript to

Agnes, so she and Jane could edit the text and place it with a publisher.

Canadian Crusoes has the kind of conventional happy-ending adventure plot that children's authors such as E. Nesbit and Enid Blyton have relied on. Set in the late eighteenth century, it involves three plucky youngsters—half-Scottish, half-French siblings called Hector and Catharine Maxwell, and their French-Canadian cousin Louis—who get lost in the bush. Together the trio rescue Indiana, a young Mohawk woman, from death, and (largely thanks to Indiana's skills at canoeing, hunting and fishing) they survive for two years in the bush. When the children are finally rescued, they discover that they have been no more than eight miles from home. At the end of the story, Louis marries Catharine and Indiana marries Hector, the happy foursome representing a blending of Canada's British, French and native heritages.

Canadian Crusoes is really a barely disguised survival manual, a kind of *Backwoods of Canada* for British children. In fiction as in conversation, Catharine burned with the impulse to pass on useful tips. When one of the girls makes tea from a wild fern, for instance, the reader not only learns what the fern looks like and where to find it ("a graceful woody fern, with a fine aromatic scent like nutmegs; this plant is highly esteemed among the Canadians as a beverage, and also as a remedy against the ague; it grows in great abundance on dry sandy lands and wastes, by waysides"), but there is even a footnote giving its Latin name ("*comptonia asplenifolio*"). Every chapter of *Canadian Crusoes* is packed with information about flora and fauna native to Upper Canada, Mohawk and Ojibwa history and culture, and hunting practices. And Catharine endowed the two British children with all the missionary zeal so popular amongst Victorians as they set out to convert Indiana: "Simply and earnestly they entered into the task as a labour of love, and though for a long time Indiana seemed to pay little attention to what they said, by slow degrees the good seed took root and brought forth fruit worthy of Him whose Spirit poured the beams of spiritual light into her heart."

To Catharine's dismay, it took Agnes nearly two years to find a publisher. Part of the reason was that Agnes spent some time on the manuscript adding a preface and once again rewriting illegible sections. But Agnes was also preoccupied with another issue. In 1850, the Pope had appointed Cardinal Wiseman, an extremely aggressive cleric, as Archbishop of Westminster—head of the Roman Catholic Church in Britain—and a large new body of distinguished converts, including the Reverand Henry Edward Manning of the Church of England, went over to Rome. The whole of London was in an uproar over the perceived threat to the established Church of England. This was just the kind of furor that Agnes, now the acknowledged expert on Victoria, loved: her opinion on the Queen's role as head of the Anglican Church was sought from one end of Mayfair to the other. She was much too busy to devote attention to a tale of scruffy children lost in the bush. She wrote to her sister that *nothing* could be done while "the whole attention of the public is taken up with the Catholic question, which has ruined literature for the present." An anxious Catharine confided in her friend Frances Stewart that she had replied to Agnes's letter, "hinting at our necessity—though I dared not tell her how pressing it really was."

Canadian Crusoes finally appeared in London in 1852. Its didactic tone and overtly Christian message found an appreciative audience. Elizabeth Strickland wrote to Catharine to tell her that her "Crusoes are very much admired," and the book was well reviewed. The *Observer* praised the "freshness" of the text and the "truth and gracefulness" of its "description of American backwood scenery, animal and vegetable productions." *John Bull* said it was "a prettily-conceived tale," and "elegantly illustrated" (there were twelve engravings by William Harvey, a well-known illustrator). *Tait's Edinburgh Magazine* was as enthusiastic as it had been for *Backwoods*. The reviewer was intrigued by descriptions of Indian settlements that were "very different from the delineations of the American novelists, and are probably nearer to the truth." According to *Sharpe's London Magazine, Canadian Crusoes* was "a very pretty book . . . full of interest and information."

Despite the critical success of *Canadian Crusoes*, the book did not solve the Traills' financial problems. Her London publishers paid Catharine only fifty pounds for the first English edition. Five years later, Agnes tried to negotiate a further fifty-pound payment for the second edition, which appeared in 1858. However, Arthur Hall, of Hall, Virtue, discovered he could get a far better price if he dealt directly with penniless Catharine rather than her virago of a sister. He managed to beat Catharine down to twenty-five pounds. Agnes was furious with Hall's deviousness and Catharine's naive interference in business negotiations: "My poor unlucky Catharine, I cannot say how annoyed I am at the cold-blooded villainy of that wretched man, and the worst of it is that I cannot do you any good because you have invalidated my agency. . . . Alas! that all my pains should have been thus circumvented! It is for you I grieve for it would have done me no other good than the pleasure of getting you out of your pecuniary straits through my good management of your books."

In subsequent years, sales of *Canadian Crusoes* continued to go from strength to strength in Britain. Catharine was thrilled when the Edinburgh firm of Thomas Nelson showed some interest in a third edition in 1867. This time, however, Catharine had a better sense of the value of her copyright. When Nelson and Sons offered her forty pounds for both *Canadian Crusoes* and a second children's book she'd published in 1856, *Lady Mary and her Nurse*, she considered the figure "shabby." But she was too broke to argue, and decided that she had better accept. She was soon referring in her correspondence to her publisher as "that old humbug Nelson," since in return for his fee Thomas Nelson also demanded extensive corrections and additions, and a change of title to *Lost in the Backwoods. A Tale of the Canadian Forest* (a "very stupid" title in the author's opinion). Nelson then delayed publication, and payment, for fifteen years. By 1882, Catharine had earned from the English editions of *Canadian Crusoe* only 115 pounds—10 pounds less than she had earned from *The Backwoods of Canada* nearly fifty years earlier.

Even on her own side of the Atlantic, Catharine received a derisory reward for her work. The American publishers C.S. Francis, of Boston and New York, brought out an American edition at the end of 1852.

Initially, Catharine was happy to have Francis as publisher because he promised her fifty dollars for the copyright. In 1853, Catharine wrote a joyful letter to Ellen Dunlop: "Francis sent me a nice present, and promised me more next year, and highly praised my book which was he said likely to be of great advantage both to author and publisher." But the absence of any international copyright law left British and Canadian authors unprotected against pirates. American publishers routinely issued low-cost editions of works that sold well in Europe before British copies had crossed the Atlantic, and without any payment to the authors or the original publishers. Canadian readers didn't object to this flagrant piracy; it gave them easy and cheap access to popular British authors like Charles Dickens and Walter Scott. They were outraged when the British government made a half-hearted attempt to protect authors with the 1842 Imperial Copyright Act. In the end, Francis never forwarded any further royalties to Catharine, although he himself did well with *Canadian Crusoes.* It rapidly went through nine impressions.

Like so many authors before and after her, Catharine raged against publishers who made more from her books than she did. But her eagerness to write made her a sitting duck for unscrupulous businessmen. And what choice did she have? Her other attempts to raise cash—needlework and knitting, selling pressed flowers to neighbours, acting as midwife—were even less lucrative. Writing was the only means she had to make some money while raising her children. And the act of putting pen to paper was her only release from the relentless pressure of daily worries.

Chapter 12

The Secrets of the Prison House

In the spring of 1847, a stout figure, in black bonnet and shawl, made her way east across the bridge over Belleville's Moira River. Susanna Moodie paused for a few minutes to watch the French-Canadian raftsmen, armed with long poles, leap from log to log as they steered rafts of timber through the foaming waters below her. Susanna's sense of fashion had not deserted her in her mid-forties: as photos from this period show, she enjoyed wearing the latest style of collar on her dark gowns, and her hair was carefully dressed. But the years of hardship had taken their toll on her looks, as they had on her sister's: the auburn in her hair had faded, deep grooves stretched from her nose to the corners of her mouth, and her thin lips were set in a straight, grim line. The lids of her deep-set brown eyes drooped; her shoulders hunched forward as she leaned over the balustrade of the bridge. The sight of the turbulent water brought back unhappy memories of Johnnie's death only three years earlier. She quickly moved on, her chin thrust forward in the sharp wind. Once she reached Front Street, she turned north, ignoring the large sign over the first building she passed, advertising in large letters, "Intelligencer: George Benjamin, proprietor." Susanna was on her way to see Belleville's other proprietor and publisher, Joseph Wilson.

Joseph Wilson was the owner-manager of the Victoria Bookstore on Front Street. He had first appeared in Belleville around 1843 when he'd set up a bookbinding business and printing press. He loved the book trade and was eager to become a publisher as well as a distributor. In the mid-1840s he decided that the colony was ripe for some home-grown publications, and he started a whole batch of periodicals, under such titles as *Wilson's Experiment* and *Wilson's Canada Casket.* They were done on the cheap—Wilson just stuck into their pages any stories or news items that came his way. But his ambition was always to get on his payroll Belleville's best-known writer, whose work was now appearing regularly in publications on both sides of the border.

The citizens of Belleville held in awe this accomplished woman who smoked a clay pipe as she hoed her vegetable garden or scattered seed for the hens in the backyard. But Susanna was also a controversial figure. First there was her treatment of George Benjamin in her widely circulated story "Richard Redpath. A Tale." Then there was the Moodies' troubled relationship with the new Congregationalist Church that they had helped to found in 1844. Apparently the couple had been considered a little too keen to argue church doctrine, and reluctant to perform church duties. They were expelled for their "disorderly walk and neglect of church fellowship"—a mysterious phrase that appears in the church records, which Susanna never explained in her letters or books.

Wilson didn't care about ornery conduct or small-town gossip: he wanted the famous Mrs. Moodie. But Susanna, though flattered by his attention, was too hard-headed to contribute to publications that didn't pay. She didn't trust Wilson: he was glib, and as one of her friends suggested, too driven by "a sordid love of the 'Dimes and Dollars.'" Susanna felt herself sufficiently established as a writer to require a certain deference. Wilson now made her an interesting offer. He told her how delighted he would be to publish a periodical edited by her. It would be cheap enough for working Canadians to afford, so that it might have a wide circulation.

Joseph Wilson was not the only entrepreneur eager to give uncouth Upper Canada some literary polish. Magazines that included Canadian material for Canadian readers, rather than reprinted material from British annuals, were multiplying. Most of them (then as now) were short-lived. As Susanna grumbled, they folded because they had to compete with American monthlies "got up in the first style, handsomely illustrated, and composed of the best articles, selected from European and American magazines [and] sold at such a low rate, that one or other is to be found in almost every decent home in the province." But a handful of Canadian writers were at last beginning to produce home-grown material. Whenever Susanna or Catharine received an issue of John Lovell's *Literary Garland,* they saw not only their own contributions but also steel engravings of the St. Lawrence River or the port of Montreal. They read pieces by the likes of John Richardson, Charles Sangster and Rosanna Leprohon. These writers slotted accounts of life in the colony into the mélange of hack escapist fantasies about fashionable aristocrats in romantic European castles that were still the mainstay of nineteenth-century periodicals. Richardson's contributions included an article about Indians in Upper Canada. Charles Sangster's poetry dealt with the familiar St. Lawrence landscape. Rosanna Leprohon portrayed life amongst the Hurons, and the trials of a destitute immigrant.

The letters that Susanna and Catharine wrote home rarely mentioned the growing literary self-consciousness of British North America: their letters covered news of harvests, children and friends. Yet both women organized their lives very differently from any of their neighbours. They structured their days, and their family duties, around what had become their main occupation: the composition of poems, sketches and stories for publication. They saw themselves as professional writers, earning money on which their families' welfare depended. A few other educated female immigrants kept journals of their daily lives: on Sturgeon Lake, just north of Peterborough, Ann Langton sat down each evening to record the comings and goings at her brother's farm. But none shared what critic and biographer Michael Peterman has called the Strickland sisters' "developed sense of literary self and attentiveness to audience." Other women didn't have the Stricklands' ruthless (or obsessive) self-discipline, which enabled them to turn their backs on domestic tasks and pick up a quill pen. It often felt like a useless occupation. Susanna regretfully noted, "The low esteem in which all literary labor is held in this country renders it every thing but a profitable employment." Yet the faint outlines of a new culture were starting to appear, and the Strickland sisters were both in its vanguard.

On that blustery spring day in 1847, Susanna was on her way to tell Wilson that she would accept his invitation to edit a publication, but only on her own terms. It was nearly ten years since Susanna had written from their farm on Lake Katchewanooka to John, while he was serving as paymaster, suggesting that they might co-edit a newspaper: "I could take all the light reading Tales, poetry &tc. and you the political and statistical details." Whenever she had dreamed of her own publication, she had envisaged a partnership with her beloved John. Susanna recognized that, although she was the more creative writer, her husband had supplementary strengths. His knowledge of facts and figures strengthened the framework for Susanna's lively narratives.

Susanna also intended to demand from Wilson complete control over all editorial contributions. No matter what Wilson was prepared to pay her, she had no intention of associating her name with material she didn't like. Susanna was always generous to younger writers, and now she was keen to use this opportunity to promote new talents, such as the romance writer Louisa Murray who lived near Kingston, and who had sent the revered Mrs. Moodie examples of her work for comment. Susanna was happy to aim the periodical at "yeomen and mechanics" (as she referred to them, with artless condescension) because in her contributions to the *Literary Garland* she had already begun to experiment with a new style and subject matter. She had broken out of the literary conventions of fiction and was producing personal accounts of her early years as an immigrant. She knew such sketches would resonate with anybody who had shared such experiences, and two-thirds of Upper Canada's citizens had been born elsewhere. But she would do nothing to jeopardize her continuing relationship with John Lovell and the *Literary Garland*, a consistently reliable source of income. She didn't want to compete with Lovell's more upmarket, Montreal-based readership.

As Susanna sat in Wilson's office, laying out her demands, Wilson nodded happily. Within the past few months, several new magazines had appeared in Cobourg, Hamilton, Toronto and Montreal, for circulation throughout the United Provinces. An entrepreneur, Wilson would have agreed to anything (other than payment for contributors) that would bring the famous Mrs. Moodie onto the masthead, giving his new venture an edge in an increasingly crowded market. Wilson was eager to get started. By the time Susanna left his office, they had decided that the publication should be called *The Victoria Magazine: A Cheap Periodical for the People*. "Victoria" combined the district's original name most satisfactorily with that of the beloved Queen. It had a regal ring that balanced the less-attractive connotations of the word "Cheap." The first issue would appear in late summer.

The first challenge facing the editors of any new publication in Upper Canada was to find subscribers. It would be another thirty years before periodicals started covering their costs by selling advertising space. Wilson wrote a prospectus for *The Victoria Magazine* which appeared in local newspapers and promised a monthly publication of "twenty-four pages in each number, printed on new type and upon good paper." The annual subscription, to be paid in advance, was one dollar: "The low price at which the Periodical is placed is in order that every person within the Colony, who can read, and is anxious for moral and mental improvement, may become a subscriber and patron of the work." The Moodies assured their readers that they would "devote all their talents to produce a useful, entertaining and cheap Periodical . . . Sketches and

Tales, in verse and prose, Moral Essays, Statistics of the Colony, Scraps of Useful Information, Reviews of New Works, and well selected articles from the most popular authors of the day, will form the pages of the Magazine."

The prospectus was sufficiently attractive (and Susanna's name sufficiently well known) to bring in 781 subscriptions. About one-third were from Belleville's population of 3,000, but a smattering came from as far afield as Toronto, Ottawa and Montreal. The Moodies' good friend Robert Baldwin subscribed: so did the Governor-General, Lord Elgin. It is unclear how many genuine yeomen and mechanics embraced the idea of paying for "Moral essays [and] Scraps of Useful Information"; literacy standards were low in the colony. But there were plenty of doctors and lawyers on the subscription list. The Moodies started to map out the first issue.

Since there was no budget for contributors, most of the material in *The Victoria Magazine* would come from the pens of Susanna and John Moodie. They aimed high, describing themselves as "literary philanthropists wishing hearty and heartfelt success, to every sincere pioneer in the exalted and noble cause of mental improvement." Despite (or, perhaps, because of) all the scars they carried from John's unhappy experiences as sheriff, they also hoped to avoid political controversy. Any writing "which awakens angry and resentful feelings, rarely tends to improve the heart, or produce those great moral changes, which must take place before we can hope to realise a permanent improvement in mankind individually or in the mass."

The first month's issue included Susanna's account of her arrival at Grosse Ile in 1832, with its vivid description of the hairy Irishman who had shouted, "Whurrah! my boys! Shure we'll all be jontlemen!" In later issues, she wrote about her first view of Quebec City from the St. Lawrence River and a hurricane in Douro. But Susanna quickly found that she had little time to shape and polish these "Canadian" pieces, as she and John struggled to fill twenty-four pages each month. The Moodies fell back on formulaic historical tales and romance to provide the promised "entertainment" for readers. Most were set in England and Scotland, but several more that they wrote were set in exotic locales, like Italy and Persia, that they had never visited. Susanna recycled tales she had published in the London annuals fifteen years earlier. John reused anecdotes about the Cape Colony that he had already published in *Ten Years in South Africa.* Susanna also put the squeeze on her sisters for articles. Catharine, now living in Wolf Tower and eager to help her "beloved Suze," obliged by sending to Belleville stories she had been unable to sell elsewhere. Agnes sent several pieces, including one of her stirring and sycophantic odes to royalty, entitled "Death of Edward, Prince of Wales." John tried to spice up the pages (and fill in space) with puns, riddles, acrostics and funny rhymes. "Whizz, whizz—buzz, buzz— dotti, dot, dot, dot, dot, / Here's lots of news, but we can't read a jot," read his cheerful verse entitled "The Magnetic Telegraph."

However, the Moodies were keener on "moral and mental improvement" than on amusement, and there was a tut-tutting tone to *The Victoria Magazine.* Even an article on practical jokes is a finger-wagging catalogue of public ridicule and humiliation. Their thinly disguised editorial priority was to promote a system of "common schools" in Upper Canada.

The Moodies had the best of intentions in their campaign to establish an educational system in the United Provinces. They realized that the colonies desperately needed men of education to fill all the public offices. The colonial government relied on immigrants educated in Britain to become the registrars, attorneys, sheriffs and court officials in cities like Montreal and Toronto, and towns like Peterborough, Belleville and Cobourg. Most first-generation Canadians, especially those raised in the backwoods, were barely literate. Susanna and Catharine had taught their own children to read and write, but in their letters, they bemoaned the sketchy education of their offspring. The children attended local public or private schools (usually run by enterprising widows who charged tiny fees) only when they had decent clothes and weren't needed at home. Catharine's eldest son, James, wrote despairingly to his aunt Susanna that his only option in life seemed to be to remain at home, "droning out my existence on an uncultivated farm, merely doing work that a common Irish servant can do much better." He envied his mother's education: "What I would not give to have sufficient talent and education to employ myself in writing." Catharine's second son, Harry, spent a few months at a Peterborough grammar school, but Catharine worried that all he learned was "moral evil" from his "low companions." The two women winced when they compared their five daughters' and seven sons' knowledge of literature, languages, mathematics or history with what they themselves had acquired in Suffolk. The English sisters —Agnes, Elizabeth, Sarah and Jane—would have regarded their Canadian nieces and nephews as little better than ignorant savages. When *The Victoria Magazine* advocated universal training in the three Rs, its editors had their own children in mind.

But there was a larger motive at work, too. If children of dramatically different backgrounds all attended the same common schools, a new cohesion would develop within a fractious society. Public schools would break down class barriers and create a "meritocracy based on education and manners," Susanna wrote in an early issue of her magazine, "composed of the well-educated, not necessarily of the well born and wealthy." Class tensions imported from the Old Country would crumble. "The want of education and moral training is the only *real* barrier that exists between different classes of men," the Moodies insisted. And it is no coincidence that such a system of common schools would also elevate and guarantee the Moodies' own position at the top rather than the bottom of the New World's social scale. By British standards, the Moodies had sunk low—they had scarcely any money, and the genteel accents that gave them status in Britain were worthless in Canada. But if the key to social position in Canada was education, the Moodies—like the cream they always felt themselves to be—would rise to the top. They would be among the most respected and socially established citizens of Belleville.

The Victoria Magazine's lofty idealism was received warmly. The *Cobourg Star* described it as "well worth a whole year's subscription." The *Huron*

Signal considered that John Moodie possessed "shrewd practical common-sense. . . . We love his manner and the honest goodness of his heart." The *Montreal Weekly Pilot* praised the publication as an "excellent journal of polite literature." But Joseph Wilson quickly realized that he had a major problem: the publication was yawningly polite. Readers found the periodical stuffy and boring, and most did not renew their subscriptions. They wanted the political gossip and polemics that were regularly provided by editors like William Lyon Mackenzie, George Benjamin of Belleville's *Intelligencer* and John Edward Barker of Kingston's *British Whig*. These gutter polemicists, eager to deploy low blows in defence of high ideals, ripped into opponents with reckless slanders. Susanna abhorred "low and vulgar abuse"—but it sold well. Royalism, romance and sermons about education didn't. After thirteen issues, *The Victoria Magazine* was forced to fold.

However, Susanna had learned a lot as the magazine's editor. *The Victoria Magazine* was produced for a native Canadian audience, not the distant British audience she knew from her London days, or the up-market, urban readers of the *Literary Garland* who liked stories that reminded them of home. Susanna had managed to banish from her imagination the ringing tones of Agnes, her elder sister and literary rival, who insisted that Stricklands were ladies and should act and write accordingly. In her autobiographical contributions to both *The Victoria Magazine* and the *Literary Garland*, she had written for her neighbours. Susanna had found a new voice as a writer.

By the time that *The Victoria Magazine* folded, Susanna Moodie had already published several Canadian sketches within the colony, two in her own magazine and six in the *Literary Garland*. Now John urged her to publish in England a book about her experiences in the Canadian bush. She had plenty of material; she had kept copious notes.

Her sisters' achievements undoubtedly spurred her on. After all, Catharine had published her breezy account of her own immigration, *The Backwoods of Canada*, only three years after setting foot in the New World and was now hard at work on *Canadian Crusoes*. And in England,

Agnes and Elizabeth were forging their way through *The Queens of England* with terrifying speed; the ninth volume had just appeared, after the two Strickland sisters had spent months in the royal archives of England, Scotland and France reading old letters and documents. Agnes Strickland's prose grew more lush with every crowned head she chronicled. Mary Beatrice of Modena, wife of James II, "comes before us," the author claimed in the throbbing introduction to the new volume, "in her beauty, her misfortunes, her conjugal tenderness, and passionate maternity, like one of the distressed queens of tragedy, or romance struggling against the decrees of adverse destiny." Perhaps it was the relentlessly uplifting tone of her sisters' work that turned Susanna Moodie into a cold-eyed realist. If Susanna was going to be a myth-maker, her myths would be darker and more menacing than Agnes's and Catharine's rosy visions. Susanna had never shown any tolerance for hypocrisy and pretension. The young woman who had turned her back on the Church of England because it was too smug was not going to pretend that Upper Canada was a Wordsworthian paradise of charming rustics and noble empire-builders.

With customary single-mindedness, Susanna embarked on a record of her first seven years as a settler in Canada, from 1832 to 1839—"this great epoch of our lives," as she called it. She jigsawed together into a coherent narrative the sketches and poems that had already been published, along with various anecdotes that she had been polishing for years. In addition, John prepared four chapters (covering such "factual" material as the operation of village hotels and land sales). By 1850, the Moodies had completed a manuscript that contained twenty-five chapters, eleven of which had already appeared in Canada. The bulky package of several hundred handwritten pages was sent off to the London publisher Richard Bentley, who had published John Moodie's book, *Ten Years in South Africa*, fifteen years earlier.

Bentley, a clever, cosmopolitan man who always dressed immaculately in starched wing collar and cuffs, had the most prestigious list of authors in the English-speaking world. He had bought up the copyrights to Jane Austen's six novels, and he published works by Anthony Trollope, Maria Edgeworth, Wilkie Collins and Lady Mary Wortley Montagu. Bentley's office on New Burlington Street, close to Piccadilly, hummed with literary gossip as authors and literary patrons came and went. So it was a coup for Susanna when Bentley offered her fifty pounds as an initial payment for the new manuscript, plus a share of the profits. It was a modest advance: Bentley paid most of his authors between two hundred and three hundred pounds. But Susanna, it appears, was satisfied. The book was published in two volumes, priced at a one pound, one shilling, under the title *Roughing It in the Bush*, in 1852, the same year that Catharine's children's novel, *Canadian Crusoes*, appeared.

Susanna Moodie would never have claimed that her sketches added up to autobiography (such a term was barely known outside literary London in these years). She didn't even have the temerity to call them "memoirs" or "reflections." Her only non-fiction model was the kind of travel writing exemplified by Anna Jameson's account of a visit to Canada, *Winter studies and summer rambles in Canada*, published in London in 1838. But she knew her own strengths as a writer. "A scene or picture strikes me as a whole, but I never can enter into details," she explained to her publisher. "A carpet must be very brilliant, the paper on a wall very remarkable before I should ever notice either, while the absurd and the extravagant make lasting impressions, and I can remember a droll speech or a caricature face for years." In her description of pioneer life, she exploited to the full her sense of the ridiculous, her ear for dialogue and her fascination with human behaviour. She strayed close to fiction at some points, as she obscured the identities of her subjects, stretched the facts to make a better story, and skewed the truth by filtering it through her own sensibility. The result is an enthralling account of life in the bush, featuring characters that are as fresh today as when Susanna wrote about them more than 150 years ago. *Roughing It in the Bush* is a far livelier, more original work than any of the clichéd poetry and sentimental fiction she had been churning out for more than twenty years. Of all the books that she and Catharine wrote, it is the best.

Susanna's stated intention in *Roughing It in the Bush* was to describe the experience of emigration without the misrepresentations that hucksters like Cattermole had spread in the early 1830s. "Oh, ye dealers in wild lands—ye speculators in the folly and credulity of your fellow men— what a mass of misery . . . have ye not to answer for!" Susanna wrote in her introduction. She accused the land speculators of persuading the gullible that "sheep and oxen . . . ran about the streets [of the New World] ready roasted, and with knives and forks upon their backs." She was committed to the truth, as she made plain in her opening epigraph:

I sketch from Nature, and the picture's true;
Whate'er the subject, whether grave or gay,
Painful experience in a distant land
Made it mine own.

Susanna was at pains to show the dark underbelly of experiences that her own sister Catharine had written about with gentle joy. In *The Backwoods of Canada*, for example, Catharine had described the "bee" during which the Traills' neighbours had helped the newcomers raise the walls of their first log cabin. Catharine had made the communal feast of whisky, salt pork and rice pudding sound like a dainty tea party: "In spite of the difference of rank among those that assisted at the bee, the greatest possible harmony prevailed, and the party separated well pleased with the day's work and entertainment." In *Roughing It in the Bush*, Susanna told a very different story. Bees presented "the most disgusting picture of a bush life. They are noisy, riotous, drunken meetings, often terminating in violent quarrels, sometimes even in bloodshed."

There was a vivid immediacy to Susanna's descriptions. In a passage describing the Moodies' arrival at their first home in Hamilton Township, she wrote, "I was perfectly bewildered—I could only stare at the place, with my eyes swimming in tears; but as the horses plunged down into the broken hollow, my attention was drawn from my new residence to the peril which endangered life and limb at every step. The driver, however, was well used to such roads, and, steering us dexterously between the black stumps, at length drove up, not to the door, for which there was none to the house, but to the open space from which that absent but very necessary appendage had been removed. Three young steers and two heifers, which the driver proceeded to drive out, were quietly reposing on the floor. . . . I begged the man to stay until [my husband] arrived, as I felt terrified at being alone in this wild, strange-looking place. He laughed, as well he might, at our fears, and said that he had a long way to go, and must be off; then, cracking his whip . . . he went his way, and Hannah and myself were left standing in the middle of the dirty floor."

Susanna also included anecdotes that capture the community humour of life in the bush. For all her disgust at the behaviour of some of her neighbours at logging bees, her prose dances with her love of regional accents and earthy humour when she writes about one that took place on the Moodies' property. One of the Irish settlers who helped at the bee was "Old Wittals . . . with his low forehead and long nose [who] ate his food like a famished wolf." A fellow logger was "funning Old Wittals for having eaten seven large cabbages at Mr. Traill's bee, a few days previous. His son, Sol, thought himself as in duty bound to take up the cudgel for his father. 'Now, I guess that's a lie, anyhow. Father was sick that day, and I tell you he only ate five.' . . . Malachi Chroak had discovered an old pair of cracked bellows in a corner, which he placed under his arm, and applying his mouth to the pipe, and working his elbow to and fro, pretended that he was playing upon the bagpipes, every now and then letting the wind escape in a shrill squeak from this novel instrument. 'Arrah, ladies and jintlemen, do jist turn your swate little eyes upon me whilst I play for your iddifications the last illigant tune which my owld grandmother taught me. Och hone! 'tis a thousand pities that such musical owld crathers should be suffered to die, at all at all, to be poked away into a dirthy, dark hole, when their canthles shud be burnin' a-top of a bushel, givin' light to the house.' And here he minced to and fro, affecting the airs of a fine lady."

Susanna wrote of herself as a wife and mother: there was always a baby in her arms or a child by her side as she faced the challenges of bush life. In a chapter set in the bitterly cold winter of 1837 ("During the month of February, the thermometer often ranged from eighteen to twenty-seven degrees below zero"), she recorded how she coped alone when the roof of her log cabin caught fire. "Large pieces of burning pine began to fall through the boarded ceiling. . . . The children I had kept under a large dresser in the kitchen, but it now appeared absolutely necessary to remove them to a place of safety. To expose the young, tender things to the direful cold was almost as bad as leaving them to the mercy of the fire. At last I hit upon a plan to keep them from freezing. I emptied all the clothes out of a large, deep chest of drawers, and dragged the empty drawers up the hill; these I lined with blankets, and placed a child in each drawer, covering it well over with the bedding, giving to little Agnes the charge of the baby to hold between her knees, and keep well-covered until help should arrive. Ah, how long it seemed coming!"

Roughing It in the Bush was more than a collection of "events as may serve to illustrate a life in the woods," as Susanna modestly claimed. It was the dramatic story of her own journey of self-discovery, as she faced the rigours and disorientation of pioneer life. She presented herself as the delicate young lady that she had been when she arrived in Canada, and with whom English readers would identify, rather than the toughened, middle-aged woman who had survived the loss of two children and now lived in a prosperous town. When the hopelessly naive Moodies arrive in the New World, "All was new, strange and distasteful to us; we shrank from the rude, coarse familiarity of the uneducated people among whom we were thrown; and they in return viewed us as innovators, who wished to curtail their independence by expecting from them the kindly civilities and gentle courtesies of a more refined community." Susanna dwelt on her incompetence as a farmer's wife, her inability to bake bread or organize a bee. She didn't brag about the fact that, before they all left the woods, Catharine acknowledged her as the best baker of breads and pies in the district.

Susanna carefully reworked the sketches to appeal to English sensitivities, and she gentrified her language: "face" became "countenance," "bite" became "masticate." In an 1847 issue of the *Literary Garland*, she had revelled in the gory details of a man who had tried to cut his own throat in a botched suicide attempt, and quoted the words of Ned Layton, the rescuer, directly: "I then saw that it was a piece of the flesh of his throat that had been carried into his windpipe. So, what do I do, but puts in my finger and thumb, and pulls it out, and bound up his throat with my handkerchief . . ." But Susanna decided that a British reader wouldn't have the stomach for such a vivid description. In the account of the same incident in *Roughing It in the Bush,* Susanna prudishly remarked: "Layton then detailed some particulars of his surgical practice which it is not necessary to repeat."

A decade after she had lived through these experiences, Susanna was able to put some distance between herself and her life. She was candid about the hardships of the immigrant life. She explained that Canada was the country for the "industrious working man" who knew how to work the land and could tolerate hardship as he slowly acquired property and prestige that were out of his reach back home. However, she warned, a penniless gentleman with no experience of manual labour could never prosper. Addressing the reader directly, she explained that any gentleman who crossed the Atlantic in order to reestablish social position lost at home would be ruined and disappointed: "If these sketches should prove the means of deterring one family from sinking their property, and shipwrecking all their hopes, by going to reside in the backwoods of Canada, I shall consider myself amply repaid for revealing the secrets of the prison-house, and feel that I have not toiled and suffered in the wilderness in vain." She confessed that she and her husband had discovered that sustained effort and faith in God's goodness were no guarantee of success in the backwoods.

Susanna had high expectations for sales of *Roughing It in the Bush*. She deliberately flagged her famous connections by dedicating it as "a simple Tribute of Affection" to "Agnes Strickland, Author of the 'Lives of the Queens of England.'"

The London reviews were everything that the Moodies had hoped for. The *Athenaeum* praised the author's ability to present "the dark side of the emigrant's life" without being "needlessly lachrymose." The *Literary Gazette* admired the author's patience, noble mind and unaffected outlook and recommended the book for its "great originality and interest," despite its occasional coarseness. *Blackwood's Magazine* carried lengthy extracts, interspersed with lavish praise of the author's moral courage and good humour in the face of adversity and rude neighbours. The magazine beseeched its female readers to "behold one, gently nurtured as yourselves, cheerfully condescending to rudest toils, unrepiningly endur-ing hardships you never dreamed of." Bentley quickly ordered a second printing of *Roughing It in the Bush*, paid Susanna an additional fifty pounds and asked her to send him more material to publish. He published fur-ther editions in 1854 and 1857.

Within weeks of its appearance in England, a pirated edition of *Roughing It in the Bush* was published in New York. The American pub-lisher, George Putnam, brought out a two-volume version, in which most of the poems were omitted, in his Semi-Monthly Library for Travellers and the Fireside series. The reviewers were equally enthusiastic there. The New York *Albion* praised the book's "obvious stamp of truth." American writers commented with admiration on the author's bravery in the remote "wilds of Canada," as though the district Susanna wrote about was in the High Arctic rather than just across Lake Ontario from New York State.

Susanna was buoyed up by her sales. Within a year, *Roughing It in the Bush* was close to outselling one of the all-time bestsellers in nineteenth-century America: Harriet Beecher Stowe's *Uncle Tom's Cabin*.

Chapter 18

Mortification and Madness

In 1852, the year that Susanna's *Roughing It in the Bush* and Catharine's *Canadian Crusoes* were published, their sister Agnes Strickland was at the height of her fame in England and grand beyond belief. Whenever Agnes visited her publisher Blackwoods in Edinburgh, "the Scottish papers announce all my arrivals and departures as if I was a Queen myself," she told Susanna. When she travelled from Reydon to Norwich to make some purchases, the tradesmen begged her to accept without payment any goods she fancied. She was a permanent fixture of gatherings at London's Kensington Palace, where, she gloated, she met "rooms full of lords and ladies."

Her elaborate costumes were reported in *The Times*: on one occasion she wore a "robe of rich Lyons brocade à l'antique, yellow roses, buds, and foliage, on pale silver-coloured ground," a long lace train and "double skirts of white glacé silk, edged with mauve velvet and covered with a tunic and deep flounce of Honiton point lace." Fearless of gilding the lily, Agnes wore both a tiara and a plume of white ostrich feathers on her head. The Prime Minister, Benjamin Disraeli, sought out this fearsomely well-upholstered figure at a Park Lane *soirée* to compliment her on her "graceful and romantic pen." Clearly, Thomas Strickland's mercantile origins had been left far behind: at a Scottish gathering of peers, Agnes was suffused with snobbish relief to see "an assembly of genuine nobles of gentle blood, no dirty cotton-spinners or stock-jobbers." And the market for royal biographies appeared bottomless. Now that *The Queens of England* series was completed, she and Elizabeth had already embarked on another set of carefully researched hagiographies, *The Lives of the Queens of Scotland*, which appeared between 1850 and 1859.

Agnes's three sisters in England—Elizabeth, her antisocial writing partner who lived in London; Jane, the dumpy homebody at Reydon who adored Agnes; sweet-tempered Sarah, now living in Northumberland and married to Richard Gwillym, a Church of England clergyman—were content to sit on the sidelines, basking in the reflected

Agnes Strickland, premier royal biographer in Victorian England, and a woman of commanding presence.

glories of this Lady Bracknell figure. They knew that Agnes's cultivation of blue-blooded friends was as much strategic as snobbish: it gave her access to the fabulous, and uncatalogued, collections of official and personal papers at stately homes all round the country. Her friendship, for instance, with William George Spencer Cavendish, sixth Duke of Devonshire, allowed her to root around in the archives of Devonshire House in London and in his two homes in Derbyshire: Hardwick House and Chatsworth House, the famous "Palace of the Peaks."

In August 1851, Agnes was happy to include a fourth sibling in her admiring family audience in England. Her brother Sam, nine years her junior, had returned with his eldest daughter, Marie Beresford, on an extended visit. Both father and daughter had recently lost their spouses. Ostensibly they were in England to visit Sam's mother, confined to her bedroom at Reydon Hall in Jane's care. Mrs. Strickland was now a crusty eighty-year-old, and from her old-fashioned four-poster bed she continued her lifelong habit of issuing a barrage of orders, disapproval and complaints. However, the real reason for Sam's return was to woo another wife—his childhood sweetheart, Katherine Rackham.

Sam's English sisters were all swept off their feet by their brother. Twenty-six years earlier, they had waved goodbye to an unruly, curly-headed twenty-year-old; now they found themselves embracing a stout and prosperous Canadian landowner. He was "so frank, good-natured and intelligent," reported Jane, "and so full of sense and sensibility." Agnes adored playing the *grande dame* of Suffolk and showing her brother what strides the county had made in his absence. When Sam wasn't paying his respects to the Rackham household, he was available to accompany his sisters to church, to the market, or to London. And since Katherine Rackham's elderly mother refused to release her middle-aged daughter into matrimony, Sam was often available. He had to wait until Mrs. Rackham died, in 1855, before Katherine was able to join him in Canada.

In January 1852, a parcel arrived at Reydon Hall that shattered all this cosy Strickland congeniality. Inside, Agnes found a copy of *Roughing It in the Bush*, hot off the press and sent by the publisher Richard Bentley. Initially, she was pleased to feel the quality of the leather binding. She smiled as she read the warm inscription: "to Agnes Strickland . . . this simple Tribute of Affection is dedicated by her sister, Susanna Moodie." However, as she read on, her smile evaporated. The book was full of disgusting scenes and ghastly people. While Agnes had been writing about glorious coronations and royal maidens, her sister had chosen to describe vulgar foreigners living in squalor. While Agnes had been mingling with the mighty, Susanna had been mixing with servants, farm labourers, drunks and "barbarous Yankee squatters." While Agnes had stayed at Chatsworth, Susanna had lived in a pigsty. Susanna had written pages about tasks that no lady would be interested in, let alone perform: making sugar from maple trees, milking cows, digging potatoes. It was all too mortifying for Agnes Strickland. What would her good friends the Duke and Duchess of Somerset, or Countess Newburgh, or Dean Pellew of Norwich Cathedral, or Bishop Monk of Gloucester think?

Within days, an angry letter was on its way to Belleville, insisting that the dedication to Agnes be removed from all subsequent editions of *Roughing It in the Bush*. Agnes also rebuked Susanna for rehashing old experiences simply to make money. In her eyes, Susanna's discovery of her own "Canadian" voice was simply a whining account of past wretchedness which would have been better forgotten. Agnes herself knew better, she wrote, than to make such a silly move: "I had the prudence to commit four whole volumes to the flames years ago, and many a production has followed it that might have proved a scorpion to myself and others when the money they would have realized would have been expended and nothing but vexation left." Agnes reported that she had seen some Suffolk friends of the Stricklands, whose nephew was the Moodies' fellow emigrant Tom Wales. In *Roughing It in the Bush* Susanna had described meeting Tom (whom she called "Tom Wilson") in Cobourg, and his complaints about the poor diet, the blackflies and swamp fever. She ridiculed him as "a man as helpless and as indolent as a baby [who] would have been a treasure to an undertaker . . . he looked as if he had been born in a shroud, and rocked in a coffin." Agnes knew that Susanna's book would cause trouble within the Reydon Hall neighbourhood. "What they will say about Tom Wales, alias Wilson, I don't know," she sniffed.

Removing her name from the frontispiece and ticking off her sister wasn't enough for Agnes. She also wanted the good name of Strickland, and the family's position as landed gentry, restored. So she sat Sam down and told him that he was to write his own pioneering memoirs—and she and Jane would be his editors. Agnes then negotiated a deal with Richard Bentley, Susanna's London publisher, whereby Sam would receive one hundred pounds per thousand copies of his book—far more than Susanna, conducting her negotiations by transatlantic mail, had managed to get for *Roughing It*.

Sam's memoir, *Twenty-seven years in Canada West*, is a no-nonsense account of emigration, adventure and success. Sam had none of the professional writing skills that his two sisters in Canada had spent over

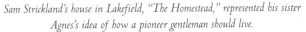

Sam Strickland's house in Lakefield, "The Homestead," *represented his sister Agnes's idea of how a pioneer gentleman should live.*

thirty years polishing; he shared neither Catharine's powers of observation nor Susanna's wit. The prose is stiff, and Sam's repertoire of adjectives for his fellow emigrants is limited. Most of the men are characterized as "a jolly set of fellows"; women, "the fair sex," are perfunctorily complimented as wives and mothers. Sam's prose flows most easily when he is describing his success as a sportsman. His stories of adventures while hunting bears, deer and wolves had their origins in the belly-laugh anecdotes with which he regaled his fellow members of Peterborough's Orange Lodge.

Sam spent an agonizing few weeks sitting in the damp and dilapidated dining room at Reydon Hall, staring out at the old sycamore tree as he tried to compose while Agnes and Jane chivvied him to keep writing. Their influence pervades most of his book's 655 pages. Agnes insisted that Sam call himself "Major Strickland" on the title page, although he never called himself "Major" at home. She helped him shape a preface that contradicted Susanna's account of the misery of a colonist's life. "Unless [an author] has experienced all the various gradations of colonial existence," wrote Sam, "from that of a pioneer in the backwoods and the inhabitant of a shanty, up to the epoch of his career, when he becomes the owner . . . of a comfortable house and well-cleared farm, affording him the comforts and many of the luxuries of civilization, he is hardly competent to write on such a subject." The implication was clear: since Susanna had never reached the upper echelons of such an existence, she must be "incompetent." Both Agnes and Jane Strickland made Sam clean up his language, so that many of his merry hunting stories sound rather pompous. ("Jane . . . insisted on turning out everything that she considered vulgar," Susanna reported to her publisher Richard Bentley, after a conversation she had had with her brother. This had "shorn the work of its identity," she added smugly. "Rough Canadians don't use the fine language of an English drawing-room.") And Agnes put her own name on the title page twice, as both editor and the author of a short verse:

And when those toils rewarding,
Broad lands at length they'll claim,
They'll call the new possession
By some familiar name.

Those of Agnes's friends who read her brother's book would know that the good major was the owner of "broad lands" on the other side of the ocean. Unlike his sister, who had written about "painful experience in a distant land," Sam lived a thoroughly civilized life and was a credit to the Strickland name. Sam's book did well. *Bentley's Miscellany* liked the work's "rough, hearty, genuinely English tone." The *Spectator* thought its "Robinson Crusoe character" splendid.

In Belleville, Susanna was shocked by Agnes's stinging reproaches. "Could I have foreseen her reception of [the dedication]," Susanna wrote to Richard Bentley in London, "thousands would not have induced me to place it there. She has wounded my feelings so severely . . . that it is to me a perfect eye sore in front of my unfortunate book." Anger soon took the place of hurt. Susanna was furious that Agnes had dismissed *Roughing It in the Bush* in such a snobbish fashion. She thought Sam's book was pretentious and boring. "My brother is dreadfully ridiculed by the Canadian press by adopting that absurd Major." And she was outraged when Sam, on his return to Canada, boasted of his royalties. Susanna was a fighter, and she thought up a nasty little scheme to sabotage Agnes. She suggested to Richard Bentley that he find an author in England to write a biographical work entitled "The Memoirs of Royal Favourites." (Such a book would be direct competition for her sister's biographies. Bentley, who was in the curious position of being both Sam's and Susanna's publisher, did not take up the suggestion.)

Susanna was particularly incensed because Agnes, she suspected, had exerted her influence over many of the London reviewers. "Hers is a *ready* and a *clever* pen," she wrote to Bentley. "It is more than probable, that to her, both my brother and I, are indebted, he for the good, I for the bad reviews of our respective works." Most of the reviews of *Roughing It in the*

Bush in London's influential literary papers were in fact very positive. But this was the first time since 1830, when Susanna had published her lengthy poem "Enthusiasm," that, instead of turning out formulaic pap, she had poured out her own heart and soul to her readers in England, and she was abnormally sensitive to criticism. The most negative London review was in the *Observer*, which took exception to Susanna's anti-Irish bias: "She describes the Irish emigrants in terms which a reflective writer would scarcely apply to a pack of hounds—as 'filthy beings sullying the purity of the air and water (of Grosse Ile)' . . . 'vicious, uneducated barbarians, far behind the wild man (Indian savage) in delicacy of feeling and natural courtesy.'" The reviewer pointed out that it was thanks to Susanna's Irish servants, particularly John Monaghan and Jenny, that the Moodies survived the bush. However, the reviewer added that *Roughing It in the Bush* was "one of the most valuable books hitherto published on that ever-novel, and always interesting subject, the customs and manners of large classes of people."

For Susanna, ten good reviews could not heal the hurt of one snarky comment. She was particularly upset because the London *Observer's* review was reprinted in the Montreal *Pilot* in March 1852. Moreover, once copies of *Roughing It in the Bush* started to arrive in Canada, Susanna found she had touched sensitive nerves in a young and self-conscious literary community, in which writers had first-hand knowledge of the bush. Charles Lindsey, editor of the *Examiner* and son-in-law of William Lyon Mackenzie, went after her for putting on airs. He called her "An ape of the aristocracy. Too poor to lie on a sofa and too proud to work for her bread." Such a glib quip was hardly fair, and Susanna pretended to laugh it off. "I can bear the castigation," she assured friends. Another reviewer in the *United Empire* accused her of penning "an unfaithful portrait of a settler's life"; she had either "greatly overrated her sufferings in the bush, or . . . very bad management must have occasioned them." This reviewer pointed out that, by colonial standards, the Moodies were well off: they had arrived in Canada with enough money to buy a cleared farm; they had received a handsome legacy; and they had benefited from both John's commission and then his salary as a captain in the militia. All these reviews, and their disparaging comments, left a nasty taste in Susanna's mouth. She convinced herself that Canadians hated her. "Will they ever forgive me for writing *Roughing It?*" she wrote Bentley. "They know that it was the truth, but have I not been a mark for every vulgar editor of a village journal, through the length and breadth of the land to hurl a stone at, and point out as the enemy of Canada?"

Good reviews in three Toronto newspapers—the *Globe,* the *British Colonist,* and the *Anglo-American Magazine*—did not calm her down or alter her view that Canadians were "vindictive, treacherous and dishonest. They always impute to your words and actions the worst motives, and no abuse is too coarse to express in their public journals." To outsiders, Susanna seemed cool and self-possessed, but in private she could be thin-skinned and unsure of herself. The bad reviews and Agnes's anger triggered all the insecurities of her childhood, when she had felt unloved by her father and sisters. As usual, she now turned to John for support, and as usual, John was there for her. Whatever the trials of living in Canada, Susanna's happy marriage was a source of strength. She acknowledged this in a touching letter to her publisher: "As a wife and mother, I have been so blessed, that one day spent in the company of my dear white-haired husband, is worth all the joys and sorrows of those sad years of home."

Blessed as a wife she might be. But she was not so blessed as a mother. Just when Susanna was feeling most vulnerable, she was finding that she could not look to her own children for much support.

The first of the Moodie offspring to cause problems was Agnes, the delicate and willful second daughter. Agnes and Susanna had had a difficult relationship since Agnes was six, when she was farmed out to live with Mary Hague in Peterborough during Susanna's final months in the bush. When the Moodies were at last ready to move to Belleville, Mary had not wanted to give the little girl back. She and Aggie adored each other, and Aggie had screamed resentfully when she was reunited with her own family. Susanna described Agnes as "lively and volatile" (which makes her sound suspiciously like Susanna herself) and felt that the Hagues, however well-meaning, had spoiled Agnes. She criticized her daughter for being selfish and obsessed with her own good looks.

The constant fault-finding drove Agnes into the arms of her beau, a charming Toronto lawyer named Charles Fitzgibbon, whom she insisted on marrying in 1850 when she was only seventeen. Charlie and Agnes made a handsome pair: she was the daughter of a famous author and he was the son of Colonel James Fitzgibbon, a hero of both the War of 1812 and the Rebellion of 1837. Susanna kept telling her daughter that her precious Charlie was a gambler who would throw all his money away, but Aggie ignored her and was pregnant soon after the wedding. Susanna foresaw trouble.

Susanna got on better with her eldest daughter. Katie was a sensible, although rather humourless girl who was her father's favourite and who had done more than her share of housework and childcare for her mother. But both the older boys, Dunbar and Donald, were starting to exasperate their parents with their lackadaisical attitudes. Neither showed any great ambition to make his own way in the world and help Susanna and John. Only Robert, the youngest child, who had never known the hardships of the bush, could still bring a sparkle to Susanna's eyes.

At the same time, the Moodies were once again finding the wolf at the door. John's income as sheriff was falling, largely because of the hostility of Belleville's Tory lawyers. And Susanna's main source of income in Canada had disappeared with the collapse of John Lovell's *Literary Garland* in 1851.

Perhaps it was all these worries, alongside the stress of her row with Agnes, that caused Susanna's descent into serious illness for much of 1852. Two physicians were called in, which meant heavy medical bills. They recommended a recuperative boat trip to Toronto (where she could visit Agnes) and to Niagara Falls. She underwent the voyage, but it didn't do her health much good—by November, she was "a sort of living skeleton," she told Bentley, "the very ghost of my former self." Nevertheless, it provided her with some new literary material with which she could fulfil her publisher's request for a sequel to *Roughing It in the Bush.*

Eager to capitalize on Susanna's success, Bentley had asked her for "an account of the present state of society in the colony." Eager to earn some money fast, Susanna supplied something rather different: a manuscript in which she cobbled together some reflections on Canada at mid-century, three pieces she had intended for *Roughing It* and a couple of character sketches she had already written. She decided to structure the book around her voyage to Niagara Falls, inserting the other pieces plus some new material along the way. The device didn't really work, the style (imperious rather than confessional) was less attractive than *Roughing It*, and the resulting book, *Life in the Clearings versus the Bush*, never came together. Nevertheless, it tells us a lot about both Susanna and Canada.

Susanna started off by defending herself from the criticisms of her first book. She went out of her way to talk about Canada's potential, particularly for honest labourers. "Canada has become almost as dear to me as my native land," she insisted, and the country "appears to us a giant for her years, and well worthy the most serious contemplation." She explained to readers that her references to Irish immigrants were "drawn with an *affectionate*, not a malignant hand," and that her comments on life in the bush were intended to warn "well-educated persons not to settle in localities for which they were unfitted by their *previous habits and education.*" She took a swipe at her sister Agnes, by quoting "An English lady" who told her to stop writing about Canada because "Who, in England, thinks anything of Canada?" Such an attitude, sniffed Susanna, "savoured not a little of arrogance, and still more of ignorance, in the fair writer who, being a woman of talent, should have known better."

Susanna was more careful in *Life in the Clearings* than she had been in *Roughing It*: she scarcely mentioned her own family, and she certainly didn't caricature her neighbours. Fame had put Susanna on the defensive, and made her a self-conscious commentator. She often ducked serious debate ("It requires the strong-thinking heart of man to anticipate events, and trace certain results from particular causes"), although she could not resist riding some of her favourite hobbyhorses, such as the absurdity of expensive mourning clothes and the importance of universal education.

The book gives us a glimpse of a middle-aged woman who had become a personality within the society that she was writing about, and while she was travelling, she was invited to tour some of the colony's most interesting sights and meet some of its most notable citizens. Had Agnes been presented with such an opportunity, she would immediately have suggested an introduction to the Earl of Elgin, then Governor General of British North America. If the same opportunity had been offered to Catharine, she would have been thrilled to meet a learned Victorian botanist at a university who might help her identify the flora of the Rice Lake Plains. But Susanna's choice was characteristically ornery. She chose to visit Toronto's Provincial Lunatic Asylum, whose inmates during this period were put on show like animals in a zoo. And she chose to write about an individual with no aristocratic or intellectual significance, who was nevertheless of enthralling interest to a student of human nature. She devoted a whole chapter of *Life in the Clearings* to one of the most notorious women in nineteenth-century Canada, Grace Marks.

Grace was a young Irishwoman who had been convicted, along with a male accomplice, of murdering her employer, a gentleman called Thomas Kinnear, and his housekeeper Nancy Montgomery. Susanna first encountered Grace Marks in 1849 at Kingston Penitentiary—a "house of woe and crime," as she called it. She described with gruesome delight the brutality of the crime in which Grace had been involved. Kinnear (or Captain Kinnaird as Susanna erroneously called him) had been shot at point-blank range, and Nancy Montgomery ("Hannah" in Susanna's account) was felled with an axe. Grace's accomplice had wielded the weapons of murder, but Grace was convicted of egging him on. At Kingston, Susanna was struck by the dramatic contrast between the savage murder and Grace's good looks: "Her complexion is fair, and must, before the touch of hopeless sorrow paled it, have been very brilliant. Her eyes are a bright blue, her hair auburn, and her face would be rather handsome were it not for the long curved chin, which gives, as it always does to most persons who have this facial defect, a cunning, cruel expression." When the penitentiary's matron introduced Susanna to Grace Marks, the young convict must have found the intense stare of the self-assured, middle-aged author quite unnerving. For her part, Susanna watched the young woman quail before her penetrating gaze: "Grace Marks glances at you with a sidelong stealthy look; her eye never meets yours, and after a furtive regard, it invariably bends its gaze upon the ground."

Three years later, on her way home from Niagara Falls, Susanna was shown around Toronto's Lunatic Asylum and she made a special point of seeking out Grace, who had recently arrived there because "the fearful hauntings of her brain had terminated in madness." Grace now presented the author with an even more enthralling image. She was "no longer sad and despairing, but lighted up with the fire of insanity, and glowing with a hideous and fiend-like merriment." Susanna was mesmerized by this vision of monstrous beauty. As a writer, she longed to give narrative shape to what had happened to the young Irishwoman. She invented a few gruesome details to make the crime fit the Victorian taste for melodrama: Kinnear's body, according to her account, was cut into quarters by the guilty duo. And she decided that Grace's madness had a redemptive purpose: it was a punishment inflicted by God, who would not let the "unhappy girl" forget the horrible bloodshot eyes of her victim. "When will the long horror of her punishment and remorse be over?" she asked with portentous gravity. "When will she sit at the feet of Jesus, clothed with the unsullied garments of his righteousness, the stain of blood washed from her hand, and her soul redeemed, and pardoned?"

Roughing It in the Bush and *Life in the Clearings versus the Bush* are the two books for which Susanna Moodie is best remembered. However, she published a further four books, all novels, in the early 1850s. In 1853, the same year as *Life in the Clearings* appeared, Bentley brought out *Mark Hurdlestone*. The following year, *Flora Lyndsay, or Passages in an Eventful Life* and *Matrimonial Speculations* appeared. In 1856, came *The Moncktons*. Versions of these works had first appeared in the *Literary Garland*, and most of them were old-fashioned Gothic romances. Susanna's impressive output in these years was prompted by simple need. Her agreement with Richard Bentley was for an initial payment for each of her books, plus a half-share of the profits. To her chagrin, none of the later books did as well as *Roughing It*, and her income quickly dropped off. "I begin to feel a mortifying certainty that my style does not suit the generality of readers," she confessed to Bentley. "It belongs like me to *the past*."

She was right: her London reviews were increasingly crabby. One went so far as to say that the story and characters in *The Moncktons* "appear to have been brought out of a dusty toy-box." The comment unnerved Susanna, who had been struggling to stay abreast of literary fashions. Sometimes she and John borrowed from their wealthier friends the latest works by British authors such as Dickens, Thackeray, Tennyson and Macaulay, or American authors such as Longfellow and Emerson; sometimes Bentley sent them some titles. And there were always Mr. Duff and Mr. Harrison, the two booksellers on Belleville's Front Street, who had regular shipments from London and New York. But British fiction in the mid-nineteenth century reflected a society entirely foreign to someone who had left Britain before Victoria ascended the throne. By mid-century, British writers were tracking a society in flux, with tension between town and country and between rich and poor. The fiction teemed with types and plots unknown to Regency era writers: *nouveau riche* factory owners, embattled aristocrats, scheming politicians, ambitious women and the pathetic victims of industrialization. The great Victorian novels were written with an intellectual slant very different from that of Susanna's flowery tales, featuring stock heroes and fainting ladies. Dickens's *Oliver Twist* and *Bleak House* and Thackeray's *Pendennis* and *Vanity Fair* (all of which Susanna read hot off the press) included not only the social comedy familiar from Jane Austen's novels but also a steady flow of ironic and moral comment. Susanna was happy enough to make such comments in her non-fiction work (a little too happy, if truth be told: parts of *Life in the Clearings* read like a church tract), but she had neither the skill nor the confidence to incorporate her own ideas into the conventional plots of her fictional works.

By the time that *The Moncktons* appeared, Susanna felt less confidence in herself as a writer than she had felt since she'd arrived in Canada. She didn't belong anywhere. English critics regarded her work as passé; Canadians, she felt, had rejected her. She was an outsider in both her native and her adopted lands, and she was angered by what she perceived as non-stop criticism. Only John could always cheer her up and make her feel both talented and lovable. When they were parted, Susanna was unsettled and miserable. John took a trip into the United States in 1856, and Susanna wrote to Catharine: "Time lengthens into ages while he is away. Will age never diminish my love for this man . . . he is as dear to me after five and twenty years of intercourse as he was when we first met. The kind darling sent me a beautiful gold locket and chain containing a capital likeness of himself. You would laugh to see me regarding that white bearded face with the devotion of old times. The old romance of my nature is not quite dead. The poetry of life still lingers about my heart."

Despite sales in the United States, Susanna's writing income continued to shrink. Susanna could expect no help from home. "I never hear from Reydon now," she told her publisher. "They have ignored me and my books." The rift with Agnes was still not mended, and the only news that Susanna got was via Catharine.

Years later, after Agnes's death in 1874, Susanna's and Catharine's sister Sarah—the only non-author among the six Strickland sisters—wrote to Susanna's daughter Katie Vickers to explain the lengthy gap in correspondence during the 1850s between Susanna and her English sisters. "The publication of that disgusting book *Roughing It in the Bush* made the very name of Canada hateful to us all," she recalled. "We had always striven hard to keep up the respectability of the family in spite of loss of property, and it was very mortifying to have a book like that going the round of some vulgar upstarts. . . .You cannot imagine how vexed and mortified my dear sister Agnes was, and at the time when she was at the very height of her fame to have passages from that book commented upon and ill-natured remarks made by people who were envious of her great fame. This will in a slight degree give you some idea of the state of things, and explain the backwardness of much correspondence."

Chapter 14

Good Advice

Catharine hated finding herself caught in the middle of the row between two angry, sharp-tongued sisters. By nature a peacemaker, she herself would do anything to avoid confrontation. She felt especially threatened by this particular family rift because she depended so much on both Agnes and Susanna.

John and Susanna Moodie were Catharine's closest relatives in Canada—her only relatives while her brother Sam was wife-hunting in Suffolk. The two sisters wrote to each other on their birthdays, and they traded children's clothes, suggestions for herbal cures and items that arrived in the care packages from England. Her link with Susanna was a crucial psychological prop to Catharine. Of course, Catharine had other friends, particularly Frances Stewart and her daughter Ellen Dunlop, in Peterborough. They provided the day-to-day conversational intimacy that a talkative and outgoing woman like Catharine appreciated. They wrote to Catharine frequently, and Frances often sent a few dollars when Catharine was desperate. Mindful of the destruction Susanna's pen had wrought, Catharine confided to Ellen in a letter her relief that, "I have written nothing which my children need regret to have my name attached to, or the dear friends who have ever taken so kindly an interest in my career read with pain."

But Susanna was the person that Catharine turned to in a crisis. In 1852, the bailiffs once again knocked at the Traills' door, looking for payment of outstanding debts. Thomas was by now far too enmeshed in despair to cope, and since he had never talked about business affairs with his wife, Catharine felt equally helpless. She had no idea what the court was allowed to claim. Could the bailiffs seize the flour and pork in her larder? Could they carry off the crops that were still in the ground but had already been sold to the neighbour? Did the Traills have any say in the value of the items that would go into a bankruptcy sale—Thomas's gold watch, the kitchen stove, the gun that Thomas had carried in '37, his books? She wrote a frantic letter to her sister describing her predicament. "I have been vainly waiting and hopelessly hoping to go down to Belleville," she told Susanna. "I have many questions to put to Moodie which would possibly save me some embarrassment and blunders . . . so very desiring [am] I of being with you even for two days [that] I would let no obstacle stand in the [way] of it as I think it might be of great service to us in many ways beside the great comfort to me of seeing you."

This particular crisis was averted, but by mid-century, clearly the tables were turned between the two sisters. Twenty years earlier in the colony's backwoods, Catharine had been the strong, sunny-tempered elder sister who reassured and comforted her sibling. Now it was Susanna, living in a comfortable stone house in a prosperous town, who could offer a hand to her sister trapped (in Susanna's words) in a "cold comfortless house on the plains." Catharine's visits to Susanna were her only respite from worry. Being stuck at Oaklands throughout the long winter eroded her ability to sail through life with hope, resolution and perseverance. "During the cold weather I feel unable to write or stir myself. I appear to stagnate to become wrapped up in self, only thinking of the present ill and how to keep myself warm. . . . My dear husband is sadly depressed again. This is the season of the year when one's creditors are sure to remember us if no one else does."

During the early years of the 1850s, travelling in winter meant that Catharine had to wait until packed snow made country roads passable, then cadge a ride to Belleville on the horse-drawn sleigh of one of the Rice Lake merchants. In the summer, she endured bumpy, dusty rides in the stagecoaches that travelled from Rice Lake south to Cobourg, then east to Belleville. Thomas would be left in the care of Katie and Annie, his oldest daughters. But soon travel got a whole lot easier. In 1854, a perky little railroad called the C&P—the Cobourg and Peterborough Railway—made its inaugural run. It was one of a tangle of small rail-roads, badly financed but enthusiastically welcomed, that suddenly sprouted throughout the more settled regions of British North America. From then on, if Catharine wanted to visit Susanna, she could take the train south from Harwood, on the south shore of Rice Lake, to Cobourg, and then travel on to Belleville by either the Grand Trunk Line

The three-mile trestle bridge over Rice Lake, an over-ambitious project
of the Cobourg and Peterborough Railway, opened in 1854.

or by stagecoach. This cut down her travelling time by at least a day. To visit Frances Stewart and her daughter Ellen Dunlop in Peterborough, she had the excitement of crossing the C&P's ambitious causeway and trestle bridge over the three-mile width of Rice Lake to the Indian reserve of Hiawatha on the north shore. When the bridge was opened in December 1854, one thousand Cobourg citizens enjoyed a free fifteen-mile-an-hour trip over the thirty miles of track to Peterborough. Unfortunately, its builders had underestimated the impact of winter weather on the flimsy structure: by 1860, the trestle would become too rickety for use.

The railroads made a huge difference to everybody's lives. Travel became relatively comfortable. The coaches—with their padded seats, stoves and kerosene lamps—were a vast improvement over stagecoaches jolting over muddy roads, or steamers tossed about by lake storms. The poignant wail of the train's whistle and the clickety-click of steel wheels on rails knitted together the scattered settlements and isolated farms of Upper Canada. Catharine knew the C&P would benefit the backwoods townships and was glad to reach Belleville more easily. However, she resented the clamour, dirt and destruction of the wilderness that they created. "As a lover of the picturesque," she admitted, "I must confess that I have a great dislike of railroads."

Susanna had none of Catharine's reservations; she embraced progress. Canada's first railway artery was the Grand Trunk, reaching from Montreal to Sarnia. When it opened its loop line through Belleville in 1856, connecting the wharves with the main Toronto line, she was thrilled. "I never saw a Locomotive engine at work before," she reported to Richard Bentley. "The sight filled me with awe." From Belleville, Susanna could now reach either Toronto or Montreal within a few hours. One of the greatest excitements in her life was the train trip she took with John to Portland, Maine, the following year. "My first visit to the sea, after an absence of five and twenty years," she recorded. "The dear, old familiar sea, by whose side I had been bred and born, with whose every tone and phase I was familiar in my English days. How my heart sprang to meet it." The "iron horse," as she called the GTR locomotive, had enabled her to unlace her shabby black leather boots and dip her toes in the ocean that lay between her and "home."

Catharine's visits to Belleville during this period allowed her to forget the stress of life in Oaklands and enjoy diversions she could only dream of when she was stuck there. In winter, she could walk down Front Street, peering into hardware stores, boot stores and dry goods stores. She might finger the new novels from London and New York in Harrison's Bookstore, admire the latest design of stoves at the shop of Thomas Linklater the ironmonger or buy patent medicines and flower

Before the arrival of the railroad, Belleville's wharves were a centre of thriving commerce. Three-masted schooners criss-crossed Lake Ontario.

seeds at Chandler's drugstore. She and Susanna would go for sleigh rides over the frozen surface of the Bay of Quinte, and Catharine would remind herself that winter was extraordinarily beautiful as well as savage. "The Bay is a solid plain just now," Susanna wrote to her publisher one February, "traversed in all directions by sleighs and pedestrians. It is so safe after these iron frosts, that you quite forget the waters imprisoned beneath the coat of snow that covers them. . . . Nature [is] dressed in a rich tissue of white and silver, and every twig enwreathed with pearls and diamonds . . . the frost King works such miracles, and the sun lights up his doings with such a glory of dazzling brightness."

In the spring, Catharine could wander down to the new stone wharves, and watch steamers and double-masted schooners jostle for a mooring. If she felt so inclined, she could even join her brother-in-law and sister at one of the evening parties that had lately become so fashionable. As Belleville's population doubled and its wealth grew, the local bourgeoisie moved beyond the humdrum six o'clock supper of meat and potatoes that had been the custom when the Moodies first arrived there in 1840. By 1852, manners and habits aspired to the standards set in the drawing rooms of Edinburgh or London. "Evening parties [today] always include dancing and music, while cards are provided for those gentlemen who prefer whist to the society of ladies," Susanna had explained in *Life in the Clearings.* "The evening generally closes with a splendid supper. . . . The ladies are always served first, the gentlemen waiting upon them at supper; and they never sit down to the table, when the company is large, until after the ladies have returned to the drawing-room."

What Catharine most enjoyed, however, were the times during summer visits when she and Susanna, and as many friends and relatives as possible, set off for a picnic. Along the Bay of Quinte there were several pretty spots, only an hour's carriage ride from Belleville, where a convivial crowd could settle on the grass and admire the magnificent scenery. As the high blue sky of a Canadian summer's day arched above the picnickers, they could watch sailboats skim across the sparkling bay and look

Belleville's Victoria Park was a favourite picnic spot, from which families could watch sailing races or take the ferry to Prince Edward County.

out at Prince Edward County, across the water. The hampers of food must have taken poor Catharine's breath away: "hams, fowls, meat pies, cold joints of meat, and abundance of tarts and cakes, while the luxury of ice is conveyed in a blanket at the bottom of one of the boats," according to Susanna. The women would stroll about, picking flowers and fruits, while the gentlemen fished. Children would play tag along the shoreline; young men would set up the stumps for an informal game of cricket. Susanna and Catharine would sit together, as comfortable with each other as they had been twenty years earlier as pioneers in the bush.

The two stout matrons, both in their fifties, must have made an intriguing pair. They were unmistakably sisters: the broad Strickland brow and deep-set eyes were emphasized by the way each woman had scraped her hair back under a lace bonnet. Their accents were as crisply English as the day they'd left Suffolk, although their speech was peppered with the Scottish expressions and pronunciations picked up from their husbands. Their dress must often have occasioned comment, since each still had a few of Agnes's cast-off collars, shawls, sashes and parasols to liven up her outfit. Both were as alert to all the life around them as ever: Catharine rhapsodized about the blossoms of the "dear little Linnae Borealis" at the edge of the wood, while Susanna kept an amused eye on which of the young people were "sparking" or flirting.

A topic of conversation to which the sisters regularly returned was their children. As young mothers they had lived so close that they continued to regard each other's family as an extension of their own, and they shared each other's maternal delights and concerns. The Traill offspring remained a tight-knit group who adored their mother, although the open contempt that James and Harry, now tall young men, showed for their father upset Catharine. Resentful of the endless farm tasks they were expected to do, they were often surly and rude. Catharine appealed to Susanna to tell the boys to curb their "want of respectfulness and deference of manner." Catharine's two older daughters, Katie and Annie, had far more compassion for the old man. The Traill household expanded in 1855 when a nineteen-year-old emigrant, Clinton Atwood from Gloucestershire, arrived to board and learn farming. This meant more work for the women: "My dear girls are kept busy from morning till night and I can hardly keep the clothing in order for the four boys and Mr. Traill and now Clinton is added to wash iron and mend for as well," Catharine complained. But he and Annie were soon "walking out" together. A compulsive matchmaker, Catharine was torn between delight in the romance and apprehension that she might soon lose Annie, a mainstay of the household, who kept an eye on the two youngest boys, William and Walter. Catharine's youngest daughter, Mary, frequently stayed with her Aunt Moodie for long spells. Catharine fretted that when Mary came home, she would "feel the change from a house of great plenty and every comfort to ours which is not so. . . . How good my sister has been to my little one."

Susanna's house was undoubtedly more comfortable than Catharine's, but her family was less harmonious. There didn't seem to be any emotional glue to keep her five children close to home. Susanna's eldest son,

Dunbar, disappeared west to join the California gold rush. Her second son, Donald, a charmer with his father's *joie de vivre* whom Susanna adored, was costing his parents one hundred pounds a year (several thousand dollars in today's currency) because he had persuaded them to send him to the new medical school at McGill University. Rumours were already reaching Belleville that Donald was spending more time in the bars than the lecture halls. He lacked, in Susanna's eyes, "that energy which alone ensures success." And Susanna's dire predictions about Agnes Fitzgibbon's marriage had been fulfilled: by the time she was twenty-one, Agnes had three children, was expecting her fourth, and was constantly appealing to her parents for help. In 1856, Susanna thanked her publisher Richard Bentley profusely for his latest remittance: "It enabled me to help one very dear to me, in sickness and in sorrow, when I had no other means of doing so." Her relief was short-lived: Agnes's fourth baby died (probably of scarlet fever or meningitis) when it was four months old. "We bask for a few days in the warm sunshine of domestic happiness," reflected Susanna, "and awake one morning to find the shadow of death resting upon our own threshold." Ill health drove Agnes back to her parents' roof: she and her three children spent several weeks in Belleville so her mother could nurse her through sickness and depression.

There was further disruption in the Moodie household in 1855 when the Moodies' eldest daughter, Catherine, married a young businessman who had just moved from Belleville to Toronto. John Joseph Vickers ran his own delivery firm and was soon so successful that he could afford a well-built stone mansion, with separate servants' quarters, on Adelaide Street. A stolid, reliable man, Vickers was a support to his in-laws from the moment he entered the family. But like Agnes, Catherine Vickers was plagued by health problems: the doctor diagnosed chronic bronchitis. Such a condition, Susanna knew, was often confused with tuberculosis. The diagnosis "made me too anxious to think of any thing else," she wrote. And with Catherine's departure from Belleville, Susanna had lost the mainstay of *her* household. Only Robert remained at home.

There was another topic of conversation that was of equally compelling interest to the sisters: outlets for their writing. New magazines, dishonest publishers, literary trends, money-making subjects—Susanna and Catharine each knew that her sister was more helpful on these topics than anyone else in the colony. No other women they knew combined motherhood and authorship; none of their neighbours carved out time from family responsibilities to write articles and stories for publication. Each sister encouraged the other's ideas and commiserated with her disappointments. And Susanna kept Catharine up-to-date on some of the new English authors. Anybody overhearing Susanna's critical judgments would have found them irresistibly crisp. She declared Tennyson's poem *Maud* "a ridiculous rhapsody of affectation" and Longfellow's *Hiawatha* "the most readable absurdity."

But the sisterly and literary companionship between Catharine and Susanna faltered after the family row over *Roughing It in the Bush*. Catharine's enthusiasm for visits to the Moodies was tempered by the knowledge that Susanna would try to recruit her as an ally against Agnes. Since the publication of *Roughing It*, Agnes no longer deigned to write to "My dear Susan" and "Dearest Brother Moodie" as she had once addressed them. So as soon as Catharine arrived in Belleville, Susanna would pump her for news from Reydon Hall. The conflict of loyalties unsettled Catharine, who continued to rely heavily on the money and annual boxes of fabric, boots, clothing and books that Agnes sent. In 1854, Agnes had given her a muslin dress with blue-edged flounces, a cashmere jacket trimmed with military braid and a woollen petticoat. Catharine never dared tell her English sister how wildly inappropriate were some of the items that lay on the top of Reydon parcels—the long white gloves, the fichus of Honiton lace, the cravats for Agnes's Canadian nephews.

Catharine felt uncomfortable when Susanna criticized Agnes, because she herself was so eager for Agnes's help in London publishing circles. It was Agnes, after all, who had found her a publisher for *Canadian Crusoes,* and on whom she depended for news of reviews and sales of further magazine pieces. But Agnes's anger at Susanna had seeped into her relationship with Catharine, and there was a note of snippy irritation in some of her letters these days. When Catharine sent Agnes a manuscript of a children's story that she had written several years earlier, which took the form of a conversation between its subjects, Agnes's response was curt: "No-one attends to books in dialogue."

Catharine already had a new project in mind that might capitalize on her success twenty years earlier with *The Backwoods of Canada.* She planned a how-to manual for female emigrants on "Canadian m[anage]ment and all such things, in cooking and making and baking, as are needful." She explained: "I want to supply a book that will give instruction in every branch that may be needed by the family of a new settler. A book such as I should have been glad to have had myself when I came out." When she first mentioned the idea to Agnes, her elder sister commented tartly, "Be sure you warn ladies not to make the worst of everything." Agnes was even snippier when Catharine sold some chapters to a Toronto periodical: "Nothing that is first published in Canada will sell in England. So never deceive yourself again with the idea that it will." Jane was more helpful: she sent Catharine some recipes for food and wine that Catharine could include ("I am a famous wine maker"); an English cookbook so Catharine could copy the format; and instructions on how to compile an index ("a plague to do, but easy when learned"). But Elizabeth Strickland turned down Catharine's request for editorial help so rudely that Agnes felt obliged to try and repair the damage. "I am very sorry Eliza has written so unkindly to you; but it is *her way,* and you must not let it distress your mind."

When Catharine had finished compiling her manual, she titled it "The female emigrant's guide, and hints on Canadian house-keeping" and shipped it off to England. Agnes knew Catharine depended on her, so she did try to place the manuscript with several London publishers. But as Agnes had anticipated, London publishers were not prepared to purchase a work to which they didn't have first rights. In any case, according to Agnes, they were all far too busy with the Crimean War, which had disrupted supplies of paper and preoccupied London's chattering classes from the moment it broke out in 1852. "Nothing sells now but newspapers or books on Russia, Turkey and this horrid mess," she wrote to Catharine in 1855.

Catharine knew all about the British campaign against Russia in the Crimean peninsula. After the mother country, alongside its allies France and Turkey, defeated the enemy at the battles of Balaclava and Inkerman, loyal Canadians, on the other side of the world, built bonfires and set off fireworks. But Agnes was right. This obsession with military glory was diverting publishers' attention from any other subjects. So Catharine decided to try her luck in Toronto, although the potential readership was far smaller and the handful of Toronto publishing houses that had sprung up were notorious cheapskates. They insisted that authors themselves finance the costs of publication by selling subscriptions to their friends and acquaintances, in the same way that magazines were financed. Catharine did her best. On one of her trips to Belleville, she signed up many of Susanna's circle as subscribers. In Peterborough, she persuaded both Ellen Dunlop and Frances Stewart not only to become subscribers themselves, but also to sell subscriptions to their neighbours. Armed with supporters, she made plans to go and butter up the Reverend Henry Payne Hope of Toronto, a recently established Toronto publisher who had used extracts from Catharine's manuscript in his monthly magazine. It was a major undertaking for Catharine to get as far as Toronto: "I have not the means either for supplying myself with decent outer clothes or to pay for a week's board and lodging at some decent house," she complained to Ellen Dunlop. Somehow, however, she did manage to talk the Reverend Payne Hope into publishing her complete manuscript. It appeared as *The Canadian Settler's Guide* in 1855.

The Canadian Settler's Guide fulfilled to the letter the purpose that Catharine had in mind. It contained instructions on how to make bread, carpets, candles, cheese, pumpkin pie, soap, maple sugar, bean soup, hemlock tea, dandelion coffee, treacle beer, potato starch, rag rugs, fabric dyes . . . amongst other items. Sam Strickland, who was always ready to help his sisters, allowed her to use the section from his book that described how to build a log cabin and organize a logging bee. Catharine gave advice on how to furnish a log house ("A stove large enough to cook food for a family of ten or twelve persons will cost from twenty to thirty dollars") and how to make an easy chair out of a common flour barrel. *The Guide* encompassed all Catharine's hard-won wisdom, and embodied the Strickland attitude to life. "In cases of emergency," she wrote in the chapter on house fires, "it is folly to fold one's hands and sit down to bewail in abject terror: it is better to be up and doing."

Once again, Catharine's book did well and Catharine did badly. The Reverend Mr. Hope was a smart businessman: he persuaded the minister of agriculture of the United Provinces to purchase six hundred copies of the guide, and the British government to make a large bulk purchase for distribution to encourage emigration. Soon copies of Catharine's guide were being passed around on the emigrant ships that continued to cross the Atlantic and dock at Grosse Ile. Catharine rapidly became the Martha Stewart of the backwoods, setting standards of taste and endurance that few other women could achieve. But Henry Payne Hope himself behaved in a thoroughly unchristian fashion. He printed more than ten editions of *The Canadian Settler's Guide*, and he used Catharine Parr Traill's name ruthlessly to promote his own career as an adviser on immigration. However, he withheld almost all the proceeds of her sales from the author.

Catharine struggled on through the 1850s, sending manuscripts to publishers in England, Scotland and Canada and receiving rejection slips for most of them. The scant rewards she received from her pen demoralized her. Little sympathy was forthcoming from her sisters in England, who were irritated with her constant pleas for help and still nursed their grudges against Susanna. But Susanna was always willing to offer consolation. She knew the uphill struggle that writers in Canada faced. "I can sympathise with you on the rejection of your ms. as Horace Bentley brought back mine," she wrote in a reassuring note to Catharine. "In these times, people want bread more than books. Authors have but a poor chance of success." She empathized with her fellow author when Catharine confided her fear that she had "no brains left" and that her writing talents were in decline. By 1858, Susanna herself was in the same fix: her own income from writing had dwindled away to nothing, John's job was getting more and more difficult, Aggie Fitzgibbon's husband was sick, and the Moodies had summoned Donald home from McGill. "Poor Aggie is penniless and I have not the means to help her, even with clothes of my own, for I am literally in rags—a misfortune which has seldom happened to me before," Susanna wrote to Catharine.

But during these years, Susanna had found a diversion from day-to-day anxiety. She had a new interest in her life, which provided her with the kind of catharsis that, when she was stuck in the bush, writing had once supplied. She and John were caught up in one of the nineteenth century's more bizarre trends and she was already using the language of the movement. "May better and brighter days be in store for us both," she wrote to Catharine, when they were both going through a difficult period. "And may we so improve the material present, that it may open the door of the dear spirit land to our weary longing souls."

Catharine would soon be swept along too in what her sister recognized as a "glorious madness."

Chapter 15

Rap, Rap, Who's There?

As Susanna Moodie sat at her writing desk on a September day in 1855, she heard her Irish servant Jane clattering out of the kitchen to answer a knock at the front door of the Moodies' house on Bridge Street. A few minutes later, Jane stuck her head into the drawing room and announced that a Miss Fox and her cousin were on the front step and would like a word with Mrs. Moodie. Jane had tried to tell them that Mrs. Moodie was busy right now, but Miss Fox had explained that she was leaving Upper Canada the next day and insisted that Jane at least let Mrs. Moodie know they were here.

Jane was astonished to see how fast Mrs. Moodie, who always discouraged social calls, threw down her quill pen and swept past her to greet her visitors. But Susanna had wanted to meet this afternoon's visitor for a long time. Kate Fox was one of the famous Fox sisters. She and her sister Maggie had ignited an extraordinary transcontinental flare of interest in "spirit adventures" in 1848 when they gave a public demonstration of their psychic abilities. By 1850, the new practice of spiritualism was already claiming an estimated two million adherents across North America—a fantastic figure considering that the total population was only twenty-five million. The Fox sisters and their followers claimed to be able to communicate with the spirits of the dead.

The spiritualist "religion" had begun when Maggie, then thirteen, and Kate, twelve, moved with their parents from Upper Canada to northern New York State. Strange sounds began to plague the family at night—raps and knockings for which there were no obvious causes. The noises always occurred around the girls. Neighbours crowded into the Foxes' cramped parlour to hear the mystery raps. Mrs. Fox insisted that it was a

The famous Fox sisters: Maggie, Kate and Leah Fox Fitch. Pretty Kate Fox (centre) was John Moodie's "spiritual muse."

"disembodied spirit" which would answer questions—three raps for "yes," silence for "no." Next, the "spirits" that the girls attracted extended their conversational range, thanks to an ingenious device invented by the girls' brother David that allowed the spirits to go through the alphabet. When the appropriate letter was reached, the spirits rapped. It was laborious, but it eventually yielded whole sentences.

Soon tales of the Fox girls' strange powers were being passed round at every general store, church hall and drinking house scattered through upstate New York. A public demonstration of their powers was staged in Rochester's splendid Corinthian Hall. Several of the city fathers were deeply sceptical, insisting that the raps must be made either by ventriloquism, a newfangled machine or lead balls sewn into the girls' hems. But each hypothesis was proved wrong, and nobody could furnish any proof that the girls were frauds. Their lucrative careers as spiritualist mediums were launched. They moved to New York City and conducted seances at P. T. Barnum's Hotel; participants paid one dollar each to attend. Big names such as Horace Greeley, editor of the *New York Tribune,* and the author James Fenimore Cooper became converts to their cause. Others quickly jumped on the bandwagon: clairvoyants, hypnotists, trance-speakers, levitationists, table-tappers.

Why did the spiritualist faith catch on with such fury? Why did an essentially mystical movement thrive during an age dedicated to scientific innovation and engineering triumphs—steam-driven ploughs and railways, gas lamps, suspension bridges and daguerreotypes? In London, the Great Exhibition of 1851 celebrated the glorious products of the Industrial Revolution: mass-produced lace, electroplated silverware, steel surgical implements, Lisle stockings—all housed in the Crystal Palace, a giant glass house. William Makepeace Thackeray described the show as "A noble awful great love-inspiring gooseflesh-bringing sight . . . the vastest and sublimest popular festival that the world has ever witnessed." Agnes and Elizabeth Strickland toured the Crystal Palace and were captivated with its glories. Yet in the midst of all this machine-made production, interest in the occult flourished.

Ironically, it was the ability of spiritualism's supporters to talk about phenomena like the "Rochester rappings" in quasi-scientific terms that gave the activity a bogus scientific credibility. At a time when scientists were investigating invisible sources of energy, spiritualists argued that the Fox sisters were harnessing another kind of unseen force, which could connect souls of this world to those that had already reached the next. Samuel Morse's invention of the electrical telegraph allowed thoughts to travel mysteriously from one location to another; perhaps the Foxes were operating a kind of spiritual telegraph.

Such a theory was particularly tenable in a deeply religious society that believed in a life after death, and nowhere was the population more prone to religious excess in the mid-nineteenth century than in the state of New York. It had experienced so many religious revivals (usually during the cold, dark days between Christmas and spring) that it was known as the "burned-over district"—burned over by Holy Rollers preaching fire-and-brimstone sermons to labourers, storekeepers and farmers assembled in lonely barns. Gothic horrors had an equal appeal for the educated: throughout the 1830s and 1840s, Edgar Allan Poe, master of the Gothic *frisson*, published stories in newspapers up and down the East Coast. The most chilling effects in Poe's tales centre on the blurring of the boundaries between life and death, the "fatal frontier." The paraphernalia of the Fox sisters' seances—mysterious rappings, darkened rooms, voices from beyond the grave—combined the notion of scientific inquiry with both a steadfast belief in the immortality of the soul and the fascination of the occult.

It didn't take long for interest in spiritualism to spill over the border. At the Belleville Mechanics' Institute, Susanna and John regularly heard lectures on "mesmerism, phrenology, biology, phonography, spiritual communication &tc.," according to Susanna. At first, John admitted, he thought that the "Rochester Knockings" were so "utterly ridiculous and puerile, that I only looked upon it as a money-making scheme." However, he started to wonder whether spiritualism's success demonstrated God's benevolent interest in their well-being: was it, as he put it, "a great instrument ordained by God to harmonize the human race"?

By the mid-1850s, newspapers were full of accounts of various phenomena, and there were at least a dozen periodicals devoted exclusively to the subject. Susanna was fascinated by the ghoulish mystery of it all. She pored over books like *Spiritualism*, published in 1853 by Judge John Edmonds and Dr. George T. Dexter of New York, which was supposedly the product of spirit-writing, employing Dr. Dexter as the medium. She also read *Experimental Investigations of the Spirit Manifestations, Demonstrating the Existence of Spirits and Their Communion with Mortals* by Robert Hare, a University of Pennsylvania chemist, and E.W. Capron's *Modern Spiritualism: Its Facts and Fanaticisms; its Consistencies and Contradictions*. As a girl, Susanna had believed in telepathy between friends. As a middle-aged woman, her strong religious faith made her respectful of man's spiritual potential, while her curiosity drove her to dig deeper into these mysterious goings-on. Whenever Catharine came to stay, Susanna discussed spiritualism with her in tones of both awe and amusement. "There is a capital article in the last *Albion* on table turning," she wrote to her sister in 1852. "I read it twice with infinite glee."

Catharine was not so sure about the whole business. Her God was a God of nature and beauty, who clothed pastures with flocks of sheep and made the valleys "stand so thick with grain that they laugh and sing." He was not a God who rocked dining-room tables or produced discordant rappings at the bidding of adolescent girls. But she did like the idea, as she told Ellen Dunlop in a letter, that "one of the offices of the released spirit [of someone who died] may be to watch over and care for those that were united to them by bonds of love or friendship during its sojourn upon earth."

Susanna had been introduced to Kate Fox on the streets of Belleville in the summer of 1854, when Kate Fox (then living in New York City) was visiting her oldest sister Elizabeth Ousterhoust in the nearby village of Consecon. On that occasion, Susanna recalled, she was "much charmed with her face and manners." The nineteen-year-old's pale oval face, waist-length dark hair and dark purple eyes beguiled the author.

"She is certainly a witch," Susanna wrote in a letter to Richard Bentley, "for you cannot help looking into the dreamy depths of those sweet violet eyes till you feel magnetised by them."

Kate Fox's visit to the Moodie cottage the following September provided Susanna's first opportunity to see the young woman's powers with her own eyes. After a few minutes of small talk in the dining room, Miss Fox asked if Susanna would like to hear some rappings. Susanna replied that she would: "Very much indeed, as it would confirm or do away with my doubts." So Kate Fox closed her eyes and asked the spirits if they would communicate with Mrs. Moodie. Straightaway, there were three loud raps on the table. "In *spirit language*," Susanna later wrote to Bentley, this meant yes. "I was fairly introduced to these mysterious visitors."

Miss Fox told Susanna to write a list of friends, some of whom were dead and some alive. The medium turned her back on Susanna as the latter wrote, then told her hostess to run her pen slowly down the list. Every time Susanna's pen lingered on a dead friend, the spirits would rap five times; for a living friend, they would rap three times. "I inwardly smiled at this," Susanna later wrote to Richard Bentley. "Yet strange to say, they never once missed." Next, Susanna wrote, "Why did you not keep your promise?" under the name of Anna Laural Harral. Anna was the daughter of Thomas Harral, who had published Susanna's work in *La Belle Assemblée*, and she had been Susanna's best friend before her early death in 1830. In their twenties, the two young women had promised each other that the one who died first should appear, if possible, to the other. Susanna was startled when the spirits immediately rapped out, "I have often tried to make my presence known to you." Susanna then asked the spirit to spell out its name. It was instantly done. "Perhaps no one but myself on the whole American continent knew that such a person had ever existed," she wrote.

Susanna was shaken by these revelations, but her guard was still up. So Miss Fox put the spirits to work in different ways. First, Susanna felt a table vibrate under her hands as if it had a life of its own. Then, at Kate Fox's suggestion, she stood by a door in such a way that she could see both its sides, and felt similar vibrations in the door. Miss Fox took Susanna out to the garden, where a few Michaelmas daisies still glowed mauve in the late afternoon light. Susanna felt strange vibrations under her feet, in the stone path and in the earth. "Are you still unbelieving?" the medium inquired. Susanna was torn between her eagerness to believe and intelligent scepticism. "I think these knocks are made by your spirit and not by the dead," she finally told her visitor. Kate Fox was determined to convince this well-known Canadian writer, who could be such a useful supporter. "You attribute more power to me than I possess," she insisted. "Would you believe if you heard that piano, closed as it is, play a tune?" The piano was not played by invisible fingers that afternoon. But Susanna convinced Kate Fox to postpone her trip and come back for the evening two days later, when John would be present.

To a casual observer, it appeared to be a charming scene of mid-Victorian domesticity: the oil lamp on top of the upright piano glowed, and Kate Fox's long dark hair glinted in its light, while Susanna's eyes sparkled with interest. Jane, the maid, stood demurely by the door, in case she was needed. John Moodie picked up his flute, and suddenly, while Susanna and Kate were standing by the piano's closed lid, they heard its strings play the accompanying melody. "Now it is certain that she could not have got within the case of the piano," Susanna mused.

When John stopped playing, the piano notes softly died away. John and Susanna looked at each other with wonder. Jane was open-mouthed. John turned to the slim young woman between them and asked the spirits to tell him what was engraved on the inside of a mourning ring, enclosing a curl of his grandmother's hair, that he always wore. As Kate stood gracefully listening, they all heard the spirits' obedient raps. The number of raps correctly identified the dates of his grandmother's birth and death. John himself had to take the ring off to check the spirits' accuracy, since he had forgotten the dates himself. "I thought I would puzzle them," Susanna later wrote to Bentley, "and asked for them to rap out my father's name, [and] the date of his birth and death." She thought it was a trick question because there were so many eights in the answer: Thomas Strickland had been born on December 8 and died on May 18, 1818. Without a pause the spirits rapped out the right name, dates and even the cause of death.

Susanna was intrigued—but unconvinced. Perhaps she suspected that Kate Fox had either been lucky or had been able to pick up clues to the correct answers from her audience's body language. Perhaps the answers given by the spirits were more open to interpretation than Susanna's account, in her letter to her publisher, suggested. Susanna rationalized the phenomenon by deciding that Kate Fox was simply a clairvoyant. She certainly didn't think her parlour tricks had much to do with Christianity. A few weeks later, she discovered how to produce raps and knockings identical to those that Kate had produced: "I can make the same raps, with my great toes, ancles [*sic*], wrist joints and elbows." Her maid Jane, who had watched Kate Fox carefully, turned out to be an even more effective rapper: "she exceeds me in the loudness of these noises."

Much as she might have liked to, Susanna couldn't tell her sisters in England about these fascinating developments; this was only a couple of years after the publication of *Roughing It*, and the British Stricklands were still treating Susanna as a pariah. Had she written to her sister Eliza, though, she would have found a kindred spirit. Eliza, like Susanna, was swept up in the greatest fad of the century. One summer, when she and Agnes were in Paris researching French queens, Eliza had spent her evenings attending seances while Agnes hobnobbed with the well-born. Eliza had watched a Parisian mesmerist hypnotize people on trains, in public gardens and in churches. On her return to London, Eliza had become convinced of the validity of spiritualism when she was put into a trance during a seance. Even Agnes would not have turned up her nose at the Moodies' new recreation: her beloved Queen Victoria had enjoyed a demonstration of clairvoyance at Osborne House and presented a gold watch to the medium, Georgiana Eagle.

Susanna knew nothing of this. Instead, she turned to her publisher in London. "Can such a thing as witchcraft really exist?" she wrote to Bentley. "Or possession by evil spirits? I am bewildered and know not what to answer." She continued her reading, and she was particularly impressed by *The Healing of Nations,* written under "divine inspiration" by the trance medium Charles Linton, and with an introduction by no less an authority than Nathaniel Tallmadge, a former U.S. senator and governor of the state of Wisconsin. Most of the book was taken up with generic Christian proverbs and homilies. "I am no friend to spiritualism, but I cannot doubt for a moment the truth of this wonderful book," she told Bentley.

While Susanna maintained a cautious distance, John Moodie rushed into this new adventure with characteristic impetuousness—he had swallowed spiritualism hook, line and sinker. John regularly attended seances at the homes of various distinguished Belleville citizens, including those of their neighbour J.W. Tate, a railroad engineer, Mayor John O'Hare and Benjamin Fairfield Davy, a Belleville grain merchant and former mayor. In the brick mansions along Bridge Street East and Queen Street, behind heavy velvet curtains, wealthy couples like the Davys and the O'Hares and their friends would sit solemnly on straight-backed chairs, with their hands flat on the polished surface of solid wooden dining tables. The host or hostess would lower the flames of the gas lamps and, as participants peered nervously at the shadows, instruct a medium to call spirits from the vasty deep.

Mrs. Davy—in John's view "a very intelligent and sincere woman"—managed long conversations with everybody's deceased relatives, while her living guests sat around a table that rocked backward and forward violently. Through her agency, John heard from nearly every long lost relative he could remember—his father, his mother, a dead brother—and some of Susanna's family, too. Miraculously, the spirit of Agnes Strickland appeared, just at the point when relations between his wife and her English sisters were at their worst, and asked for Susanna's forgiveness for the way that she had treated her. The fact that Agnes was alive on the other side of the Atlantic rather than dead and on the other side of the fatal frontier didn't faze John. He admitted that some of the spirits' communications to him were "absolutely and uselessly false," but such minor details didn't puncture his faith for an instant. Even the false communications, he insisted, exhibited "extraordinary intelligence and knowledge of matters only known to myself."

John also visited the Fox family in New York and took part in a seance in which a spirit tried to unbutton his boot straps. In 1857, he bought himself a large album bound in blue leather, labelled it "Spiritualist Album" in gold block letters and began to record occult adventures in Belleville and Toronto. He constructed devices to facilitate spiritwriting. He sent lengthy accounts of his activities to the *Spiritual Telegraph*, a weekly periodical published in New York. The only disappointing aspect of the regular spiritualist sessions at the Davys' was that the spirits told him he could not become a medium himself because, "You are too energetic."

John's unbridled enthusiasm for knockings and table-turnings led to arguments with his wife. Susanna remained scornful of darkened-room mumbo-jumbo; it offended her respect for reason and restraint. She also shared much of Catharine's uneasiness about an activity which suggested that God was a sort of celestial doorman, rather than a primal creative force. And she must have found the exchange of family secrets which it often involved most upsetting—she didn't want the whole of Belleville knowing about her row with Agnes, for instance. When she heard that the spirit of a notorious local philanderer had appeared at a tea and table-moving party soon after his death, she snapped that she was surprised he had even got as far as heaven, since "he had a number of illegitimate children while in this world." While John watched tables rock and listened to spirits moan on Queen Street, Susanna remained in the stone cottage on the wrong side of town, disgruntled by her husband's absence. She had always been able to handle physical distance between them, but the psychological separation from her beloved John unnerved her.

Then, early in 1858, an event occurred that dissolved even Susanna's scepticism. She and John had had "several sharp mental conflicts . . . which grieved me much," she explained to Richard Bentley. One evening when John strode off to yet another seance, Susanna stomped upstairs, threw herself into the button-back chair in her bedroom and "wept very bitterly, over what I considered the unpardonable credulity of a man of his strong good sense. As I was sitting alone by a little table . . . I suddenly laid my right hand upon the table, and feeling very angry in my own mind at all spiritualists, I said tauntingly enough, 'If there be any truth in this doctrine let the so-called spirits move my hand against my will off from this table.' You would have laughed to have seen the determined energy with which I held my hand down to the table, expecting the moon that was then shining into the room to leave her bright path in the heavens as soon as that my hand should be lifted from that table. You may therefore guess my surprise, not to say terror, when my hand became paralyzed, and the fingers were slowly wrenched up from the table, and the whole hand lifted and laid down in my lap. Not dropped nor jerked suddenly, but brought forward, as if held in a strong grasp and placed there."

It is easy today (although perhaps too glib) to explain this phenomenon away as auto-suggestion, and to assume that Susanna's need to share John's beliefs and be reunited with her husband overwhelmed her doubts. But for a nineteenth-century woman, it could only have meant that there was a disembodied presence in the room that had grasped her hand. Susanna was shaken. She slowly rose and went downstairs into the empty dining room. She found the "Spiritoscope" that John had invented—a wood-and-brass contraption that allowed spirits to spell out words quickly. Up to then, she had always ridiculed the Spiritoscope and refused to touch it. Now, with nobody looking, she put her hands on it and asked, "Was it a spirit that lifted my hand?" The Spiritoscope spelled out, "Yes." Susanna asked, "What spirit?" The contraption spelled out "A friend," and then, "Thomas Harral." Susanna was amazed; she had no idea whether her old mentor was alive or dead. But soon, through the agency of the Spiritoscope, she was conversing with Harral, who, unknown to her, had died in 1853.

In subsequent nights, with a devoted John looking on, there were further exchanges with the disembodied Harral, and additional ones with another character from Susanna's past, "my dear friend Thomas Pringle, the abolitionist from whose house I was married," who had died in 1834. The spirit of Pringle apparently assured Susanna (quite erroneously, as it turned out) that she would never live to see the end of slavery. Soon Susanna was in regular communication with the spirits, who told her to trust in God. "God is a perfect Unity," a particularly enlightened spirit told her through John's busy little contraption. "The great circle and centre of existence. Death is but the returning wave of life flowing back to him. All created existence lives through and to Him, and no man lives for himself alone. He is a link in the chain of life which would be broken without his ministration."

The kind overtures of the two dead editors were part of a pattern: what Susanna found in the spirits' communications was usually what she wanted to hear. At a difficult time in her own life, it must have been a welcome sensation to be in contact with the two men who, thirty years earlier, had been her literary mentors—almost as good, indeed, as having an apology from Agnes. Now that she had overcome her suspicion of spiritualism, she embraced its message (as she interpreted it) that God is perfection, and that it is man's proper condition to move towards that perfection by struggling against limitations of reason, worldly pleasures and evil spirits. She also found herself very comfortable with a faith that didn't need an autocratic male cleric as its arbiter. As a woman who had rejected the Church of England in Suffolk, and been thrown out of the Congregationalist Church in Belleville, she enjoyed her seemingly direct line to heaven.

Catharine Parr Traill arrived for a visit while the Moodie Spiritoscope was working overtime. Being a more ingenuous woman than Susanna, and encouraged by her sister's arguments, she allowed herself to succumb to the spiritualist fervour. "My sister Mrs. Traill, is a very powerful Medium for these communications," Susanna remarked, "and gets them in foreign languages." But poor, long-suffering Catharine didn't have so much fun. Susanna recorded that "her spirits often abuse, and call her very ugly names." There was, however, one aspect of the occult that both women loved: it allowed them to talk to their dead children. The Moodies' son Johnnie, drowned fourteen years earlier, sent his father a message that, "I love him, and am ever at his side trying to overthrow the evil influence of bad men, who presumptuously deny the divinity of my Lord." For her part, Catharine was made happy, according to Susanna, "by the intercourse of her dear children, which has quite overcome her fears of death that she till lately entertained."

By now, John was chomping at the bit. Spiritualism was a very welcome distraction from financial worries and his mounting problems in the sheriff's office, and he yearned to get more involved. He wanted to be a medium through which messages were sent, rather than a passive recipient of the messages. In 1858, he visited New York City again and called on "my amiable friend, Kate Fox," with whom he had often discussed his enthusiasms. And his wish was granted. Speaking through Kate, his dead mother told him to be "faithful to your new vocation, and great Spirits will aid you." When he inquired as to what his new vocation would be, his mother told him that it was "Healing in every form."

Spiritualism had been linked to healing from its earliest days. In Europe in the late eighteenth century, followers of the Viennese physician Franz Anton Mesmer had claimed that they could cure patients of ailments ranging from blindness to rheumatism by controlling the flow of electrical energy through their bodies—which usually meant putting them into a trance. Once "mesmerism" arrived in the New World, where there was no medical establishment to authenticate its claims, it quickly became the subject of sensational demonstrations at fairs and carnivals. The charismatic preacher Henry Ward Beecher mesmerized his sister Harriet Beecher Stowe (the future author of *Uncle Tom's Cabin*) and threw her into delicious convulsions: "spasms and shocks of heat and prickly sensation ran all over me." The orgasmic overtones of this new touchy-feely therapy are unmistakable. Similar techniques rapidly became part of many spiritualists' arsenal as enthusiasm for spiritualism spread across the continent. Soon the young Victoria Woodhull, who would later scandalize America with her outspoken feminism and her candidacy for presidential office, was operating as a spiritual healer in Indianapolis. According to Theodore Tilton, her first biographer and third husband, "She straightened the feet of the lame; opened the ears of the deaf . . . she solved psychological problems; . . . she prophesied future events." Her technique, which involved gently stroking a sufferer's body and limbs with both hands to stimulate healing electrical energy, sounds remarkably like the "therapeutic touch" technique practised today. And she earned a staggering amount of money, approximately $100,000 in one year alone.

John Moodie embarked on his practice as a spiritual healer with some trepidation. The only advice that the spirits gave him was to be abstemious in his diet and refrain from drinking tea or coffee. He must have known all about "mesmeric passes" (perhaps from Kate Fox), because that was what he used in his first attempt. His guinea pig was his sister-in-law, Catharine Parr Trail, who had been complaining about pain in her knees resulting from gout that she thought she had inherited from her father. John made a few passes over her joints and down her lower legs. It must have been a little unsettling for both of them: Catharine would rarely have bared her knees, and John was not in the habit of stroking his sister-in-law's limbs. Catharine claimed instant relief from the pain— perhaps through the power of John's healing hands, perhaps through sheer embarrassment.

John was thrilled with the result. "This encouraged me to try my heal- ing powers in other cases," he wrote in the Spiritual Album, "and I have been successful beyond my most sanguine expectations." Catharine must have enjoyed the sensation of spiritual healing because she was soon back for more. John next relieved the rheumatism in her shoulder and arm by laying his left hand on her bare shoulder while holding her hand in his right. John healed a neighbour's chronic rheumatism by gentle manipu- lation of his arm, and cured his neuralgia and sore eyes through massag- ing his eye sockets. When his daughter Agnes Fitzgibbon arrived from Toronto with a streaming cold and congested lungs, he drew his hands "from her ears downward to her stomach, and passed them off outward several times. She felt as if warm water were running down one side of her lungs." She was better in no time. "I can hardly tell how many cases of bilious and nervous headache I have relieved by similar means, in a few minutes," John recorded with delight in his album.

What was going on? A large part of John's effectiveness as a healer was probably psychological: his subjects believed that he could cure them, and every success reinforced their belief. He himself acknowledged, in one of his lengthy letters to the *Spiritual Telegraph*, that faith was an essential ingredient. It is also likely that, by promoting drainage of the sinuses or the lymph system (in the neighbour with sore eyes, for instance), John was doing some good. John himself took his role as a healer very seriously: he recorded different techniques, homeopathic remedies and accounts of his activities in his Spiritual Album. Nevertheless, news that the sheriff spent his afternoons in darkened drawing rooms, "healing" some of the town's most respectable matrons, must have spread like wildfire through gossipy Belleville. It cannot have done John's reputation much good amongst the stony-faced Tory lawyers who met on the first Monday of every month at the Orange Lodge.

John's career as a spiritual healer didn't last long. Soon after it was launched, the sisters' interest in spiritualism began to nose-dive. Perhaps it was the local tittle-tattle. Perhaps it was because the claims of spiritualists were coming under increasingly rigorous scrutiny, and the pseudo-scientific claptrap became too much for Susanna's and Catharine's more mainstream, modest Christian faith. Most likely, it was because both sisters had more pressing issues in their lives: Catharine's household was already engulfed in disaster, and John Moodie's position as sheriff was being challenged. For whatever reason, Catharine decided that she had been "under some peculiar influence of Animal magnetism during my so-called medium state," and she summoned up "the mental courage to abandon all that sort of thing." Susanna simply turned her back on the mumbo-jumbo.

By the end of the 1850s, the Moodies had largely abandoned their spiritualist activities. John continued to keep up his album for a few months, but he didn't have the energy for frequent submissions to the *Spiritual Telegraph*, or the money for more trips to see sweet Kate Fox in New York. And his children, particularly his eldest daughter, ridiculed him for indulging in sorcery. Katie Vickers, now a member of Toronto's social establishment, disapproved of her elderly father's tactile healing activities. Several years later, she destroyed over fifty pages of John's Spiritual Album, including those (she explained) that dealt with her father's "homeopathic medical prescriptions . . . all of which my dear Father lived to see the fallacy of."

South of the border, spiritualism was rapidly falling out of fashion and its practice had become decidedly tacky. Some spirits turned out to be rather opinionated, radical folk. There were mediums who claimed that the spirits believed in free love; others who insisted that they endorsed votes for women; still others through whom the spirits lobbied for the abolition of slavery. With the outbreak of the Civil War in 1861, the mania for spiritualism disappeared. In Britain, Professor Michael Faraday subjected the movement to a barrage of withering contempt in the columns of the *Times*. The eminent scientist wrote that he was "aghast at the hold which the table-turning mania had gained on all classes of society, and at the loose thinking and presumptuous ignorance which the popular explanations revealed." He described experiments that showed that the movements of tables and the "rappings" could be produced by unconscious muscular pressures exerted by the sitters. The novelist Charles Dickens was equally caustic: "I have not the least belief in the awful unseen being available for evening parties at so much per night."

And in October 1888, before a sold-out audience at the New York Academy of Music, Maggie Fox publicly confessed that spiritualism, as far as she was concerned, had been nothing but a fraud from the start. She demonstrated that the mysterious "Rochester rappings" had been produced by an abnormality of her big toe, which she had developed through assiduous practice. Kate Fox, who was sitting in a box overlooking the stage, confirmed her sister's statements. Susanna Moodie had been right all those years earlier when she had divined the source of Kate Fox's rappings as the cracking of toe and ankle joints.

Chapter 16

Tottering Slowly On

A couple of hours after midnight on August 25, 1857, Catharine woke up and smelled smoke. Her stomach twisted with fear, and she pulled herself into a sitting position as she gathered her thoughts. Perhaps she was dreaming. Perhaps it was just the whiff of a bush fire a few miles away. But a second later, she heard an ominous crackle. She shook her husband, slumbering next to her. Her voice rising with panic, she told him to get up and wake their children, who were asleep on the floor above. Hurriedly, she swung her feet to the floor, groped for a shawl and felt for her moccasins with her feet. Oaklands was on fire. Catharine knew that an old log house with a shingle roof would burn like a tinderbox.

"I had barely time to awake the sleepers upstairs, and we got out a part of our bedding, wearing apparel, a few books, 3 chairs and 3 tables before the whole house was in a blaze," recorded Thomas in a journal he kept intermittently. "I am so thankful that all our lives were saved, particularly our dear Walter, whose room was full of smoke when he was called, that I hardly regret what is lost. Thanks to God for all his mercies."

The Traills watched the blaze from beyond the snake fence round the property, where they were out of reach of the searing heat. But as the flames finally subsided, the family made a pathetic sight. They stood amidst the stubble as the sun rose and illuminated the smouldering wreck of their home with the cool light of dawn. Relief that they had all survived evaporated when they realized what they had lost. Thomas's maps and prints, and all save a handful of his books, were gone; the first-edition novels of Sir Walter Scott that he had so carefully transported from home to home were now just a pile of ash. All the beds, chests and stools were charred fragments, and the cooking pots and pans were bent and blackened. Catharine had lost everything she had carefully preserved for winter: dried apples, herbs, bottled vegetables and fruit, maple sugar and syrup, wild rice, bags of flour. Most of their clothing was gone, as were their candlesticks, plates, cutlery, rag rugs and Catharine's carefully worked quilts. The Traills had lost all records of their family history: letters from England and Scotland, drafts of Catharine's published books, all the treasures—antlers, pressed flowers, fossils, squirrel skins, awkward drawings—that recorded the children's upbringing in the bush. The only batch of papers that Catharine had manage to rescue were her botanical notes on ferns, flowers, trees and shrubs.

The Traills were left worse off than when they had first arrived in the colony twenty-five years earlier: they were now both homeless and penniless. Friends and relatives came to their aid. Sam Strickland gave them ten pounds to replace household goods, and a cheque for twenty pounds arrived from Agnes for "My poor unlucky Catharine." For a few weeks, the whole family stayed at Thorndale, a nearby farmhouse in which Clinton Atwood, the young man from Gloucestershire, was now living. Catharine looked around for a new house. "I am very desirous to procure a home before the cold sets in as I cannot feel settled here," she told

Ellen Dunlop. But Catharine had no money with which to rent a decent property, and the Traills were forced to scatter around the region, dependent on the kindness of others. Thomas and Catharine went to stay with Sam Strickland at Lakefield. Kate, now twenty-one, and nineteen-year-old Annie, the two eldest daughters, were taken in by friends at Gore's Landing. Mary Traill, a sixteen-year-old with fragile health, was invited to stay with Ellen Dunlop. Catharine's eldest son, James, was now married: he and his wife Amelia took in thirteen-year-old William and nine-year-old Walter. Twenty-year-old Harry stayed on with Clinton Atwood.

For Catharine, the fire was simply another crisis that God would help them overcome. "We trusted in Him and were helped." She began to plan how they might restart their lives. "If we let our farm [land]," she wrote to Ellen, "we can live at a small expence and earn something in a quiet way by needle-work and knitting, pressing flowers and other matters." She discussed with her sister Susanna the idea of taking in a couple of boarders. But for Thomas Traill, the fire was the last straw. He tried to play his part in getting the family ship afloat again, appealing for help from his first wife's brother, in the Orkneys: "We were poor enough before but the fire has made us of course still poorer." As the winter of 1857–58 dragged on, however, he emerged less and less frequently from his bedroom. By now, both the sons he had left behind in Scotland had died. Thomas's health deteriorated; his cough became more and more pronounced. The following summer, Catharine moved her ailing husband to a cottage in the grounds of Frances Stewart's house, Auburn, on the outskirts of Peterborough. She nursed him devotedly, but Thomas had lost the will to live. He died on June 21, 1859.

Catharine had always loved her sweet, bewildered husband. She believed that it was her duty "as a wife, and now as a widow," as she wrote in her journal, "[to] bear testimony to my husband's worth. With some foreign eccentricities of manner, and some faults of nervous irritability of constitution, he was a true hearted loyal gentleman, faithful in deed and word—a kind & benevolent disposition, a loving father, husband and friend—a scholar and a true gentleman, whose virtues will be remembered long after his faults have been forgotten." Susanna too had always had a soft spot for her brother-in-law, who was so painfully unsuited for roughing it in the bush. But as we consider his career today, we can't help wondering: could Thomas Traill ever have made a happy immigrant? If he had been able to settle in Toronto in 1832, where he might have taught at the newly founded Upper Canada College, might he have found his niche in the colony? Perhaps. But during most of the last century, immigrants who relied solely on their learning and social position in Britain rarely did well in the New World. Those who thrived in British North America were men far more ruthless, ambitious and brave than "a scholar and true gentleman" like Thomas Traill.

During the anguished months between the Oaklands fire and Thomas's death, Susanna Moodie reached out to Catharine as much as she could. Catharine spent several weeks with the Moodies in early 1858. (Catharine's son James had now moved to Belleville, and he and his wife Amelia had a son—Catharine's first grandchild—in January). Susanna fussed over her elder sister in a quite uncharacteristic way, dosing her with wild cherry balsam because she had a cough and trying to keep her in bed when she had bronchitis. It was during this visit that John "healed" Catharine's rheumatism by laying his hand on her shoulder. Catharine did not mention her adventures in spiritual healing in her letter to her own daughter Mary, but she did write, "Your Aunt . . . is much concerned at my illness."

Susanna was probably glad to have her sister close, so she could confide her own concerns. John Moodie's long-running, corrosive and expensive battle with his Tory critics in Belleville was reaching a climax, and it did not augur well for the Moodie family.

For more than twenty years, Belleville's Tories (most of whom were active Orangemen) had made life difficult for John Dunbar Moodie, sheriff of Hastings County. In nineteenth-century Canada, the sheriff was responsible for collecting court-ordered debts on behalf of creditors. If for any reason the debtor did not pay, the unsatisfied creditor could sue the sheriff on the grounds that it was the sheriff's fault that the court action had failed. John's Tory critics, led by Thomas Parker (who still resented Moodie's appointment to the job he himself had wanted), had indulged in protracted "sheriff-baiting," suing John for non-collection of debts, but protecting themselves from his counter-suits with legal tactics. John's income was eroded by all his legal bills, incurred as he tried to defend himself from his enemies. The sheriff's prime source of income was drawn from the fines levied by the court, but John's income from this source had steadily fallen, because Parker and his friends made sure that most cases were settled in the lower courts, where John had no access to any fines levied. Susanna railed against the weasel tactics of lawyers: "They are a set of finished rascals, and swarm everywhere."

The struggle to do his job despite Thomas Parker and his ilk had aged John. By the time his brother-in-law Thomas Traill died, sixty-one-year-old John was a white-haired, limping old man. He had lost the military swagger of his youth; thanks to the accident with the pioneer harrow just before the 1837 uprising, and a knee injury he had sustained in a fall in 1845, he dragged his left leg as he walked. Although he still loved to laugh, an expression of permanent anxiety had settled on his ruddy face. Life was getting harder, not easier.

Hastings County covered a large area, and John found himself travelling farther and farther, in the bitter cold of winter and the furious heat of summer, in order to supervise the administration of justice and collect what little income he could. It all got too much for him in the mid-1850s. So he agreed with the former district court bailiff, Dunham Ockerman, that if Ockerman, as deputy sheriff, took on the "outdoor work" in outlying parts of the county, John would allow him half the fees he collected. John took Ockerman off to a lawyer to have the legality of the arrangement checked and a formal agreement signed.

John's enemies smelled blood. Although the appointment of a deputy sheriff was legal, the "farming of offices" was against the law. Judge Allan Ramsey Dougall, an Orangeman and another old adversary of

John's, watched Ockerman's conduct with eagle-eyed attention. As soon as he had enough evidence to prove Ockerman was acting with far too much independence to be described as a mere "deputy," Dougall pounced. In October 1859, four months after Thomas Traill's death, Dougall brought a formal court action against John for "the purpose of bringing before the Court of Queen's Bench the legality or otherwise of the proceedings of Mr. Sheriff Moodie in reference to his office." John was summoned to appear before the assizes in Belleville in December to answer the charges.

Susanna was convinced that the charges against her beloved husband would be dismissed, but she was wrong. The presiding magistrate at the Belleville Assizes ruled against John. In the spring of 1860, the case went to the Court of Queen's Bench in Toronto, which ruled that Moodie was technically guilty of infringing the statute regarding the farming of offices. But the whole issue of John's future as sheriff was left in a dreadful limbo. On the one hand, the Reformers who dominated the United Provinces government were reluctant to terminate John's appointment as sheriff. He had been a loyal, hard-working, honest sheriff, and Belleville's Orangemen were notorious for their vicious partisanship. On the other hand, the government was not prepared to come to his aid: they didn't want to offend Belleville's cabal of Tory lawyers. So the case was left hanging in a crossfire of appeals and petitions.

Susanna was stunned by this turn of events. She insisted to Catharine that John had the "sympathy of the whole county" against the "malignity of the men who have done this. . . . So do not grieve for me, my sister, my dear tried friend." She also realized that the case could drag on for months: "I wish it were over. . . . Uncertainty is always worse to bear than the pressures of sorrows known. When we know what we have to expect, the mind rises to meet the emergencies of the case, and we can mature plans for the future." The behaviour of their Belleville neighbours both enraged and scared her. Anger made her insist that she and John would turn their backs on Belleville as fast as possible if they lost the case: "I have no ties to bind me to Belleville, beyond the dear home that has sheltered us for so many years, and the trees I have with my own hands planted, and last, not least the graves of my dear boys." But this anger was a defence mechanism against a much more deep-seated emotion: fear. Susanna was worried about John: "The blow fell very severely, and I never saw him look so pale and worn." Susanna had just watched her strong, stalwart sister Catharine accommodate herself to widowhood, and she was terrified of facing the same prospect. By now, she knew that Catharine had an emotional stamina that she lacked.

John Moodie was not the only person to fall victim to the obstinate determination of members of the Orange Order in British North America. At the Order's annual parade on July 12, there were always Orange-Green brawls between Protestants and Catholics on Belleville's Front Street. "It appears a useless aggravation of an old national grievance to perpetuate the memory of the battle of the Boyne," Susanna had written indignantly in *Life in the Clearings.* Orangemen had also been central in the election rioting in Toronto in 1841 that left one man dead. Small wonder that Susanna insisted that the activities of the Orange Order "pollute with their moral leprosy the free institutions of the country." But in 1860, a few weeks after the Court of Queen's Bench in Toronto ruled against the sheriff of Hastings County, the Orangemen outdid themselves in a display of muscle. This time, the victim was none other than Edward, Prince of Wales, the nineteen-year-old heir to the British throne.

Prince Edward, eldest son of Queen Victoria, had arrived in the colony for the first ever royal overseas tour. One of his first public appearances was in Montreal, where he was to lay the last stone of one of the most splendid structures in the British Empire: the Victoria Bridge, which spanned the two-mile width of the St. Lawrence River and was named in honour of his mother. The bridge, designed by the great British engineer George Stephenson with an innovative construction of tubular girders, had taken almost five and a half years to complete and was the longest bridge in the world. On August 25, the slim young prince clambered onto a train pulled by a huge Grand Trunk Railway locomotive and was taken

One of the first steam engines (with a cow-catcher at the front) of the
Grand Trunk Railway. Canada's Railroad Era had arrived.

to the centre of the bridge to hammer into place the final rivet. He and
his entourage then clambered back into the train and returned to the
immense locomotive shed at Pointe St. Charles, where the City of
Montreal had laid on a luncheon for one thousand guests. "'God save the
Queen' was played as His Royal Highness entered, and when he was
seated the whole company sat down and fell to," reported *The Daily Globe*.
With the opening of this engineering masterpiece, the Prince of Wales
had inaugurated Canada's magnificent Railroad Era.

The Victoria Bridge was more than just an engineering triumph. Its
glorious opening ceremonies allowed the young, sprawling colony, with
its rapidly swelling population and fractious politics, to show itself off
to its future sovereign. For the first time in most of their careers, cabinet
ministers donned the British civil uniform designed for colonial officials.
It was a flattering costume that included a sword and navy jacket with
lashings of gold braid and facings. The *Globe* carped that John A.
Macdonald, joint premier (along with George-Etienne Cartier) of the
United Provinces, had no idea how to walk with a sword sheathed at his
side, and with his "devil-may-care air, managed to get his cocked hat

Ottawa's splendid Gothic Parliament Buildings in the 1860s, during construction.

stuck on one side . . . in a most ridiculous fashion." But none of those present at Montreal could be oblivious to a shared pride in the dignity and autonomy of their own government.

From Montreal the Prince of Wales proceeded to Ottawa, to lay the cornerstone of the new Parliament Buildings. Susanna was one of the few people in British North America to laud Queen Victoria's choice of the swampy lumber town as the new capital, instead of either Toronto or Montreal. "A very few years will make Ottawa worthy of the royal favour. In natural beauty it far surpasses all its more wealthy rivals. . . . The Queen showed much taste in picking it." The young Prince must have been overwhelmed by his welcome, and by the peculiar Canadian tradition of building triumphal arches of leafy boughs along the official route. "Here is the universal programme," declared one newspaper reporter. "Spruce arches, cannon, procession, levee, lunch, ball, departure; cheers, crowds, men, women, enthusiasm, militia, Sunday school children, illuminations, fire works, etcetera, etcetera, *ad infinitum.*"

It soon became evident, however, that the wild enthusiasm for the Prince was getting out of hand. John A., in particular, was perturbed by a nasty undercurrent in the outpouring of loyalty to the British Crown, thanks to the machinations of the Orangemen. In the United Kingdom, the parades and banners of the Orange Order were illegal, so the Prince of Wales's advisers had told Canadian authorities that the Order could make no public demonstrations during the royal visit, because Edward could not acknowledge an illegal organization. Most Canadian Orangemen reluctantly accepted the veto. However, the fiercest among them bristled at this insult to their independence. Since Orange Order parades were perfectly legal in Canada, why should Canadians follow English rules? The Orangemen in Kingston, John A. Macdonald's own riding, built a particularly glorious arch of evergreens, put on their orange-and-blue uniforms, tuned up their fife-and-drum band and clamoured to be allowed to join the parade when the Prince disembarked at Kingston's docks.

The result was a stand-off. The Prince refused to disembark from the

Wherever the Prince went, he passed under massive temporary arches of spruce branches: this one welcomed him to Sparks Street, Ottawa.

steamer on which he was travelling down the St. Lawrence River; the Orangemen refused to back down. So the royal steamer weighed anchor and set off towards the Bay of Quinte and the next stop on the royal itinerary: Belleville. But the infuriated Kingston Orangemen got there first, by train. They persuaded their zealous colleagues in Belleville to insist that the loyal Order of Orangemen be allowed to make their demonstration there.

As sheriff of Victoria County, John Dunbar Moodie was part of Belleville's welcoming committee, and Susanna, now one of the best-known writers in the colony, was at his side amongst the other civic dignitaries. Early that bright September morning, the Moodies had walked from their house down to the wharf, admiring as they went all the decorations in the centre of town. Belleville had gone overboard with preparations: the streets were lined with sheaves of wheat, cornstalks, bunting, Chinese lanterns and glowing bunches of orange day-lilies. Ten triumphal arches were positioned along the Prince's scheduled route. Farmers from the surrounding countryside had loaded their wives and families onto their wagons and converged on the town to see the show. A bevy of fifty young ladies on horseback were scheduled to meet the Prince when he set foot on firm ground.

But once again, the Prince of Wales never stepped ashore. In the face of yet more Orange intransigence, the steamer bearing the royal party simply chuffed away. It wasn't until Edward reached Cobourg that he and his retinue were finally able to enjoy one of the balls organized in his honour—and that was largely because the train in which Kingston's Orange troublemakers were pursuing him had broken down ten miles from the town. Back in Belleville, the townspeople "chaffed with suppressed rage," according to *The Daily Globe*'s correspondent: "Though the gilded crowns, many coloured flowers and flags give an air of gaiety to the place, yet such a quantity of sullen, discontented faces I have never before witnessed."

The Moodies were outraged by the discourtesy to the royal party. But it would have been foolish for John to have tried to stop the Orange

Order's demonstration—too many of the most prominent townsfolk, and all his political enemies, were involved. George Benjamin, publisher of the *Belleville Intelligencer* (whom Susanna had caricatured so viciously in her writings), was one of those who organized the pugnacious defence of Orange Order rights in Belleville. Benjamin's role came as no surprise to John and Susanna, since John's old adversary was still pursuing the sheriff with equal zeal: Benjamin told Premier John A. Macdonald that John Dunbar Moodie's dismissal from office was "the most important" of all the issues in his riding.

The uncertainty of the court case, the belligerence of the Orangemen, the hostility of George Benjamin—the sheriff was under a lot of stress. In July 1861, John Moodie suffered a stroke that paralysed his left side. A hysterical Susanna quickly called in Dr. Lister, the well-known Belleville physician, and watched aghast as he applied the favourite all-purpose remedy of the nineteenth-century: cutting open a vein to bleed the patient.

Twelve days after his stroke, John wrote a cheerful letter to his favourite daughter, Katie Vickers, in Toronto. He told her that his left arm was gradually regaining its strength: "I can now open and shut my hand, put it on the top of my head and take hold feebly of my right elbow and other gymnastic feats of the same kind. . . . I believe some of my *friends?* here expected I was used up. However I laugh at them and tell them I am going to join the Cricket Club in a few days." But John's impaired health unnerved his wife. She couldn't sleep at night. She suffered a chronic, settled pain and uneasiness in the pit of her stomach. For the first time in her life, when she sat down to write, "Ideas will no longer come. . . . My mind is neither so lively nor so elastic as formerly."

For the next few weeks, John pretended to go back to work. But an invalid sheriff was an even greater embarrassment for the government than one facing charges of corruption, and eventually John's old friend Lewis Wallbridge, the Speaker of the Assembly, persuaded him to resign his position before his appeal was heard. Early in 1862, John Dunbar Moodie resigned as the sheriff of the County of Hastings after twenty-three years of service. At sixty-four, he was old, sick and broke. The Moodies' only assets were their cottage and fifteen acres of land, heavily mortgaged, and the various debts still owed to John as sheriff. He continued to hope for another job, and received a vague indication that something might be found for him, but his wife was the greater realist. "I build very little upon these promises," Susanna wrote sadly to her sister. "I wish the dear husband would cease to hope, and resign himself to the probability of disappointment. The anxiety and uncertainty of his position is killing him by inches."

Susanna was scared about the future, but, as usual, she was resourceful in a crisis. The only way she knew how to earn money was through writing, so she picked up her pen again. She sent two sketches to a new Toronto periodical, the *British-American Magazine.* She encouraged John to prepare a collection of all his past writings and publish them with a biographical introduction. Despite his trembling hand and failing eyesight, John managed to produce *Scenes and Adventures as a Soldier and Settler during Half a Century,* which would appear in 1866. Susanna explained their predicament to Richard Bentley and requested his help in getting a story that she wrote years earlier published, to keep "the gaunt wolf poverty from the door."

Her loyal old friend could not have responded more sympathetically. "Your letter just received gave me very sincere grief," Bentley replied in April 1865. "It is indeed very hard that after the faithful discharge of arduous duties for many years, and in the decline of life as your good husband is, when personal comforts may be acceptable and frequently required, a public officer should lose his means of support without any pension." Tears came to Susanna's eyes as she read his letter, and when she reached the second page she ran out onto the verandah to show John the kind words before sitting down to express her fervent gratitude. "God bless you for your goodness," she scrawled, and went on to thank God "for raising me up a true friend." Bentley was confident that he could secure for Susanna a grant from the Royal Literary Fund in

London. In due course, a bank draft for sixty pounds arrived from Octavian Blewett, the Fund's secretary.

This was the only formal recognition, in England or Canada, that Susanna Moodie ever received for her work during her lifetime. The meagre grant was soon consumed by the Moodies' living expenses and legal bills, but in Susanna's mind, it compensated for the meanness of both her Canadian critics and John's political friends. "I hold, perhaps, the first place among the female authors residing within the Colony," she told Bentley, "and my contributions to their periodical literature [have] always enjoyed great popularity. But this has not made them more ready to give my dear husband a small place under the government, to keep us from the Author's fate—a dry crust and the garret."

John knew his memory was failing and his strength draining away, but his native ebullience was unquenched: he continued to read the *Globe* each day, to write to the editors of various publications and to visit his daughters in Toronto. Even when fatigue struck and his leg ached, he tried to be cheerful, not least because he knew how much Susanna feared widowhood. Susanna refused to acknowledge her husband's steady deterioration. As one of her daughters later admitted, "whatever her husband did or said was right in her eyes . . . not even her own children dare hint to the contrary."

There was one trip John was determined to make before he died. Since the Moodies had left the backwoods for Belleville after the 1837 Rebellion, John had never returned to Lake Katchewanooka and the community now known as Lakefield. However, he and Susanna had heard a great deal about its development during the intervening years from Catharine, who had settled there after Thomas died. Her brother Sam, who lived in a grand brick house and was acknowledged as Lakefield's founding father, had helped his widowed sister build a small cottage close by. So in July 1865, John and Susanna Moodie scraped together the money to pay a two-week visit.

Susanna and John travelled by train as far as Peterborough. The journey tired the elderly couple, who clung to each other's arms and hung on to bags filled with their clothes, writing pads and gifts of baked goods and jam for their relatives. A stagecoach collected them from the Peterborough railroad station and took them into Lakefield. They were overwhelmed. "How rapidly the face of this country changes!" wrote Susanna. "I left the woods of North Douro, 26 years ago. Only three houses all composed of logs and of the smallest dimensions were to be found within three miles of us." Now, the Otonabee River no longer raced and foamed through the dense forest, overwhelming a handful of settlers with the raw power of the landscape. Instead, the water rippled in the calm millponds next to the huge waterwheels of two prosperous sawmills. Clapboard houses, with gardens full of hollyhocks, delphiniums and roses, lined the main street. There were four taverns, a frame schoolhouse where Catharine's daughter Mary taught, a post office, three stores, a doctor's office and a bakery. All the scars of a pioneer settlement—the mud holes in the road, the stumps and bare earth around every dwelling, the vegetable peelings outside the kitchen doors—had disappeared. There was even a brand-new plank sidewalk down the main street. It was only eleven years earlier that Sam Strickland had organized the building of the village's first church—Christchurch, a little stone building that looked as though it had arrived ready-made from an English village—but its congregation had already outgrown it and was in the process of building a larger Anglican church, St. John's. In addition, the Baptists and the Presbyterians had each built brick churches and the Wesleyan Methodists had built a frame church.

Lakefield would never rival Susanna's memories of Southwold—there were none of the village trades she remembered from her English youth, such as the wheelwright, barrel-maker and potter. But Lakefield had fulfilled the promise that both Catharine and Susanna had described in their letters home before the 1837 Rebellion: it was a community in which a gentleman could live in comfort. The canal system first promoted in the 1830s, linking Lake Ontario with Lake Huron, would not be completed for another fifty-five years. But Lakefield had flourished because immigration was booming again. A half-century of back-breaking work had pushed the "frontier" dividing cultivated land and wilderness hundreds of miles beyond the town to the north and the west. British North America still lacked men with capital, but the rail-roads were stimulating the economy and the five colonies were moving towards political union. Among English-speaking Canadians, there was a slowly emerging national identity that combined loyalty to the British Crown with the levelling instinct (what Trollope called "the corduroy braggadocio") of their American neighbours.

The visit raised the Moodies' spirits. Old friends stopped John and Susanna in the street and recalled the youthful adventures they had all shared (Susanna mistook many of the grey-whiskered men for their fathers). "I do not remember that I ever spent a happier or more enjoyable fortnight in my whole life," Susanna told Richard Bentley. "My dear old husband forgot for a few days his cares, and enjoyed himself as much as I did." There were family reunions in The Homestead, Sam's mansion. "My brother," Susanna told Bentley, "has a handsome and commodious house and a beautiful garden which would amply satisfy the taste of any gentleman of moderate fortune." Sam himself was in poor health; his muscular body was aging rapidly, and his eyes were clouded due to diabetes. His pretensions soon began to grate on Susanna, who preferred cosy evenings in Catharine's pretty little cottage, on the banks of the Otonabee. Their sister Agnes's successive triumphs in literature and society were a recurrent topic of conversation. In a recent letter to Catharine, Agnes had described a visit to the fifth Earl Spencer, at Althorp, "where I found the finest library in England." It is easy to imagine Susanna's expression as she read her sister's smug account of "three weeks in these classic shades having much homage paid to me."

John and Susanna made one more pilgrimage, a poignant one, to the property, a mile outside Lakefield's centre, that had been their home from 1832 to 1839. "I did not know the place," Susanna noted. In Lakefield, nature might have been tamed and shaped to suit colonists' tastes, but out there, it was back in control. Their lakeside log cabin had disappeared, and most of the acres had reverted to cedar swamp. The only evidence of the Moodies' sojourn were the stones of their well—mute testimony to the blood, sweat and tears they had expended on survival.

Susanna stood at the edge of Lake Katchewanooka, watching the yellow water-lilies rocking up and down on the lake and the iridescent blue dragonflies hovering over them. Memories of her younger self flooded back. She thought about how hard they had worked to clear the land, and the miseries of hunger, disease, cold and disappointment they had endured. But she also remembered the twilight sails that she and John had taken on the lake, and the cheerful laughter of Peter Nogan and Mrs. Tom, their Chippewa friends. She had been a slim, active woman in those days who, for all her grumbles, firmly believed that her backwoods trials were the dark hours before the dawn. Now she was a tired, grey-haired sixty-two-year-old, convinced that she had never been "among fortune's favourites." What had she achieved with all those struggles? The Moodies had left England in order to give their children more opportunities in the New World. So far, their children's lives were no easier than Susanna's and John's. Had it all been worth it?

On their return to Belleville, Moodie fortunes went from bad to worse. Dunbar created the first problem. When John gave up the sheriff's job, he'd given the Bridge Street house to Dunbar, in the expectation that his oldest son would look after his parents in their old age. But Dunbar had quickly sold the house so that he and his new wife, Eliza, could travel to Delaware and buy a farm there. Eliza and her sister, Julia Russell, had first entered the Moodie household as boarders, from Jamaica, a few years earlier. In those days, Susanna had found them "a great comfort." She told Catharine that "dear Lizzie . . . is a daughter to me in my trouble and dear little Julia does her best with her angelic voice to drive away care." But once Eliza had married Dunbar, Susanna began to blame her for Dunbar's shortcomings and constant requests for money. All of Susanna's broad-minded liberalism deserted her when

John and Susanna with thier daughter-in-law Eliza: "a selfish, cold-hearted, arrogant Quadroon."

she came to blows with a daughter-in-law who had negro blood. She described Eliza as a "a selfish, cold-hearted arrogant Quadroon, a woman of *little intellect* and who despises it in others."

John's decision to give Dunbar the Bridge Street cottage, and Dunbar's decision to sell it, provoked endless family rows and recriminations. Katie Vickers and her husband, who thought little of Dunbar and his wife, were so exasperated that they stopped talking to the Moodies. This meant that John and Susanna had lost the support of their only child who was comfortably settled. Next, Susanna decided that she and John could not go to Delaware with Dunbar, as they had originally planned; she could not bear to leave Belleville. However, they now had neither a roof over their heads nor any equity. And in the midst of all this confusion, news reached them from Toronto that the feckless Charles Fitzgibbon had died suddenly, leaving Agnes a penniless widow with six young children. Susanna ached to help her poor daughter, but she had no money. Nor could she help Donald Moodie, her second son, who was also in a fix. "His heedless extravagance has been a sore burthen and trial to us," Susanna complained in a letter to Bentley (although she refrained from admitting that Donald was well on his way to becoming an alcoholic). Only Robert, the sturdy youngest son, continued to express concern for his parents. But since he too was now married, with a delicate wife and young family but no job, he could offer only sympathy. Family turmoil made Susanna sick with anxiety for the future. In her weakened state, she contracted typhoid fever—rampant in every small town due to the primitive wooden drains, but in Susanna's view, due in her own case to "mental anxiety."

Thanks to her sturdy Strickland constitution, Susanna recovered from the fever. Bowing to the inevitable, she gave up any thought of living with one of their children. Instead, she and John rented a modest wood-frame cottage a mile outside Belleville and found an elderly servant to look after them. From her front windows overlooking the Bay of Quinte, Susanna could watch schooners unload cargoes of coal on the wharves, then return to Oswego, on the American shore of Lake Ontario, loaded with lumber. Various grandchildren came to stay. Friends brought baskets of apples, onions, beans and carrots, and took Susanna out for a spin in their carriages. Susanna eked out a living by selling paintings of flowers. But her letters are steeped in the anguish of infirmity and fear. Often, her only diversion was to watch the antics of Quiz, her Skye terrier, and Grim, a steel-grey cat. She wrote to her faithful patron, Richard Bentley: "My dear husband is not very well, low-spirited and anxious. . . . My heart has been nearly broken. I often wonder that I am alive." Neither she nor John enjoyed old age. "Old age is selfish," she exclaimed to her niece Mary Traill, now married and living in Belleville. "It covets companionship, which the young too much immersed in the pleasures and hopes of their happy prime, have no time or inclination to give, and when your own nestlings are all flown, the lonely hours hang heavily on your hands and the shadows lengthen in the dark valley as you totter slowly and sadly on."

Death hovered in the shadows, and Susanna shrank from its touch. Her mother had finally passed away in 1864, her ninety-two years belying her constant complaints of ill health. Both her brother Sam and Catharine's son James Traill died in 1867. Her sister Sarah's husband, Richard Gwillym, died in 1868 ("Dear Thay . . . looks sweet in her weeds," wrote Agnes). Agnes had at last resumed her correspondence with Susanna, but her letters were full of medical grumbles. "Dr. Wilson . . . said I had a liver complaint of long-standing and my illness in the spring had been wrongly treated by leeching and blue pills," she moaned.

One brisk October day in 1869, John Moodie sat on the porch of his cottage attempting to split some firewood with his good right hand. Susanna, who was returning from a walk, put her hand on his shoulder as she passed through to the kitchen door. "You naughty creature," she teased her husband. "Did you take the opportunity of my being out to kill yourself?" John laughed: "I feel quite well and strong, today. I mean to cut all the wood for the parlour stove, it will give me a good appetite for dinner."

The two old people pottered their way through the day. In the evening, they settled into chairs on each side of the parlour stove, and John read aloud while Susanna knitted new socks for him. After thirty-eight years of marriage, they still delighted in each other's company. "He looked so beautiful," Susanna recalled a few days later. "The silky snow white hair waving on his shoulders. The noble face illumined by the lamp and the pure fair complexion just tinged with a bright glow, that gave to lip and cheek almost the bloom of youth." At nine o'clock, Susanna brought her husband a tumbler of milk and a bun and remarked that it was time "for respectable old people like you and I to be in bed." She helped him into the bedroom, where he still slept in their iron bedstead and she slept on a low couch nearby, and started unbuttoning his shirt for him. "Dear Susy," John grinned, "I give you a deal of trouble." Susanna smiled back. "It is no trouble. I always bless God that I am here to help you."

John manoeuvred his stiff left leg awkwardly into bed, then Susanna plumped up the pillows to make him comfortable. She leaned down and kissed his broad brow, and "bade God to bless my old darling, and give him a good night's rest." John reached up to her, pulling her down to his breast, and said in an exaggerated Scots accent, "My dear auld wife, may He bless you." They were the last words of love Susanna ever heard from John.

It was still dark when Susanna awoke with a start. Someone had cried out, "Mother!" She quickly struggled off the couch and went to his bedside. "Dear Johnnie, are you ill? What is the matter?" John appeared quite coherent as he replied, "Mother, I did not call you. But I am very thirsty. Have you any drink here?" Susanna lit the oil lamp, and brought him a glass of water.

As she watched John brush the glass away and struggle to speak again, Susanna realized that something was wrong. She rose to send the servant for the doctor, but John insisted that, "Doctors can do me no good . . . Get me over the bed and open the window, I want more air." By now, the sky was gradually changing from inky black to luminous blue, but the wind from the open window was icy. John, in the grip of a second stroke, was struggling for breath. Susanna wrapped a cloak round him, but he promptly threw up a quantity of slimy foam. He was dying, and Susanna knew it.

John leaned heavily on the window sill, gasping for air. Susanna finally got him back into bed. Desperation creeping into her voice, she begged him to say a few final words—a final message of love to his children. He waved his hand, took two deep breaths, closed his eyes and, as Susanna tearfully put it, "passed through the dark river as peacefully as a child going to sleep." As Susanna stared in horror at his body, she heard the mill bell tolling six times in the distance. It had all been so quick, so abrupt. How could John have left her in such a rush?

Robert Moodie, his sister Agnes and brother-in-law John Vickers arrived by train the same day to help Susanna with the funeral arrangements. Neither Dunbar nor Donald showed up to mourn their father, but the town of Belleville came out in force to honour John Dunbar Moodie. The *Belleville Intelligencer* noted that, "Mr. Moodie was a man of warm social affections, had a great many personal friends, and died very generally regretted." The town council moved a resolution expressing its sympathy to Mrs. Moodie and family in the loss they had sustained. The funeral procession, led by a horse-drawn hearse, straggled almost the full length of the road from the Moodies' humble cottage to St. Thomas's Anglican Church on Bridge Street East, on the smart side of town. "Even the men whose persecutions had shortened his days paid respect to his remains," Susanna wrote to a friend. Nevertheless, black-coated Tory well-wishers like Allan Dougall and Mr. Mackenzie Bowell (a protegé of Benjamin's, and future prime minister of Canada) were received with a steely, unsmiling glint as they clutched their top hats and mouthed clichés about her husband's kind heart and service to the community. One of John's most important enemies was not amongst the throng at St. Thomas's Church that chilly autumn day. George Benjamin, the Jewish immigrant who had made a strategic conversion to Christianity years earlier, was already buried in the Anglican graveyard.

After the service, Susanna wailed as John's body was lowered into his grave. "What sorrow is equal to this sorrow?" she sobbed. "It is a strange new feeling to feel so desolate and alone. I ought to be glad. I ought to rejoice that his exit was so easy and painless, that he had for months looked forward to death with pleasure, that the merciful Father saved him from what he most dreaded, a long, lingering death of helplessness and suffering." Instead, she was plunged into "the gloom of grief." Her children stared at her anxiously, not knowing how best to comfort her.

For Susanna, widowhood was a death sentence. She was desperately lonely. John had been the centre of her existence; she depended on his love, good humour and enthusiasm to give her own life shape. He had made her laugh, and stopped her taking herself too seriously. He had always read everything she wrote before she sent it off to editors. With him, she felt clever, loved and appreciated. John had protected her from both her own storms of feelings and others' criticisms. She couldn't even imagine life without him. "Never, never, can I hope to be so happy again," she wept. All her children had left home, and anyway, she had never been as close to any of them as she had been to her dear John. "For him I painted, for him I wrote, and I now feel that my occupation is gone," she wrote to an old friend in England. "Poor Susy is alone—has no motive to live for herself."

Chapter 17

"A Wail for the Forest"

Widowhood, which was so threatening for Susanna, had proved a liberation for Catharine Parr Traill. It meant she no longer had to put a brave face on the grim life with an ailing, failing husband. After Thomas's death in 1859, she continued to struggle with the poverty and ill health that had dogged her; her correspondence is liberally speckled with references to lumbago, neuralgia, rheumatism, gout and sciatica. But in none of the hundreds of letters that have survived does Catharine mention that she misses the companionship of her husband. While Susanna confided to her sister, two years after John Moodie's death, that she still clung "with passionate love to the long, long ago," Catharine scarcely paused for breath before she was "up and doing."

Loneliness was not a problem. Catharine's devoted oldest daughter Kate lived with her and ran the household. And Catharine was soon far more comfortably settled than she had been in years. Although she'd had

Widowhood suited Catharine, who was sustained by her sense of humour and faith in God's benevolence. Photo taken at Port Hope by R. Ewing in 1867.

only a few dollars in her purse at the time of her husband's death, with her brother Sam's help she soon scraped together the capital required to buy some land in Lakefield that sloped steeply down to the river. There she built a little frame cottage that she called Westove, the name of the bankrupt Traill family estate in the Orkneys that she had also given to her first log home in Upper Canada, twenty-seven years earlier. The new Westove had clapboard walls, long windows opening onto a view of the water and gingerbread trim round the eaves of the high-peaked roof. Her bedroom was on the ground floor, and in the early hours of each day she could lie awake listening to the dawn chorus. It was cosier than any of the houses the Traills had previously lived in: the east wind didn't blast through the bedrooms, as it had in Oaklands, or whistle up the staircase, as it had at Wolf Tower. Catharine put colourful rag rugs on the floor and curtained all the windows in secondhand red velvet drapes, with net curtains. For someone who loved to gossip with neighbours and exchange news in the general store, life in the close-knit community of Lakefield was heaven.

Catharine immediately began to plan for Westove an English country garden full of violets, scarlet geraniums, primroses and dahlias. When she focussed the same talent for organization on the lives of her children and grandchildren, she began to sound like a Strickland matriarch. Her eldest daughter Kate was commissioned to do most of the weeding in the garden. Her second son Harry fenced in the backyard so his mother could plant potatoes. Catharine's son-in-law Clinton Atwood, now married to Annie Traill, found his sturdy horse and carriage commandeered if Catharine needed a ride to visit Frances Stewart in Peterborough or Annie at the Atwoods' farmhouse near Gore's Landing. An echo of Agnes's imperiousness crept into Catharine's manner.

Hither and thither Catharine swept between friends and relatives in Belleville, Brockville and the Peterborough region, dispensing family news, medical advice and geranium clippings to an ever-widening circle of acquaintances and relatives. She acted as a sort of human information exchange, connecting the rapidly reproducing ranks of Stricklands, Traills and Moodies. Among them, the three Strickland siblings who had left Suffolk for Canada in the early years of the century would eventually have 111 grandchildren who survived childhood. "The family being so scattered calls for longer letters," was Catharine's happy complaint, as she wrote to her two youngest sons, William and Walter, who were both

Catharine's beloved Westove, at Lakefield: any Strickland relative was warmly welcomed.

working west of the Red River with the Hudson's Bay Company. She was always at hand when a new addition was expected to the families of her children, nieces, nephews or friends. "Percy [Strickland's] wife . . . was confined on the 12th of this month with a fine little girl," she wrote her friend Frances Stewart in 1862. "Of course dear old Percy looked much to me to see that matters went on rightly."

Now in her sixties, Catharine beamed at the younger generation even as she cast a disapproving eye at their values. When she stayed with Agnes Fitzgibbon in Toronto in 1863, she clucked at the way that young women in the city behaved, declaring herself "rather disgusted with the way in which they dress for effect in public." While Agnes and her Toronto friends revelled in the arrival of music halls, London fashions and racy novels, Catharine shared her disapproval with Frances Stewart: "The luxurious style of dress, amusements and idleness of the young men and women of the last few years have encouraged a greater laxity in their manners and ideas. You and I perfectly agree in our opinion, respecting the want of deli-cacy in the fast dances, besides the effect on the moral charac-ter." Yet for all her busybody gregariousness and talk of the "good old days" (tales of which must have horrified her nieces and nephews), Catha-rine had a kind heart and was a welcome guest in many households. Her white hair neatly tucked under a starched cap, her black gown (a castoff

Kate Traill, Catharine's eldest daughter, who devoted her life to her mother's welfare.

from Agnes) frayed at the cuffs and her bright blue eyes sparkling with life, she quickly determined what needed to be done. She would sit up all night with a feverish child, teach a musical grandchild to pick out a melody on the piano, talk about old times with the dying, or help lay out a corpse. Small wonder that her shy, stay-at-home daughter Kate regularly received notes that Catharine's return from some sociable little trip would be delayed because her hosts "all want to keep me longer with them."

However, Catharine was far from a merry widow—she still needed to earn money. The first entry in her journal for 1863 begins: "On examining the state of my purse I find just $4.30. This is all the funds I have to begin the year with. It is true that I have half a barrel of flour, and some meat and I have often been without meat and money. God will provide as heretofore."

Catharine had known from childhood that God only helps those who help themselves; and for her that meant writing. Over the past thirty-five years she had worked in a variety of genres—children's stories, romances, sketches of nature and autobiographical narratives. Although none of her books had made her a fortune, they sold well and had established her reputation in both Britain and Canada. She continued to churn out stories for educational and children's magazines, and she knew which subjects were the perennial favourites of European readers, then and now —"Snow, ice storms, forest scenery . . . a flight of snowbirds would make a pretty little poem." But her submissions were returned with demoralizing frequency, and with advancing age, she had less tolerance for hustling unsympathetic publishers or pleasing periodical editors. Like Susanna, she felt out of touch with the tastes of the main audience for her publications: the British. Her attention was increasingly focussed on the world at her own doorstep, within British North America—in particular, the natural world.

Ever since she had crossed the Atlantic, Catharine had collected and studied flowers, grasses, mosses, lichens and ferns. Nature study was a relief "from the home-longings that always arise in the heart of the exile, especially when the sweet opening days of Spring recall to the memory of the immigrant Canadian settler old familiar scenes . . . when all the gay embroidery of English meads and hedgerows put on their bright array." Nature, for Catharine, was pervaded with divine purpose—its beauty and harmony illustrated God's power and goodness. She never found a plant that she couldn't love both for its looks and as an example of God's creation. The bud of the water-lily, lying just below the surface, "is ready to emerge from its watery prison and in all its virgin beauty expand its snowy bosom to the sun and genial air," she observed in a letter home in her first months in Upper Canada. Every year, she watched the changing seasons with a delight that always crept into whatever book she was writing at the time. "The pines were now putting on their rich, mossy, green spring dresses," reads a passage in her *Canadian Crusoes*. "The skies were deep blue; nature, weary of her long state of inaction, seemed waking into life and light." In *The Female Emigrant's Guide*, she provided a month-by-month description of natural events, which covers everything from croaking frogs to wildflowers. In August, "the squirrels are busy from morning till night, gleaning the ripe grain . . . they seem to me the happiest of all God's creatures, and the prettiest."

But Catharine's nature study wasn't all Wordsworthian reverie and nostalgia for Suffolk's daisies, bluebells and buttercups. She took a serious interest in every aspect of a plant: its appearance, its life cycle, its medicinal and food value, its relation to other plants. During her first decade in the silent and unexplored backwoods, she searched for the name of any unfamiliar species in the only botanical text she could lay her hands on: Frederick Pursh's *Flora Americae septentrionalis* (*North American Flora*), published in 1814, which Frances Stewart had lent her. Since Catharine had never studied Latin, she stumbled through Pursh's descriptions, "and when I came to a standstill I had recourse to my husband." She copied Pursh's use of the Linnean classification system of plant species, largely based on the number of stamens and pistils in the flower. Her husband's books were lumpy with all the pressed specimens she had inserted between their pages. Her journal was full of careful notes.

Had Catharine been born a hundred years later, she would have become a serious scientist. But stuck in remote Douro Township, or on the Rice Lake Plains, Catharine had as much hope of mingling with professors of botany, who could tell her exactly how to mount and label her specimens, as she had of mingling with important authors in the London publishing business. She was so poor that she was never able to afford to visit the greatest natural wonder of her adopted land, Niagara Falls. She couldn't even do accurate plant drawings; unlike Susanna, she had never mastered the art of flower-painting. She was an avid collector, and her "herbarium," or collection of dried specimens, was one of her greatest sources of pleasure. Album after album was filled with elaborate arrangements of dried material.

Today, Catharine's scrapbooks are lodged safely in the archives of the Museum of Nature in Ottawa. Their decaying pages, with their fragile red lichens still adhering to the rag paper and the blossoms of fireweed still purple 130 years after they were picked, give us a warm insight into their creator's mind. The books bulge with lovingly handled plants, many of which she was the first to identify in the countryside around Lakefield. Specimens are arranged artistically on the page. One album begins with an inscription encircled by a wreath of pressed sphagnum moss and pearly-white everlastings. Another features sprays of pressed ferns, anchored on white birch bark and decorated with faded maple leaves. But vital scientific information—a plant's Latin name, or the habitat and date on which it was found—is often missing. Catharine was as likely to accompany her specimens with biblical quotations (especially from the Psalms or Revelations) as with proper notation. Her albums include tiger moths, their delicate wings flaking with age, and the orange feathers of a northern oriole.

In the mid-nineteenth century, there was a market for Catharine's type of collection and display. Friends bought her artistic arrangements of pressed flowers, just as they bought Susanna's flower paintings, as aesthetic pleasures and keepsakes of their creator. Catherine sent the dried seeds of unusual plants to a professor of botany (probably Robert

Graham, who held the chair from 1819 to 1845) at Edinburgh University. Provincial flower shows had special sections devoted to amateur herbariums: Catharine's collection of dried native plants won a prize at the Kingston Provincial Fair in 1856, and in 1862 another collection was awarded second prize at the Provincial Exhibition in Toronto. Catharine knew her albums were well put together, and when her fern collection did not win a prize at the same show, she took umbrage: "They were without doubt the best things there of the kind . . . it has now become so partial a thing the awarding of the prizes that I shall make no further attempts to send any collection to the Provincial Shew." When fire swept through Oaklands in 1857, instead of grabbing old letters, clothes or keepsakes, Catharine rescued from the crackling flames a half-finished manuscript on plants. Once she was settled at Westove, she decided to focus on her botanical interests as her next publishing project.

With some difficulty, Catharine managed to update her limited collection of botanical texts to include Maria Morris's *Wildflowers of Nova Scotia* (published in 1840). She also got hold of a copy of the 1833 classic *Flora Boreali Americana*, by the illustrious Sir William Jackson Hooker, since 1840 director of the Royal Botanic Gardens at Kew. Like Pursh's, however, Hooker's tome was written for professional scientists, not enthusiastic amateurs like Catharine. Catharine's preferred model for botanical writing was *The Natural History and Antiquities of Selborne* by the eighteenth-century naturalist Gilbert White, which had first appeared in 1789 and which she had read as a child. White, a country parson who lived in Hampshire, kept a careful record of the seasonal changes in his beloved birthplace. His work reflects a poetic affection for wild life and nature, and a love of the picturesque in landscape. Catharine decided to devote herself to writing a usable botany manual for Canada, written in the literary style of Gilbert White.

The potential value of British North America's plant life had been recognized as early as 1730, when company surgeons of the Hudson's Bay Company began to include botanical descriptions and specimens of native plants in the regular reports that they sent back to London.

During the eighteenth century, most specimens collected by explorer-naturalists were shipped straight to Kew Gardens in London. However, by the time the Strickland sisters arrived in British North America, a handful of the colony's more affluent residents were showing some curiosity about the flora and fauna that surrounded them. Natural history societies had been established in Quebec, Montreal and Halifax during the 1820s. Toronto finally got its own Horticultural Society in 1834, and a botanical garden near Government House soon afterwards. The learned lectures and field expeditions offered by these societies were even considered suitable "scientific" activities for highbrow women—animal biology involved blood; mineralogy involved dirt; while horticulture involved only plants and flowers. The stylish Lady Dalhousie, wife of the Governor-in-Chief of British North America from 1820 to 1828, regularly swathed her head in muslin, to keep off the bugs, and set off with specimen box, magnifying glass and a retinue of attendants into the farmlands around Quebec City. Once her specimens were dried, university-educated members of the Literary and Historical Society of Quebec (an organization founded by her husband) showed "M'lady" how to label them properly. Lady Dalhousie, whose articles appeared in the Society's *Transactions*, was one of the few women of her time to be published alongside male botanists.

Catharine lacked the instruction that Lady Dalhousie enjoyed, but she had far more opportunity to concentrate on her botanical interests. From her earliest years in the bush, she would try to cultivate the plants she had found growing in the wild, or had seen Indian women using for their healing properties. She sold more than a dozen natural history articles to the *Anglo-American Magazine*, published in Toronto, and the Rochester-based *Horticulturist*. She was as maternal with plants as she was with her own children. She oohed and aahed over every discovery with protective pride, and in her published articles she used familiar and maternal metaphors alongside scientific terminology. When she could not discover an existing name for flowers and plants in the "wild woods," she wrote soon after her arrival, "I consider myself free to become their floral godmother and give them names of my own choosing." The longer she remained in the colony, however, the more she wondered whether progress towards permanent settlement was such a marvellous advance. So much was being lost as forest was cleared, roads constructed and towns founded.

Much of her concern for the wilderness was expressed in the *dum-de-dum* of sentimental doggerel:

> O wail for the forest, the proud stately forest,
> No more its dark depths shall the hunter explore,
> For the bright golden main
> Shall wave free o'er the plain,
> O wail for the forest, its glories are o'er.

But she also tried to alert others to the slow erosion of native Canadian species. In 1852, she protested to the editor of the *Genesee Farmer* that in the rush to clear land, stock greenhouses and cultivate annuals for gardens, indigenous forest plants were disappearing. "Man has altered the face of the soil," she wrote with despair. "The mighty giants of the forest are gone, and the lowly shrub, the lovely flower, the ferns and mosses that flourished beneath their shade, have departed with them. . . . Where now are the lilies of the woods, the lovely and fragrant Pyrolas, the Blood-root, the delicate sweet scented Michella repens? Not on the newly cleared ground, where the forest once stood."

Catharine's first priority, in the early 1860s, was to find a publisher for the manuscript on Canadian plant life she had rescued when Oaklands went up in flames. Her visit to Toronto in 1863 gave her the opportunity to hawk it round the publishing houses. Vincent Clementi, the Anglican minister at Lakefield, had sketched a few of the flowers mentioned in Catharine's manuscript. Armed with these scrappy efforts, and five dollars that the Reverend Mr. Clementi had lent her, Catharine laid siege at the door of the newly established Toronto branch of the Scottish publisher Thomas Nelson. But the door never opened. "My patience has not been rewarded," she wrote to stay-at-home Kate, explaining that she

must return home before she ran out of money. She left the manuscript
with friends in Toronto: "May be Mr. Nelson will write to me soon and
some good may yet come to us through what as yet seems a fruitless
expenditure of time and money."

The following year, it seemed as though the manuscript might be
published as "The Plants of Canada" by the Hamilton Horticultural
Society, which was hosting the Provincial Agricultural Fair that year. But
Catharine's hopes fell when she was told that the Society had decided it
could go ahead only with the help of a government subsidy. She dismissed the president of the Horticultural Society as "a man not to be
relied upon" and despaired of the colonial government ever having the
imagination to put money into a comprehensive catalogue of Canadian
plants. In the opinion of Sir William Hooker, she had been told,
"Canada was behind every one of the British Colonies and all civilized
nations in Scientific literary effort especially in Botany." Strickland
amour-propre came to the fore as Catharine emphatically concurred with
the director of Kew Gardens: "I think the Great Man was right—there is
certainly a want of encouragement in this country for literary talent."
But she was driven as much by financial as scientific imperative: "I am so
anxious to earn what will pay our bills that I write even when I have no
hope of a market."

Catharine refused to be discouraged. She laboriously copied out her
manuscript, then sent it off to all the people she could think of who
might recognize the value of her work and give it a public endorsement.
One copy landed on the desk of Professor John Dawson, a geologist
who had become principal of McGill College in Montreal; another
arrived at the doorstep of William Hincks, professor of natural history
at the University of Toronto. Catharine also sent a copy to George
Lawson, a Scot who had published more than fifty articles on botany
before his thirtieth birthday, and who had arrived at Queen's College,
Kingston, in 1858 to teach natural history. In 1860, he'd founded the
Botanical Society of Canada, which was soon busy cataloguing Canadian
plants and advising farmers on pest control.

In the end, it was none of these well-positioned or ambitious men who helped Catharine get her work in print, but her own niece, Susanna's daughter Agnes Fitzgibbon.

The older Agnes Moodie Fitzgibbon got, the more she resembled her mother. She had Susanna's delicacy of appearance and air of vulnerability that hid an iron will. She shared her mother's sense of humour, wicked temper and stylish dress sense: her bonnets reflected Parisian modes, and her skirts were always as wide as fashion dictated. Sharp-featured and proud, with a penetrating gaze, Agnes was extremely beautiful. Since her marriage in 1850, Agnes had lived in Toronto, and, now in her twenties, she far preferred the diversions of a big city to those of rural life. She found Toronto at mid-century just as thrilling as Susanna had found London in the 1820s. And Toronto *was* exciting as it swelled from a muddy little port to a booming railroad city. Men were making fortunes in the milling, transportation and banking industries, and building monuments to their success in the form of splendid stone banks and office buildings.

Unfortunately, Charles Fitzgibbon was not one of the Toronto entrepreneurs making his fortune. He and his wife had little time and less money to enjoy many of the new civic amenities—the library and music hall of the Mechanics' Institute on the corner of Adelaide and Church, built in 1854, or the splendid row of new glass-fronted stores on King Street, offering clothing, dry goods, carpets, curtains, books and boots. Agnes spent the fifteen years of her marriage to Charles Fitzgibbon in the usual Victorian cycle of repeated pregnancies, births and intermittent deaths. Four of the eight children born to Agnes and Charles died before they were ten years old. She had some help from a succession of teenage Irish girls (the only domestic servants that the Fitzgibbons could afford), but she could rarely leave home. There were few opportunities for strolling down King Street's plank sidewalks, or watching games of cricket at the Old Garrison Reserve during the summer, or ice-boating in the harbour in winter. Most of her excursions were walks in the nearby valley of the Humber River, where the children played on the riverbank and she sketched wildflowers. Her mother had taught Agnes how to paint flower pictures when she was a little girl, and Agnes's skill had quickly surpassed Susanna's.

Catharine had always had a close relationship with Agnes; aunt and niece got on much better than mother and daughter. Agnes "was always my own dear child when she was a baby," Catharine confided to her sister Sarah in England. "I always had her with me when dear Susanna was ill or confined, and she has been like one of my very own daughters all her life and very dear to me she is." It suited Catharine that Agnes Fitzgibbon lived in Toronto, which was starting to rival Montreal as a centre for Canadian publishing. The Fitzgibbon house on Dundas Street had quickly become her base on her occasional trips to Toronto to hustle publishers, and Catharine would moan to Agnes about their reluctance to take on her manuscript unless she could produce better illustrations.

In 1865, Charles Fitzgibbon died, and thirty-two-year-old Agnes was abruptly widowed, with a family to support. "Having only the proceeds of my husband's life insurance upon which to feed, clothe and educate them, it was necessary for me to replenish my purse before its contents were exhausted," she later wrote. But her only salable skill was her dexterity with a paintbrush. She decided to put together a volume of flower illustrations, with text provided by Catharine from her lengthy manuscript.

It was a wildly ambitious project. Agnes's mother and aunt could have thrown cold water on any hope that such a book would make much money. But when Agnes set her mind to something—whether it was marriage when she was only seventeen, or authorship when she had no experience in the book trade—she usually achieved it. Agnes displayed the same Strickland drive that had kept both her mother and her aunt scribbling during their wretched years in the backwoods. She certainly cut a more impressive figure in publishers' offices than her aunt, whose country-mouse clothes and eagerness to distribute gingerbread recipes were out of place amongst Toronto's new entrepreneurial elite.

Agnes began by approaching John Lovell, her mother's publisher in

Montreal, to buy the idea of an illustrated volume of Canadian wild-flowers. Lovell was a great champion of the need for a vibrant Canadian publishing industry, and he liked Agnes's determination that her book should be an exclusively Canadian production. He agreed to be the publisher. Next, Agnes co-ordinated efforts to sign up five hundred subscribers for the proposed volume. At five dollars a volume, it was an expensive proposition, but Agnes bullied all her family, friends and acquaintances into agreeing to buy the book before it was even in print. Then she sketched out the ten illustrations required for Catharine's text and looked around for a printer who could reproduce them by means of the newly developed process of lithography.

Lithography, perfected by the Munich printer Aloysius Senefelder in 1796, was a popular medium amongst nineteenth-century artists such as Goya and Daumier. By Agnes's time, it was well-known in the United States through the colourful scenes of horses, yachts and newsworthy events published by Currier and Ives. But it had only reached Upper Canada in the 1830s, and was used there exclusively for maps, charts, cheques and banknotes. The colony's artists considered the quality of local lithography far too poor for illustrations; Cornelius Krieghoff's *Scenes in Canada* were sent back to Munich to be lithographed. Agnes did enough research to convince herself that it was the perfect medium for her drawings because hundreds of illustrations could be taken from one stone. However, no Toronto printer could undertake the production of such sophisticated designs, so she decided that "if no one else could, I must endeavour to do it myself."

She acquired a specially prepared block of limestone from a printer called Ellis and drew a trillium on it. Under Ellis's guidance, she etched around the lines with chemicals, then greased the plate, rolled ink over the design, and pressed a damp sheet of paper onto the stone. A perfect reproduction of the trillium appeared on the paper. Fired up by success, Agnes drew the first of her own exquisite floral designs onto the stone and printed out five hundred plates. Then she cleaned off the first design and repeated the operation with the second design for five hundred copies. She worked on methodically, reusing the same stone each time, until she had five hundred copies of each of her ten designs.

Both Agnes's aunt and her mother were in awe of Agnes's achievement. Catharine recognized that this was "a gigantic effort to be executed by one person"—especially when the person was a single parent with a limited budget. Susanna, ever the pessimist, felt that her daughter had taken on far too much. She wrote to Catharine that if Agnes tried to paint all the plates herself, "it will well nigh kill her . . . I much fear either of you embarking in such a hazardous enterprise which if it did not succeed would be utter ruin." But Agnes ignored the Cassandra chorus. She and her three eldest daughters—Maime (then sixteen), Cherrie (thirteen) and Alice (ten)—sat down at the dining-room table of their house on Dundas Street and coloured the whole edition of five thousand illustrations by hand. Some of the illustrations featured a single plant, such as *Sarracenia purpurea,* or purple pitcher plant. Others showed an unrelated group of three or four flowers, such as *Veronica americana* (American brooklime or speedwell), *Rubus odoratus* (purple-flowering raspberry), *Moneses unifloea* (one-flowered pyrola) and *Pyrola elliptica* (shin leaf). Had the book been published in England, with a professional lithographer and artist preparing the illustrations, she later discovered, the cost would have been 1,500 pounds ($7,500).

It did not take Catharine long to assemble from her plant life manuscript the brief literary descriptions to accompany Agnes's lithographs. Each mini-essay (thirty-one altogether) was vintage Traill, combining a detailed description of the plant, its medicinal qualities, references to previous botanists' writings about it, a smattering of poetry and Catharine's personal opinion of its merits. She included the English, scientific and native names for each plant. And some of the information has a modern ring: for example, she described the medicinal qualities of coneflower, commonly known today by its Latin name, Echinacea. She mentioned that wintergreen could cure rheumatism, balsam made a good dye, and Indian herbalists used turnips as a remedy for colic. Of the species *Pyrolae* (wintergreen), she wrote an admiring description that is a

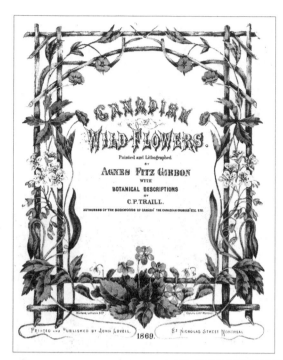

Frontispiece for "a most valuable addition to the literature of Canada," to which citizens of the newly-minted Dominion eagerly subscribed.

Agnes Moodie Fitzgibbon's lithograph of a trillium: she and her daughters hand-coloured 5,000 illustrations.

botanic variation of something Agnes Strickland might have said about a particularly good-looking branch of the British aristocracy: "Every member of this interesting family is worthy of special notice. Elegant in form and colouring, they add to their many attractions the merit of being almost the first green thing to refresh the eye, long wearied by gazing on the dazzling snow for many consecutive months of winter."

Catharine chose her tone deliberately. She wanted the large-format, literary volume to "foster a love for the native plants of Canada" and persuade readers to pay attention to the "floral beauty that is destined sooner or later to be swept away, as the onward march of civilization clears away the primeval forest, reclaims the swamps and bogs, and turns the waste places into a fruitful field." Her preface acknowledged that "the scientific reader may possibly expect a more learned description of the plants, and may notice many defects and omissions," but Catharine was writing for people like herself, not for lofty scientists.

Once Agnes had finished her lithographs, *Canadian Wild Flowers* took most of 1867 to put together. "I got the proof sheet and Agnes's design of the specimen sheet for the book of Canadian Flowers," Catharine wrote to her daughter Kate in February that year. "I re-wrote one article and corrected and sent it by post to Lovell." Although she acknowledged that it was mostly her niece's work, she was soon getting as irritated with Lovell and Agnes as she had been with the Hamilton Horticultural Society. "I have been writing at my flower book but have not heard from Lovell . . . how very uncourteous these publishers are." She resented the way that Agnes failed to consult her on every detail. She complained to Susanna that "I do not even know who is correcting the press for Agnes writes hasty letters and seldom comes to the point on business matters." She knew Susanna would sympathize with her exasperation—Susanna knew Agnes's haughty manner all too well.

Exasperation apart, Catharine did her bit to sell subscriptions. She and Kate did the rounds of likely readers in the Peterborough area. Loyal friends like Frances Stewart bought several. "Your approval dear friend of the book," Catharine wrote to her, "cheered me not a little for I was much disappointed with my share of the work." But other potential buyers looked askance at the high-priced, large format volume. Catharine described to her daughter Annie how "[a] hard-fisted, hard-headed hardware merchant . . . looked . . . as if he would have liked nothing better than throwing one of his hammers or hoes at [Kate's] head when he paid down hard cash for his book. One man kept us a long time in suspense, and at last declined on the plea that his children always tore all the books in his wife's drawing room to pieces, calling on a lean, ill-favoured vinegar bottle of a wife to endorse the fact which she did saying, 'I guess they do.' I merely hinted that it was rather a bad plan to let them destroy things. 'Wal I guess it is but they will do it so it's no use buying things to be tore up,' she said—so there was an end to the matter."

The proposed volume received a better reception amongst the English relatives. By now, Agnes Strickland had resumed a regular, if frosty correspondence with Susanna, who had described to her English sisters her own and Catharine's various writing projects. Agnes was in a forgiving mood, because she had discovered yet another rich run of royals for Elizabeth Strickland and herself to write about: the Tudor princesses. She loyally promised to support *Canadian Wild Flowers*. "I hope that [the work that] your interesting daughter Agnes . . . and dear Kate are preparing will answer," she wrote to Susanna in 1868. "I have not heard the price, but I will subscribe for a copy."

The first edition of *Canadian Wild Flowers* appeared at the end of 1868, and it was an instant triumph. It was the first botanical book for the general reader; it had been put together by two indomitable women; and it was a proudly Canadian production at a most propitious moment. The previous year, to the accompaniment of brass bands, blazing fireworks and sonorous speeches, the United Provinces (present-day Ontario and Quebec) and two of the British colonies on the Atlantic seaboard (New Brunswick and Nova Scotia) had come together to form the Dominion of Canada. Prime Minister Sir John A. Macdonald, knighted at Confederation, was determined to expand and promote the newly minted nation. There was a popular hunger for the symbols of nationhood: in

England, the Staffordshire potter Thomas Furnival replaced the pictures of Niagara Falls on ironstone dinner services destined for Canada with pictures of beavers and maple leaves. A book celebrating the Dominion's flora had instant appeal.

The *Montreal Daily News* wrote: "This beautiful work must be regarded as a most valuable addition to the literature of Canada. It is a joint production of two ladies, Mrs. Agnes Fitzgibbon of Toronto and her aunt, Mrs. Traill of North Douro, a lady well-known to the literary world, sister of Miss Agnes Strickland, the celebrated authoress of the Lives of the Queens of England . . . Between them these ladies have produced a work of great merit; and we rise from its perusal full of hope for the future literary reputation of the Dominion." The periodical *New Century* referred to the book as "[o]ne of the most remarkable works ever attempted by a woman." Agnes Fitzgibbon, who had stayed in Montreal to oversee the first printing, easily found subscribers amongst that cosmopolitan city's literary set for a second and then a third edition within a few months.

Spurred by success, Catharine and Agnes planned English and American editions, and further botanical collaborations. Catharine must have hoped that this triumph would stimulate interest amongst publishers for her longer manuscript about plants. But all these hopes and plans were quickly overtaken by events. A more attractive proposition than literary sweat and toil came along for pretty, clever Agnes Fitzgibbon: a new suitor. While selling subscriptions for *Canadian Wild Flowers* in Ottawa, she had been introduced to Colonel Brown Chamberlin. Chamberlin, a lawyer who owned the Montreal *Gazette*, was active in the militia and was the Conservative member of Parliament for the Eastern Townships riding of Missisquoi. Moreover, the dashing Colonel Chamberlin had served Sir John A. Macdonald, his political boss, so well that a patronage plum came his way: in early 1870, he was appointed Queen's Printer, which gave him a very comfortable annual salary of $2,000. Within a year of first meeting, Agnes and her suitor were married. Agnes had achieved what every young widow of the era prayed for:

a second chance. Moreover, unlike Charles Fitzgibbon, Brown Chamberlin offered the three Rs—he was rich, respectable and reliable. In 1871, thirty-eight-year-old Agnes Chamberlin gave birth to her fourth daughter and (counting the four earlier deaths) ninth child. She no longer had the time or inclination to scrape a living in the book world.

In July 1870, tragedy struck Catharine Parr Traill's family. Her son Harry had recently got a job as a guard at Kingston Penitentiary. One day, while he was supervising a limekiln within the prison grounds, two convicts attacked and killed him in the course of a planned escape. It was a brutal crime: Harry's head was split open by a crowbar wielded from behind him. The newspapers covered the trial and conviction of the murderers the following November with ghoulish interest—it was the first time a prison guard had been murdered in the line of duty in Canada.

The loss of her second son devastated Catharine. She told Frances Stewart how she desperately tried to forget "the terrible details of this most disastrous event, and to think only that he is gone from amongst us." Susanna's sympathy for her sister was unstinting—although clothed, as usual, with snatches of her own enduring grief. "Oh dear, dear Katie, you have my fullest, deepest sympathy. . . . The poor wife will feel it most, for in the course of Nature, you and I will soon join our dear ones again, but she poor thing has a long sad life of widowhood before her."

Catharine worried about Harry's widow, Lily, and three children. She prayed that "God who is the father of the orphan, and the protector of the widow will not leave them comfortless . . . to His gracious care we must commend poor desolate-hearted Lily and her children." More practically, she invited Harry's only daughter and her own namesake, three-year-old Katharine Parr, to stay with her and her daughter. There were now three Catharine Traills (with variations in the spelling) living at Westove: the writer Catharine, sixty-eight; "Aunt Kate," as Catharine's thirty-four-year-old daughter was now called; and "Little Katie." The two older women found Little Katie "a source of great interest yet of anxious care." Most of the child-rearing fell on the shoulders of Aunt Kate, but Catharine took on herself the responsibility of teaching Little Katie the letters of the alphabet and names of wildflowers. She had less time to pursue botanical research and a publisher for her plant life manuscript.

It was not simply Catharine's preoccupation with family affairs that kept her long manuscript on plant life unpublished during the 1870s. The more fundamental problem was that Catharine was a nineteenth-century woman writing in an eighteenth-century idiom. Botany was changing; natural history was giving way to scientific technique; laboratory work was replacing nature study. Charles Darwin had rocked the intellectual establishment of the English-speaking world when he published *The Origin of Species*. Professional botanists now sought evidence of evolutionary change rather than divine intervention when they studied the propagation of plants. Catharine's writing style—the attractive mix of scientific nomenclature and literary elegance that she had learned from Gilbert White—was increasingly out-of-date. Interest faded in books that reflected sheer love of nature's bounty and admiration of God's handiwork. There was no room for female gifted amateurs amongst the academically qualified male scientists in professional associations. In 1897, when D.P. Penhallow, professor of botany at McGill University, published a review of Canadian botany from 1800 to 1895, there was not a single woman mentioned in his list of over one hundred people who had contributed to the subject.

But Catharine, who was as little interested in intellectual fashions as she was in clothing fashions, remained determined to get her manuscript in print. "Nothing is done, my dear," she remarked to her daughter Katie, "without trying, and if one thing fails I must try another." Her dog-eared manuscript on plant life would see the light of day during her own lifetime because of her persistence and because, for all its faults, it had its charms.

Chapter 18

A Trip to Stony Lake

Susanna leaned heavily on the arm of her nephew, Percy Strickland, as she hobbled along the dusty road. It was a sultry June morning—the hottest day so far of 1872—and the distance from Westove, Catharine's cottage, to the Lakefield steamer dock seemed longer than she recalled. She regretted that she had agreed to walk with Percy when she could have been riding with her sister in his horse-drawn buggy. But Percy had put her on her mettle with a careless remark, as he looked at his two stout aunts, that the buggy would "scarcely hold two fairies" like them. Determined not to let her seventy-year-old sister show her up, sixty-eight-year-old Susanna had insisted on walking the mile to the dock situated just behind the little Anglican Church built by her late brother Sam, who had died five years earlier. Now her lace-up black leather boots were pinching her corns. She would have loved to stop and mop the "glow" from her brow.

Once the landing dock was in sight, however, her good humour returned. It had been a pleasant surprise when Percy had arrived at Catharine's front door that morning to invite his aunts to join a family excursion on the steamer to Stony Lake. Susanna had not seen Stony Lake for years. She vividly recalled the expedition that she and John had made in 1835 by canoe from their log home on Lake Katchewanooka. They had been in Canada less than three years and were still enjoying their "halcyon days" in the bush. The trip been an epiphany for her—a moment when the sheer grandeur of the Canadian landscape had blotted out the endless gnaw of homesickness. The opportunity to revisit such an achingly beautiful landscape was irresistible.

When Percy and Susanna stepped onto the dock, a small crowd was already waiting to board the steamer *Chippewa*. There was Catharine's friend, the Reverend Vincent Clementi, and his wife and niece; Catharine and her daughter Kate; Percy's brothers George, Robert and Roland Strickland, and Roland's wife and Robert's two daughters; plus a handful of other Lakefield residents. There was also a pile of luggage. The gentlemen all had fishing rods and baskets; the ladies had straw hats, parasols and reticules filled with remedies for seasickness and sunburn; Catharine had the basket she always carried for rock, fern and flower specimens; Mrs. Vincent Clementi and Mrs. Roland Strickland had the makings of a picnic.

Catharine and Susanna settled themselves on the wooden seats in the cabin of the little vessel, while the men stood on the deck overhead, by the engine room. Acquaintances often confused the two sisters, with their sharp blue eyes, white hair and lacy widows' bonnets. But differences were more apparent than similarities when they were together. "I am dark and much older looking," Susanna insisted, "and she is a pretty old lady with a soft smiling face and nice pink cheeks." The *Chippewa*, which had been plying the Lakefield to Stony Lake route since the previous year, was emitting an urgent hiss: it had got up enough steam in its boiler to cast off. Its red-painted funnel gave a resounding whistle as the boat headed upstream through Lake Katchewanooka towards Clear Lake.

With every passing year, more of the forest disappeared and the log booms
from Clear Lake down the Otonabee River grew larger.

Susanna's two nephews, Roland and George, had a particular interest
in showing off the delights of Stony Lake. They co-owned the eighty-
foot *Chippewa* with its nineteen-horsepower engine. Roland Strickland,
one of the most important timber merchants in the area, used the
steamer in the spring to tow his log booms from Stony Lake to
Lakefield, and he was eager to drum up passenger traffic for the vessel
during the summer months. Aunt Moodie, the well-known author, might
be very useful in his campaign to promote the attractions of the waterways above Lakefield. She still received invitations from Montreal magazine editors to contribute to their publications: perhaps she might turn
her descriptive talents to the Strickland enterprise?

As the *Chippewa* churned through the water, Catharine chatted away to
anyone who settled near her, but Susanna was silent as she eagerly
searched the scenery for familiar landmarks. As she gazed out the cabin
window at the east shore of Lake Katchewanooka, she could scarcely
make out the property on which she and John had worked so hard in the
1830s. She knew from her visit in 1865 that their old house had collapsed,
but only now, as she took in the entire setting, did she appreciate the

change in the landscape that ruthless logging had wrought. "The woods about it are all gone, and a new growth of small cedars fringes the shore in front," she wrote later to her son-in-law, John Vickers. "There is a tolerable looking modern cottage on the spot that the old log house once occupied, and the old barn survives on the same spot on which it was built, more than 30 years ago, but the woods that framed it are all down, and it has a bare, desolate look."

To Susanna's eyes, the land looked plucked and shaved with its stubble of stumps. The giant pines, oaks and maples that had topped the skyline were felled, and wispy second-growth birch and cedar were only starting to replace them. Huge quantities of lumber had been taken out of the area. The limestone falls down which water had once roared and foamed from Clear Lake had been blasted out in 1871 to make a lock, so that logs could be floated into Lake Katchewanooka more easily. Banks that were once covered in brilliant red cardinal flowers and orange tiger-lilies had been flooded to make a millpond. The magnificent emptiness of sparkling Clear Lake was interrupted by scattered habitation along its west shore. Susanna, who did not share her sister's concerns about vanishing species, was happy to see these signs of life. She decided that "a pretty Catholic church, and burying ground, and a small picturesque group of cottages, gives an air of civilization to the once romantic place."

In 1835, the Moodies had pulled their canoe up at the mill by Young's Point Falls and been served a feast of "bush dainties" by the Young family. Susanna had been particularly startled to be offered coffee that had been boiled in the frying pan—"for the first and last time in my life," she would remember thirty-seven years later. Now, Susanna was delighted to discover that the recently appointed master at the new lock between Lake Katchewanooka and Clear Lake was none other than Pat Young, son of the old miller: "He greeted me with intense Irish glee, and asked after the two pretty little girls he carried down in his arms asleep to put in Moodie's canoe at night," she told John Vickers, Katie's husband. "And sure, was he not delighted to hear that they both had married Irish husbands and that little Katie was the mother of nine children. 'Sure, she was always the clever stirring little thing.'"

The steamer continued through Clear Lake, and the temperature rose in the *Chippewa*'s cabin as the hot yellow sun climbed in the sky. Susanna fanned herself with the latest issue of the *Canadian Monthly and National Review*, and Catharine undid the button at the throat of her black gown. Finally, when the sun was directly overhead, the *Chippewa* nosed its way into Stony Lake. Although thirty years of logging had wiped out the mighty oaks and white pines from its shoreline, the lake itself was as dramatic as Susanna recalled. She stared about her at the great red-granite rocks along the north shore, heaved steeply up "like the bare bones of some ancient world." She looked at the reflections of dark woods "frowning down from their lofty granite ridges" into the cold, blue water. She heard Percy insisting that there were over 1,200 islands, and she wondered how long it would be before this marvellous, vast, lonely place became as popular amongst sightseers as the English Lake District.

Thanks to the efforts of the Strickland family, it didn't take long for Stony Lake to be discovered. The first tourists started arriving to disrupt the "wild and lonely grandeur" as soon as there was a regular steamer service each summer through Lake Katchewanooka and Clear Lake. And three years after Susanna and Catharine took their trip, a new train service from Peterborough to the Lakefield wharf doubled the steamers' business. Soon the fighting qualities of Stony Lake muskellunge, the delicate pink flesh of its salmon trout, the profusion of private islands, the azure clarity of its waters and the abundance of deer, partridge and ruffed grouse in the surrounding woods were famous amongst fishermen and hunters as far south as Ohio and New York. Local entrepreneurs built shoreline hotels with well-stocked bars and acted as guides for sportsmen. The *Canadian Illustrated News* named Stony Lake "possibly the prettiest locality in Canada." In 1893, Catharine's daughter Kate bought a three-acre island, Minnewawa, where Catharine spent happy summers. She slept in the rustic cabin and delighted in the island's "*most beautiful oaks and pines,*" as she told her son William, "and the wild picturesque outline of the rocky mounts and deep valleys." Within twenty years of Susanna's and Catharine's summer trip in 1872, the whole area had acquired a new name, the Kawartha Lakes (a corruption of the Ojibwa word *kawatha*, meaning "bright waters and happy land"), and become an established part of the summer cottaging ritual for many Canadian families.

In 1872, however, the two sisters were still looking at an empty expanse of glistening water and an unbroken shoreline. As the *Chippewa's* paddle slowed, and the vessel came to a halt about twenty-five miles from Lakefield, the men in the party retrieved their fishing rods and baited their hooks. The Reverend Mr. Clementi and Percy Strickland were particularly lucky, and soon several plump black bass and salmon trout were gutted and ready to be fried on a portable stove. They made "a capital dinner," in Susanna's opinion. Then the party disembarked on the north shore, where there was a natural landing place, called "Julien's landing" after an old French-Canadian fur trader who had built a shack there. Kate Traill set off to climb a nearby hill, called "the big sugar loaf rock," while the elderly members of the party sought the shade of the woods. Some aspects of the wilderness had not changed in three decades: the black-flies and mosquitoes were still relentless. Catharine, hot on the trail of a delicate fern that she just *knew* lingered in these woods, brushed them off with an imperious wave of her hand. But Susanna had *never* made the best of things, and she was not about to start now. As she angrily tried to swat the insects, she almost stepped on a snake. It was enough to send her marching back on board. Nevertheless, she described the trip to friends as "a grand party."

After she was widowed, in 1869, Susanna had been slow to take up Catharine's invitations to stay with her at Westove, in Lakefield. Susanna never displayed either the sense of family or the instinct for survival that Catharine always had. When Catharine was vulnerable, she retreated without hesitation into the comforting Lakefield fold of the Strickland clan. She had done this both in 1832, when the Traills first arrived in Canada, and in 1859, after Thomas Traill's death. But Susanna floundered after John's death, just as the Moodies had floundered after their arrival in Upper Canada in 1832. She had no roof to call her own, and she spent the rest of her life ricocheting amongst various friends and relations. The trip to Stony Lake took place at the start of one of her longest sojourns with Catharine at Westove, after Susanna had tried and rejected a variety of other options.

Immediately after John's death, Susanna had joined her youngest son, Robert, in Seaforth, sixty miles northwest of Toronto. Of Susanna's five children, only her youngest son had felt the full force of this passionate woman's love. Robert had been born in the relative comfort of the Belleville years. By the time he was a toddler, Susanna had lost one child in infancy and another child, Johnnie, in a drowning accident. Little Robert was infinitely precious to her—and like his father, he could always raise her spirits. After John's death, he was the first to insist that Susanna should come and live with him. He had recently been appointed

stationmaster at Seaforth, which was on the Grand Trunk Railway branch-line between Goderich and Stratford. His offer to Susanna was more than generous, since it meant that he would have to support, on a very limited salary, not only his delicate wife Nellie and their three small children, but a mother and a mother-in-law who couldn't stand each other. They were all crammed into a badly built, four-room house, the front door of which opened directly

Susanna, alone and lonely.

onto the platform. Every time a train thundered by, or drew to a shuddering halt, the house shook. Nellie's mother, Mrs. Russell, constantly shrieked at the children or slapped them, setting off gales of tears. Susanna spent most of her time in her own bedroom, painting, knitting or writing, and wishing she had somebody to talk to. "Ah my dear sister," she wrote to Catharine. "My poor, sore heart is so *empty*. . . . The days seem so long and sad."

After a year of the chaos in Robert's household, Susanna had had enough. Catharine entreated her sister to come and stay with her, but Susanna yearned to return to Belleville and John's grave. "Whenever, lately, I visited my husband's grave, it appeared to me such a blessed haven of rest, that I longed with an intense longing to lie down beside him. Poor darling, the harebells and Ox-eyes were growing upon his lowly bed . . ." She decided to take lodgings in Belleville with some old friends, Mr. and Mrs. Frederick Rous. But this arrangement soured,

Robert Moodie, Susanna's beloved youngest child, with his wife Nellie and one of their seven children.

because Susanna found the Rous daughter "selfish, indolent and conceited" and Mrs. Rous's stews and hashes indigestible. "It is quite a misfortune to have been a good cook," she wrote to Catharine. "It makes one very dainty, but I can't help it." She moved on to rooms with Mrs. John Dougall, on the Kingston Road. But she grumbled that Mrs. Dougall was not feeding her properly, despite the ample rent she was paid. Her health deteriorated. "I have suffered awful agonies from inflammation of the stomach and bowels and frightful haemorrhage which has reduced me to a bag of bones," she complained to friends.

Susanna's health problems weren't helped by two worries. She wanted to continue her literary career—in particular, she was eager to publish some of her husband's work. But without John's guidance, her writing and editing skills deserted her. She agreed to let George Maclean Rose, of the Toronto publishing house Hunter, Rose and Company, bring out a new edition of her own *Roughing It in the Bush*, but she couldn't even draft an updated introduction. "You must help me with matter for the Canadian preface," she implored Katie Vickers. "I forget all the subjects dear John told me to write about on the present state and prospects of Canada." It took her months to draft an introductory chapter in which she defended herself against her critics, celebrated the progress of the previous forty years and insisted that "some of the happiest years of my life" had been spent in the colony.

The second source of stress for Susanna was her family. Susanna's relations with her eldest four children continued to deteriorate. As adults, both Katie and Agnes found their mother exasperating. When she stayed with them, she was demanding and critical. Susanna was a little too free with her opinions on child-raising and sketch-writing ("I think her publishing has not been profitable," she wrote to her sister Catharine, about Agnes Chamberlin, "but she would not listen to my advice"). Susanna's devotion to her husband had been particularly hard for the two boys, Dunbar and Donald, who always felt second-best. In 1866, to his mother's consternation, shiftless Donald had married Julia Russell, the sister of Dunbar's wife Eliza. Susanna had now decided that she didn't like either of the two Jamaican sisters, and she could never resist being catty about them in her letters to Catharine ("It is only that horrid woman," she told her sister, that prevented Donald from writing home). By the 1870s, both men were living as far away from their mother as they could afford on very limited means. Dunbar was in Colorado, in an experimental agricultural community. Donald was an alcoholic, who was constantly scrounging money from relatives and whose wife eventually left him. Neither ever visited their widowed mother, although she always kept in touch with both of them.

Robert Moodie was more sympathetic to his mother than his elder brothers and sisters. But he was struggling with health and financial problems of his own, which worried Susanna. "The dear kind fellow has a shocking cough," Susanna wrote to Catharine, "and is very thin and delicate." As though he did not have tribulations enough, an additional blow struck in 1871. His wife Nellie was overcome with what Susanna described as *"raving madness."* Today, Nellie would be diagnosed as suffering from postnatal depression: she had just given birth to her fourth child, and was subject to alternating fits of weeping and rage. But there was no clear diagnosis one hundred years ago. Instead, she was committed to the grim wards of Toronto's Lunatic Asylum, whose "raving maniacs" (including the murderess Grace Marks) Susanna had visited twenty years earlier. Robert was left with four young children, an unpleasant mother-in-law and bills for both Nellie's treatment and his baby's wet-nurse.

Susanna was stuck. She didn't like her Belleville lodgings, but she could not return to Robert's cramped household. Sensing her sister's unhappiness, Catharine continued to press her to come and live in Lakefield. Susanna did not really want to be her sister's guest—she valued her independence, and she knew that Westove had become a refuge for lame ducks. Every fatherless child, ailing friend and grumpy adolescent within the extended Strickland network knew that Aunt Traill's door was always open to them. But there were few alternatives for Aunt Moodie. So in the spring of 1872, Susanna accepted her sister's invitation and boarded the train to Peterborough.

Catharine always loved family reunions. She and her daughter Kate put a stove, a carpet and a cherrywood dresser in the unused bedroom on the second floor for Susanna, and Catharine wrote in delight that "my dear sister Moodie" was going to be "an inmate with us." At first, Susanna was profoundly relieved to have found such a pleasant home. "Nothing could exceed the kindness of my dear sister and her good daughter," she told her daughter Katie Vickers. "We live twice as well as I did at Mrs. D.'s, without the miserable and begrudged scarcity and eternal liver and fish dinners. If I feel hungry I can get a bit of bread and butter without having to keep a store of food in private." As summer approached, she sat in Catharine's garden, "in a dreamy sort of rapture communing with nature and my own soul," smelling the lilac and honeysuckle that her sister had planted and watching "the bright winged birds and butterflies disport themselves." Catharine's carefully nurtured collection bed of twenty-five different kinds of fern did not interest Susanna, but the summer riot of roses and delphiniums brought back pleasant memories of Suffolk. Often, she would take Catharine's four-year-old granddaughter Katie Traill down to the water's edge to watch the perch and sunfish darting through the shadows just below the surface.

The arrangement appeared to suit everybody. From England, Sarah Strickland Gwillym wrote to Susanna to express the satisfaction felt by all four English sisters, now well into their seventies and in varying degrees of health: "I cannot say how glad I am that you have arranged to live with dear Kate. I think it will be a mutual comfort to you both." Agnes and Sarah probably hoped that if their Canadian sisters shared living expenses, they would need fewer handouts from home.

However, the English sisters might have guessed that Susanna and Catharine would not be happy under one roof for long. They themselves had refused to contemplate living with each other. To Agnes's chagrin, she had been unable to bully Sarah into allowing her to move into Sarah's comfortable home in the Lake District. Agnes, in turn, had refused to allow Jane to share her elegant Georgian house in Southwold, purchased after their mother's death and the sale of Reydon Hall. Jane had had to content herself with buying a humble cottage next door to Agnes. Elizabeth wouldn't live with anybody: she preferred a reclusive life in her own house, Abbott's Lodge, in Tilford, Surrey. The only relative she visited was her brother Tom, now retired from the merchant navy. Given this pattern of scratchy relationships, it is no surprise to discover that harmony did not prevail for long at Westove, either.

Susanna and Catharine were too different, and by now too set in their ways, to live together. If anyone was sick, Catharine would start boiling roots and herbs, according to old Indian recipes. Some of her remedies sound terrifying: the limewater gargle that she recommended for a sore throat consisted of diluted quicklime. Susanna, on the other hand, would insist on producing Brown's Bronchial Troches or Ayre's Liver Pills—nostrums that were all the rage in the late nineteenth century but were rarely effective. When Catharine's daughter Annie Atwood arrived with an unruly swarm of children, Susanna would get snappy. ("You must just turn a deaf ear to criticisms on the little ones as though you heard it not," Catharine told Annie. "It is just her way you know.") Susanna objected to the number of people continually trooping through the house, and the consequent expense. ("Aunt has only a few dollars in the Bank," she wrote to her daughter Katie Vickers. "But she will *enter-tain . . .*") Sarah Gwillym, on the other side of the Atlantic, got the impression that the household was messy and disorganized. When an envelope arrived in England with unfinished scraps of two letters from Catharine, Sarah wrote back: "Tell her with my love that her last letters were rather disappointing. . . . I suppose that as she seemed to have more than a houseful of people with her that she had more on her hands than she could well get through, poor dear, though I suppose that in Canada all visitors help till all the duties are done."

Susanna spent more and more of her time in her bedroom, reading and going through old papers rather than joining the endless family gatherings in the drawing room downstairs. She refused to join Catharine for overnight visits to relatives' houses. She had been asked by a collector for a copy of her famous sister Agnes Strickland's autograph, and as she searched through a pile of old letters, she was often moved to tears. "I had no idea that I had so many, and such long letters from Agnes, and until my unlucky book was published, so full of affection," she told Katie Vickers, adding triumphantly, "Mrs. Traill seemed quite *astonished* that Agnes had written *such letters to me!*" As the months went by, Susanna's thoughts of Agnes became increasingly fond and she barely remembered how Agnes's reaction to *Roughing It in the Bush* had stung her.

In 1872, Susanna and Catharine were disturbed to hear that Agnes, now seventy-six, had suffered a serious fall on the stairs of a friend's house and broken her leg. Jane Strickland wrote from Southwold that the accident had been a prelude to serious bronchial problems for Agnes: "the attack was both paralytic and apoplectic, but you must not name it to her or let any of her relatives in Canada mention it as that would make her unhappy." Agnes's health slowly collapsed, and she died in July 1874. A few weeks later, her brother Thomas Strickland passed away.

Susanna expressed quite as much grief as Catharine at Agnes's death. She was quick to correct various errors made in an obituary that appeared in the Toronto *Globe*, and to add a eulogy of her own: "An affectionate, loving daughter, a faithful sister and friend, kind and benevolent to the poor, and possessing warm sympathies for the sick and suffering; she never let the adulation of the world interfere with the blessed domestic charities."

But indomitable Agnes had never forgiven her youngest sister for that "unlucky book." At her death, she was not going to give Susanna the pleasure of believing that she could rival Catharine as the family favourite. Susanna must have been stunned when, a few weeks later, she heard the contents of Agnes's will. Agnes left the copyright to her *Lives of the Queens of England*, still a bestseller in Victorian England, jointly to Catharine Parr Traill and Percy Strickland. (Her sister Elizabeth was furious, since by rights half belonged to her; however, Elizabeth died the following year). There was no specific bequest for Susanna. Agnes did not leave her sister even a single keepsake from Reydon, "which was rather mean I must say," Catharine acknowledged.

In the fall of 1874, a large box arrived in Lakefield from Sarah Gwillym. It contained a treasure-trove: the splendid wardrobe in which Agnes had made her entrances at various royal, noble and civic occasions. Catharine pulled out black silk and brocade gowns, jet and gold jewellery, pearl-encrusted collars and intricate lace flounces, whalebone corsets and horsehair petticoats, muslin underskirts and voluminous velvet cloaks, elaborately decorated bonnets, shawls and gloves. "It is so many years ago since I looked upon articles so rich and costly," she marvelled. Most articles were distributed amongst various granddaughters and great-nieces. The only items Susanna received were a bracelet and a jasper brooch.

Soon after the parcel arrived, Susanna decided to leave Lakefield. Perhaps she had simply had enough of Westove's endless stream of relatives with their crying babies. It must have been hard for her to stomach the contrast between Catharine's children, who showered their mother with affection and worried about her health, and her own offspring, whose attention to her was fitful at best. Or maybe she left because Agnes's will, with its ostentatious concern for Catharine and disregard for Susanna, pushed her youngest sister's nose painfully out of joint. For whatever reason, Susanna packed her bags and took the train back to Toronto.

From now on, Susanna stayed only a few weeks at Lakefield each summer, and spent the rest of the time in Toronto, where Robert now lived, and where she could be close to her Moodie and Vickers grandchildren. There was a more varied stream of visitors in Toronto than in Lakefield to amuse Susanna with talk of exotic new fashions, such as spotted veils and women's rights. It was still not very comfortable living with Robert (he moved house seven times in less than three years), but Nellie Moodie had returned home after three years in the asylum and was willing to cherish her cantankerous mother-in-law.

Susanna was a petulant old woman, but she always kept her sense of humour. Her own children found her moods hard to bear, but her grandchildren appreciated her mischievous stories about their relatives. Who wouldn't be amused by a grandmother who wrote funny verse, as Susanna did to fourteen-year-old William Vickers, the fourth of Katie Vickers's ten children? William, a student at Upper Canada College in Toronto, had lost the gloves she had knitted for him and written to her requesting another pair. Susanna replied:

> You careless fellow!—What, lost your mitts?
> Aren't you afraid I'll give you fits?
> Punch your head, or slap your face,
> Or send to a corner in dire disgrace?
> Were I a lady young and fair,
> You would certainly take the greatest care,
> Of the smallest thing her love could proffer,
> So what excuse my lad can you offer?

By 1876, Susanna's eyesight was no longer sharp enough to knit, but her wit was quite sharp enough for verse.

> When I take up the pins in your behalf
> I give you leave my boy to laugh—
> At old Knitty Knotty, who loves you well,
> And hopes to see you a learned swell.

When Catharine and Susanna were apart, they thought fondly of each other—even though they knew that, together, they got on each other's nerves. They exchanged frequent letters, never forgetting to mark each other's birthdays. Susanna wrote to "my beloved sister of old" whose face "seems looking at me through the dim mist of years in its youthful bloom." She assured friends that "My dear sister Catharine is as amiable and loveable as ever. . . . We still love with the old love through weal or woe." The sisters were now in their seventies, and with each passing year, more ailments filled their letters. Catharine's lumbago made writing uncomfortable; Susanna had an "odious hernia" which prevented her from walking very far. Both women complained of failing memories (although each could reel off the name of every single family member on each side of the Atlantic). More poignantly, Susanna began to suffer spells of dementia. "I had no idea," she wrote sadly in 1882, "that age was such a ruthless destroyer of the senses and so perfectly obliterates the past, by mingling it up with the present."

In 1883, Catharine received a summons from Robert Moodie: Susanna was sick. As Catharine boarded the 2:30 pm train to Toronto at Lakefield Station on a gloomy November afternoon, she wondered whether she would ever see any of her sisters again in this world. "There are only four of all the old Stricklands left," Catharine had written sadly to Ellen Dunlop that morning. "Two in England—Mrs. Gwillym 85—Jane Margaret 83—myself 81—and dear Mrs. Moodie in her eightieth year— an aged sisterhood." After a seven-hour journey, she stepped onto the platform at the yet-unfinished Union Station and was immediately bewildered by the throng of people, the whistles and clangs of huge locomotives, the white brightness of the huge station's new electric lights. But Robert Moodie, reliable as always, was there to greet her, carry her shabby cloth bag and find a cab to take them to his house on Wilton Crescent, between Jarvis and Sherbourne streets.

Catharine slowly clambered up the narrow staircase of the brick duplex to the bedroom overlooking the back garden, where Susanna had spent most of the previous two years. She was shocked when she saw Susanna: "She looked *aged* and feeble and I found the fine intellect much weakened . . . more than I could have supposed. Only at times she would brighten up, and seem more like her old self; but it was like flashes of light on dull cloudy days." Catharine's ten-day visit proved a tonic for both these sturdy women. Susanna insisted on struggling down the narrow stairs to Robert's parlour, where her old piano now stood. Then Catharine would sit down and pick out the hymns they had learned in their Suffolk childhood. Susanna insisted that Charles Wesley was "the king of hymn writers," and the sisters' quavery sopranos would join together in the words of "Jesu, lover of my soul" or "Forth in thy Name,

O Lord, I go." Many of the poignant verses must have recalled for the sisters their hard times in the backwoods, when they and their young families had assembled on Sundays in Catharine's parlour to sing the same verses:

> Other refuge have I none,
> Hangs my helpless soul on thee;
> Leave, ah! leave me not alone,
> Still support and comfort me.

Catharine's visit gave Susanna a new lease on life. For a few months, the shadows of dementia retreated from her mind, and she recovered her appetite for visitors. When a dapper, middle-aged Englishman, with shiny black boots and a jaunty self-assurance, turned up at Robert's house, she was eager to talk to him. The visitor was James Ewing Ritchie, a well-known English travel writer. Ritchie had been commissioned by the London periodical the *Christian World* to cross the Atlantic in order to prepare a series of articles on the pros and cons of emigration to Canada. But Susanna knew Ritchie as the son of Andrew Ritchie, once the pastor of Wrentham Congregational Church, three miles north of Reydon. It was Pastor Ritchie who had converted the young and spiritually restless Susanna to Congregationalism in 1830.

James Ritchie had inquired into the whereabouts of Agnes Strickland's sisters as soon as he arrived in Canada. He knew that their stories, and their link to the famous royal biographer, would make great copy. Before he had even tracked them down, he'd drafted a few dramatic paragraphs about two "delicately nurtured ladies" who had been "familiar with the best of London literary society" and had then arrived in the "waste, howling wilderness" of Canada and slaved as "no servant girl slaves in England." Now he had finally located Susanna in Toronto, and he reported that she possessed "a mental vigour and active memory rare in one so aged." They talked for hours about her memories of her Suffolk childhood and of Regency London.

After talking to Susanna, Ritchie knew that both sisters had incredible stories to tell. So he made a special side trip in order to visit Lakefield and knocked on the door of Westove. Catharine, who had fussed over James when he was a little boy, was even more delighted to see him than Susanna had been—it is easy to imagine a smart London journalist flinching from the garrulous flow of reminiscences he had sparked. Ritchie told his readers that he was bowled over by Mrs. Traill's "queenlike" manners and enthusiasm for nature: "In spite of all the hardships she has had to undergo as wife and mother in the wilderness, her face still retains something of the freshness and fairness of her youth. She is a wonderful old lady." Ritchie lavished praise on the literary output of both women, and on their role as "pioneers of Canadian literature." Much of Ritchie's interview with Susanna was reprinted in the *Globe*, and his whole collection of articles was published in London in 1885 under the title *To Canada with Emigrants*.

Even after all these years, the English sisters winced when they saw references in the London press to their Canadian sisters' humble circumstances. All that *Roughing It in the Bush* mortification flamed again in Jane Strickland, who wrote a tetchy letter to Susanna. Jane dismissed James Ritchie as "Sir Snob" and deplored his patronizing style: "While praising [Catharine's] elegant arrangements he takes care to inform his readers 'it is only a wooden house.' . . . We all thought him a disgusting child. He must have written in pure spite."

Susanna's interview with James Ritchie was amongst the last encounters she had with anyone outside her family circle. Strange fantasies began to flood her mind—fantasies that she had been robbed and was now penniless. The fantasies intensified over the next few months as Susanna's sanity slowly slipped away. She could no longer read; she could not walk without assistance; she confused her children with her grandchildren. By the end of 1884, she required constant nursing, and Robert Moodie and his sister Katie Vickers decided to move their mother to Katie's mansion at 52 Adelaide Street.

Yet it was not until March 1885 that the old lady seemed ready to

Susanna's daughter Katie and her husband John Vickers, with seven of their ten children, in the parlour of their opulent mansion on Toronto's Adelaide Street.

relinquish her hold on life. Catharine arrived to sit with her and listen to her inchoate ramblings. Susanna was a wreck of her former independent, private self. Catharine wrote to Ellen Dunlop: "I cannot leave her as she frets if I go away and when she comes in to me she keeps talking and rambles so that I lose all thought of anything and every one else. . . . My sister who used to rail against dolls to play with and call them hideous idols and find fault with mothers for giving little children dolls to play with has a great wax doll dressed like a baby and this she nurses and caresses—and believes it is her own living babe and cannot bear it out of her sight. . . . This is to me the saddest sight for it shews the entire change that has come over her fine intellect. She is a child again in very truth."

It was a wretched, anguished death. On Easter Sunday, the new bell of St. Andrew's Church on King Street began to clang. Susanna grew dreadfully agitated. She got it into her head that the bell tolled for a murderer who had cut off her head, and she struggled out of bed to kneel on the floor and pray for his soul. For the next thirty-six hours, the poor old woman was repeatedly startled awake by fearsome delusions and nightmares. Finally, as her nurse, daughter and sister slumped exhausted by her bedside, she fell into a coma. Catharine listened to her laboured breaths. "The total loss of your dear aunt's faculties," Catharine told her daughter Annie Atwood, "had indeed reconciled us to the final close of her life on earth . . . the restful peace of God seemed to have taken the place of all the sad harassed pained expression that was for so long sad to witness on that beloved face." Staring at her sister's face, Catharine was transported to the bedroom of Reydon Hall, where she had last seen her own mother "calmly sleeping" fifty-two years earlier. As she watched and prayed, Susanna drew her last breath.

Robert Moodie arranged for his mother's remains to travel to Belleville by train. Susanna Moodie was buried in the newly laid-out graveyard to the west of the city, overlooking the Bay of Quinte. The bodies of her husband John and her two sons were taken from the old graveyard, in the centre of town, and buried next to her. John Vickers paid for a splendid white marble angel, wearing a Moodie-like expression of fierce pride and holding a star aloft, to be erected at the grave. *The Globe* published a long obituary, applauding Susanna's determination to help create a Canadian literature: "Many a struggling Canadian author has reason to thank her for encouragement and advice kindly given." The obituary writer described *Roughing It in the Bush* as the best-read book ever written in Canada and made the prescient comment: "Its pictures of patient suffering and endurance will last long after the landmarks with which they are associated will have disappeared."

Chapter 19

Apotheosis in Ottawa

n 1884, when she was eighty-two, Catharine went to stay in the Dominion capital and found that she was a celebrity. "I am paid more attention to here in Ottawa," she wrote with delight to her sister Sarah Gwillym, "than I ever have been [elsewhere]." She was fussed over by "the heads of the society of the place . . . for my literary talents, which of course few care for at Lakefield."

A prophet is always without honour in her own country: Catharine's Lakefield neighbours knew her not as a famous author, but as Sam Strickland's sister who was a walking encyclopedia of flowers. Catharine recognized that her newfound status as a celebrity said a lot about Canada, too. "Education has made vast strides since even our flower book appeared," she explained to Sarah. "There is not now the struggle for *mere bread* that there was—the cultivation of the mind is extending far and wide even to the remotest parts of the country. You cannot think the progress that a few years have made among all ranks of the people."

The progress of the new nation in the late nineteenth century was phenomenal. The population of British North America, only 800,000 when the sisters arrived in 1832, now numbered 4.5 million. The Canadian landscape had been transformed from bush farms and mud roads to open countryside, railways and industrial towns. There were seven provinces now, stretching from the red earth of tiny Prince Edward Island in the east to the unexplored vastness of British Columbia in the west. Sir John A. Macdonald, first Prime Minister of the Dominion of Canada, was well on his way to achieving his dream of a railway that reached to the Pacific Ocean. The economy had begun to flag, but most families continued to have large numbers of children, and settlers surged into the prairies and beyond. Thanks to the efforts of education pioneer Egerton Ryerson, a strong-willed Methodist minister and provincial politician, Ontario now had a first-rate system of primary and secondary schools. No child at the end of the century had to forego instruction in mathematics, literature and history the way that Catharine's and Susanna's children had. Every small community in southern Ontario aspired to a small brick schoolhouse and some kind of lending library (although most banned works of fiction). Specialized journals flourished, particularly those that covered religious or agricultural issues or promoted the benefits of temperance.

Nowhere was the speed with which Canada had been civilized more evident than in the capital. When the Traills and Moodies had crossed the Atlantic to the New World half a century earlier, there had been only a muddy, rowdy lumber town on the banks of the Ottawa River, just below the roaring Chaudiere Falls. Now Ottawa boasted a viceregal court at Rideau Hall, the residence of the Governor-General of the Dominion, and the town was graced with a magnificent set of copper-roofed Parliament Buildings that constituted, according to the novelist Anthony Trollope, "the noblest architecture in North America."

For all the pomp and ceremony, however, Ottawa was still a lumber town. James Ewing Ritchie called in there before he carried on to Toronto and Lakefield to visit the Strickland sisters. The author of *To Canada with Emigrants* described it to his English readers as "a curious compound—almost Irish in that respect—of splendour and meanness. There are magnificent shops—and then you come to the wooden shanties, which in such a city ought long ere this to have been improved off the face of this earth." Like so many visitors from the rarefied literary air of London, Ewing was astonished by the medley of characters who congregated in the Canadian capital: "I met there statesmen, adventurers, wild men of the woods or prairie, deputies from Manitoba, lawyers from Quebec, sharpers and honest men, all staying at one hotel; and it seemed strange to sit at dinner and see great rough fellows, with the manners of ploughmen, quaffing their costly champagne, and fancying themselves patterns of gentility and taste." Nonetheless, Ewing reflected that the horrors faced by Susanna, Catharine and other early pioneers "are now amongst the pleasant reminiscences of the past."

This was the Ottawa to which Catharine, a cheerful octogenarian with lively blue eyes, came to visit her favourite niece and co-author, Agnes Fitzgibbon Chamberlin, in January 1884. She boarded the smoky carriage of the Grand Trunk Railway at Brockville, where she had been staying with friends, then changed at Prescott onto the Ottawa & Prescott Railway line. During her

Agnes Moodie Fitzgibbon Chamberlin, a respected figure in Ottawa during the 1880s, had her mother's spirit and intelligence.

three hours of jolting train travel, a familiar dread of station crowds at the other end began to suffuse her. She worried that she would never manage to clamber down unaided from the train with all her baggage. She stared anxiously out the window, noting snowbanks so high that the farmhouses and Dutch barns were almost buried. But thirty miles from the capital, a cheery voice called out, "Oh Auntie! I am so glad you are here!" It was Agnes's eldest daughter, thirty-three-year-old Maime Fitzgibbon, who years earlier had helped colour the lithographs for *The Wild Flowers of Canada,* and had now joined the train to ensure her great-aunt's comfort. "All the weary feeling and the anxious thoughts fled like melted snow away," Catharine wrote to Ellen Dunlop.

Maime, or Mary Agnes as she had been christened, was a particular favourite of Catharine's because she herself was now an author. In 1880, she had published a lively account of a trip she took by rail, steamer and road to Manitoba, where she spent some months as governess to the children of a CPR engineer. Maime was no fool: she had capitalized on her famous grandmother, Susanna Moodie, by calling her book *A Trip to Manitoba, or Roughing it on the Line,* and in an attempt to snare a valuable patron she had dedicated it to Lady Dufferin. Maime chatted away to her great-aunt as the train chuffed north. "You will I am sure like your great niece Miss Fitzgibbon," Catharine wrote to Sarah Gwyllim, who had invited Maime to spend some time in England with her, "She is clever, practical and very agreeable—not pretty, but nice and lady-like and possesses much general knowledge and taste and the talent for writing which still belongs as a source of heirloom to the Strickland race."

When the train drew into Ottawa's fussy little station, cab drivers looking for fares and boys eager to earn a few cents carrying baggage swarmed onto the platform. "I should have been perfectly bewildered by the jostling crowd of men and horses and boys pulling at one's sleeve," Catharine recorded. But capable Maime elbowed a path through the throng, helped Catharine into a cab, bundled her up against the piercing east wind that cut through the town and told the surly Irish cab driver to take them to New Edinburgh, a small village about a mile east of the

Parliament Buildings. The cab bumped along the unploughed road and over the two rickety wooden bridges that spanned the frozen Rideau River. Soon Catharine was settled in front of a warm fire at 52 Alexander Street, the Chamberlins' pleasant brick house, barely two hundred yards from the Governor-General's gates at Rideau Hall.

Within a few days of Catharine's arrival, she was swept up into the social life of the capital by "the good kind [Colonel] and my dear Agnes C." Agnes introduced her aunt to a social ritual that had not reached Lakefield: weekly "At Homes," at which ladies received friends and acquaintances. "On Monday Mrs. C took me to call with her on Mrs. Macpherson," Catharine wrote to Ellen Dunlop, "and it was *her day* . . ." Catharine, who had never had much time for social rituals, was both impressed and uncomfortable. "I saw several strangers . . . but they were all *rather* grand." Next, Agnes hired a cab to take her aunt through Rideau Hall's wrought-iron gates and up to the viceregal front door so Catharine could write her name in the visitors' book. This would alert the Marquess of Lansdowne, recently arrived to serve as the Dominion's fifth Governor-General, to the presence in town of a distinguished visitor. "Oh Ellen! How I enjoyed the drive through the beautiful grounds and the dear snow laden evergreens of the woods—it was a treat and took me back to old times but the deep, deep snow! . . . and the *cold*—last night was 26° below Zero."

The greatest excitement came in February, when an engraved and crested invitation arrived for Catharine from Rideau Hall. His Excellency the Governor-General, and his wife Lady Lansdowne, requested the pleasure of the company of Mrs. Traill at a winter soirée. On the evening of Saturday, February 23, Catharine, the Chamberlins and Maime Fitzgibbon swaddled themselves in buffalo robes for the short drive through the icy evening air under a star-studded sky. Catharine was in ecstasy: "The drive through the avenue among the snow laden trees was delightful . . . a splendid young moon just above the dark pine woods gave light enough to make every old leafless oak and silvery birch stand out from the darker evergreens in bold relief." As the party neared the Hall, they saw "a great vapoury cloud of smoke rising into the still air and spreading in fold after fold upwards above the trees, the lower part gilded till it appeared like a golden veil over the great solid banks of snow." The next turn in the driveway revealed the flames of a giant bonfire leaping skyward and illuminating the toboggan slide. The toboggans "flashed past on their downward descent with a speed that almost took my breath to see their lightning-like swiftness as they flew past us," Catharine wrote to Sarah Gwyllim.

Lady Lansdowne made the old lady feel very welcome. She took her arm and escorted her along a path, illuminated by Chinese paper lanterns hung from tree branches, to see the skating rink. The belles of Ottawa, cheeks flushed and eyes sparkling in the cold air, spun around as a brave little band played Viennese waltzes: "It was a pretty lively sight, the girls skating on this wood-encircled sheet of ice lighted up by torches on a little islet in the far end of the rink." By now, Catharine was feeling chilled, so she and Lady Lansdowne went into what the latter called the "log cabin" to warm up by the stove. Catharine chuckled as she compared this Petit Trianon fantasy of life in the woods with her own memory of the real thing. "It was not a real log cabin, for it was . . . handsomely panelled with varnished wood inside . . . not rough and chinked and plastered as log houses used to be. This would have been a palace for a settler in the old settlement days of the Backwoods. We should have been thought too luxurious altogether and the house out of keeping with the rude furniture, diet and dress of that time."

Up until this moment, Catharine had been enjoying herself. But she suddenly realized that people were staring and pointing at her. She heard people whisper, "That's her, that's Mrs. Traill." Several of the voices spoke in the kind of aristocratic English accents that she thought she had left far behind her when she waved goodbye to England. A tidal wave of self-consciousness rushed through her. She felt out of her element, just as, years ago, she had felt unsettled within the unfriendly class system of Britain. Had her sister Susanna been the literary lion at this gathering, she would have watched with cool amusement the Henry

The 1884 skating party at Rideau Hall, organized by the Governor-General.
Catharine found the log cabin "a palace . . . far too handsomely panelled."

James world of cigar smoke, rustling silk skirts and social nuance, as she
had once enjoyed them in Thomas Pringle's house in Hampstead.
Susanna would have risen to the occasion and revelled in being the centre
of attention. But Susanna at that time was close to death in Toronto, and
Catharine was acutely uncomfortable. Perhaps her nonchalance about her
own appearance caught up with her in this plummy crowd; her coiffure
might have suddenly felt dishevelled and her black silk gown (another
Agnes hand-me-down) shabby. "Short people stood on tiptoe, and
others peered over shoulders and pushed those before them aside peering at poor me as if I had been the shewpiece of the play," she confessed
to Ellen Dunlop a couple of days later. "The poor old lioness squeezed
herself into a corner (I believe some people expected her to roar or wag
her tail) not being accustomed to be gazed at in that way—it was a little
oppressive."

Kind Lady Lansdowne rescued her guest and took her into Rideau
Hall for refreshments. Catharine admired the platefuls of cakes and
fruit, but contented herself with a cup of hot coffee. She was not

impressed by the manners of her fellow guests: "all seemed bent on making the *most* of the liberal hospitality of His Excellency." But she herself made quite an impression on others. When Agnes Chamberlin told her friend Mrs. John Thorburn, wife of the librarian of the Canadian Geological Survey, that her elderly aunt was present, Maria Thorburn made a beeline for Catharine and introduced herself. "I do love nice old ladies," Maria wrote in her journal. "And she is so interesting, over eighty . . . I wonder if it is her love of nature that has kept her young and cheerful. Mrs. Traill has that pretty pink complexion that you see sometimes in old English ladies, a nice forehead and soft white hair."

Catharine enjoyed her glimpse of viceregal life, but she had a particular motive for attending the Governor-General's party. She knew that James Fletcher, a botanist and entomologist who was then sub-librarian in the Parliamentary Library, was likely to be present, and she wanted to ask his advice about her plant manuscript. Towards the end of the evening, wrote Maria Thorburn, "Mr. Fletcher made his appearance. I vacated my seat to him and left him and the old lady to consult on the matter."

Catharine had got to know James Fletcher in the early 1880s, when she had tentatively sent him her manuscript for comment. Fletcher, who was born in Kent, England, was still a young man, but he became an instant ally to Catharine because he was a natural historian of the old school. "I am charmed with your style and find it so attractive after the irreverent materialistic philosophy, falsely so-called, of too many of our contemporary naturalists," he had replied. "It is very charming for me to see such love for our beneficent creation, and reverence for His perfect works." He read her manuscript carefully, marking with a red tick those flowers that he thought she had identified incorrectly, or for which she had given the wrong geographic locale. But he was a tactful editor. He suggested he send her specimens of the plants he had queried, so she could check. And he assured her that he had "seldom enjoyed any 'communing with nature' more than I have the perusal of your thoroughly and patently original notes on our loveliest treasures, the flowers of the field."

Catharine's Ottawa visit in 1884 allowed her to see other prominent scientific men in the capital. An extraordinary collection of self-educated and gifted engineers, geologists and biologists had gravitated to Ottawa after Confederation. These were men eager to participate in the great enterprise of discovering, mapping and developing the vast territories at Ottawa's doorstep. Many were associated with the Geological Survey of Canada, which had moved from Montreal to Ottawa in 1881; most were charter members of Canada's Royal Society, founded in 1882. Armed with specimen boxes and notebooks, they accompanied each other into the Gatineau Hills on the congenial field trips organized by the Ottawa Field Naturalists' Club (of which James Fletcher was secretary-treasurer). In 1884, and during a handful of visits Catharine subsequently made to Ottawa, these distinguished scientists went out of their way to pay homage to the old lady who had written *The Wild Flowers of Canada.* They recognized the value of Catharine's own painstaking efforts to record and celebrate Canada's native plants and Indian folklore.

The most significant of Ottawa's scientists to call at 52 Alexander Street was Sandford Fleming. Fleming, the surveyor and engineering genius behind the Pacific Railway, bubbled over with ideas to improve mail service, science education and communications. At the time of Catharine's visit, he was going full bore on the campaign for which he is best remembered: the need for global uniformity in time-keeping. (Before the nineteenth century drew to its close, the whole world would adopt his idea of dividing the world into one-hour time zones, with a mean time based on the prime meridian through Greenwich, London). He was also a generous teddy-bear of a man: instead of trying to remember the individual birthdays of his many grandchildren and their friends, he sent them all presents on his own birthday.

Fleming had met Mrs. Traill years ago in Peterborough, where he had arrived as an eighteen-year-old Scottish immigrant in 1845. When he heard she was in town, he immediately came calling. He cut a wonderful

A brilliant engineer, Catharine's friend Sandford Fleming (1827–1915) was the inventor of Standard Time and a man of irrepressible charm and boundless energy.

figure, with his huge bushy beard and powerful gait, as he strode through record-breaking snowdrifts from his mansion in Sandy Hill to the Chamberlins' house. Catharine was thrilled by his visit. "He was so kind and cordial it was pleasant to meet with the old dear and he said he would come again soon."

Catharine, indefatigable as ever, packed in plenty of sightseeing in the capital. She saw the fish hatchery organized by Samuel Wilmot, the Dominion's superintendant of fish culture, where trout, salmon, whitefish, herring, bass and pike were being bred to stock lakes and rivers. She admired the Dominion collection of stuffed animals and birds, and the collection of Indian canoes and artifacts, in the newly built Victoria Hall. Leaning heavily on Agnes Chamberlin's arm, she walked through the marble corridors of the Parliament Buildings and into the ornately carved elegance of the Parliamentary Library. She was almost overwhelmed when the Prime Minister, Sir John A. Macdonald, appeared "and greeted me very cordially." These glimpses of scientific inquiry and national purpose were of much greater interest to her than Viennese waltzes.

The best news came when, largely thanks to James Fletcher, the Ottawa publisher A.S. Woodburn agreed to publish her manuscript under the title of *Studies of Plant Life in Canada*. It would be a more modest production than *Wild Flowers of Canada*: Woodburn wanted to bring it out as a quarto-sized volume, with twenty chromo-lithographs from drawings by Agnes Chamberlin. The introduction was quintessential Catharine, and encapsulated all the themes she had developed in half a century of botanical study. She wrote how, during her early years in the backwoods, forest flowers and shrubs "became like dear friends, soothing and cheering, by their sweet unconscious influence, hours of loneliness and hours of sorrow and suffering." She insisted that her careful cata- logue of plants, which included the Latin name for each plus a host of botanical and literary references, was "not a book for the learned." The flowers of the field, she wrote, were good reminders of the teachings of Christ. And she deplored the fact that so little effort was being made to record native plants before they vanished "as civilization extends through the Dominion."

Studies of Plant Life in Canada appeared in 1885, a couple of months before Catharine travelled down to Toronto to sit with her dying sister. The book's reception lightened Catharine's mood as she watched Susanna's steady decline and heard her sad, unhappy rantings. The Toronto *Globe* wrote of Catharine's publication: "There is in it enough of technicality to make it extremely useful to the student, while there is about it a literary charm that will lead even the reader most ignorant of botany to go through that book from one end to the other." The *Week* acknowledged Catharine as "an authority upon the flora of this country" and praised her for her "simplicity of style." The Marquis of Lorne, who had been Governor-General of Canada from 1878 to 1883, and to whom the book was dedicated, told Agnes Chamberlin that Catharine's work "will add a great deal to our pleasure in discerning the different species." And Professor Fletcher wrote her: "With regard to your disclaiming the title of botanist, all I can say is, I wish a fraction of one percent of the stu- dents of plants who call themselves botanists, could use their eyes half as well as you have done. I think indeed your work of describing all the wild plants, in your book, so accurately that each one could have the name applied to it without doubt, is one of the greatest botanical triumphs which anyone could achieve, and one which I have frequently spoken of to illustrate how one can develop their powers of observation."

Catharine knew how she wanted her "little work," as she called it, to be regarded. She opened with a verse from Sir Walter Scott, and she addressed her "dear reader." In the introduction, she stated that she hoped the book might become "a household book, as Gilbert White's *Natural History of Selborne* is to this day among English readers." White's eighteenth-century classic was an anachronism to muscular post-Darwinian botanists at the turn of the nineteenth century. Yet Catharine always understood the book's gentle appeal, based on literary as well as scientific merit. Had *Studies of Plant Life in Canada* been received as a literary rather than a scientific text, it might have been seen alongside works by contemporaries who shared her concerns. Catharine Parr Traill would have been comfortable in the company of the nineteenth-century American poet Walt Whitman, who wrote, "A morning-glory at my window satisfies me more than the metaphysics of books," or the Russian writer Anton Chekhov who, in *Uncle Vanya*, bemoaned the fact that, "Whole Russian forests are going under the axe. . . . We're losing the most wonderful scenery for ever, and why?" *Studies of Plant Life in Canada*, however, was assessed not as a literary work but alongside straightforward field-guides. It had a short shelf-life: it was reprinted in 1906, then virtually forgotten.

In the short term, Catharine's age alone gave *Plant Life* a novelty value that led to sales. Most octogenarian authors would have regarded this triumph as their last hurrah and retired to rest on their laurels. But Catharine couldn't. Her impulse to tell the next generation of Canadians about the natural beauty around them remained unquenched.

Chapter 20

The Oldest Living Author in Her Majesty's Dominion

Catharine was seated in her favourite rocking chair near the French windows of Westove's parlour. From this vantage point, she could look out at the lilacs in her garden and watch the plump Canadian robins strutting about on the grass. On one side of her chair was a sewing basket, filled with brightly coloured scraps of fabric from which she was making a patchwork quilt for the Indian Missionary Auxiliary. On the other side was a knitting bag, in which was tucked a half-finished woollen hat for one of her grandsons. Today, however, Catharine was busy with the activity she most enjoyed of all her pursuits: writing. On her lap was a portable writing desk, with a fresh sheet of paper and an inkwell filled with thick black ink. Her steel-nibbed pen hovered over the page as her mind drifted back to her Suffolk childhood.

She was trying to capture in words the atmosphere of Reydon Hall in the early years of the century, when she and her five sisters were growing up there. In 1887, her sister Jane Margaret Strickland had published *Life of Agnes Strickland*. Jane's book was an adulatory account of her sister's biographical achievements, describing Agnes in glowing terms as a sort of literary Madonna: "We must remember that Agnes Strickland was really more of the woman than the author. She had a feminine love of dress and female employments, was fond of fine needlework, and, till she had a maid, mended her own stockings." Jane's biography of Agnes received some cruel reviews. *The Athenaeum* announced that it was "one of those books which might as well not have been written . . . [the author] is perpetually reminding us of the number of balls to which her sister was taken, the number of country houses which she visited, and the number of genteel persons who drove her out in their own carriages." Jane's loving, but banal, memories of her dauntingly intelligent older sister provided an excuse for Agnes's male rivals to dismiss her achievements with misogynist glee. "We have not yet arrived," sniffed *The Northern Whig*, "at that stage of evolution when women can rank as historians of the first order." Jane was crushed by these comments. Her health, already poor, suffered. Within a few months, she was laid in a grave next to Agnes's splendid marble monument in the graveyard of St. Edmund's Church, Southwold.

Catharine didn't want to belittle Agnes's leather-bound royal biographies. She was too fond of Jane, and had too much experience herself of misogynist brushoffs from professional men, to reply to these unkind reviews on Jane's behalf. However, she was saddened by Jane's book because Jane had scarcely mentioned either Susanna or Catharine herself. Samuel Strickland was allowed a walk-on part as the author of *Twenty-seven years in Canada West*, "which contains everything necessary for a settler to know." But there was no reference to the literary achievements of Agnes's youngest sisters, who had written much better, more helpful books about Canada. Catharine wanted to record a fuller picture of the gifted Strickland family.

Scratch, scratch, scratch . . . the steel nib started moving quickly across the page. Catharine had always been a fluent and fast writer, and old age

IN
LOVING MEMORY OF
JANE MARGARET
FOURTH DAUGHTER OF
THOMAS AND ELIZABETH
STRICKLAND.
BORN APRIL 18.1800.
DIED JUNE 14.1888.

*Agnes and Jane Strickland's gravestones in the graveyard of St. Edmund's
Church, Southwold. A great-niece of Catharine sent her this picture.*

had not slowed her down. "We passed our days," she wrote, smiling at
the Reydon memories, "in the lonely old house in sewing, walking in the
lanes, sometimes going to see the sick and carry food or little comforts
to the cottagers; but reading was our chief resource." Catharine enjoyed
penning these "pictures of old world life," as she described them to one
publisher, "which will amuse if not astonish the reader taking him back
into bygone scenes even to the past days of the former century . . ." At
the other end of her own lifetime and on the other side of the Atlantic,
she acknowledged that she and her sisters had been part of an extraordinarily rich literary tradition, a uniquely Old World legacy which she had
absorbed, and of which her own children and grandchildren had no
notion. Before Thomas Strickland's death, the household at Reydon Hall
had included servants to cook, clean, launder, press, garden, dust, sweep,
preserve and bake. Thomas's young daughters had the time to furnish
their minds from his library. Catharine scribbled down her memories of

how they had penned historical dramas, "embellished according to the invisible genius of their fertile minds," and "ransacked the library for books." She described how Agnes, when only twelve, could recite from memory whole scenes from Shakespeare and lengthy passages from Milton's *Paradise Lost.* She smiled as she remembered how she had thrown herself into the role of Ariel in a Reydon Hall production of *The Tempest.*

Scratch, scratch, scratch . . . the pen moved faster and faster as memories flocked back. Catharine recalled how Elizabeth had excelled at quick sketches of village characters, including John Fenn the rat-catcher, old Catchpole the mole-catcher and "some old women reputed to be witches but really very harmless creatures." She wrote of Jane's cloud of curls and Sarah's sense of style: "When dressed in her riding habit and Spanish hat and feathers she certainly made a striking appearance." But the sister she recalled with the deepest and most familiar affection was the one to whom she had always been closest.

It was more than five years since Susanna had died, and Catharine missed her. These days Catharine remembered her sister not as the cantankerous widow or the demented old woman on her deathbed, but as the lively, headstrong girl with "an inherent love of freedom of thought and action." She wrote about her with a love and longing she had never expressed about Thomas Traill after his death. "We two lived in child-like confidence and harmony, as we grew up side by side as loving friends, our lives remaining in parallel grooves, and this continued even after we married and left the old home at Reydon to share the untried fortunes of the new world in our forest homes in what is now Ontario." In particular, she remembered her youngest sister's intensity. "Susie was an infant genius. . . . Her facility for rhyme was great and her imagination vivid and romantic, tinged with gloom and grandeur. . . . As is often found in persons of genius, she was often elated and often depressed, easily excited by passing events, unable to control emotions caused by either pain or pleasure. . . . I was not of so imaginative a disposition."

Whatever wistful thoughts of Susanna she harboured, Catharine undoubtedly comforted herself with the pleasure she continued to take in her own huge family. Five of her seven children were still alive in 1890, and she had twenty-one grandchildren. Kate Traill continued to look after her mother, and Annie Atwood and Mary Muchall, Catharine's two married daughters, lived close by. But both her sons, like so many young men in the late nineteenth century, had been forced to travel west in order to find work. William and Walter were now both settled in western Canada and had started families thousands of miles away from Lakefield. Catharine ached to see them and her "little Nor'wester grand-children." Even when her right hand was swollen with rheumatism, or her eyes cloudy with cataracts, she managed to write them lengthy letters. "See dear how I have blotted the sheet well you must not mind the blot but take from the hand of the aged mother," she wrote to William Traill, now a chief trader dealing in furs for the Hudson's Bay Company

Catharine's son William Traill (seated, right), who worked for the Hudson's Bay Company before becoming a farmer in Saskatchewan, with his wife Harriette and nine of their ten children.

in the remote northwest of the Dominion. William wrote affectionate letters home, filled with vivid descriptions of native uprisings, natural disasters and adventurous canoe trips. He sent his mother dried ferns and grasses from the Peace River region. But Walter's letters arrived infrequently these days, and were often gloomy. Catharine confided to William her concerns about Walter's mental health. "I fear for that morbid temperament so like his dear father's."

In sheer volume alone, Catharine's correspondence is extraordinary. Judging by what has survived, during the last few years of her life she sat down to write a lengthy epistle to a relative or a friend, or a formal letter to a publisher or fellow writer, at least once or twice a week. Moreover, letter-writing was light afternoon entertainment for the elderly author. Most mornings, while Kate Traill did the housework, Catharine worked away at her writing projects. Often her eyes ached after she had been writing or reading too long; then she would open the windows and step outside. "I long for air," she explained to her daughter Annie, "and pottering about the garden." Kate looked after beds of flowering perennials, while Catharine was still in charge of the vegetable patch. Since the two women could rarely afford meat in their diet, they depended on Catharine's harvest of peas, beans, root vegetables, raspberries and strawberries. Despite her white hair, arthritic knees and aching back, the octogenarian would dig, plant, weed and pick just as she had done throughout her life in Canada.

Besides the family memoir, Catharine had two other writing projects on the go: an account of her first seven years in Canada, and a book of essays on natural history for young readers. Catharine's determination to get into print never flagged, despite endless rebuffs from publishers. "Canada is a poor market for literature," she complained to her niece Katie Vickers. Household bills gnawed away at Catharine, but there was also a secondary motive: "I wished to leave something myself for my grandchildren as I have neither gold nor silver nor any personal property to leave . . ." Often, publishers didn't even bother to return Catharine's carefully hand-copied manuscripts to her. Those that did offered only vague indications of interest. By now, Catharine knew that her sister Agnes's description of publishers' "cold-blooded villainy" was deadly accurate. "He is a real hum-bug," she wrote of one unctuous editor. "I have no faith in his promises and his *flattery* as *that does not pay.*"

Catharine's struggles to find a publisher were particularly exasperating since she was now clearly a *bone fide* Canadian celebrity herself, rather than simply the sister of either Agnes Strickland or Susanna Moodie. Successive governors-general paid obeisance to her. Six years after being lionized in Ottawa by the Lansdownes, Catharine was invited to preside over the hospitality offered to Lansdowne's successor, Baron Stanley of Preston, and his wife Lady Stanley when they made a two-hour visit to Lakefield in September 1890. The village residents threw themselves into the viceregal reception. They built arches over the main street, decorated the village hall in flowers and wreaths, draped clean white linen cloths over the rugged trestle tables and appointed twelve girls to wait upon the tables at tea. Catharine was not impressed. Her discomfort with snobbery and formality erupted. "I had a bad headache and felt unequal to the fatigue," she wrote to her son William. She smiled graciously throughout the Governor-General's generous compliments to her—"a lady whose name is known . . . in England as well as here"—although her advanced deafness and the clatter of teaspoons meant she couldn't hear a word. However, a lifetime of authorship meant that Catharine knew how to take advantage of such a situation: she was more than happy to present Lady Stanley with a copy of *Studies of Plant Life in Canada.* For all the excitement, as soon as the Stanleys had been escorted off to a night train "amid huzzahs and a torchlight procession and God Save the Queen by a Lindsay band," Catharine was relieved to get back to Westove.

Once again, it was not the important men with fancy titles amongst Catharine's acquaintance who came to her rescue on the publishing front but her own family. Soon after the Stanleys' visit to Lakefield, Maime Fitzgibbon came to live there. "I shall be busy writing," Catharine told William, "as she wants us to bring out a volume together." Maime had become friendly with Edward Caswell, the eager young literary editor at the Toronto-based Methodist Book and Publishing House. Caswell was working with Maime on her second book, a biography of her maternal grandfather entitled *A Veteran of 1812: The Life of James FitzGibbon,* which was eventually published in 1894. Both Maime and Edward were caught up in the craze for "wheeling," or bicycling, that swept Toronto in the 1890s. Maime was just the kind of woman to embrace the liberation that the bicycle offered. Still single at forty and an intrepid traveller who had gone west by train and crossed the Atlantic by steamer, she loved to swathe her head in a veil, her legs in bloomers, and go for a good wheel. Mr. Caswell pedalled as fast as he could to keep up with her as she sped around the streets of Toronto, or along the Don Valley ravine. One August, she persuaded him to put his bicycle on the train to Peterborough, and to cycle from there to Lakefield to visit Catharine Parr Traill at Westove.

Edward was captivated by the genial, white-haired author, now in her nineties, who sat on the verandah and seemed to recognize each individual bird that flew through her garden. Maime soon had him interested in her great-aunt's manuscripts. The editor particularly liked the short essays that she had written for children about different aspects of nature—the smell, sounds and sight of the Canadian woods in spring, for example, or the behaviour of such Canadian birds as pine grosbeaks and the increasingly rare scarlet tanagers. Edward asked Maime to write a biographical sketch of Catharine as an introduction to a volume that he decided to call *Pearls and Pebbles, or Notes of an Old Naturalist.* To Catharine's excitement, when the book was published in mid-December 1894, it did well. Within three months, 750 copies, at one dollar a copy, were sold, and it received favourable notices in both Canada and England. Sandford Fleming, an enthusiastic fan and reliable friend, dashed off a quick note from Ottawa to the author. "Receive dear Mrs. Traill an order for seven copies. I long to see the latest production of yours. You are indeed a wonderful woman."

The review that must have given Catharine the most pleasure was by the redoubtable Professor Goldwin Smith, the former Regius Professor of Modern History at Oxford University who now lived in splendour in Toronto with his wealthy wife, the former Mrs. Henry Boulton of The Grange. Smith, who delighted in the title "the Sage of the Grange," was a roaring snob who knew little about the countryside and usually sneered at anything too sentimental. But in his review in the London *Illustrated News*, which was reproduced in the Peterborough *Daily Evening News*, he pronounced *Pearls and Pebbles* "a sort of Canadian counterpart to White's 'Selbourne.'"

Caswell was sufficiently encouraged by the success of *Pearls and Pebbles* to publish a further volume of Catharine's essays the following year, *Cot and Cradle Stories*. Maime helped her great-aunt organize the manuscript for, as the ninety-three-year-old author confessed to her niece: "I get dreadfully bewildered now with MS papers, lose time through want of memory. A thousand things flit through my brain—like dreams—good for a few minutes—then gone." But *Cot and Cradle Stories* did not do well.

Catharine had never had two cents to rub together—she derived no royalties from the books that had been published in England, and the two little volumes published by the Methodist Book and Publishing House brought slim proceeds. She had always depended on the generosity of relatives like her brother Sam, her sister Sarah and her son William. But now she was the only member of her generation left. Her sister Sarah Gwillym had died in 1890, two years after Jane. "I stand alone," wrote a saddened Catharine, "the last and only one living of the sisters."

Both Catharine's English sisters left her modest legacies, which she invested (along with Agnes's legacy of $2,500) in a Peterborough enterprise run by a Mr. John Burnham. Mr. Burnham, however, went bankrupt in late 1897, and Catharine, at ninety-five, was left virtually penniless.

Catharine received the dire financial news with her usual "The Lord will provide" stoicism. She had borne many hardships before, and she prepared to weather this latest storm. Several younger members of the Strickland clan, however, thought she deserved better. Mary Strickland, wife of Sam's grandson Arthur, decided Catharine needed official assistance. Without Catharine's knowledge, an urgent plea was sent to the British Prime Minister, at 10 Downing Street, for help for the "oldest living author in the British Empire."

A secretary to Lord Salisbury, the Prime Minister, sent a stuffy reply, indicating that her service to the Empire did not make Mrs. Traill eligible for a civil list pension. However, he added, she might receive a donation from the Royal Bounty Fund of 150 pounds "if the people of Canada generally, or her friends and admirers in particular, are willing to show their appreciation of her literary merits and character by raising a Testimonial Fund for the purpose of making some permanent provision for the future." Such a grant, it was made clear, was made on account not of Catharine Parr Traill's own achievements, but simply because she was the sister of Agnes Strickland. And the Royal Bounty Fund put stingy limits on its largesse. If Mrs. Traill should die before the grant was awarded, the money could not be redirected to her daughter Kate Traill, who was equally needy, because she was too distant a relative of Agnes to qualify.

By the summer of 1898, Catharine had outlived two of her four sons and one of her three daughters (Mary Muchall died in 1892) and, in her own words, "all the great men and women of the past. Soldiers, sailors, statesmen, three sovereigns, the poets, the novelists, artists, historians." At ninety-six, she was a Canadian icon—one of the few souls alive who could remember the celebrations after the Battle of Waterloo, and who knew the Dominion of Canada when it was still a wilderness. She appeared to be immortal. The journalist Faith Fenton made a pilgrimage to Lakefield to profile Catharine for her new magazine, the *Canadian Home Journal*. She was captivated by the welcome she received. "What a picture she makes as she sits in her rocking chair: blue eyes, bright as a child's; silky white hair, parted over the high forehead and tucked away beneath the pretty cap, whose pink ribbons are not more delicately coloured than the wrinkled cheeks; a smile full of kindliness, and lips curving humourously." As their grandmother chatted away to the smart

Catharine on the porch at Westove in 1898, with two of her granddaughters: undeniably, "a wonderful old lady."

lady journalist from Toronto, Katie Traill (Harry's daughter) and a couple of Annie Atwood's daughters exchanged significant looks. They had seen so many visitors fall under their grandmother's charm. When Faith Fenton finally rose to leave, Katie Traill said, "Don't call her a 'wonderful old lady.' Everybody does, and we get so tired of it." Fenton couldn't resist using the label: "There is no other phrase so true."

But Catharine's ready smile could not hide the fact that she suffered all the handicaps of her advanced age. Her eyes were cloudy, her ears deaf, her hands shook, and she was too frail to scramble over the rocks of the Stony Lake islands, searching for lichen, moss and ferns. "The fund should be started at once," Mary Strickland insisted, "and only kept open for a few weeks, fearing that anything should happen to Mrs. Traill which is only too likely at her great age." The family knew exactly who to approach to raise a Testimonial Fund for Catharine: her good friend Sandford Fleming, who had recently been knighted in Queen Victoria's Diamond Jubilee honours of 1897, alongside Prime Minister Wilfrid Laurier.

In June 1898, Sir Sandford threw himself into the campaign to raise funds for his old friend. He arm-twisted colleagues, sent out a circular to everyone he had ever worked with and persuaded the Governor-General and his wife to head the list of donors with a generous contribution of fifty dollars. "Those of the present generation . . . may not be familiar with the life and work of Mrs. Traill . . ." read the note he sent round. "She has rendered service of no ordinary kind in making known the advantages offered by Canada as a field for settlement, and by her very widely read writings she has been instrumental in inducing very many emigrants from the United Kingdom to find homes in the Dominion."

The list of signatories to the testimonial was a Who's Who of the intellectual establishment of 1890s Canada. It included George Grant (principal of Queen's College, Kingston), John Bourinot (chief clerk of the House of Commons) and all the senior staff of Ottawa's Experimental Farm. It included Toronto lawyers and Quebec City businessmen. It included the librarian of the British Columbia legislature, the president of the Winnipeg Board of Trade and the wife of Sir William Van Horne, president of the CPR. By December, when Sir Sandford wrote and told Catharine about it, the fund stood at over $1,000.

Catharine finally had more financial security than she had known for years. "Dear valued friend," replied Catharine, in a script as firm as it had been twenty years earlier, "You can hardly think how welcome [your letter] proved. . . . How can I thank all the kindness of the generous givers of this large sum of money awarded to the aged authoress. It does seem too great for such small services. . . . And in what words dearest Friend shall I thank you, and all my known and unknown friends in England and Ontario. I can only adopt the hearty simple phrase used by the Indian women of Hiawatha village—'I bless you in my heart.'"

The formal presentation came early in 1899. The tribute acknowledged Catharine's major literary works, and concluded: "We cannot forget the courage with which you endured the privations and trials of the backwoods in the early settlement of Ontario, and we rejoice to know that your useful life has been prolonged in health and vigour until you are now the oldest living author in Her Majesty's dominion. Nearing the close of the century we desire to pay tribute to your personal worth, and we ask your acceptance of this testimonial as a slight token of the esteem and regard in which you are universally held."

A few months later, Kate Traill took her ninety-seven-year-old mother to Minnewawa, her cottage on Stony Lake. Catharine sat on the shady verandah, scattering crumbs for her beloved birds and watching canoes skim across the azure water. She loved "the wild and picturesque rocks, trees, hill and valley, wild-flowers, ferns, shrubs and moss and the pure, sweet scent of pines over all, breathing health and strength. If I were a doctor," she had once written, "I would send my patients to live in a shanty under the pines." In the summer of 1899, she would occasionally ignore Kate's protests and, cherrywood staff in hand, totter off to the

Kate Traill's island of Minnewawa, on Stony Lake, where Catharine loved to smell the pines and scatter crumbs for warblers and orioles.

woods behind the cottage to look for berries and flowers. Very occasionally, she would pick up a pen to write to distant relatives.

As the August nights lengthened, and the evening breezes grew cooler, Kate helped her mother board the steamer for the return journey to Lakefield. Soon after Catharine was settled back in her beloved Westove, she began a letter to a cousin in England about a London publisher's decision not to publish one of her children's stories. "I had many misgivings as to the merits of the composition," wrote Catharine, with typical self-deprecation. "I never see anything good in my writings till they are in print and even then I wonder how that event came to pass."

Catharine's head began to nod before she had finished the letter. Kate gently took the pen out of her hand and, as her mother jerked into wakefulness again, Kate suggested to Catharine that she could finish the letter later. The old lady gave her faithful daughter a grateful, sweet smile, and settled back into her chair as the evening shadows began to lengthen.

Catharine's final hours were far more peaceful than those of her sister, Susanna. With the blessed calm she had radiated throughout her life, she died quietly in her sleep two days later, on August 29, 1899.

Postscript

The best memorial to the lives of Catharine Parr Trail and Susanna Moodie is the angel above the Moodie grave in Belleville cemetery. A stalwart figure in her carved robe and mossy wings, she towers over her neighbours and holds her arm aloft in defiance of the winds from the Bay of Quinte. In her hand she clutches a star—symbol, perhaps, of the immigrant's hope that a better future lies ahead, and that he or she can control it.

It is unlikely that the two Strickland sisters who came to Canada ever felt in control of their destiny. Yet as each neared the end of her own long life, with beloved children close by, she would have acknowledged that the journey had been worthwhile. Each had arrived in the New World a writer, and had continued writing despite hardship. Each had seen most of her children happily settled. Both had watched the rough-and-ready colony of 1832 embark on its transformation into a remarkably vigorous, prosperous nation. And through their books, both women had themselves helped to shape the culture of their adopted country—Catharine through her descriptions of landscape and natural history; Susanna through her portrayals of pioneer experiences and colonial society.

Yet today, one hundred years after Catharine's death, she and Susanna would find modern Canada unrecognizable. Only two of their various dwellings survive: the Moodies' pleasant stone cottage on Belleville's Bridge Street and Catharine's beloved Westove in Lakefield. These homes are now jostled by brick and clapboard neighbours of much more recent date, with car ports, swing sets and gas barbecues in their yards. The rest of the log

cabins and cramped cottages in which the sisters scraped and scribbled in Ontario are long gone. We have moved far beyond sagas of wilderness survival and tales of rural life.

Hamilton Township, where the Moodies spent their miserable early months, is now dotted with gentrified farmhouses to which Torontonians drive, along a six-lane highway, for country weekends. Trailer parks and campgrounds crowd onto the south shore of Rice Lake, which Catharine described so

The marble angel that marks the Moodie grave in Belleville cemetery.

lovingly in *Canadian Crusoes*. You can find historical plaques here and there, commemorating Susanna's log cabin on Lake Katchewanooka, or the sites of Wolf Tower and Oaklands, the Traill homes on the Rice Lake Plains. But on the plaque that is planted firmly in the middle of Lakefield to mark Susanna's connections with the village, Catharine's name is misspelled. The most handsome mansion in Lakefield remains The Homestead: a yellow brick reminder that the only Strickland who was a successful pioneer was Sam.

Yet the legacy of Susanna and Catharine is as sturdy as Sam's mansion or the Moodie angel in the Belleville cemetery. Their most important books are still in print. More than a century has passed since the sisters' deaths, but plenty of contemporary Canadians have shared the feelings they captured on paper about emigration, and their ambivalent relationship with a landscape both majestic and savage. Every new Canadian who thinks longingly of "home" and every brave adventurer who sets off into the bush, brushing off black-flies and marvelling at nature, is following in the sisters' footsteps.

Family Trees

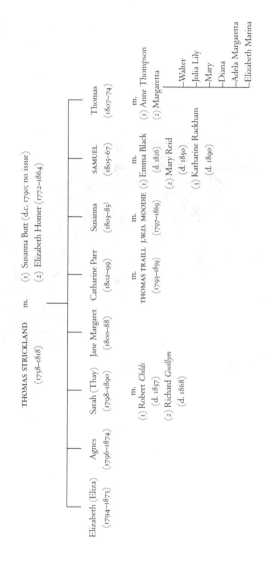

THOMAS STRICKLAND   m.   (1) Susanna Butt (d.c. 1790; no issue)
(1758–1818)   (2) Elizabeth Homer (1772–1864)

Elizabeth (Eliza)   Agnes   Sarah (Thay)   Jane Margaret   Catharine Parr   Susanna   SAMUEL   Thomas
(1794–1875)   (1796–1874)   (1798–1890)   (1800–88)   (1802–99)   (1803–85)   (1805–67)   (1807–74)

                                   m.   m.   m.   m.   m.
                                   (1) Robert Childs   THOMAS TRAILL   J.W.D. MOODIE (1) Emma Black (1) Anne Thompson
                                   (d. 1837)   (1793–1859)   (1797–1869)   (d. 1826)   (2) Margaretta
                                   (2) Richard Gwillym   (2) Mary Reid
                                   (d. 1868)   (d. 1850)
                                                                                                        (3) Katharine Rackham
                                                                                                        (d. 1890)

Walter
Julia Lily
Mary
Diana
Adela Margaretta
Elizabeth Marina

JOHN WEDDERBURN DUNBAR MOODIE   m.   Susanna Strickland
(1 Oct. 1797–22 Oct. 1869)   4 April   (7 Dec. 1803–8 April 1885)
1831

Catherine Mary Josephine
(14 Feb. 1832–24 Dec. 1904)
m. 1 Aug. 1855
John Joseph *Vickers*
(b. 1818)

Agnes Dunbar
(9 June 1833–1 May 1913)
(1) m. 23 Aug. 1850
Charles Thomas *Fitzgibbon*
(d. 22 Feb. 1865)
(2) m. 14 June 1870
Brown *Chamberlin*
(22 March 1827–13 July 1897)

John Alexander Dunbar
(20 Aug. 1834–14 May 1927)
m. 20 March 1862
Elizabeth Roberta Russell
(1834–2 March 1882)

Donald
(21 May 1836–27 Dec. 1893)
m. 16 Feb. 1866
Julia Ann Russell

John Strickland
(16 Oct. 1838–
18 June 1844)

George Arthur
(19 July 1840–
8 Aug. 1840)

Robert Baldwin
(8 July 1843–3 Feb. 1889)
m. 27 June 1863
Sarah Elizabeth (Nellie) Russell
(17 Nov. 1847–8 Feb. 1930)

Children of Agnes Dunbar:
- Georgina Eliza (b. 28 May 1856)
- John Alexander Dunbar (b. 22 May 1858)
- Katie Moodie (b. 28 June 1860)
- William Wallbridge (b. 6 Aug. 1862)
- Isabel Josephine (b. 7 Aug. 1864)
- Victor Gilmore Ridgeway (b. 1 June 1866)
- Ethel Rosina (b. 4 March 1868)
- Henrietta Moodie (b. 2 March 1870)
- Arthur Algoma (b. 26 March 1872)
- Agnes Strickland (b. 6 Nov. 1874)

Children of John Alexander Dunbar:
- Mary Agnes (Maime) (b. 18 June 1851)
- James Gerald (b. 2 Feb. 1853)
- Geraldine (Cherrie) (b. 31 Oct. 1854)
- Eliza Dunbar (24 Feb. 1856–14 July 1856)
- Charlotte Alice (b. 8 Aug. 1857)
- Katie (b. 10 Feb. 1859–8 Aug. 1859)
- John Wedderburn Dunbar (18 June 1860–16 March 1865)
- William Winder (12 April 1862–18 Oct. 1866)
- Agnes Gertrude Mary (b. 7 April 1871)

Children of Donald:
- Agnes Strickland Dunbar (b. 11 Feb. 1863)
- Robert Russell (b. 28 Nov. 1864)
- Elizabeth Dunbar (b. 24 Aug. 1866)
- Janet Ethel (28 Aug. 1868–20 Dec. 1881)
- Alice Dunbar (14 Aug. 1870–16 Dec. 1881)
- Clutha Roberta (b. 28 Nov. 1873)
- Elsie Helen (b. 6 Aug. 1877)

- Daniel Edward Prodhead (b. 1 Jan. 1867)
- Walter Brewster (Nov. 1868–13 June 1870)
- Charlotte Peachy (b. 1 Jan. 1872)
- Julia Edith Strickland (b. 4 Oct. 1875)

Children of Robert Baldwin:
- Bessie Perry (b. 12 April 1864)
- Nellie (b. 17 Sept 1865)
- John Wedderburn Dunbar (b. 4 March 1868)
- Thomas Edward Strickland (b. 8 May 1871)
- Esther Edith (b. 23 July 1875)
- Susanna (b. 15 May 1878–1878?)
- Catherine Agnes (b. 13 Dec. 1881)

THOMAS TRAILL   m.   (1) Anne Fotheringhame (d. 1828)
(1793–1859)   (2) Catharine Parr Strickland (1802–99)

Children of Thomas Traill:

- (1) Walter (1815–45)
- (2) John Heddle (1819–47) — m. Eliza Dunbar Heddle (d. 1844)
- James George (1833–67) — m. Amelia Keye Muchall
- Katherine Agnes Strickland (Kate) (1836–1922)
- Thomas Henry Strickland (Harry) (1837–70) — m. Lilias Grant Maclean
- Anne Traill Fotheringhame (Annie) (1838–1931) — m. James Parr Clinton Atwood (1836–1912)
- Mary Ellen Bridges (1840–1)
- Mary Elizabeth Jane (1841–92) — m. Thomas W. Muchall (d. 1898)
- Eleanor Stewart (1843 d. infant)
- William Edward (1844–1917) — m. Harriette McKay (1847–1920)
- Walter John Strickland (1848–1932) — m. Mary E. Purdy

Children of John Heddle & Eliza Dunbar Heddle:

- Francis (Frank) (b.c. 1842)
- Henrietta Anna (b. 1841)
- William Henry (1843–1902)

Children of James George & Amelia Keye Muchall:

- Richard Henry (1857–1940)
- Thomas Edward Strickland (1859–1931)
- Catherine Amelia (1861–2)
- Agnes Strickland (b. 1863 d. infant)
- George Frederick (b. 1863 d. infant)
- George Herbert (b. 1866)

Children of Thomas Henry & Lilias Grant Maclean:

- Charles Henry Strickland (1865–1949)
- Katharine Parr (Katie) (b. 1867)
- George James McManus (1869–1950)

Children of Anne Traill & James Parr Clinton Atwood:

- Henry Arthur Strickland (1860–4)
- Emily Grace (1863–1940)
- Clinton Arthur Strickland (1865–1952)
- Katharine Stewart (1868–1954)
- George Evan (1869–1964)
- Anne Traill Fotheringhame (1871–1972)
- Florence Marion (1874–1957)

Children of Mary Elizabeth Jane & Thomas W. Muchall:

- Hargrave Henry (b. 1865)
- Evelyne Mary (b. 1867)
- Caroline Gwillym (1871–96)
- Norman Stewart (1873–92)

Children of William Edward & Harriette McKay:

- Walter (1870–1932)
- Katherine Barbara (1871–1918)
- William McKay (b. 1875)
- Henry (1877–8)
- Ethel (b. 1879)
- Jessie (b. 1881)
- Mary (b. 1883)
- Maria (b. 1884)
- Harriet (b. 1888)
- Annie (b. 1892)

Children of Walter John & Mary E. Purdy:

- Walter Archibald Strickland (1882–)
- Cora Gilbert
- Hardesty Gilbert

SAMUEL STRICKLAND m. (1) Emma Black (d. 1826)
(1805–1867)   (2) Mary Reid (d. 1850)
                             (3) Katherine Rackham (d. 1890)

(1) Richard (1826–9)

(2) Maria Elizabeth (1829–84)
m.
1. Benjamin *Beresford* (d. 1850)
2. Kivas *Tully*
(1) ┌ Elizabeth Rowan (1850–1)
(2) ├ Agnes (b. 1853)
    ├ Mary Katherine (d. infant)
    ├ Louisa
    └ Sydney (f) (b. 1860)

Robert Alexander (1830–1916)
m.
Caroline Charlotte Ellis
┌ Katherine Charlotte (b. 1856)
├ Agnes (1858–80)
├ George Arthur (b. 1859)
└ Ethel Ellis (b. 1864)
  d. infant

Emma Susanna (1832–1913)
m.
Frederick *Barlee*
┌ Frederick Ross (b. 1855)
├ Amy Herbert (b. 1863)
├ William Roland (b. 1865)
└ Grace Emma (b. 1868)

George William Ross (1833–90)
m.
1. Frances Rothwell
2. Amadelena Clementi
3. Ellen Mary
(1) ┌ Samuel George (b. 1859)
    ├ Percy Wade (b. 1861)
    ├ Clara Frances (1867–79)
    ├ Frances Mary (b. 1865)
    ├ Henry George (b. 1867)
    │ d. infant
    ├ George Gordon (b. 1869)
    └ Julia Georgina (b. 1871)
(2) ┌ Kathleen Irene Sylvia (b. 1874)
    │ d. infant
    ├ Cecil Hamilton (b. 1875)
    ├ Cecilia Mary (b. 1878)
    ├ Algernon
    └ Vincent

Henry Thomas (1835–1908)
m.
1. Margaret Rogers
2. Ann Morgan
┌ Mary Eliza (b. 1860)
└ Emma Margaret (b. 1862)

Francis Arthur (1838–58)

John Percy (1839–1909)
m.
Susan Sherwood
┌ Alice Maude (b. 1862)
├ Walter D'Eyencourt (b. 1864)
├ Susan Josephine (b. 1865)
├ Percy D'Eyencourt (b. 1867)
├ Katherine Mary (b. 1869)
└ Alexander William (b. 1871)

Walter Reginald (1841–1915)
m.
Charlotte Amelia Morgan
┌ Violet Charlotte
├ Henry Frederick (b. 1870)
└ Reginald

Jane (1843–1902)
m.
Charles James *Blomfield*
┌ Frank (d. infant)
├ Dorothy Henrietta
├ Mary Emmalene
├ Edith (d. infant)
├ Frederick Charles
├ Isabel May
├ Edward Valentine
├ Ethel Rose
├ Reginald
├ Kathleen Rollaston (b. 1885)
├ Charles
└ Alfred

Roland Clement (1844–1929)
m.
1. Mary Jane Boulton
2. Eleanor Crickmore
(1) ┌ D'Arcy Edward (b. 1868)
    ├ Edith Julia (1869–72)
    ├ Clementina
    ├ Katherine (b. 1870)
    ├ Roland Hugh (b. 1872)
    └ Mary (b. 1874)
       d. infant
(2) ┌ Edith Roper (b. 1878)
    ├ Eleanor Firth
    ├ John Clement (b. 1879)
    ├ Mary Stuart (b. 1880)
    ├ Sylvia Agnes (b. 1882)
    └ George Roper (b. 1885)
       (b. 1887)

Richard (1845–6)

Richard Gwillym (1847–1925)
m.
Emily Caddy
┌ Florence May (b. 1868)
├ Edith Julia (1870–72)
├ Olive Mildred (b. 1872)
├ Maud Millicent (b. 1874)
│ d. infant
├ Alfred Roger (1876–78)
├ Emily Grace (b. 1878)
└ George

Son (1849 d. infant)

Mary Agnes (1850 d. infant)

Acknowledgments

I would not have had the material, the time or the nerve to write this book had it not been for Professor Michael Peterman of Trent University. Thanks to Michael and his two colleagues, Professor Carl Ballstadt of McMaster University and Professor Elizabeth Hopkins of York University, I was able to draw on three volumes of Traill and Moodie correspondence as sources. The three academic authors collected, edited and published all the extant letters by John and Susanna Moodie, and 136 of the approximately 500 letters written by Catharine Parr Traill. The three volumes saved me from months of labour in the National Archives of Canada, squinting over copperplate handwriting and cross-written letters. In addition, throughout the gestation and birth of this book, Michael has provided information, access to his research, suggestions for further reading and feedback. He showed me around Lakefield and Peterborough, and he and his wife Cara welcomed me to their home. After our first meeting, Michael said, "Well, I think the ladies will be safe with you." I hope I have justified his confidence.

Both Beth Hopkins and Carl Ballstadt were also generous with their support. The insights into the sisters that I gained from Beth, as she drove me across southern Ontario one fall evening, gave valuable shape to my own impressions. I have drawn extensively on journal articles by all three authors.

I am also indebted to two rigorous and enthusiastic readers. My good friend Sandra Gwyn rescued a first draft of the book with imaginative and clear-headed suggestions. Dr. Sandy Campbell, who teaches in the English Department of the University of Ottawa, helped place the two sisters in their literary context and drew my attention to Susanna's slave narratives. In addition, she eagerly joined me in my exploration of the sisters' complicated personalities and relationship, as well as their importance as nineteenth-century authors.

It was a joy for me to rely once again on the professional advice of my agent, Jan Whitford, and to return to Penguin Books, and the careful attention of Meg Masters. Ramsay Derry, my editor, brought a sharp pencil and a sharper eye to my manuscript, and improved it in more ways than I care to admit. I would like to thank Catherine Marjoribanks for being a dream copy-editor, Susan James for her time-consuming work on production, and Laura Brady for the imaginative design of the book. Jeanne Simpson knew exactly what I meant when I asked for "maps that tell a story," and she created four wonderful examples. She also produced the elegant illustrations of Reydon Hall and Middleton Square.

I always enjoy walking into any of the great Ottawa repositories of national memory and discovering not only the treasures they house, but also the enthusiasm and knowledge of their staff. Both Brian Murphy and Jennifer Mueller were a pleasure to work with at the National Archives of Canada; at the National Library of Canada, Michel Brisebois searched out letters and rare books for me; the staff at the Parliamentary Library tracked down obscure titles and entries in biographical dictionaries. I was particularly thrilled to discover that the Canadian Museum of Nature had in its collection many of Catharine Parr Traill's botanical specimen books. Mike J. Shchepanek, chief collection manager, botany section, and Micheline B. Bouchard shared my excitement as we turned the pages, and they explained to me the strengths and weaknesses of Catharine's approach to natural history.

In England, I should like to thank Mr. LeGrys for opening Reydon Hall, Suffolk, to me, and my friend Tosh Potts for joining me on research trips in Southwold and London. In Canada, I would like to thank David Staines, Dean of Arts at the University of Ottawa, for supplying me with the New Canadian Library editions of Catharine's and Susanna's most important books. I am grateful to Gerry Boyce, who shared his extensive knowledge of Belleville with me, and to Betsy Boyce, who guided me through the photographic archives of the Hastings County Museum. Three people in the Peterborough area went out of their way to provide me with assistance: Connie Thompson at Hutchison House, and Jean Cole and Kathy Hooke, who fleshed out my knowledge of Stony Lake. Kathy Hooke generously sent me maps, photos and booklets and read the Stony Lake chapter for me. In Ottawa, Liz Kane walked me round her house in New Edinburgh, where Catharine stayed in 1884 as a guest of her niece Agnes Fitzgibbon.

Much of the fun of writing this double biography came from discussions with friends and new acquaintances about the sisters. Norman Hilmer and Christopher Moore helped me with historical background. Ann Schteir discussed nineteenth-century natural history with me. Designer Paddye Mann helped me imagine what the women would have looked like and how they dressed. Clara Thomas shared her astringent (and well-informed) views on which sister would have been the most likable. Roger Hall gave me reading lists and good advice on how to deal with the value of money in the nineteenth century. Fay Sharman gave me expert advice on both sailing and plant life. Jennifer Southam allowed me to talk through my ideas as we walked. Sheila Williams, Chaviva Hosek, Barbara Uteck, Wendy Bryant, Maureen Boyd, Cathy Behan, Kyle

McRobie and Judith Moses all once again convinced me that there is considerable public interest in how women in any century live their lives. Ernest Hillen convinced me that I could write a book about these two particular women. And several others gave me and my family the kind of support that allowed me to stay in my third-floor study for hours on end: they include Violeta Bonales-Hollmann, Christie Murray, Katie Plaunt, Gloria Cardoza, Monic Charlebois and Wayne McAlear.

My parents generously and enthusiastically helped facilitate my research trips in Britain, and waited patiently as I tramped around Leith, Norwich and Suffolk. My deepest thanks, as always, go to my husband George Anderson, who always provides unconditional support and encouragement, as well as useful feedback and good suggestions on the manuscript. And I could not have written this book without my sons Alexander, Nicholas and Oliver, who make my own life worthwhile.

This book would not have been possible without the financial assistance of the Canada Council and the Arts Committee of the Regional Municipality of Ottawa-Carleton. I am grateful to both for their continued support of Canadian writers.

Sources

Susanna Moodie and Catharine Parr Traill are themselves the main sources for this book. Thanks to the New Canadian Library imprint of McClelland and Stewart, Catharine's *The Backwoods of Canada* and Susanna's *Roughing It in the Bush* and *Life in the Clearings versus the Bush* are still in print. The University of Ottawa Press has recently issued a collection of Susanna's short narratives, under the title *Voyages* (1991, edited by John Thurston), and a collection of Catharine's sketches, under the title *Forest and Other Gleanings* (1994, edited by Michael A. Peterman and Carl Ballstadt). Carleton University Press has reissued Catharine's novel *Canadian Crusoes, A Tale of The Rice Lake Plains* (1986, edited by Rupert Schieder). I found original copies of all the other books that the sisters wrote in Canada in the Parliamentary Library and the National Library of Canada.

The sisters' published works tell only half the story. For their personal letters I relied heavily on three volumes of their correspondence, published by the University of Toronto Press and edited by Professor Carl Ballstadt of McMaster University, Professor Elizabeth Hopkins of York University and Professor Michael A. Peterman of Trent University. The volumes are *Susanna Moodie, Letters of a Lifetime* (1985), *Letters of Love and Duty, The Correspondence of Susanna and John Moodie* (1993) and *I Bless You in My Heart, Selected Correspondence of Catharine Parr Traill* (1996). I used the Traill Family Collection in the National Archives of Canada, and the Patrick Hamilton Ewing Collection in the National Library of Canada, for additional letters from Catharine, and for letters from other members of the Strickland, Moodie and Traill families.

Given the importance of the Strickland sisters for students of both Canadian history and Canadian literature, there have been surprisingly few attempts to describe their lives in nineteenth-century Canada. The best, Audrey Y. Morris's *The Gentle Pioneers*, appeared in 1966. Other useful biographical assessments of Catharine and Susanna are G.H. Needler's *Otonabee Pioneers, The Story of the Stewarts, the Stricklands, the Traills and the Moodies* (1953); Clara Thomas's essay on "The Strickland Sisters" in *The Clear Spirit*, edited by Mary Quayle Innis (Toronto, 1966); Marian Fowler's *The Embroidered Tent* (1982). Michael Peterman's *Susanna Moodie: A Life* (1999) elegantly traces the links between Susanna's books and her life. Sara Eaton's *Lady of the Backwoods* (1969) is a cheerful account for young readers of Catharine's life.

There are two biographies of the formidable Agnes Strickland. The first is her sister Jane's hagiography, published in 1887. The second is Una Pope-Hennessy's *Agnes Strickland, Biographer of the Queens of England* (1940).

PREFACE

In *Brittania's Daughters, Women of the British Empire* (1983). Joanna Trollope gave a moving account of the great outflow of people from the British Isles to the overseas colonies, and the endurance of the women who helped sustain the British Empire. Professor Michael Peterman discussed the way that subsequent Canadian writers have treated the sisters in *This Great Epoch of Our Lives: Susanna Moodie's Roughing It in the Bush* (1996).

CHAPTERS 1, 2, 3

Details of the Strickland family in England come from a variety of sources. They include Catharine's reminiscences published in her book *Pearls and Pebbles* (1894); an interview with Susanna Moodie that I found in an 1884 issue of the Toronto *Globe*, in the Belleville Public Library; and material from the Traill Family Collection. Carole Gerson's article on "Mrs. Moodies's Beloved Partner" (*Canadian Literature*, No. 107, Winter 1985, pp. 34–45) was a corrective to much of the criticism John Moodie has suffered over the years.

To round out the picture of Suffolk in the early nineteenth century, I turned to *Suffolk Scene* by Julian Tennyson (1939); Rachel Lawrence's *Southwold River, Georgian Life in the Blyth Valley* (1990); and *A History of Suffolk* by David Dymond and Peter Northeast Phillimore (1995). The comparison with the Austen family came to mind after I read *Jane Austen, A Life* by Claire Tomalin (1997).

I learned about the position of women in Regency England in Muriel Jaeger's *Before Victoria, Changing Standards of Behaviour 1787–1837* (1967) and in *Hyenas in Petticoats* by Robert Woof, Stephen Hebron and Claire Tomalin (1997). Another book that provided useful background for lives of women during this period was *A Passionate Sisterhood: The Sisters, Wives and Daughters of the Lake Poets* by Kathleen Jones (1998). I learned about London in the late 1820s from James Morris's *Heaven's Command, An Imperial Progress* (1973). Information about Mary Prince and Ashton Warner comes from Dr. Sandy Campbell, of the English Department at the University of Ottawa.

CHAPTER 4

I learned about Leith during a personal visit, and from Hamish Coghill's *Discovering the Water of Leith* (1988). I never found a good modern account of Atlantic crossings in the 1830s, but I did discover Edwin C. Guillet, a prolific historian who wrote on a wide variety of topics I wanted to know about. His book *The Great Migration, The Atlantic Crossing by Sailing-Ship 1770-1860* (1963) and his pamphlet *Cobourg 1798-1948*, written for the

Business and Professional Women's Club of Cobourg (1948), were both useful sources. Dr. Bruce Elliot of Carleton University and Caroline Parry (author of *Eleanor's Diary*) both shared their knowledge of the emigrant ships with me.

CHAPTERS 5, 6 AND 7
I was able to imagine Cobourg in 1832 thanks to Katherine Ashenburg's *Going to Town, Architectural Walking Tours in Southern Ontario* (1996) and a wonderful little memoir of "the early days" written by a longtime resident, Mrs. David Fleming, and published by the Oshawa and District Historical Society (1960). I got a sense of what Upper Canada looked like, and how newly arrived travellers responded to it, from *Early Travellers in the Canadas, 1791-1867*, edited by Gerald M. Craig (1955), and from three first-hand accounts: *Our Forest Home, Being extracts from the correspondence of the late Frances Stewart* edited by her daughter E.S. Dunlop (1902); *A Gentlewoman in Upper Canada, The Journals of Anne Langton* edited by H.H. Langton (1950), and from John Langton's *Early Days in Upper Canada* (1926).

    Gentlemen Emigrants by Patrick Dunae (1981) explained what ill-suited pioneers the Traills and Moodies were. John Thurston's *The Work of Words, The Writing of Susanna Strickland Moodie* (1996) dealt with Susanna's shock at her first taste of the New World. Carole Gerson explored the two women's attitudes to native peoples, and pointed out how sympathetic they were, in her article "Nobler Savages: Representations of Native Women in the Writings of Susanna Moodie and Catharine Parr Traill" (*Journal of Canadian Studies*, Summer 1997, Vol. 32, No. 2). Joan Holmes explained to me who the "Chippewa Indians" were.

CHAPTERS 8 AND 9
William Kilbourn gave us the best biography of William Lyon Mackenzie, and the liveliest account of the 1837 Uprising, in *The Firebrand* (1956). Donald Creighton provided more general accounts of the history of this period in *The Story of Canada* (1959) and in his magnificent biography *John A. Macdonald, The Young Politician, The Old Chieftain* (reprinted in one volume, 1998).

CHAPTER 10

I spent happy hours in Belleville Public Library's Canadiana Room, looking through old almanacs, county atlases and local histories for details of life in nineteenth-century Belleville. Information on George Benjamin came from Sheldon and Judith Godfrey's lively and sympathetic *Burn This Gossip: The True Story of George Benjamin of Belleville* (1991). Information on Robert Baldwin came from J.M.S. Careless's essay about him in the book he edited entitled *The Pre-Confederation Premiers: Ontario Government Leaders, 1841-1867* (1980). For these two personalities, and most others mentioned in this book, I turned again and again to one of our greatest national publications: the *Dictionary of Canadian Biography*.

CHAPTER 11

Three local historians supplied me with a wealth of wonderful detail about the residents of the Rice Lake area during the last century. *Gore's Landing and the Rice Lake Plains* (1986) by N. Martin, C. Milne and D. McGillis brought home to me the spirit and eccentricity of so many early settlers. Rupert Schieder's introduction to the Carleton University Press edition of *Canadian Crusoes, A Tale of the Rice Lake Plains* (1986) and Michael Peterman's introduction to the Carleton University Press edition of Catharine's *The Backwoods of Canada* (1997) covered Catharine's experience with publishers, and the receptions accorded her books.

The most useful source on the slow and tortured development of the Canadian publishing industry is George L. Parker's *The Beginnings of the Book Trade in Canada* (1985). I also looked at Royal A. Gettman's *A Victorian Publisher, A Study of the Bentley Papers* (1960) and H. Pearson Gunday's *Book Publishing and Publishers in Canada before 1900* (1965).

CHAPTER 12

This chapter would have been impossible without a thoughtful and exhaustive thesis by Klay Dyer, entitled "A Periodical for the People, Mrs. Moodie and *The Victoria Magazine*" (unpublished thesis presented at the University of Ottawa, 1992). It shaped all my reactions when I read the original *Victoria Magazine*, now reprinted by the University of British Columbia Press.

Since *Roughing It in the Bush* is by far the best-known book by Susanna, it has repeatedly been put under the academic microscope. Among the most helpful analyses are two by Michael Peterman: "*Roughing It in the Bush* as Autobiography," in *Reflections: Autobiography and Canadian Literature*, edited by K.P. Stich (1988); and *This Great Epoch of Our Lives: Susanna Moodie's Roughing It in the Bush* (1996). A collection of essays which cast a new light on many aspects of Canadian women's writing, and which I found helpful and provocative, was *Re(dis)covering our Foremothers*, edited by Lorraine McMullen (1990). I learned a lot from Alec Lucas's contribution, "The Function of the Sketches in Susanna Moodie's *Roughing It in the Bush*," and Bina Freiwald's "'The tongue of woman': The Language of the Self in Moodie's *Roughing It in the Bush*."

CHAPTERS 13 AND 14

Most of the information in these chapters is contained in the exchange of letters between the Strickland sisters on each side of the Atlantic, and in Pope-Hennessy's biography of Agnes Strickland. Samuel Strickland's pioneer memoir, *Twenty-seven years in Canada West*, was first published in 1853, and was reprinted in 1970 by Hurtig.

CHAPTER 15

Most of the Moodie material in this chapter comes from Susanna's letters, and from "'A Glorious Madness,' Susanna Moodie and the Spiritualist Movement" by Carl Ballstadt, Michael Peterman and Elizabeth Hopkins (*Journal of Canadian Studies*, Vol. 17, No. 4, Winter 1982-83). The nineteenth-century fascination with spiritualism has often been ignored by serious historians, while attracting the attention of twentieth-century believers. One of the best and most dispassionate accounts of the Fox sisters' activities appears in *The Spiritualists, The Passion for the Occult in the Nineteenth and Twentieth Century* by Ruth Brandon (1983). I also looked at *Mediums and Spirit-Rappers and Roaring Radicals* by

Howard Kerr (1972), and Geoffrey Nelson's *Spiritualism and Society* (1969). For information about Victoria Woodhull, I read Barbara Goldsmith's *Other Powers, The Age of Suffrage, Spiritualism and the Scandalous Victoria Woodhull* (1998) and Mary Gabriel's *Notorious Victoria* (1998). Ramsay Cook's *The Regenerators, Social Criticism in Late Victorian English Canada* (1985) gives the social context for the Moodies' spiritualist activities.

CHAPTER 16
My principal sources for information about Orange Order activities in 1860 were Donald Creighton's *John A. Macdonald, The Young Politician, The Old Chieftain*; Gerald M. Craig's *Upper Canada, The Formative Years*; and *Early Travellers in the Canada 1791-1867* (1955) edited by Gerald M. Craig. Audrey Y. Morris (*The Gentle Pioneers*) has produced the best account of John Moodie's travails as sheriff.

CHAPTER 17
No aspect of the Strickland sisters' achievements has been more neglected than Catharine's interest in natural history. Two articles that explore Catharine's activities are "'Splendid Anachronism,' The Record of Catharine Parr Traill's Struggles as an Amateur Botanist in Nineteenth Century Canada" by Michael Peterman (*Re(dis)covering Our Foremothers*, edited by McMullen, 1990) and "Science in Canada's Backwoods" by Marianne Gosztonyi Ainley (*Natural Eloquence, Women Reinscribe Science*, edited by Barbara T. Gates and Ann B. Schteir, 1997). Another essay in the Gates and Schteir volume was also useful: Stephen Jay Gould's "The Invisible Woman." For background on science in nineteenth-century Canada, I read Suzanne Zeller's *Inventing Canada, Early Victorian Science and the Idea of a Transcontinental Nation* (1987). Information on Catharine's botanist friends comes from the *Dictionary of Canadian Biography*. I was also helped by *The Pioneer Woman* by Elizabeth Thompson (1991) and "Catharine Parr Traill and the Picturesque Landscape," a paper prepared for the Lakefield Literary Festival in 1998 by Elizabeth Hopkins.

CHAPTER 18

There are marvellous local histories and early photographs of the Stony Lake area. Among those I used were Enid Mallory's *Kawartha, Living on These Lakes* (1991); Jean Murray Cole's *Origins: The History of Dummer Township* (1993); James T. Angus's *A Respectable Ditch: A History of the Trent-Severn Waterway, 1833-1920* (1988); Katharine N. Hooke's *From Campsite to Cottage, Early Stoney Lake* (Peterborough Historical Society, 1992); and Richard Tatley's *Steamboating on the Trent-Severn* (1978). The quotations from James Ewing Ritchie come from his travel book *To Canada with Emigrants* (1885).

CHAPTERS 19 AND 20

For a sparkling social history of late-nineteenth-century Ottawa, there is nothing to compare with *The Private Capital: Ambition and Love in the Age of Macdonald and Laurier* by Sandra Gwyn (1984). The quotation from Maria Thorburn was kindly sent to me by her great-great-granddaughter, Jane Monaghan. All the other family information in these pages comes from the Traill Family Collection in the National Archives of Canada and the Patrick Hamilton Ewing Collection in the National Library of Canada.

I found additional useful material in *Ottawa, An Illustrated History* by John H. Taylor, and in "Making Science Beautiful: The Central Experimental Farm, 1886–1939" by Julie Harris and Jennifer Mueller (*Ontario History*, Vol. LXXXIX, No. 2, June 1997). Maime Fitzgibbon's *A Trip to Manitoba, or Roughing It on the Line*, appeared in 1880 and has not been reprinted.

Picture Credits

162 Hastings County Museum, Belleville
164 NAC C 31493
169 NAC C 9556
212 NL 22012
215 NAC C 67335
229 NAC PA 127486
231 Hastings County Museum, Belleville
233 Hastings County Museum, Belleville
242 Collection of The New York Historical Society
265 NAC C 5164
266 NAC C 606
267 NAC C 2183
275 Hastings County Museum, Belleville
282 NAC C 67346
283 Katharine Hooke, Peterborough
284 NAC C 67327
296 NAC C 145223, C 145224
304 Katharine Hooke, Peterborough
308 NAC C 7043
309 NAC PA201403
320 NL 17457
324 NAC C 67343
328 NAC PA 13248
331 NAC PA 26304
336 NAC C 67334
338 NAC C 55562
344 NAC PA 117832
346 NAC PA 67353
349 Hastings County Museum, Belleville

Index